WISDOM'S JOURNEY

WISDOM'S JOURNEY

Continental Mysticism and Popular Devotion in England, 1350–1650

STEVEN ROZENSKI

University of Notre Dame Press

Notre Dame, Indiana

CONTENTS

FIGURES

ACKNOWLEDGMENTS

It is a true pleasure, indeed, to have accumulated countless debts of gratitude to so many over the past decade. I ought to start even earlier: the
priceless gift of passion for literature was given to me by Barbara Newman and Regina Schwartz. I could never have imagined where I would
end up when I first took classes with them at Northwestern from 1998 to
2002. Having a *Baccalaureusmutter* like Barbara is truly a pearl without
price, and my gratitude to her is unending. So many marvelous scholars
in Evanston were remarkably supportive of an overly ambitious blue-
haired kid. My deepest thanks to Richard Kieckhefer, Julia Stern, Jeffrey
Masten, Helen Thompson, Larry Lipking, Mary Kinzie, Clare Cavanaugh, Louisa Burnham, Lianna Farber, Pheng Cheah, Ed Muir, Sara
Vaux, Tim Stevens, Stephen Alltop, Wallace Best, Jacob Kinnard, and the
late Larry Evans. Eric LeMay, years later, would come up with the title
of this book: special thanks to him and to Kristin LeMay for their friendship both in Evanston and in Cambridge. Studying theology with David
Jasper at the University of Glasgow and medieval German in Cologne
with Ursula Peters and Hans-Joachim Ziegeler also proved important
early moments in the prehistory of this project. Opportunities to speak at
the International Piers Plowman Conference in Birmingham in 2003 and
Ad Putter and Carolyn Muessig's conference, Envisaging Heaven in the
Middle Ages, in Bristol (2004) were also crucial for my early interest in
becoming a part of this field.

When I was a graduate student at Harvard, many scholars gave gen-
erously of their time in training me in their fields: Nicholas Watson was
simply everything one could wish for in a rigorous yet supportive *Dok-
torvater*. Similarly, I am exceedingly grateful to have learned from James
Simpson, Dan Donoghue, Joe Harris, Gordon Teskey, Elaine Scarry, and
Stephen Greenblatt in English, Beverly Kienzle and Bill Stoneman in

paleography, Jan Ziolkowski in Latin, Jeffrey Hamburger and Hugo van der Velden in art history, and Stephen Mitchell in Old Norse. Those years were enriched deeply by sharing the joy of learning with fellow graduate students Anna Traverse Fogle, Katie Deutsch, Stella Wang, Joey McMullen, Chris Barrett, Brandon Tilley, Misha Teramura, Shirin Fozi Jones, Anna Zayaruznaya, Julie Orlemanski, Taylor Cowdery and Helen Cushman, Kaye Wierzbicki, Erica Weaver, Margaret Healy-Varley, Alexis Becker, Sara Gorman, Larry Switzky, Timothy Michael, Rachel Smith, Laura Wang, and the late Sally Livingston. Anna McDonald, Gwen Urdang-Brown, Lauren Bimmler, Giselle Ty, Case Kerns, and Sol Kim-Bentley made the English Department a truly delightful academic home for eight years. Harvard's Villa I Tatti, the Ruusbroecgenootschap of the University of Antwerp, and the English Department at Oxford all proved extraordinary temporary berths during graduate school; my gratitude to Joseph Connors, Thom Mertens and Veerle Fraeters, and Vincent Gillespie for welcoming me to those institutions. Géraldine Veysseyre's warm welcome into her OPVS working group funded by the European Research Council during this period was also immeasurably helpful in forging relationships with an amazing team of European manuscript scholars.

Since leaving Harvard, I have been especially grateful for funding from the National Endowment for the Humanities, the Alexander von Humboldt Stiftung/Foundation, the US-UK Fulbright Commission, the Folger Shakespeare Library, Houghton Library, and the University of Rochester Humanities Center. Sarah Blick and Laura Gelfand led an extraordinary NEH seminar in York; Julia Perratore and Elisa Foster were ideal coeditors of the essay collection that followed: *Devotional Interaction in Medieval England and Its Afterlives*. My hosts in Göttingen—Dirk Schultze, Winfried Rudolf, Paul Langeslag, and Chris Voth—made my time in their splendid and storied department a delight. Nancy Bradley Warren's 2016 seminar at the Folger Institute was a true tour de force of intellectual exploration. At Queen Mary University of London, Julia Boffey not only welcomed me into the School of English and Drama for a year, but even sang the Verdi *Requiem* with me at the Royal Festival Hall; she and A. S. G. Edwards have been richly supportive of my work. Here in Rochester, New York, I have benefited from a trio of especially dedicated chairs: Rosemary Kegl, John Michael, and Katie Mannheimer.

Similarly, my colleagues Laura and Bruce Smoller, Jen Grotz, Nigel Maister, Tom Hahn and Bette London, Greg Heyworth, Sarah Higley, Joel Burges, Jeff Tucker, Will Miller, Matthew Omelsky, James and Debbie Rosenow, Morris and Georgia Eaves, and my illustrious predecessor Russell Peck have all contributed profoundly to my development as a scholar and teacher. Rossell Hope Robbins librarians Alan Lupack, Marie Turner, and Anna Siebach-Larsen have also done marvelous work in promoting and fostering medieval studies on campus.

I have so many generous and thoughtful colleagues in medieval studies and related fields to thank. First, invitations to speak from Juliette Vuille, Denis Renevey, Klaus Pietschmann, Dirk Schultze, and Laura Saetveit Miles at their institutions were especially welcome. Many thanks too to Anthony Bale, Susanna Fein and David Raybin, Claire Waters, Barbara Zimbalist, Joshua Byron Smith, Jessica Barr, José van Aelst, Rabia Geha Gregory, Amy and Suso Nelson, Michael Sargent, John van Engen and Kathryn Kerby-Fulton, Spencer Strub, Monika Otter, Susanne Sklar, E. A. Jones, Ian Johnson, Rhiannon Purdie, Paul Patterson, Bernard McGinn, Sara Poor, C. J. Jones, David Watt, Arielle Saiber, David Wallace and Rita Copeland, Alaric Hall, Mary Kate Hurley, Carissa Harris, Michael Van Dussen, Hetta Howes, Anthony Mandal, Alastair Minnis, Kellie Robertson, Andrew Albin, Racha Kirakosian, Tison Pugh, Shannon Gayk, Miri Rubin, Mary Flannery, Katherine Zieman, Virginia Blanton, Liza Blake, Arthur Bahr, and Matthew Sergi for their kind support and helpful advice across the years.

It would be imprudent and impossible to attempt to summarize with any degree of concision just how much the following friends have meant to me. The moment I click *save*, I have no doubt I'll immediately and unforgivably remember many I've left out. Still, my deepest, deepest thanks to Scott Perkins, the Zadeh family, the King family, Chris and Delilah Blum, Stephanie Guerette, Colin and Melissa Barringer, Saumitra Saha, Brian Perkins, Nicole Valentino, Julia Schlozman, Kelly Hoffman, Lisa Zelljadt, Aaron Lanou, Alisan Funk, Wendy Browne Henoch, Jessica Corwin, Sheila Heffernan, Michael Ravita, David and Anne Truman in King's Lynn, Melissa Stewart, the Ayanna family, Alan Brown, Amber Ying, Raha Nasseri, Susanna Guarino, Mevin Peña, Sarah Hofferbert, Shawi Cortez, Margo Vallee, Riley Dekeyser, Leah Whitehouse, Wayne Alber, Robert Palmer and Ward Pedde, Anja Viberg Jackson, Britt

Temme, Fay Capstick, Caroline Bisk, Allie Nichols, Brenn Whiting, Teddy Scheuerman, Julia Josfeld, Daniela Holler, and Venetia Bridges. Thank you all, from the bottom of my heart.

My friendship with Andrew Kraebel and Leah Schwebel deserves its own paragraph, if not a different font, to hope to hint at just how important it has been over the years.

So too, Klaus Pietschmann, Caprice Jakumeit-Pietschmann, and Anno Pietschmann have been like a second family on the Rhine for almost fifteen years, since we first met in Florence. Jeoffry, Jujeh, Vincent, and Jerome have been the very finest of house companions, but sadly Jeoffry and Jujeh did not live to chew or sit on the final product of my research; the arrival of Vincent and Jerome in March 2020 made the pandemic year so much more bearable. Finally, and most profoundly, my stepfather, Henry Colangelo, and my mother, Mary Colangelo, have made me feel so very loved and supported in every step of this process.

Devotional Theology
and Devotional Mobility

Although literary study has never strayed too far from the ancient belief that much of literature's strength dwells in its fundamental ability
to instruct and delight, didactic literature has nevertheless long been
given short shrift. Instruction manuals, cookbooks, religious pamphlets,
medical or psychological self-help books of all stripes: these have to
fight with exceeding vigor to be considered as having any part, however
minor, in literate and literary culture.[1] Perhaps this exclusion has some
justification in an era as saturated with surviving texts in the vernacular
as our own, but medieval didacticism constitutes the vast majority of
the surviving manuscripts of the Middle Ages—whereas *Beowulf*, *The
Book of Margery Kempe*, and *Sir Gawain and the Green Knight*, among
many other quite commonly taught texts, survive in a single manuscript.
When the didacticism in question is religious, critical bias against it only
seems to grow fiercer still. Most of the texts surviving in the greatest
number of medieval English manuscripts are didactic in one sense or
another, and all are connected to the dominant religion; yet the notion
of "popular" literature in contemporary critical discourse has nevertheless almost always been defined in opposition to both the religious and
the didactic. In this realm of scholarship, the popular may represent the
remnants of paganism (however faint), the development of courtly romance in the vernacular, the persistence of the folkloristic, traces of oral-
formulaic storytelling, and so on.[2] Somehow, what was copied most often
by medieval scribes, presumably to be read by the greatest number of

readers—literature by ecclesiastical authors—is almost never treated as part of the sphere of "popular literature" by scholars today (just as today, the millions of self-help books sold annually, to take just one instance, are similarly excluded from nearly all modes of contemporary literary or scholarly consideration).[3]

I am sympathetic to the many attempts medievalists and early modernists have undertaken to recover medieval literature created outside of the church (broadly construed). But attempts to use such literature to define medieval or early modern "popularity" have the distinct disadvantage of lacking any empirical evidence. Instead, whatever contemporary scholarship decides *should* represent the "popular" tends to define how the study of popular literature proceeds. This may be a result of a range of contemporary biases shaping how we view the medieval past in the present: generally, overt didacticism of the sort found in so many medieval texts has little place in contemporary popular media (both dramatic and comedic), let alone even higher-brow categories of art. When there is a moral to the story in contemporary "literary" narrative, it tends to be muddled, implicit, or deeply multivalent. There is one genre, however, in which narrative's dual function of entertainment and instruction is still openly and indisputably visible: media for children, be it books or television shows. Here, there is little worry that the text or narrative can become too preachy, and perhaps the contemporary descendants of medieval didactic literature can be most clearly recognized therein. Five or six centuries in the future, Nobel Prize–winning novelists and Pulitzer-winning poets may well be studied wherever literary scholars gather to think and write on the literary culture of the early twenty-first century, but there will nevertheless be considerable cultural value, I believe, in studying books written in our time for the entertainment and edification of children, for those seeking to diet more effectively, and for those learning how to recover emotionally from divorce, addiction, or abuse.

Translation, particularly nonbiblical translation, is also often neglected in literary and religious history. The central role of translation in shaping the reading habits and devotional practices of the medieval and early modern European is often acknowledged in one way or another, but our contemporary investment in authorial personality and creative originality continues to limit our collective understanding of the theological and literary significance of the continued movement of texts from one language to another across the centuries. So too have the Reformations of the early sixteenth century proved a powerful and enduring roadblock in historical and literary research: too often scholars on either side of the divide, despite seeing some kinship with the period adjacent to their own, have yet stopped well short of truly overturning the barriers of periodization.

Similarly, England has often been treated as a conservative insular backwater when compared to "the Continent" (which is in turn reified to include, somehow, every aspect of sophisticated, daring theological work). English contemplative texts are always held up to the impossible standard of meeting the intellectual level of whichever corner of continental Europe a scholar happens to be most interested in—Paris, the Rhineland, Tuscany, or perhaps the learned members of one monastic order or another. In reality, however, the cultural topography of England and Europe is immeasurably more nuanced; no single author or textual community can be considered in isolation as representative of the whole. The intellectual atmosphere in fifteenth-century Sheen or Syon may have been far more theologically robust and philosophically experimental than, say, a roughly equivalent Carthusian or Bridgettine monastery at the same time in Italy, France, or Germany.[4] A parish priest in an Alpine village in Switzerland would have had an entirely different outlook on exegesis, catechesis, preaching, and the literature of devotion when compared to clerics tending their flocks on the outskirts of Oxford, London, or Cambridge. Each author or translator worked within a horizon of available texts that differed dramatically from place to place, library to library, and mind to mind, both in every corner of England and wherever our attention turns across continental Europe. Authors, texts, ideas, and languages were all fluid and connected, even if from today's perspective it seems as though generalized comparisons between insular and Continental piety might not be particularly controversial or hard to justify.

In this book, I hope to reinvigorate our understanding of popular piety and its most popular literary manifestations over the course of three crucial centuries. Widely read and widely translated authors such as Henry Suso, Catherine of Siena, and Thomas à Kempis have been almost erased from English literary history by generations of scholarly neglect and misplaced post-Romantic nationalisms (not to mention a variety of negative aesthetic judgments). Recent decades, however, have seen a wave of scholarship overturning traditional concepts of English religious and literary insularity and exceptionalism across the late medieval and early modern periods. So too has the scholarly neglect (or active denigration) of popular didactic translations seen considerable reversals. Thus this book aims to contribute to the ongoing reevaluation of the relationships between literature, religion, and translation in late medieval and early modern Europe.[5]

Hence, I investigate the transformations of Continental spiritual literature in England across a roughly three-hundred-year period, focusing especially on texts that—despite their considerable popularity—have received the least scholarly attention. By examining the English translation and adaptation of the works of Henry Suso, Catherine of Siena, and Thomas à Kempis, along with the common devotional culture manifested in the work of Suso and Richard Rolle, *Wisdom's Journey* reshapes our understanding of English devotional and mystical literature (in both manuscript and print) and its wider European context both before and after the Reformations of the sixteenth century. This group of texts demonstrates an array of rich and significant English contacts with literatures and cultures beyond its most widely studied neighbor, France. The *devotio moderna* of the Low Countries, the Dominican mysticism of the Rhineland, and the female spirituality of the most famous Italian saint of the fourteenth century represent three of the most important facets of Continental religion, all of which found their way into English. Adaptations and translations of devotional and mystical writings for broad new vernacular audiences were a central feature of the late medieval and early modern literary marketplace both across Europe and across what often looks like the unbridgeable divide of the Reformation. I argue that clerical and didactic literature, surviving as it does in hundreds of manuscripts and early prints, deserves to be considered a part of what we consider "popular" when considering the literary culture of the Middle Ages today. Furthermore, I demonstrate that the ongoing popularization of devotional theology in the vernacular shaped nonclerical readers' religious practices and experiences even more profoundly than did the better-known history of vernacular biblical translation; indeed, these texts often had unexpectedly long and complex afterlives that reward deeper inquiry. I continue reading past the 1470s or 1530s, in essence, because I found that the texts themselves asked me to: Suso, Catherine of Siena, and Thomas à Kempis all continued to be read, translated, and printed in England and in English decades and even centuries after England's split with Rome.

Focusing my attention primarily on these three key case studies, I study the forms and strategies of late medieval translation and early modern engagement with Continental medieval devotion and its literary afterlives in English-speaking communities. In doing so, I also argue for three distinct modes of postmedieval interaction with these texts: slow decline, Catholic interest and Protestant denunciation, and continued popularity. Suso's work demonstrates the first of these modes. He found initial widespread influence, translation, and adaptation followed by a steady, gradual decline in influence, but considerably more gradual than previously has been recognized. Works by and about Catherine of Siena, in contrast, saw continued use and retranslation in post-Reformation recusant communities (primarily on the Continent), paralleled with vehement denunciation by English Protestants as a prime example (along with Bridget of Sweden) of the embarrassing errors of medieval visionary literature. Finally, Thomas à Kempis's *Imitation of Christ* managed to attain a remarkably consistent expansion of popularity, translation, and acceptance among both Catholic and Protestant readers well into the nineteenth and twentieth centuries. Scholarship has tended to see the literature following the Reformation as representative of either an insular repudiation of the Catholic past or a robust Tridentine Counter-Reformation (usually dominated by Rome and the Jesuits), but I demonstrate instead a far more nuanced understanding of the ongoing engagement of post-Reformation English writers with some of the most widely read religious literature of the later Middle Ages.

DEVOTIONAL THEOLOGY: POPULAR AND CLERICAL?

Central to my overall argument is the contention that clerical and didactic literature and associated texts are typically excluded from the canon of popular literature without any firm reasoning whatsoever. I believe that scholars of medieval religion and literature must dissolve the dichotomy between what is often called "popular literature" and its religious, didactic, and clerical counterparts. Rather than relying on contemporary definitions of popular culture and projecting its assumptions onto the literary culture of the Middle Ages, I want to consider the popularity of medieval texts by examining the surviving manuscript evidence. How many manuscripts of a given text are extant today and in which languages? When and where was the medieval text subsequently translated and printed? How did it fare past 1517 or 1538? With manuscript numbers putting the idea of popularity on a firmly empirical basis, and the consideration of multiple languages seizing definitions of popularity from the domain of the study of national vernaculars, this perspective transforms what we think of as popular and international medieval literary culture, as a new series of texts come to the foreground: chief among them, those studied here.

As one of the categories governing this work (and much better-suited to it, I believe, than the more familiar critical modes of either mystical or vernacular theology), "devotional theology" stands in need of fuller explication. I take the term from the historian Berndt Hamm, who identifies four characteristics he associates most closely with devotional theology.[6] First, the choice of audience: the devotional theologian is not especially interested in the elite theology of the schools, particularly insofar as the universities catered exclusively to men.[7] Rather, a broader, mixed audience is sought (in terms of both gender and religious life); this choice of audience in turn informs consequent authorial decisions.

Second, the thematic choices made: themes such as the *ars moriendi* and affective meditation upon and imitation of the life of Christ prove to be especially popular, as do meditations upon the "Four Last Things." But the key criterion is the avoidance of exceedingly complicated Trinitarian theology or other such topics long debated in schools and perceived to have little relevance to the straightforwardly soteriological matters with which devotional theologians primarily concerned themselves.[8]

Third, Hamm also points to the generic choices made by authors: although these are manifold, and can include large compendia, one form that saw particular growth in the fifteenth century is the short, edifying tract.[9] In both of the fourteenth-century authors discussed in chapter 1, for instance, Henry Suso and Richard Rolle, we will see a predominance of epistles, postils, and Suso's own favorite descriptor, the *Büchlein* ("little book"). Most importantly, however, devotional theology is a fundamentally *literary* and narrative-based mode of theology, and it is a profoundly *theological* mode of literature.[10]

Hamm's fourth defining category of devotional theology points toward the linguistic style of the edifying tractates themselves: he sees devotional theology as evincing "the immediate and concomitant choice
of the theological *modus loquendi*" in which theological language "is
transformed in a style close to everyday life and piety, (more or less)
straightforward and clear." Devotional theology is "often an—if anything—affective rather than cognitive-intellectual theology of pulpit
and confessional, the burgher's parlor and the monastic cell, the everyday
world of the professions and the deathbed."[11] Throughout this book, we
will see devotional authors distinguishing themselves by their choices:
of audience, of theme, of genre, and of narrative style.

Hamm mentions as one example of the particular thematic and stylistic flexibility characteristic of devotional theology, *Die himlische funt-
grub*, a sermon cycle by Johannes von Paltz. First published in 1490, it
was reprinted twenty times before the Reformation.[12] Paltz is a prime
example, Hamm writes, for "how varied the readjustment of the theology
to an edifying style can turn out within the works of the same author: it
can, on what we might call a half-academic level, remain quite close to
scholasticism insofar as it continues to employ the *quaestio*-style . . . ;
however, it can also simplify this method by converting a discursive 'sic
et non' methodology to a straightforwardly affirming 'sic'-style."[13] The
particular strength of devotional theology dwells in its ability to move between theological and rhetorical styles in order to appeal to a broad audience, a flexibility that is further related to the increased vernacularization
of devotional theology in the later Middle Ages. In both Rolle and Suso,
for instance, we will see a similar theological flexibility and similar talent
in reframing academic theology in popular terms.

DEVOTIONAL MOBILITY: EXPERIENCE AND EXEGESIS

Chapter 1, on Henry Suso and Richard Rolle, demonstrates how these
two key devotional figures operate at the crossroads of a movement in the
history of mysticism Michel de Certeau examines in *The Mystic Fable*:
the transition from the dominance of scriptural exegesis to a heightened
emphasis on the interpretation of personal experience. This transformation, for Certeau, pivoted on the understanding of the Song of Songs as
a narrative that necessarily describes not only physical or spiritual erotic

union in allegorical terms, but also the possibility of the *personal* experience of that union. In the process of the movement from the adjective *mystic* to the substantive *mysticism*—the change from mystical interpretation of the sacred text to the discourse of mystical experience—he writes that "the word no longer modeled itself, as the adjective had done, on the noun units of one sole great ('biblical') Narration in order to connote the many spiritual appropriations or interiorizations of the biblical text. It became a text itself."[14] In both Suso and Rolle we see the intermingling of these two trends: biblical commentary and exegesis are still absolutely crucial to both, but their own presence in their narratives is a large source of the novelty, credibility, and ultimately popularity of their texts. The true "word" to be interpreted in both instances is multivalent and, in part, the story they claim to tell of their own experience.

The discursive flexibility Hamm establishes as a fundamental component of devotional theology and Certeau's account of the readjustment of mysticism from biblical commentary to personal experience together point toward a central commonality between Suso and Rolle: what I term their "devotional mobility." By this I mean not only the instances of *physical* and *spiritual* mobility inherent to both: Rolle's account of traveling between insufficiently solitary hermitages and the role of Suso's own travels and persecution while on trips in the Rhineland (physical mobility) and the shared framework of spiritual ascent within the space of the visionary event that both men employ (spiritual mobility). Also crucial, however, is their *social* mobility as devotional authors able to respond to considerably different readerships over the course of their authorial careers. Other aspects of authorial and textual mobility are also fundamental components of the devotional culture Suso and Rolle shaped, such as their ability to move between Latin and the vernacular, the ways in which their reception histories both manifest considerable adaptation by regional audiences, the circulation of their manuscripts across Europe in service of varying devotional aims, and, most concretely, in the very process of translation itself, as their ideas were transformed into new languages and changed in the presence of new local devotional cultures. Hence, it is the *translation* of Continental devotion that serves as the cornerstone of this book.

Devotional mobility did not begin with Suso and Rolle, of course. The particular strand of affectivity inherent in devotional theology can be seen to have its start in both a movement of texts across Europe and an earlier cleric's self-presentation as a uniquely exemplary author. In 1104, Saint Anselm sent his *Prayers and Meditations* from Canterbury to Countess Mathilda of Tuscany: "Some are not appropriate to you, but I want to send them all, so that if you like them you may be able to compose others after their example."[15] The text is provided from a distinctly noted distance, to replace a missing presence, and a second preface indicates that even this transit itself initially failed, and that Anselm's spiritual "son" became the bearer of a text copied by Anselm's own hand. Anselm's *physical* absence seems to be part of what leads to a heightened *textual* presence because he proposes himself, and his words, as a possible authorial model for Mathilda's own textual production.[16]

The *Meditations* themselves, too (and the larger genre of Passion meditation considered more broadly), are a similar attempt to rectify an absence: the reader was not present to witness the events of Jesus's life, especially the simultaneously horrifying and salvific moment of the Passion. Recreating these events in the mind can lead to a secondary presence that will help to reflect the original by reconstituting an emotional response similar to what one would have had had one been present: through prayer and meditation, one can *feel* the Passion even if one could not have seen it. Anselm writes, for instance: "Alas for me, that I was not able to see the Lord of Angels humbled to converse with me. . . . Why, O my soul, were you not there to be pierced by a sword of bitter sorrow?"[17] It is this awareness of a lack, an experiential deficit, that propels the reader into attempting an imagined vision of the events of the Passion. As Certeau writes, even Christianity itself "was founded upon *the loss of a body*—the loss of the body of Jesus Christ, compounded with the loss of the 'body' of Israel, of a 'nation' and its genealogy."[18] The devotional project of the *Meditations* is to struggle against the emptiness and loss Mary Magdalene suffers when she weeps at the empty tomb, when she cannot find Christ's body. Curiously, even *seeing* the risen Christ in John's Gospel—first mistaken for a gardener—does not console her; she needs to *hear* him speak to her before she can recognize him.[19] The reader of the *Meditations* needs even more: all the senses need to be employed in the Prayer to Christ. A complete interpenetration of the reader and the ecclesiastical, textual, and Eucharistic body of Christ is longed for in Anselm's *Prayer before Receiving the Body and Blood of Christ*: "May I be worthy to be incorporated into your body 'which is the church,' so that I may be your member and you may be my head, and that I may remain in you and you in me."[20]

Similarly, the attainment of *canor* (auditory union with the divine) in Rolle's *Form of Living* involves both spatial distance and spiritual movement. It is "likened to an otherworldly place where the soul not only hears heavenly song, but also can commune with the presence of Jesus."[21] Rolle's definition of *canor* involves melody, to be sure, but it is also a form of rapture, leading the reader to journey into a mystical spatiality in which love of and participation in Jesus can operate in concord with the aural experience of (and participation in) celestial music.[22] Indeed, even this music itself is a subset of movement, as universal music is generated by the very movement of the spheres of the universe themselves. And in the opening of the prosimetric Middle English epistle *Ego Dormio*, Rolle writes that the proper lover of Christ is one who is "never weary to love, but is ever, whether standing, sitting, going, or any deed doing, always thinking of his love, and often since dreaming thereof" (neuer is wery to loue, but [is] euer, standynge, sittynge, goynge, or any oþer dede doynge, is euer his love þynkynge, and oft sithe þerof dremynge), a frenetic description of constant movement amidst meditation on the beloved that is in stark contrast to the calm stability one might ordinarily expect of a hermit.[23]

In a wide range of thirteenth-century treatises on divine love—from the very title of Bonaventure's widely successful *Journey of the Soul into God*—amorous union with the Godhead is figured as movement, travel, and pilgrimage along a pathway.[24] Travel to overcome distance and separation is a frequently invoked metaphor for Rolle, too, one frequently employed to emphasize "the distance between the material and the spiritual worlds in both spatial and moral terms . . . intimating that a forced separation from one's true home is in operation during life."[25] There are also other forms of mobility at work: both the circulation of texts throughout Europe and the inherent flexibility and necessary transformations that take place in the course of translation and adaptation help shape this story.[26] On an even larger scale, indeed, the history of Christianity itself can be seen as a history of a repeated transposition of old into new, the spiritual *translatio imperii* from Israel and Jerusalem to Europe and Rome being echoed by the corresponding *translatio studii*: Stephen Greenblatt has described Christian typology as itself a form of mobility, a constantly moving oscillation in interpretation between historical and allegorical meanings of sacred texts.[27]

These textual journeys serve to connect the translational impulse of devotional theology to its broad-based, international appeal in the later Middle Ages. Berndt Hamm discusses, for instance, "the border-transcending, broadening tendency of devotional theologians," describing how "they take entirely new concepts—ones not included in academic theology—within their own theology: particular experiences of pastoral care and devout life practices in the cloister, in lifestyles similar to those of the regular clergy, or in the secular domain. Theology thus becomes not only transposed and transformed, but also attains—as devotional theology—additional religious content and intimacy with the conditions of everyday life, as well as a new mode of intensity and sympathy."[28] The omnivorous theologians themselves had these tendencies, but so did their translators. Indeed, the translators must properly be considered theologians in their own right. Typically anonymous, the translators of popular devotional works are constantly adapting their source-texts to the needs and interests of their local audience. These translations ought not be dismissed as merely "derivative" or considered utterly secondary to "native" devotional literature. Translations are often our key witnesses into the fine-grained particularities of late medieval religious belief and practice, both lay and clerical, regional and international. Moreover, fluid processes of adaptation and expansion are not always inevitably evidence of a degradation or diminution of theological content, as has often been argued in the past century of scholarship. Whether secular or religious, a central tenet of the study of translation has been to recognize it as a creative process that makes the source-text *more* present, *more* affectively significant to its intended audience than the source-text (for all its putative originality) could have hoped to be. Through this sense of translation, one comes to emphasize the revitalizing and revivifying effects so often seen in medieval translations of a source-text; they do not dull or dilute the efficacy of the original, even as they contribute to the widespread, enduring success of devotional theology.[29]

Michel de Certeau has written of the diffusion of spiritual literature across Europe in the age of print, along with the convoluted process of translations of translations, as creating "a sort of spiritual pidgin" (even though the multilingualism one encounters is often quite intricate, indeed). He describes a "language of the 'other'" that "was generated by the vast labor of these alterations."[30] This translational aspect of mysticism depends on what he calls "the obscure heroes of mystic language" (especially appropriate in this study of late medieval devotional translators because the vast majority of the translators studied here have remained anonymous, their status as authors routinely neglected today), those who "pursued the sole task of understanding the different modes of speech and making them intelligible to others."[31] These translators, just as much as the "original" authors whose texts were admired, remain one of the most important facets of medieval literary history, a component too easily neglected in our peculiarly post-Romantic concern with notions of poetic originality and creativity.

These countless acts of translation in the fifteenth and sixteenth centuries, in their vast popularity, can tell us more about the religious interests of northern European culture writ large than the more rarefied texts (often relatively unread in their own age), which seem to receive the lion's share of attention in scholar's study and classroom today.[32] The translations examined in this book, and the translation of source materials within Suso and Rolle themselves (discussed in the next chapter), all evince a textual and linguistic mobility (in making use of diverse authorities and sources, and of expertise in both Latin and their respective vernaculars) that is directly related to their successful literary and devotional mobility (in the diversity of readers they attracted in the late Middle Ages and beyond).

Intimately connected to the task of devotional translation and devotional mobility, too, is desire. Whether the mystic's yearning for expressing ineffable experience, the popular devotional author's zeal for the salvation of ever-increasing numbers of souls, or the contemporary scholar's curious quest to understand the never-ending history of books and ideas as fully as possible, desire is part and parcel of the creation of texts by and about devotion. The conclusion of Certeau's *The Mystic Fable* is perhaps the most powerful exposition of the connection between the desire produced by mystical ineffability and the consequent mobility inspired thereby:

He or she is mystic who cannot stop walking, and, with the certainty of what is lacking, knows of every place and object that it is *not that*;

one cannot stay *there* nor be content with *that*. Desire creates an excess. Places are exceeded, past, lost behind it. It makes one go further, elsewhere. It lives nowhere. . . . Unmoored from the "origin" of which Hadewijch spoke, the traveler no longer has foundation nor goal. . . . It goes on walking, then, tracing itself out in silence, in writing.[33]

Although devotional translation might at times seem, to some eyes, rather prosaic or utilitarian, it is at the very heart of mystical discourse as theorized by Certeau. Mystic speech, as Certeau writes, has always been fundamentally translational. From the first moment of writing, experience is being translated into text; human experience of the divine immediately, perforce, vanishes and the very first act of "translation" onto the page alone survives for others to read and interpret. Apophasis, despite its insistent dismissal of language, is relentlessly analyzed, reread, and translated—even the *Mystical Theology* of Pseudo-Dionysius, perhaps the most apophatic text in the Christian tradition, was translated into English in the fourteenth and the seventeenth centuries. The repeated recognition of the paradoxical inadequacy and necessity of translation, coupled with the impossible desire for a text truer than its exemplar, a translation more perfect than its source-text, has been the ongoing engine of religious discourse, and mystical discourse most especially, across the centuries.

Devotional Mobility in Fourteenth-Century England and Germany

Around the year 1400, an English hermit named Thomas Basset wrote a short defense of the texts of the Yorkshire hermit Richard Rolle (ca. 1300–1349) against the criticisms of an unnamed Carthusian detractor. Rather than situating Rolle in an exclusively insular or hermitic context, or invoking the ancient precedent of the desert fathers, however, he instead turned to one of the most popular spiritual authors of the fourteenth century: the Swabian Dominican Henry Suso (often known as Heinrich Seuse, especially in German scholarship). Born between 1295 and 1300 in Constance or Überlingen, Suso, with his vernacular preaching, his masterful defense of Meister Eckhart's condemned works, his encouragement of female Dominican authorship, and his popularization of bridal mysticism, became one of the most important German spiritual authors of the fourteenth century. Basset's main claim in his defense of Rolle is that the textual reports of mystical experiences doubted by Rolle's critics are indeed valid descriptions of lived experience.

Suso's description of the experience of mystical heat in his Latin *Horologium Sapientiae* (*Clock of Wisdom*) serves as a major component to Basset's argument that Rolle's descriptions of experience are, if not exactly independently verifiable, at least a reputable part of a tradition with analogues elsewhere in what he believes to be suitably authoritative fourteenth-century devotional writing (Bridget of Sweden is quoted at the beginning of the treatise as another example of an authentic, trustworthy visionary author). Basset writes of Suso, linking him to Rolle: "So it often happened, from these and similar experiences, that his heart would feel as if it began to be on fire from the vehemence of his love, and through a violent motion and pulse he evinced the power of love, and by his deep sighs he made known the ardor of his burning affections."[1] Particularly striking is Basset's eagerness here to extract Suso's description—quoting his very words—in order to present readers with an experience similar to Rolle's *fervor* in his defense of the Hermit of Hampole. The similarities between Rolle and Suso and their depictions of the phenomena of mystical experience were already well known, by at least one English author, at the close of the fourteenth century.

This chapter will continue to examine what Thomas Basset first briefly remarked upon. Henry Suso and Richard Rolle, two exemplary figures of early fourteenth-century spirituality, have rarely been studied in tandem, yet these two widely read figures demonstrate how several central aspects of devotional culture were shared between fourteenth-century England and Germany.[2] Devotional texts were produced on both sides of the English Channel during the period, seeking to make theological truths more widely accessible to lay and religious readers alike; the role these texts played in teaching modes of contemplation, communicating accounts of religious experience, and instructing lay and religious readers in methods of prayer and liturgical worship has long been acknowledged as among the most important developments of late medieval literature at its intersection with theology. Suso and Rolle were uniquely successful, however, as popular authors who not only offered these aspects of devotion, but also carefully cultivated their self-performance as specifically *modern*, contemporary author-characters, both learned and devout, bookish and passionate, within their own works.

Both Suso and Rolle may appear rather idiosyncratic when considered in the context of the literary output of their own national traditions. But when examined together, their numerous congruities become apparent; one begins to see the ways in which audiences of the time must have been interested in, even especially excited by, texts that featured this particular kind of self-referential author-character and the themes their texts addressed. These eponymous, pseudo-autobiographical author-character-narrated descriptions of experience lent them (and thus, by proxy, their creators) a kind of spiritual authority supplementing that of scripture or the Church.[3] These self-descriptions are delicately balanced between outward work in the world (however imaginatively constructed this world may be in their texts) and interior descriptions of their contemplative lives, their relationships with other devotees, their key moments of ascent and rapture, and their emotional relationship to liturgy and scripture.

The sheer number of weighty spiritual and historical categories Suso and Rolle alike manage to straddle is particularly significant. The textual characters performed by Suso and Rolle bridge, for instance, the lay and the clerical: Rolle is the controversially mobile hermit with a self-designed habit who flees for solitude from the rancor of Mass; Suso is the unapologetic Dominican devotee of a posthumously condemned heretic, ministering to (and corresponding with) Dominican women and regularly traveling through the world (he describes himself being accused by both Dominicans and laypeople of heresy, well-poisoning, and illicit affairs).[4] Both are proficient vernacular and Latin authors: they value (albeit in somewhat different ways) the particular attributes and valences of each language, and are concerned with the powerful capabilities of the vernacular in their pastoral care for devotees without knowledge of Latin, especially women. Both, too, are profoundly invested in the interaction between textual and aural; they regularly invoke celestial music and the experience of the aural as a mode of experience superior to the written and textual. Accounts of visual experiences of God were widespread, but it is *aurality*, for Suso and Rolle, that is commonly treated as a more trustworthy warrant of the validity of mystical experience (particularly, that is to say, when compared to visuality).

The malleable performance of gender, particularly a delicate oscillation between male and female attributes in the construction of their literary personae, is also central to their texts. Even as they are devoted to a God depicted in terms both masculine and feminine, they also make reference to male and female aspects of their own self-construction of gender. Rolle most famously transforms his sister's garb into a habit and refers to Christ as mother; Suso imagines himself both as husband of a female Christ-as-Sapientia and as the bride of the male God-Man Christ (and chooses to take his surname from his devout mother rather than his aristocratic father). They were masters of both *scientia* and *sapientia*, high theology and popular culture, of knowledge and affect, of bringing learning into devotion, and vice versa—what Andrew Kraebel has variously termed "learned devotion" or "the appeal of the academic."[5] Rolle (the Oxonian) and Suso (the theology graduate of Cologne's *studium generale*) were skilled in describing the affective experience of God's presence even as they showed themselves equals to the most sophisticated theological debates and knottiest exegetical discussions of the day. All of these commonly shared, interconnected liminalities proved crucial to their unique success as both authors and characters. Balancing themselves, their author-characters, and their texts between so many borders, just so, was a strategy that reaped rich dividends for the futures of their literary production. Rather than seeing them as theologians writing devotional literature, I believe we do better as critics to read them as literary authors keenly invested in theological matters, following, for instance, Hamm's framework of devotional theology as inherently concerned with its own narrative structure.

Something new is happening in Suso and Rolle. Compare their bodies of work to some of the other most popular texts of their time, the other devotional texts that achieved a truly broad, pan-European, multilingual readership: the Pseudo-Bonaventurean *Meditationes vitae Christi*, Ludolph of Saxony's *Vita Christi*, *Vitaspatrum*, *Pelerinage de la vie humaine*, *Legenda aurea*, and *Somme le roi* (most popularly appearing in English as the *Speculum vitae*). Temporally, there is a clear distinction: the narrative segments of these books take place either in the distant past of the New Testament or late antique Christianity, or in a dream vision (others, meanwhile, are more straightforwardly nonnarrative, that is, almost purely didactic or catechetic).[6] None of these are set so squarely in the contemporary present as are the narratives of Suso and Rolle; none are nearly as invested in the claims to personal experience of a single author-character. Suso and Rolle were neither exclusively literal nor allegorical authors; their texts neither purely dream-vision nor solely pastoral-exegetical treatise. They had no objection to, for instance, devotion to the traditional sacraments, yet they were constantly devising new experiential and affective channels into which the pious fervor of their readers could flow. Both invoked the synaesthetic experience of the divine, leaving no experiential stone unturned in their unending pursuit of wrenching unique personal affect into universally relevant text.

They largely avoided the biggest controversies of their time, and yet nevertheless managed to perform a certain appearance of *anxiety* about their orthodoxy, perhaps even deliberately imparting a touch of scandal to intrigue or excite their contemporary audiences—a middle path between a heretical attempt to reconceptualize the contemporary Church or predict the future, and a purely historical appreciation of the time of Jesus, early martyr-saints, or the desert fathers. Are they themselves eliding these tensions, offering both novelty and tradition, orthodoxy and edginess, in order to distract their readers from more suspect texts that might lead them into thornier debates? Were their texts in turn promoted by religious or secular clergy in order to achieve the same goal? Or was this creation of contemporaneity instead competing for audience attention with fiction, with romance—are their performed selves meant to function more as literary characters to entertain than true spiritual exemplars to be imitated? Some of the appeal of these texts, surely, must have extended beyond a straightforwardly pious desire for prayer, biblical exegesis, or Passion meditation: ample texts, both before and after Suso's and Rolle's own heyday, could have been read by those seeking piety alone. Suso's extensive use of floral and natural imagery—and his borrowings from Ovid and the *Carmina Burana*—make him something of a troubadour or Minnesinger for Christ; each of the episodic troubles he describes experiencing in the *Vita* can read almost like a romance *âventiure*.[7] In much the same way, Rolle's forceful personality and his elegant lyricism have often led to more interest in the flamboyant character he presents than the careful theologian and exegete behind the texts. And even though a good deal of contemporary interest in both figures tends inexorably to the biographical, it seems likely that neither the authors themselves nor their initial audiences would have seen much usefulness in mere interest in their potential historicity; it is the spiritual stories they told, and their lessons for the transformation of the reader's own life, that brought Rolle and Suso their enormous audience.

DEVOTIONAL PSEUDO-AUTOBIOGRAPHY
AND LITERATURE

Some of this historical interest, however, is doubtless warranted. Rolle and Suso constantly invite curiosity about the possible historicity of the author-characters in their texts, even as they steadfastly refuse to satisfy that interest. This is one of the key components of what Laurence De Looze has termed "pseudo-autobiography," which he sees as perhaps *the* dominant mode of fourteenth-century literature.[8] His work focuses on the rise of this phenomenon in predominantly nondevotional authors (figures of such importance to secular literary history as Chaucer, Juan Ruiz, Machaut, and Jean Froissart), but the concept applies equally well to a pivotal branch of spiritual literature contemporary to these authors. The broad outlines of the genre can be seen quite precisely in the spiritual and pseudo-autobiographical works of Suso and Rolle. De Looze sees pseudo-autobiography as "a way of reading that shifts, or at least hesitates, between readings as 'true,' 'historical,' 'autobiographical,' and ones that receive a text according to known modes of fiction."[9] Seeing the textual production of Suso and Rolle in this light can move us forward from the wearisome and oft-rehearsed arguments about the possible historicity of the events portrayed in their works (about which it is possible to know very little with any strong degree of certitude, despite the best efforts of a century of historically oriented research), and instead allows us to understand their texts more closely to the manner in which they were originally received. For Suso and Rolle did *not* aim to write history; their goal was not to shine light on the precise details of contemporary spiritual practices in Yorkshire or Swabia. They are authors in equal measure literary and devotional, local and global, and were received as such among the many keen readers of pseudo-autobiographies of their day. Indeed, to claim the existence of a truly historically accurate autobiography in *any* era is epistemologically vexed—in De Looze's words, "to read a work as an autobiography . . . means to read as though unaware that truth is always conventionally constructed."[10] Far from being a potential source of historical truth about two authors of the period, the works of Suso and Rolle must be seen from this perspective: part of a series of popular literary conventions employed in both secular fiction and devotional texts in constructing the main characters of narratives (whether exemplary or otherwise).

Fourteenth-century readers of both secular and religious literature appear to have been much better equipped to understand this literary framework than many scholars of recent decades. Indeed, this complicated interrelationship was part and parcel of the *appeal* of pseudo-autobiography; attempting to draw bold, absolute lines between fact and fiction is rather counter to the very spirit of the genre. Late medieval audiences were captivated by "texts that claimed to be autobiographical, in the sense of being retrospective first-person narratives about the author's life, but then also undermined that claim."[11] A. C. Spearing writes in similar terms of what he calls instead "autographies," that is, "extended nonlyrical writings in the first person, in which 'I' and the other first-person singular pronouns function not as labels for a real or fictional individual but as means of evoking proximality and experientiality."[12] Whether these readers had the *Canterbury Tales*, Machaut's *Le voir dit*, Suso's *Life of the Servant*, or Rolle's *Fire of Love* before them, the (pseudo-)autobiographical or autographical statements therein were not of interest exclusively—or even mainly—for their potential historicity or their ability to transmit a precise, factual account of a specific life as it was lived (or of a specific episode of religious experience in the life of a pious figure). Nor, I believe, should we today employ the traditional tools of religious historiography to evaluate such texts (few people, I hope, have ever turned to the *Canterbury Tales* purely out of interest in the conditions of late fourteenth-century English pilgrimage). Rather, it was the play *between* clearly fictional elements and claims to authenticity, between literary tradition and personal innovation—ultimately between individual invention and theological reality—that appealed to the fourteenth- and fifteenth-century audiences who appreciated the works of Suso and Rolle with such enduring fervor.[13]

And both secular and spiritual pseudo-autobiographies certainly did appeal, on a truly vast scale. Among Middle English verse, *The Prick of Conscience* survives in the greatest number of manuscripts (the pseudo-autobiographical *Canterbury Tales* comes a rather distant second), but the prose of Suso and Rolle found its way into hundreds of codices. More than 500 manuscripts of Suso's major works survive, with his Latin work translated into nearly every vernacular in Europe (with even more complicated patterns of transmission and translation in the Low Countries). The Middle High German *Little Book of Eternal Wisdom* was his most popular vernacular text, surviving in at least 121 complete manuscripts and, in excerpts, a further 145 manuscripts.[14] The Latin reworking of the *Little Book of Eternal Wisdom* (titled *Horologium Sapientiae*) was translated into Middle French (at least forty-eight largely complete manuscripts),[15]

Middle Dutch (seventy-four manuscripts, including manuscripts containing only fragments, with hundreds more of the *Hundred Meditations on the Passion* and the *Hours of Eternal Wisdom*),[16] Italian (twenty-five manuscripts),[17] a number of Middle English versions in manuscript and print,[18] Czech (eight manuscripts), Swedish (two versions—one copied by nuns at Vadstena, the mother house of the Bridgettine Order—in five manuscripts altogether),[19] Hungarian, and Polish.[20] As we will see in chapter 2, the complexities of the English tradition (one of the most thoroughly researched among the vernaculars Suso entered) reveals quite widespread excerpting—if one extends manuscript counts to include significant excerpts, he may prove to have been even more widely known in various European vernaculars than current numbers appear to indicate. Suso was also published quite widely in the opening decades of print: before 1501, his works had already been printed at least sixteen times, once each in Aalst (Belgium), London, Delft, Schoonhoven (the Netherlands), Venice, Magdeburg, Nürnberg, twice in Augsburg, three times in Cologne, and four times in Paris.[21] This is already an impressive history of international copying and reading over the course of roughly 150 years, but it omits the use of Suso in excerpts as a source-text and the extensive use of some of his prayers, Passion meditation, and liturgy (not to mention, of course, his continued sixteenth- and seventeenth-century reception). His *One Hundred Meditations on the Passion* (the third book of the *Little Book of Eternal Wisdom*) reached its greatest audience in the Low Countries: translated from German to Dutch to Latin, then retranslated into Dutch (a total of thirteen times), versions of the text survive in 274 Netherlandish manuscripts. His liturgical *Office of Eternal Wisdom* (the third book of the *Horologium*) found an eager audience among the Dutch too: translated into the vernacular by Geert Grote, founder of the *devotio moderna*, it survives in at least 354 manuscripts. It was also included in some (but not all) versions of his vernacular book of hours, surviving in hundreds more copies.[22] This liturgy also had some success in England and English: it was included in some versions of the Sarum Hours, immediately after the Hours of the Virgin, and retitled "The Hours of the Name of Jesus" (and was also translated into English for some versions of the vernacular Sarum Hours).[23] Even if they may not have always been aware of it, late medieval devotional readers were encountering Suso at nearly every turn.

Rolle did not circulate in quite these numbers, or in as many languages, but he was still copied in quantities almost singular among early fourteenth-century English authors. In the early decades of the twentieth century, Hope Emily Allen consulted more than 400 manuscripts containing Rollean or Pseudo-Rollean material in assembling her foundational *Writings Ascribed to Richard Rolle, Hermit of Hampole* (1927); the *Emendatio vitae* alone, for instance, survives in 108 manuscripts.[24] Ralph Hanna's catalogue of the 123 English-language manuscripts of Rolle's work has enriched our understanding of the details of his widespread appeal in a variety of vernacular manuscript contexts.[25] Rolle's Latin works were also found outside of England in manuscript and print: most of his biblical commentaries, for example, were printed for the first time in 1535 and 1536 in Cologne by the Dominican Johannes Faber, in the service of the Counter-Reformation.[26] The number of extant Rolle manuscripts easily demonstrates his broad popularity as an author, but Denis Renevey has also written of his particular versatility and skill across genres and intellectual spheres, considering him "the like of a Chaucer in the field of religious literature."[27] There are other authors of the later Middle Ages who survive in numbers in this range, and in this variety of Latin *and* vernacular manuscript contexts, but they are truly rare.

The manuscript contexts in which Suso and Rolle appear are especially significant in understanding contemporary perspectives on the two authors, in particular their inclusion as authorities in numerous compilations and the consequent company they kept. Both circulated widely, both were considered popular enough to have multiple texts misattributed to them, and both appear alongside a similar coterie of devotional material. In this we can see clear evidence of audience desires and expectations that led compilers to include Suso and Rolle among similar devotional reading material. From Ralph Hanna's descriptive catalogue of English Rolle manuscripts, for instance, we can see that Rolle circulated in the vernacular most commonly with works by (erstwhile enemy) Walter Hilton (fourteen manuscripts). In five manuscripts Rolle appears alongside the Pseudo-Bonaventurean *Meditationes vitae Christi*, in three with William Flete, and in two with Bridget of Sweden.[28]

In the most straightforwardly codicological terms, Suso and Rolle are connected in the English devotional imagination (and historical record) by means of their joint presence in a number of miscellanies: they appear together in five important English devotional manuscripts. Cambridge University Library MS Ff.v.45 has a two-folio inclusion of lines 1–129 of Rolle's *Form of Living* added to the main manuscript that contains chapter 5 of the *Seven Points* (on the art of dying), and tracts from *Pore Caitif* and a series of vernacular prayers. British Library MS Additional 37790 (Amherst) has an extract from chapter 4 of the *Seven Points* alongside Rolle's *Ego Dormio* and *The Form of Living*, the short text of Julian of Norwich (known as *A Vision Showed to a Devout Woman*), Ruusbroec's *Treatise on the Perfection of the Sons of God*, Rolle's *Emendatio vitae* and *Incendium amoris* (both in Misyn's fifteenth-century English translation), Marguerite Porete, and a portion of Bridget of Sweden's *Revelations*.[29] Bodleian Library MS Douce 322 again contains the most popular extract of the *Seven Points*, on the art of dying well, alongside the English translation of the *Scala claustralium*, Rolle's *Emendatio vitae* (English translation, version 1), and numerous other devout treatises. Salisbury, Cathedral Library MS 56 contains the *Visio Tnugdali* and book 2, chapter 3 of the *Horologium*, immediately followed by *Emendatio vitae*.[30] Finally, Indiana University MS Poole 126, written in England in the late fourteenth or early fifteenth century, contains Rolle's *Contra amatores mundi* on ff. 1–16v followed immediately by a unique abridgment of four chapters from the *Horologium* (ff. 17r–27r), Rolle's *Orationes ad honorem Nominis Ihesu* (ff. 28r–29v), and the *Emendatio vitae* (ff. 29v–39r).[31] Each of these assemblages offers a unique instance of overlapping devotional interests (perhaps even, in Jill Havens's phrase, distinct "narratives of faith," however difficult to uncover they may be) definitively linking Rolle and Suso in the textual production of later medieval England.[32]

Examining their central devotional and pastoral concerns in tandem thus explains a great deal about the most fundamental interests, concerns, and reading practices of one of the largest subsets of late medieval readers readily identifiable. And yet the most extensive continuous comparative study of these two figures to date is the following paragraph in Wolfgang Riehle's *Middle English Mystics*:

> The mystical styles of Richard Rolle and Suso are very akin to each other in the fervour and imagery of their language. It is quite possible that Rolle, who was a contemporary of Suso's, had learned about

him in some way. Even manuscript illuminations show a remarkable parallel between the two mystics in one particular detail. Just as the British Library manuscripts, Cotton MS Faustina B VI, pt. II (f. 8v) and Addit. MS 37049 (f. 52v)—both from the first half of the fifteenth century—depict Rolle with a monogram of Christ on his breast, so too several manuscripts of Suso's Exemplar—the earliest from the second half of the fifteenth century—portray Suso with the monogram of Christ. This parallel does not of course prove any relationship between Rolle and Suso, as the manuscripts date from well after Rolle's death, but it does highlight the important point of affinity between them, for a deep devotion to the name of Jesus, which arose in connection with the mysticism of St Bernard, permeates the works of both men.[33]

Bernard McGinn also briefly mentions that "Suso, like his contemporary Richard Rolle, is one of the premier male mystics who describe experiences of heavenly sweetness, divine fragrance, celestial song, mystical dancing, and the physical warming of the heart."[34] Jeffrey Hamburger quickly discusses the iconographic similarities in manuscript images of the authors, and also their mutual interest in the desert fathers and their engagement in pastoral care.[35] But the study of these two authors in tandem has never proceeded further than these few general observations of similarity; the implications for our understanding of late medieval readers, the devotional culture England and Germany appear to have shared, and the respective postmedieval reception histories of the two authors have all, as yet, been largely untouched.

Various strands of national literature have, over the past two centuries, separated authors into distinct language groups, but readers in late medieval literary and devotional culture rarely acknowledged such boundaries.[36] Rolle and Suso, besides their incomparable popularity among fourteenth- and fifteenth-century devotional readers, also encouraged similar patterns of devotional response and fostered a sense of spiritual authorship that rewards deeper investigation. As they wrote, their understanding and exposition of contemplation, affective response, and exegesis had the same contours; their writing shared common spiritual concerns and developed similar senses of devotion and affect in their readers.[37] As devotional theologians, they knew few peers.

EXEMPLARY AUTHORS AND IMITATIVE READERS

What does it mean for a reader to want to imitate an author? How does a devotional author create a text in which he or she appears as a character worthy of imitation? In order to understand the significance of Suso's and Rolle's position in the history of late medieval devotion, we must examine their particular understandings of selfhood, their consequent pseudo-autobiographical self-presentation as the author of their texts, the means by which they acquire status as authorial figures, and, ultimately, their self-presentation as exemplary figures that share with Christ the potential to be a model for imitation. It is in these strategies of textual self-fashioning and literary self-creation that Suso and Rolle stake their claim for authority and significance to devotional readers, and by which they gain a great deal of their affective potency.

I have written in greater detail elsewhere about the shifts in models of authorship, linked to the thirteenth-century scholastic development of the exemplar cause (as an addition to the Aristotelian four causes); this concept of authorship finds prominent expression in the authorial programs of Suso and Rolle, particularly their novel use of "exemplary causation" to redefine the purpose and power of exemplary figures for their readers.[38] The most essential piece of this argument here is the growing role of exemplary author-characters in the spiritual literature of the fourteenth century (Suso making this point especially clearly by assembling his works into a self-authorized anthology and giving it the title *The Exemplar*).[39] That is to say, not only do Suso and Rolle write pseudo-autobiography, they create pseudo-autobiographical figures as *exemplars*.[40] As Jessica Barr has written of Rolle's vernacular *Meditations on the Passion*, Rolle's narrative self, witnessing the brutal crucifixion of Christ and yearning for an appropriate emotional response to it, is "at once a rhetorically specific individual reflecting on personal experience and an open 'I' inviting the reader's participation in the scene that he describes," a literary-theological technique in which Rolle's "persona draws the reader into an idealised response to the central story of the Christian faith."[41] For both Suso and Rolle, this open-ended narrative persona not only stimulates but *creates* imitative behaviors and emotional responses in their readers.

The concept of Christian imitation stretches back, of course, to the New Testament, and sees perhaps its most emphatic expression with the rapid spread of Passion meditations in the thirteenth and fourteenth centuries.[42] Already in the Pauline epistles, of course, one sees the introduction of author-characters designed as textual intermediaries in the process of following Jesus: Paul quite pointedly places himself above the Corinthians, encouraging them to follow his own example of following Christ rather than directly follow Christ (1 Cor. 11:1—"Imitatores mei estote sicut et ego Christi").[43] The early Christian cult of imitation through martyrdom, too, encompasses a wide range of cultural, literary, and theological approaches to imitation—each account of a martyr imitating Christ through suffering "involves a particular reading of traditions about Jesus, his death, his significance, and his work."[44] That is to say, any imitation of Christ, beginning with Paul and the early church, has never been a straightforward or unmediated act, nor can it ever be a clear, one-dimensional devotional practice (even the belief that one can simply follow the Christ of the New Testament immediately runs up against the different emphases of the four Gospel accounts of his life). Its variety is mediated by both text (the text of the New Testament itself and the conceptual framework provided in the textual community in which the imitation is taking place) and by other exemplary figures who have been presented as following Christ in a mode well suited to a particular brand of Christic imitation.[45] Rolle and Suso participate in and continue this literary-devotional movement by recounting their own authorship of especially exemplary texts, even as their literary personas are seen performing a variety of exemplary pious acts.

Thus their reports of mystical experience (alongside their prayers, participation in the liturgy, acts of reading, and other pious actions) are constructed in part to be self-consciously exemplary. Even reading these texts may serve as an act of devotion in which readers imagine themselves inside the imaginative world of the text, mirrorlike. In this, of course, both Suso and Rolle had also to make a display of reluctance in imagining their texts as worthy to be imitated: in the preface to the *Life*, for instance, Suso describes how Elsbeth Stagel transcribed their conversations without his knowledge. He discovers this, and demands they be burned—until divine intervention demands he allow her authorship of his life to continue. Rolle, on the other hand, carefully prefaces many of his works to appear to limit their applicability while intensifying their immediacy.[46] Nicholas Watson writes, of Rolle's prosimetric *I Sleep, but My Heart Is Awake* (*Ego Dormio*), that its immediacy and its setting in the present affirm "the reality of two other people: Christ, whose love is presented as being always available now; and Rolle himself, who is always to be heard 'speaking' the words he has written."[47] Both this rhetoric of immediacy and the rhetoric of exclusivity in the text's self-identification as an epistle contributes to the overall effect of exemplarity: although he is distant, through the epistolary medium Rolle makes a claim for being present through his intimate speaking voice.[48] Rolle writes that "to þe I writ þis speciali, for I hope in þe more goodnes þan in anoþer, þat þou wil gif þi þoght to fulfil in dede þat þou seest is profitable for þi soule" (*Ego Dormio*, O-T 33–35), establishing a uniquely intimate bond between reader and writer. These strategies are clearly part and parcel of the more general imitative trend of late medieval devotion: the constant adaptation of clerical forms of worship for lay devotion is here amplified to the imitation of a holy hermit or friar.[49]

LATIN AND THE VERNACULAR:
BETWEEN MOTHER AND FATHER TONGUES

One of the most important distinctions between Suso and Rolle, however, can be found in their attitude toward language itself, and their varied uses of languages. Both wrote in Latin and the vernacular, but Suso began his career as a writer in the vernacular, seeming to value it above Latin as an expressive medium (or, at the very least, prizing it as a more effective language pastorally). Only later in his life did he rework his most popular Middle High German treatise, the *Büchlein der ewigen Weisheit* (*Little Book of Eternal Wisdom*, hereafter *LBEW*), as the Latin *Horologium Sapientiae* (*Clock of Wisdom*), changing its content and structure quite significantly in the process. This self-translation, however, launched Suso's work into its extraordinarily successful pan-European reception. Rolle, on the other hand, spent most of his career writing in Latin, and appears to have turned to English only rather later on in his life. This turn was also in part motivated by pastoral purposes, most especially his increased concern with the care of women, during the final stage of his career—a period described by Nicholas Watson in general terms as a pursuit of the "mixed life."[50] Even more importantly, however, it came after his authority as a mystic author and reporter of experience had been firmly established by his earlier writings. Nevertheless, one need only briefly consider the quality of the prosimetric epistles, not to mention the expanse of the *English Psalter*, to see that Rolle could use the vernacular as a powerfully expressive medium. Whereas Suso's Latin and vernacular works show relatively little theological difference—and the vernacular is certainly his preference—Rolle's Latin and vernacular works often differ quite substantially.[51] This discrepancy in their attitude toward languages sheds light on their reception of theological tradition, their authorial aims, and their intended audience—and also on the regional valences of the vernacular in northern England and the Rhineland in the first half of the fourteenth century.

The early fourteenth century saw most German-speaking regions already well past the thirteenth-century flowering of chivalric narrative and *Minnesang*, whereas Middle English devotional literature was still relatively nascent, with only relatively minor literary production in Middle English by the time Rolle began writing.[52] The issue of vernacularity also points toward their concerns about authority: although both emphasize their constant persecution by jealous and misunderstanding rivals, Suso's more traditional position as a Dominican friar is a significant contrast to Rolle's quite idiosyncratic path as a self-made hermit (and thus his use of Latin as the official theological medium to establish himself as a theological authority—despite the irregularities of his lifestyle—at the start of his career). Both received excellent Latinate educations, but Rolle's training at Oxford might have made Latin seem a more obvious choice for theological and exegetical writing, whereas Suso's period at the Dominican school of theology in Cologne saw him influenced not only by the Latin scholasticism of Albert the Great and Thomas Aquinas but also, perhaps most profoundly, by the great master of vernacular German preaching, Meister Eckhart.[53]

The greater appeal of Suso to a vernacular audience, overall, is also apparent in the reception history of Suso's Latin text: whereas the *Horologium* was translated into vernaculars across Europe, Rolle's Latin works largely remained in Latin. Important exceptions, however, are found in the reception of Rolle's *Emendatio vitae* (*Mending of Life*) and the *Incendium amoris* (*Fire of Love*), translated into English by the Yorkshire Carmelite Richard Misyn in the middle of the fifteenth century (and others). Indeed Rolle's Latin works survive in far more manuscripts in England than do either English adaptations of Suso or Latin Suso manuscripts of English provenance.[54] Rolle's success in achieving posthumous Latin *and* vernacular authority can also be seen in his later use as a source in devotional collections such as the *Donatus devotionis* and the *Speculum spiritualium*.

Suso's appreciation of the potential of the vernacular is surely based in part on his admiration for Meister Eckhart, a writer who could blend snippets of sophisticated biblical exegesis, quotations from Pseudo-Dionysius, and passing references to intellectual debates in Paris with a method of expression (especially in the German sermons) laced with vivid metaphors, profound parables, and casual examples drawn from everyday life.[55] He created a style of theological discourse, blending the colloquial and the scholastic, which Erich Auerbach refers to as "personal, familiar, one might almost say neighborly."[56] Both Latin and vernacular works of Eckhart, however, were also deemed problematic: in describing the process of condemning Eckhart for heresy leading up to the posthumous bull of 1329, Bernard McGinn points out that "Eckhart was taken to task for *both* his Latin and his vernacular works. Among the articles condemned in the papal bull, fifteen are taken from the German works and thirteen from the Latin."[57] Both languages were seen as integral to Eckhart's theological career when he was condemned by papal officials in Avignon.

Eckhart's sense of the valences of language choice is linked to a Johannine theology in which the Father speaks the Word (Jesus) and Jesus speaks words in the soul of the believer, in Eckhart's words, "according to the manner to which the spirit is receptive."[58] Eckhart describes both the Incarnation and personal experience of the divine, too, in terms of the Johannine *logos*; he sees a repetition of the Father's speaking the Word (of both creation and the Incarnation) in Jesus's own intimate speaking in the soul of the believer (a variation on one of his central themes, the eternal birth of the Son in the soul of the believer).[59] The self-revelation of the Son in the soul, however, emphasizes both the intimacy and the accessibility of the divine message: this creative speech act, transmitted from the Father to mankind through the mediation of Jesus, is meant for spiritual reception on an immediate, personal level. That is to say, the mediation provided through this speaking (or, as elsewhere, birth) of the Son in the soul takes place primarily to establish a personal, internalized acceptance of the divine message. It is a theology and rhetoric deeply and intricately invested in whatever lies closest to the emotional heart of an individual, and in many cases this proves to be best expressed in the vernacular. At the same time, however, Eckhart remains humble about the linguistic power of his own sermons, vernacular or Latin. The straightforward existence of the substance of a simple rock, he says, can teach more about the existence of God than any of his most noteworthy linguistic triumphs: "The same thing that my mouth says about God, and reveals Him, the being of a stone does too—and one learns more from works than from words."[60]

Suso expresses his use of the vernacular in still simpler terms: he claims to have straightforwardly transcribed what God said, and God happened to speak to him in German. In the prologue to the devotional manual *LBEW*, Suso most directly addresses his own understanding of the vernacular. The text opens with a description of the pious Suso standing before a crucifix and finding himself unable to focus properly on Christ's torment. Then, "as he stood lamenting, an unusual ecstasy came to his inner senses."[61] Over the course of this illumination, Suso is granted a hundred meditations on the suffering of Christ to complement his *veniae*, or prostrations (in fact, he counts the meditations from the first revelation, finds only ninety, complains to God, and then receives the final ten). Realizing that these meditations might be able to help others overcome their devotional troubles, he decides to compose the *LBEW*: "And so he wrote down the meditations and did so in German, for so they were given to him by God."[62] The vernacular here is portrayed not as a medium of accessibility or intimacy, but rather a matter of divine self-revelation. God spoke German; Suso simply transcribed.

And yet Suso later qualifies this, carefully clarifying that this revelation was not, in fact, straightforwardly auditory—nor was it explicitly visual. The intimate conversations with Eternal Wisdom

did not take place as bodily conversations nor with image-rich responses. Rather, they took place solely by meditation in the light of holy scripture (whose responses cannot lead one astray). Thus the re-sponses were taken either from the mouth of Eternal Wisdom, who Herself spoke them in the gospels, or from the highest of spiritual teachers; they have either the same words or the same sense or [ac-cord with] such truth which has been spoken from the mouth of Eter-nal Wisdom according to the sense of the holy scripture.[63]

This would seem to imply that the work is composed primarily of selec-tions from scripture and the church fathers, and commentary thereon. Rather than emphasize any potential novelty, he quickly transforms his claim to have transcribed a vernacular conversation with God under a crucifix into a more modest assertion that he has produced nothing more than a series of meditations on texts that either Eternal Wisdom spoke in the Gospels or that could be found in the authoritative works of the holy fathers (despite the fact that both would likely have been encountered in Latin).[64] Yet the seed has been planted in the reader's mind: even though these are safe and orthodox, steeped in tradition, they are also personal revelations transcribed directly from God's speech.

He continues to minimize the immediate, revelatory nature of the text by claiming that the visions described therein are but an *usgeleitú* (educational or illustrative) *bischaft* (example or parable), and he ac-knowledges Bernard of Clairvaux by name as the source of the Marian laments.[65] He then provides a pastoral explanation for his style: "The teaching is presented as a dialogue, for this is more enjoyable—not that he himself [i.e., the author] is the one discussed or that he has spoken about himself. He intends to give a common teaching in which both he and all others can find just that which pertains to them."[66] Suso distances himself from being identified with characters of the dialogue, explicitly claiming it to be a *fictional* scenario structured in the service of peda-gogical and pastoral aims; yet Suso's self-presentation within the text is also central to his authorial project. There are few spiritual authors of the period *more* concerned with how they portray "themselves" as characters in their own texts. But the absolute historicity of the self-representation is not of concern here (there is very little that can be said with any confi-dence about the possible historical truth nested in Suso and Rolle's narra-tives); rather, the *belief* of both author and contemporary audience in the exemplary power of the representation is what makes the *Vita* significant in the study of popular religious literature. Indeed, the Disciple is not even intended to be a singular creature rooted in one place and time, let alone a replica of the historical Suso. Instead, as the *Horologium* itself claims, the Disciple serves "to represent everyone who is like him."[67]

On the style of the text, Suso writes further that "the thoughts which stand here are simple [*einvaltig*]; thus the words are even simpler, for they come from a simple soul and are spoken to simple people."[68] The supposed humility of his subject matter dictates the humility of his rhetoric; the aforementioned self-distancing from divine revelation or even originality corresponds neatly to this deployment of the humble style, the *sermo humilis*. The novelty the prologue of the *LBEW* first posited (and the inherent novelty of particular human experiences worthy of being reported) is subsumed in a gesture pushing the following text toward an ideal of humility and simplicity (a significant contrast to the more intense philosophical speculation of, for instance, his *Little Book of Truth*).

Suso ends the prologue by returning to the subject of divine speech; he "apologizes" for his book by disparaging the affective potency of the written word in favor of the spoken. In a famous passage on the status of his vernacular, he writes:

> Just as to hear for oneself the sweet sound of strings being played is unlike simply hearing someone talk about music, so too are words that are received in pure grace and flowing out of a living heart and a lively mouth unlike the same words appearing on a dead parchment, and especially in the German tongue. They somehow grow cold and blanch completely like plucked roses. That joyful art—that which above all things moves the human heart—then fades away and is received in the dryness of dry hearts. There were never strings so sweet that did not grow dumb when stretched across a dry board. An unloving heart can understand a song of love just as little as a German can understand an Italian.[69]

Just as a description of music naturally pales in comparison to hearing it actually being performed, so too words on a "dead parchment" are desiccated and barren when compared to an inspired oral recitation or the warmth of private conversation. Particularly noteworthy is that Suso specifically highlights the expressiveness of his native Middle High German and its need to be recited by a "fervent mouth" in order to be fully under-stood, priming readers for sympathetic appreciation, but also preparing them for the disappointment that may come depending on their own spiritual or emotional state. He encourages the reader to overlook the short-comings of written German and bids us to understand them in light of their source "where they existed alive and in attractive beauty."[70] We are to imagine orality at all times, even if we encounter the text silently. After having imagined or experienced the beauty of the original, he is certain, one "cannot really ever read through this without his heart being deeply moved."[71] As moved as we are by the text, we are meant to imagine the experience of hearing these words directly from Suso's mouth as more moving still.[72]

And yet the rhetorical skill and literary references in the *Horolo-gium*, on the other hand, amply demonstrate his familiarity with the Latin literary and theological tradition and his facility in Latin composition. Furthermore, his theological lexis can differ significantly between the *Horologium* and the *LBEW*.[73] The two works give us the opportunity to see precisely how his message differed in vernacular and Latin versions, and it is often the case that the vocabulary chosen for the *LBEW* points to-ward an intentionally simplified pastoral style. Claire Champollion notes, for instance, in comparing the *Horologium* to the *LBEW*, that in the Ger-man text "we find hardly any corresponding terms for *ratio, intellectus, mens*. Not because the words are lacking; they exist, but they are hardly ever used."[74] Despite the most pseudo-autobiographical work, the *Vita*, being written only in German, he is sure to point readers wanting to learn more toward any version of his own works, writing in the *Vita* that a reader interested in the practices that started him on his path to piety "can find [them] in his *Little Book of Wisdom* in German and Latin."[75] Here, both the Latin and German versions of the text are lumped together as equal expressions of divine inspiration, despite Suso's own deliberate ef-fort in the prologue to humble himself and his text by downplaying the role of God and Latin in the book's composition.

In the prologue to the *Horologium*, meanwhile, Suso performs the denigration of his own Latin style: "Now, I entreat my devout readers not to be displeased by my unskilled and crude language, even though it perhaps may seem to sound barbarous to them. For I do not greatly care if I blunder into the errors that polished preachers abhor, provided that I have been able with my earnest words to correct and cure more easily the errors in men's minds."[76] His simple style, he claims, avoids the overpolishing of other authors and preachers and aims at the appropriate goal of correcting moral errors rather than being overconcerned with mere stylistic ones: "Indeed, because in the past these same matters have been expounded by many authors with such subtlety and style and such frequency that they have now become almost wearisome, I have not attempted to quote the authorities for everything; for if I had named everyone who says as I do, the object of this book would have been defeated."[77] Even in stressing the orthodoxy and lack of novelty of his treatise, he also excuses himself from the need to cite his authorities comprehensively; this prologue almost appears designed to distract a potentially critical reader from the real novelty of the self-asserted, experiential authority of the character created within.

Suso's attitude toward the vernacular seems to be somewhat malleable, perhaps even a bit opportunistic. Although he tends to associate it, as does Eckhart, with a humble and natural manner of expression, quite suitable to the kenotic subject matter their works often dwell on, he also recognizes the considerable opportunities granted by Latin—a wider, if not broader, audience, most especially. In the largest structural change made in his reworking the vernacular *LBEW* into the Latin *Horologium*, Suso replaces the *Büchlein*'s *Hundred Meditations* (book 3) with the *Cursus de Aeterna Sapientia* (*Office of Eternal Wisdom*). Both are seen as the sole ancillary section of the respective works: they alone, Suso states explicitly, may be copied separately. Here too, Suso is adapting for different audiences: the Passion meditation is provided for a vernacular readership more likely to be female religious or lay, the *Office* for the devotional and liturgical needs of Latinate, more clerical readers.

For Rolle the vernacular is seen more directly as a tool to offer greater accessibility—whether written didactically for a general audience or used in a more specific work of pastoralia for an intended recipient. Watson's assessment that the English works are largely "occasional pieces, rather than bricks in the tower of Rolle's authority"[78] is largely accurate (when restricted specifically to the category of authority-building); this makes it all the more unusual that critical attention in recent decades has largely focused on the small fraction of his output that was written in the vernacular. The size and scope of the *English Psalter*, however—though it "probably began as a response to Margaret Kirkby's desire to understand the doctrine behind the spiritual songs she was to spend so much of her life, as nun and anchoress, chanting"[79]—is a significant exception to the idea that his vernacular works were little more than an authorial afterthought. The *English Psalter* might perhaps offer instead a hint as to what his career might have come to look like had he lived another decade or two, and had he needed to respond to an ever-growing vernacular audience as the fourteenth century continued. Although it is, of course, quite difficult to imagine his becoming a Lollard, Rolle would have been strongly sympathetic with aspects of their evangelical fervor, if nothing else—and the Lollards, to be sure, deeply appreciated his vernacular biblical authorship, as the Lollard interpolations in a large number of manuscripts of the *English Psalter* testify.[80]

A later Lollard interpolator wrote a verse prologue to the Psalter, explaining the pressing need to write an exposition of the Psalms. Although it does not express Rolle's own understanding of the project, a text like this nevertheless helps to explain the status of vernacular commentary in the decades after his death. Indeed, the Psalms are acknowledged as the ideal way to praise God, but there is often a problem:

> Bot for the psalmes bene ful derke   in many a place whos[o] wol take hede,
> And the sentence is ful merke   euery row who so wol rede;
> Hit nedeth exposicyon   written wel with monnes honde,
> To stirre to more deuocyowne   & hit the bettur vndurstonde.[81]

The direct intimacy between author and reader that can be found in, for instance, the prosimetric epistle *Ego Dormio*, is again emphasized here. Beyond simply highlighting these exegetical qualities, the prologue also emphasizes the *personal* element of the Psalter—handwritten by Rolle himself, made especially for Margaret Kirkby's use—and its utility in encouraging both devotion and comprehension before continuing to describe the location of the nunnery of Hampole itself and Rolle's own saintly deeds: "This same sauter in all degre is the self in sothnes / That lyȝt at hampole in surte at Richard own berynes, / That he wrote with his hondes to dame Merget kyrkby / And thar it lyȝt in cheyn bondes in the same nonery."[82]

The prologue then goes on to discuss how exactly the translation takes the form it does, with the goal of aiding the marriage between God and the soul:

> This holy man, in expownyng   he fologth holy doctours;
> And in all his englysching   ryȝt aftur the latyn taketh cours.
> And makes it compendyous   short gode and profetabul
> To mannys soule, goddys spouse   in charite to make hym stabul.
> Errour in hit is ther non   ne deseyt ne heresy,
> Bot euery word is sad as stone   and sothly sayd, ful sykerly.[83]

The *lack* of innovation and the closeness of the vernacular to the Latin (the English itself seems more of an explanatory tool to bring the reader closer to an understanding of the Vulgate Psalter) is precisely what heightens the success of its encouraging the spiritual marriage of the soul and God. Rolle's own prologue declares that the Vulgate Psalter is an enclosed garden, a paradise "ful of all appils" and yet within which "the sange that delites the hertes & lerese the saule is made a voice of syngand, and with aungels whaim we may noght here we menge wordis of louynge, sa that worthily he may trow him."[84] This somewhat obscure passage seems to refer to the actualization of an unsounded melody (*sange*) in singing (*a voice syngand*), which in turn can lead to the pure worship found in the ineffability of angels' song.

This preface also famously addresses stylistic issues relating to Psalm commentary in the vernacular:

> In this werke I seke na straunge ynglis, bot lyghtest and comonest, and swilk that is mast lyke til the latyn. Swa that thai that knawes noght latyn by the ynglis may com til mony latyn wordis. In the translacioun I folow the lettere als mykyll as I may. And thare I fynd na propire ynglis, I folow the wit of the worde, swa that thai sall red it thaim thare noght dred errynge. In expounynge I fologh haly doctors.[85]

The project of the Psalter is not only to gloss and translate the Latin, but also to provide some degree of instruction in the Latin original; the glossing itself is seen as following in the orthodox exegetical tradition. Suso seems largely unconcerned with his audience's potential Latinity (but the German works do employ Latin tags from scripture and liturgy), but Rolle's most lengthy English work is in large part designed to guide readers toward the more authoritative Latin text it glosses. This attitude toward Latin may have been the case during and immediately after Rolle's life, but his status as a vernacular author seems only to increase as time passes. Already in 1510, in a Paris printing of the wide-ranging fifteenth-century spiritual encyclopedia *Speculum spiritualium* (likely Carthusian, the work also cites Suso, Mechthild of Hackeborn, and Bridget of Sweden), it is Rolle's English that is singled out for attention. In an otherwise entirely Latin compilation, one chapter alone is printed in English (mistake-riddled English, as it was typeset in Paris), without any editorial explanation for the language change: a chapter from Rolle's *The Form of Living*.[86]

FEMININITY AND COURTLY LOVE:
MARRYING JESUS AND GENDERING THE SOUL

þai sai þat I ame most vnmanli
—Christ speaking to Bridget, in *The Liber Celestis of St Bridget of Sweden*, ed. Roger Ellis (EETS o.s. 291, 80)

Women play a catalyzing role in the life-narratives, spirituality, and ministry of both Suso and Rolle. From the opening of their life stories (Rolle's sister providing makeshift vestments for him, Suso taking his mother's name instead of his aristocratic father's in admiration of her piety) and their overall pastoral aims to their devotion to Mary and Eternal Wisdom, aspects of femininity permeate the consciousness of their texts.[87] Their very concept of authorship itself is formed in relationship with an imagined female audience that itself is often vividly represented in their texts. In Rolle's case, several of the vernacular tracts and the *English Psalter* claim to be written for a female recluse, Margaret Kirkby, and are prefaced with dedications to her. Suso, for his part, wrote numerous letters to women under his care, collecting them into the *Little Book of Letters*, and represents the *Life*, or *Vita*, itself as being secretly transcribed by his spiritual daughter over the course of numerous conversations. Considering Rolle's understanding of gender more broadly, Nicholas Watson notes that the *Incendium amoris* contains "a discussion of *amicitia* with no clear relevance to the treatments of *canor* surrounding it, [which] seems to have been written largely for the sake of its reflections on friendship between men and women."[88] Indeed, one of the most vivid scenes of the description of Rolle's life in the *Officium* (an office written for his feast day, were he to be canonized) is his curing the recluse Margaret Kirkby, then spending the night outside her cell with her head on his shoulder; in a somewhat more awkward moment, he notoriously is reprimanded for asking unseemly questions about the size of a devotee's breasts.[89]

The lavish Latin of Suso's *Horologium*, meanwhile, is quite extensive in its mixing of the erotic and the courtly alongside exegesis and practical catechesis. It includes, for instance, a quite lengthy and elaborate description of Mary's breasts. The chapter begins soberly with Mary standing beside the cross, but then Suso soon begins to describe Mary's beauty in ways that might even outstrip his earlier (also quite florid) blazon of Eternal Wisdom. The ekphrastic banquet pauses in its journey across her body, however, and considers Mary's breasts in considerable detail. Suso takes the Song of Song's metaphor of the beloved's breasts being twin roes feeding among the lilies and elaborates on it with exuberant abandon. Some of this surely must be inspired by Bernard of Clairvaux's famous sermons on the Song of Songs, but its detailed attention to metaphorical complexity very quickly outstrips Bernard's exposition of the perfumed breasts of the bride and bridegroom of the Song of Songs.[90] Suso considers the beauty of all of creation, for instance, comparing it unfavorably to Mary's body: "See how the Founder of the universe adorned the celestial bodies with stars, the earth at its beginnings with beasts and birds, the woods with verdant foliage, the meadows with smiling flowers; but far above these, blessed Virgin, he made your body lovely with its most holy breasts."[91]

The translator, Edmund Colledge, duly notes that this passage follows a variety of earlier authors in linking God's creation to the earth's beauty, acknowledging, however, that none make the leap to praising Mary's breasts.[92] Drawing on a traditional motif for the beauty of creation, Suso nevertheless insists that this pales in comparison to the very breasts that Jesus suckled. The paragraph then continues with quotations from the Song of Songs, Zachariah, Genesis, Exodus, and Ephesians before considering the centerpiece of this quite exuberant passage, the healing power of her milk:

> For "in wine there is luxury" [Song 1:13] but in these golden phials there is the total extinguishing of the poison of concupiscence, and a delight that is heavenly and supernatural. Anyone who has tasted knows how swiftly and completely every carnal pleasure has vanished, once he has tasted the milk of your graces. Virulent serpents, terrified, fled from the fragrance of those ointments from above, and they could not endure the presence of such purity.[93]

This rhapsodic passage focuses primarily on the noncorporeal healing qualities of the milk: effective against spiritual harm, carnal temptation, and demonic threats. The paragraph then ends by imagining the souls of all men joining together to exclaim in the words of the first verse of the Song of Songs, the very words most readers have been expecting: "Thy breasts are better than wine!"

Of the many women praised in Suso's works, his intense devotion to both Mary and Jesus-as-Wisdom can create a somewhat jarring comparison between the spiritual benefits gained by suckling at Mary's breast and Jesus-as-Wisdom's breast.[94] Mary's provides perfectly nourishing and consoling milk, but nursing from Eternal Wisdom's teat yields instead a "spiritual wine" (*vinum spirituale*; K 510.2), which, though sweet, contains "a certain mixture of bitterness" (*mixta quaedam acerbitas*; K 510.4), or provides milk mixed with "as it were a sharp wine" (*quasi austeritatem vini*; K 510.8). Whatever rewards we get from nursing at Eternal Wisdom's breast, Suso claims, they are nevertheless inevitably tempered with some unwelcome chastising. We are often able to inhabit the Christ-as-(female)-Wisdom allegory for long enough stretches of text that such images become not especially jarring, but in this instance Suso then suddenly collapses the comparison between Christ-as-Wisdom and Jesus, between spiritual spouse and spiritual parent: "And when I have rejoiced to possess Him as my dearest spouse, suddenly amazed to remember His divinity, I have entreated him as my Judge. And when time to time I have asked Him for milk, He has rejected me, and He has shown me a sour severity, as if to 'a child that is weaned from its mother.'"[95] Eternal Wisdom, once an elegant bride, is here transformed into a husband again for a brief moment; the Disciple has been so deeply involved in the spiritual marriage with her that he is even able to forget her status as God-Man, and yet he still petitions Christ as a mother for consoling milk, only to be scolded, like a baby, in the words of Psalm 130.

This same alternation between maternal succor and harsher admonishment—and between masculine and feminine ideals of nourishment—is found elsewhere in the *Horologium* and is a hallmark of his elaborate structure of gender-ambiguous rhetoric. The narrator speaks to Jesus: "To me, seeking your divinity, you show your humanity; I seek sweetness, and you offer bitterness; I ask for milk from your breasts, and your gift for me is to fight in manful battles."[96] In a passage in which Eternal Wisdom acts as a comforter, Wisdom fills an excess of *male* gender roles (again blending erotic and familial ties): "I am your brother, your spouse!" (ego sum frater tuus, sponsus tuus) (K 400.17),[97] while Sin is personified as "clever little vixen" with a "whore's face" (C 93). The first words of the Disciple's Soul's response to this brother-spouse figure then turn Wisdom into a *father* also: "Oh, the unheard-of compassion of the heart of the father! Oh, stupendous love of a brother's faithfulness!"[98] Eternal Wisdom's gender is never stable, neither in the vernacular nor here in Latin; indeed, translation from Latin into other vernaculars results in an even more complicated gendering of divine characters.

Suso is not alone, however, in employing these types of gender ambiguities and fluctuations. References to femininity in the *Melos amoris* are primarily negative (warning of the fleshly enticements and distractions women provide to the contemplative), but in his commentary on the Song of Songs Rolle joins Suso in employing the motif of Jesus-as-Mother when considering the breasts of the bride of the Song of Songs:[99]

> Speaking allegorically, it can be said to any saint just as that woman said in the Gospel to Christ: "blessed be the womb which bore you and the breasts which gave you suck." For just as before we were born bodily into the world we were carried in our mother's womb, so before walking or running or taking real food it was necessary for us to take milk from our mother's breasts; thus, spiritually, before baptism or penance [we are] in Christ's womb, that is, in His patience.[100]

Although the primary example here is Christ, Rolle extends the possibility of this suckling motif to *quemlibet sanctum* (not *sanctam*), offering a still broader feminization of the reader's spiritual relationship (that is, in imitation of those male saints who can be allegorically linked to the anonymous woman in the Gospel), imagined here as a nourishing relationship of suckling, with exemplary *male* figures from Christ to the saints. This passage, asserting the maternal succor Christ offers immediately after an invocation, in Denis Renevey's words, of "the joy, the sweet kiss, the madness, the inebriation, the panting, the sighs and the melting" of the erotic relationship of God to the soul, emphasizes the wide range of allegorical roles, both erotic and parental, Christ can inhabit.[101] In an episode in the Rollean *Verba seniorum*, too, a hermit cannot find anyone to confess the "gret temptaciouns in his thoghts," presumably sexual temptations. As he plans to cope with this shame by abandoning his vocation and returning to the world, "þe same nyght, þe grace of oure Lorde Ihesu in lyknes of a madyn aperde to him,"[102] comforting him and promising that simply by sitting with Jesus-as-maiden no harm will come to him.

Suso's investment in the feminine is so profound that he reverses the conventional image in visionary literature of male scribe serving a female would-be author, and delegates all initial authorial inspiration to his "spiritual daughter," Elsbeth Stagel. He claims in the *Vita* that she secretly copied down their conversations, which, once discovered, he began to burn. A divine voice then halted him, authorizing the hagiographical project of the *Vita*—indeed, the text makes a claim for coauthorship between Suso and Stagel that contemporary scholarship has been all too eager to dismiss.[103] Hildegard Keller argues that "the use of the fictional character 'Elsbeth' for the development of the *Exemplar* is firstly a narrative tool which helps to construct the exemplarity of the Servant. . . . Women function in the *Vita* as figures of response: their attention, eagerness to learn, and readiness to be wholeheartedly trustful are expressions of recognition and approval, casting a bright light on the charismatic Servant."[104] Throughout the *Vita*, Elsbeth indeed plays the role of the ideal acolyte (even though she is, I believe, on the whole rather more active than this account warrants), tempering any potential reader's zeal to see Suso's extraordinary acts of self-mortification as perfectly exemplary and replicable. Elsbeth gives us a lens through which we might admire Suso's piety, and imitate *some* aspects of it, without taking our spiritual lives to the extremes he seems to disapprove of in others.[105]

Even further, however, Jeffrey Hamburger writes that it is "virtually unprecedented . . . the way in which Suso turns the genre of the *Vita* inside out, establishing Stagel as a virtual mother confessor to whom he reveals his innermost spiritual secrets through the letters that ostensibly provided the basis for his 'autobiography.'"[106] For the *Vita* ends, in fact, not with a glorification of Suso's life, works, and achievements. Instead, it is Elsbeth who has gained heavenly reward and posthumously appears in a spiritual vision to the Servant, consoling him and assuring him of *her* reward.[107] Rolle also believes he has a special role in ministering to women, but he is careful to point out that we are *not* to follow his example in this. Rolle emphasizes the unique role he plays in the care of women by "warning readers [in the *Melos amoris*] not to regard his engagement with women as something to imitate, implying that God has bestowed on him a special grace which frees him from the fear of succumbing to carnal love."[108]

Critics have commented on a certain femininity to their writing style and devotional habits; this has been in turn lauded or disparaged alongside changing trends in the study of gender.[109] As just two examples, Wolfgang Riehle has written of the influence of the Song of Songs on Rolle and its imagery of "sweet flowing" that "give [Rolle's] mystical language that characteristically soft, almost female tone."[110] Richard Kieckhefer, too, points out in *Unquiet Souls* that raptures and visions "generally were more important to the female than to the male saints, with few exceptions: when men did have visions, they were seldom integral to their lives as for the women. (The one most important exception is Henry Suso.)"[111] The pastoral concern both authors have for their female flock is far from superficial or born of necessity; it often pervades the very language and structure of their accounts of mystical experience.

Gender also plays a central role in their representations of God: Suso, operating largely within the tradition of bridal mysticism, fills his texts with oscillating and intertwining genders for characters both divine and human. Most notably, rather than imagining himself or his soul as a female wedded to Christ (in the tradition of Bernard of Clairvaux and

William of Saint-Thierry, among others), he describes an elaborate court-ship leading to his spiritual marriage with the courtly lady, Jesus as Eter-nal Wisdom.[112] Rolle, too, pledges his devotion to the Goddess Jesus in the guise of (feminine) Wisdom, declaring in *Against the Lovers of the World* that "this beloved [*dilecta*] of mine is Uncreated Wisdom, truly worthy of love and most gratifying in love."[113] And yet both also dedi-cate large portions of their texts to meditations on the (male) humanity of Christ; they then (usually) aim to depict their souls as female in order to respond to the bridegroom within the expected heteronormative bound-aries. In the *Horologium*, for instance, the soul laments how she has been made a "miserable woman," "a widow and desolate," and "not worthy to be called his kitchen maid," having lost her betrothed on account of her sins (C 91–92).

The prologue of Suso's *Horologium* addresses this concern for the heterosexuality of the mystical marriage quite directly. A passage de-tailing the rhetorical strategies employed within the text, and the role of the varying representations of Disciple and Wisdom, concludes by explaining that "sometimes the Son of God is presented as the spouse of the devout soul; then later the same Son is introduced as the Eter-nal Wisdom, wedded to the just man."[114] Jesus's gender fluidity within the text is addressed without any particular anxiety: Jesus can be de-scribed as the masculine Son of God when wedded to the feminine soul (*animae*), but uncontroversially becomes the feminine Eternal Wisdom when then wedded to the just man (*viro iusto*).[115] Even depictions of Jesus-as-Wisdom seem to manage to straddle this division, in fact: Ham-burger notes that although the miniatures in the earliest manuscript of the Exemplar, with their "swaying hip-shot pose identify the personification of Wisdom as unmistakably feminine, she nonetheless sports a beard."[116] When the Suso-character first encounters Eternal Wisdom in the *Horolo-gium*, for instance, the text depicts these changing genders quite suc-cinctly: "First one thought that here one had a delicate young girl, and then suddenly a most handsome youth was found" (C 72). These (and other) clearly nonbinary representations of Jesus in the heart of popular pan-European devotional discourse have yet to be fully incorporated into much of the recent theological discussion of trans issues—even as Eliza-beth Clark has pointed out the transgressive power of early Christian metaphors surrounding Jesus as "celibate bridegroom" wed to "virginal brides" (and the erasure of gender binaries in Galatians 3:27–28, which led early ascetic authors to "assure readers that since there is 'no male and female in Christ,' men as well as women can enjoy a marriage to the Heavenly Bridegroom").[117] Sophie Sexon, most recently, has written that visual depictions of the side-wound contribute to a potential for Christ's body to express "a range of genders, not limited to signifying in binary terms to a binarized audience."[118] Similarly, both alchemical discourse and the Christianization of Ovid led to late medieval hermaphroditic depictions of either Jesus or a chimeric Jesus-Mary.[119]

These moments of Jesus's gender fluidity can be seen particularly clearly on a textual level in one passage of the *Horologium*. The Disciple, seeing the pleasures of the world as nothing more than wilting flowers, soon finds high in the mountains the loveliest bloom of his life. It then quickly transforms into "what instead seemed to be a Goddess of all beauty" (quasi dea totius pulchritudinis) (K 418.20)—this is Eternal Wisdom, who, in the manner of a panther, exudes the sweetest perfume.[120] The Disciple is, at first, dumbstruck, but eventually speaks, asking her name and her lineage. She replies with a swarm of scriptural quotations, many saturated with musical imagery, then prefaces further discourse with an apophatic warning: "The secrets of my begetting are such that they surpass the wits of every mortal being."[121] Then, when Wisdom-as-Christ introduces Isaiah's prophecies of her, she quietly shifts the prophecy's object from masculine to feminine: "Ego namque sum illa, de qua scriptum est: *Generationem eius quis enarrabit? (Is 53:8)*" (K 421.11–12). Helpfully, Isaiah's *eius* is the genitive of the pronoun for either gender, allowing what would be in its scriptural context "Who shall declare *his* generation?" to be understood instead as "Who shall declare *her* generation?" without any alteration to the biblical text itself.[122]

She continues, however: "I came out of the mouth of the most high, the firstborn before all creatures. And my emergence is from the beginning, from the days of eternity" (Ego ex ore Altissimi prodivi, primogenita ante omnem creaturam [Ecclus. 24:5]. Et egressus meus sicut a principio, a diebus aeternitatis [Mic. 5:2]) (K 421.11–14). Suso here modifies the quotation from Micah: the Vulgate reads (addressing Bethlehem Ephrath): "et egressus eius ab initio a diebus aeternitatis" (Mic. 5:2). After these quotations comes a long passage from Proverbs (8:23–31)—the famous description of the generation of Eternal Wisdom herself before all creation, and her faintly seductive "playing" (*ludens*) with the Creator during creation.

Immediately after this biblical passage ends, however, Wisdom refers to herself as a masculine lover: "So I remained, always beloved in my beloved, and always, beloved, flowing out from my beloved, and always from the beginning playing in my beloved."[123] Once again, the gender of this visionary figure is effortlessly reversed. Although these shifts are not explicitly discussed in the text, Wisdom seems to aim to allay our confusion immediately after this passage by once again pointing to the ultimate ineffability behind all these words, biblical or otherwise. She tells the Disciple: "So far as full understanding of what my true essence may be is concerned, reason requires you not to inquire, because a well-ordered nature should not strive for impossible things."[124] Words are necessary here, but they are necessary failures, and reason can only take the Disciple so far in his attempt to understand her relationship to the Godhead—his exercise of reason, indeed, should teach him to reject reason. The Disciple wisely complies: rather than begin a learned discourse about the Trinity and its potential gender or genderlessness, he instead describes his great emotions, the rejoicing of his heart, and refers to Wisdom in his ecstatic response with the masculine-gendered words *dilectum sponsum* (K 422.18)—"beloved bridegroom."

Barbara Newman draws attention to a similar textual ambiguity or oscillation occasioned by a troubling thought to the practitioners of bridal mysticism: the possibility of the multitude of God's people *all* being God's lover. These motifs are all of course firmly allegorical, the consummation of the mystical marriage usually happening quite decorously offstage, but it seems that feelings from lived human experience nevertheless manage to creep into these relationships. Suso brings up this idea of the jealous lover by citing Ovid's *Remedia amoris*, dwelling on his desire to be the sole beloved of Wisdom, and even, at the passage's rhetorical climax, complaining: "You are indeed, if I dare say so, very given to loving here and there!" (valde, si audeo dicere, sparsus amator es!) (K 428.4–5). Wisdom (not a little offended) calms him, explaining that the root of his troubles is a misunderstanding of divine love: God's love can quite simply, and unconflictingly, extend to all of creation. Suso's desire to love Wisdom is overwhelmed, she says, by Wisdom's preexistent, eternal love for him (and, only secondarily, all creation). What Newman notes about this erotically charged passage, however, is the gender reversal Wisdom undergoes: "In a patriarchal society that insisted in real life on strict monogamy, God could be imagined as a king with an enormous harem, but hardly as a queen with innumerable lovers. Hence in this part of the dialogue Suso quietly changes the gender of Eternal Wisdom. . . . As soon as the discourse [on jealousy] ends, the delectable Bride returns."[125] Despite the exceptional freedom with which these authors write of a genderqueer Jesus and their sexuality, certain limits to the allegory nevertheless remain.

These oscillations, too, are not confined to Suso's Latin works. At the beginning of their spiritual courtship in the *Life*, Suso first imagines being coddled by Wisdom-as-mother, then exclaims, "O Lord! If I were married to a queen, my soul would rejoice; Ah, now you are the Empress of my heart and the giver [fem.] of all grace."[126] Christ the Mother is addressed as Lord, then quickly imagined as royal *spouse* instead of mother. Although these topoi are not by themselves particularly unusual in late medieval devotion, it is the rapid oscillation between mother, lord, and empress that seems especially jarring in this vernacular context. In *LBEW*, Barbara Newman points out, Suso "refers to his own soul as Wisdom's 'poor servant girl' (*diner armen dirnen*), and Wisdom responds to Suso as 'my daughter' (*min tohter*)."[127] These multiple transitions between genders nearly manage to seem effortless, and yet, as the careful attention to the issue in the prologue cited above suggests, one cannot dismiss that there are carefully calculated rhetorical choices being made by both Suso and his translators.[128] These feminizations vary dramatically not only in their intensity of expression, but also in their targets; both God *and* the Servant-narrator are profoundly feminized in the course of Suso's works.

And yet, both Suso and Rolle appear to subscribe to a more normative ideal of masculinity at times: "You are a womanish soldier, to fear hardships so much" (Delicatus miles es, qui adversa tantum formidas) (C I.9/K 451.4), Wisdom scolds the Servant.[129] Suso even writes to a nun tormented by evil spirits, "*Act manfully*, etc.: When an honorable knight first guides a squire into the ring, he speaks bravely to him: 'so, worthy hero, act gallantly today! . . . *Manfully*, etc., which means: conduct your-self boldly and manfully, all you who trust in God!"[130] Rolle too, shortly after declaring himself a lover of Uncreated Wisdom in *Against the Lovers of the World*, describes the soul (*anima*) as having "fought like a man against the spears of the enemy, conquered kingdoms, destroyed encampments." This soul-as-valiant-woman (Prov. 31:10) "made herself clothing out of monk's cloth. This woman is not soft, in a feminine way, and did not submit to the noxious words of young men, but . . . stood as a man in her strength."[131] The male soul, become feminine, is then re-masculinized in order to emphasize knightly, martial virtues in the resis-tance to temptations of the (male) flesh. Christian Straubhaar-Jones has argued that moments like these represent a competition between mas-culine personae—"spiritual knight" and "mystic spouse"—for the affec-tions of a female persona. The heterosexuality of mystical desire is nearly always taken for granted in the text, but there is also an ontological sys-tem in which, in Christian Straubhaar-Jones's words, "there is no sense that gender is a cosmic, eternal truth" and thus gender "remains malle-able: restrictive in performing specific personae but not overdetermined on a cosmic scale."[132]

I have been emphasizing the role of these gender oscillations in Rolle and Suso, but it is important to note, too, the wider theological orbit in which these concepts operated.[133] For instance, the thirteenth-century German Benedictine Gertrude of Helfta "uses mixed-gender imagery to describe God, Jesus, Mary and John the Evangelist as emperors, queens, soldiers, fathers, mothers, nurses and friends. To Gertrude, Christ's fa-therhood includes loving, cuddling, feeding from his breast and teaching the baby soul its letters; Christ's motherhood includes protecting the soul during a storm at sea, clothing it with fine dresses, punishing it, denying it jewels and ornaments, refusing it affection so that it learns patience, and frightening it with ugly faces or masks."[134] The only thing that seems certain about the gender of characters in these texts is that they are persis-tently oscillating; with or without grammatical gender, the ability to shift rapidly from one register to another is the hallmark of Suso's and Rolle's strategic deployment of the language of gender—whether applied to hu-mans or God. Yet despite the numerous and profound feminizations the texts enact, some of the rhetoric of misogyny seems to be inescapable to even these most feminine of medieval male devotional authors.

LOVING AND WRITING THE HOLY NAME

*The Evangelist renders the etymology of his name, saying (Matthew 1:21),
"And thou shalt call his name Savior (salvator; cf. Vulgate Iesus), for he
shall save his people." Just as "Christ" signifies a king, so "Jesus" signifies a savior. Not every kind of king saves us, but a savior king. The Latin
language did not have this word salvator before, but it could have had it,
seeing that it was able to when it wanted.*

—Isidore of Seville, *The Etymologies* 7.7.7–9 (trans. Stephen A. Barney,
W. J. Lewis, J. A. Beach, and Oliver Berghof)

The most well-known moment of the insular intertwining of Suso's and
Rolle's authorial characters is found in London, British Library MS Additional 37049. This famous Carthusian devotional miscellany appears to
conflate the two, putting the bloody letters of Christ's name, so vividly
associated in word and image with Suso, on the chest of a hermit representing Rolle.[135] Despite the discussion of Latin and vernacular above,
in one sense it is Greek that is in fact dearest to both Rolle and Suso—
or rather the first three letters of the Greek name of Jesus, *IHC* or *IHS*.
These two author-characters take great care in their textual performance
of individuality and self-fashioning, but they are rarely identified by their
own names within the text: it is the spiritual exemplarity of their characters that matter, not the names of the characters themselves.[136]

Instead, both Rolle and Suso not only associate themselves in their
narratives with the Holy Name, they also appear in multiple manuscript
images labeled with variants of that name. Suso, most famously, describes using a stylus to carve the Holy Monogram into his chest, resulting in a permanent reminder in scar tissue. This is an act of bloody
authorship dedicating himself to Christ, to be sure, but also serves as a
partial rechristening that would seek to subsume Suso's identity almost
entirely in the name of Christ (or, the name Wisdom gives him, "Amandus," the beloved of Christ). Rolle too is identified in manuscript images
as a hermit with *IHC* imprinted or gilded on his chest (even as he bears
a book reading, both simply and indistinctly, *ego* in one manuscript; for
a different depiction of the same scene, see fig. 1.3); the names of the
pseudo-autobiographical author-characters Richard Rolle and Henry
Suso (despite our interest in those two names today) are both subsumed

in their quest to become exemplary figures mediating between the reader and Christ.[137]

This marked emphasis on the importance of devotion to the divine name in both Suso and Rolle offers an intersection between the consideration of the linguistic performance of individuality and the dependence on the *reduction* of language into the (often non- or even antiverbal) auditory. The name and the monogram are both part of a system of language and somewhat distant to it—the Holy Name itself is used as an extraordinarily labile signifier, bringing to mind any number of referents in the thoughts of the devout without the certitude of narrative, dogma, or grammar. The three-lettered monogram, meanwhile, is moved beyond script and functions instead as decoration in a number of relevant manuscripts. As a trio of letters pregnant with meaning and treated as an icon by Suso, Rolle, and their scribes, it serves as a running title to devotional tracts, appears as marginal flourishes in other manuscripts, and gestures toward the Greek of the New Testament even as it employs only letters also found in the Latin alphabet.[138] The use of Jesus's name as a totemic reminder of his continued presence and continued devotion to him is also described using the rhetoric of courtly love; it is as desirable to the devout as a token of a beloved is to the lover.[139] The aspect of the compression of meaning and affect into a single word—or, indeed, into the three-letter contraction of a word—inherent in devotion to the divine name will reappear as we turn to the extragrammatical, apophatic, and experiential aspects of musical audition.

Indeed, Denis Renevey has drawn attention to a passage in Walter Hilton that testifies to otherwise little-known popular traditions of worship of the Holy Name (as part of a revision to the *Scale* that includes new sections dedicated to regulating Holy Name devotion). Hilton explains that his recommended form of devotion to the name of Jesus is "noȝt þis word ihesu peynted upon þe wal or writen by letters on þe boke, ne fourmed by lippes in soune of þe mouth, ne feyned in þe hert by trauaile of þe mynde."[140] These forms of material worship of the name of Jesus—written, painted, or spoken—and even "feigned" internal worship in heart or mind are to be avoided in favor of what he describes as a purer devotion to Christ theorized as wisdom, love, and sweetness. By his refutation of these other forms, however, he gives us a tantalizing glimpse of some of the practices of Rolle's contemporaries in the mid-fourteenth century.

There is a striking account in Suso's *Vita*, often accompanied by illustrations, of a similar practice of communal distribution of the name of Jesus. There is no mention of painting the monogram on walls, but the *Vita* recounts Elsbeth Stagel (impressed by Suso's scar tissue but proscribed from replicating it on her own body) sewing small badges with the divine monogram on them (see figs. 1.1 and 1.2 for both manuscript and print depictions of this scene). Their importance is further signaled by their treatment as something between a courtly token and a contact relic: after Elsbeth is shown a vision of Mary holding a candle inscribed with the Holy Name, she begins sewing the IHS monogram onto silk. Although she intended to wear this devotional token herself, secretly, the text then reports that she "did just this with the same name countless times, and made it so the Servant put the names all over his heart; she then sent them all over with a holy blessing to all of his spiritual children."[141] The holiness of the silk embroideries depends on their contact to Suso's original fleshy inscription for (some) of their spiritual power. The hiddenness and intimacy of their contact with his original scars heightens the effect of the courtly motif of the cloth token, even as Elsbeth changes the dynamics of the token both through its wider distribution and the description of its recipients as Suso's "spiritual children."[142]

This famous scarring scene, in which Suso bloodily carves the three letters into his flesh, appears both in the *Vita* and the Latin *Horologium*, albeit in slightly different forms. In the penultimate chapter of the *Horologium*, Suso writes that this particular story is related "since for the most part deeds achieve more than words":[143] the devout self-harm in inscribing these letters matters more than the letters themselves. Whereas in the *Vita* it is quite straightforwardly a *grifel* (stylus) that is used to cut the flesh, in the Latin Suso uses a more ambiguous *ferro acuto* (sharp iron) to do the cutting. There are some classical metonymic uses of the term *ferrum* as stylus, but medieval lexicons do not provide evidence for this use in postclassical Latin. The use of one's own skin as a wax tablet on which the stylus cuts the text, so vivid in the *Vita*, is made somewhat more generic in the Latin.

This passage, included in the *Horologium*'s main English translation, is quite heavily compressed. The scene in Suso's Latin, however, is described in terms almost as grisly as are employed in the German text:

There was a certain youth, a fervent lover, who, when he had renounced earthly loves, chose for his mistress this heavenly spouse

FIGURE 1.1. Einsiedeln, Switzerland: Stiftsbibliothek MS 710 (322), fol. 89r
(https://www.e-codices.ch/en/list/one/sbe/0710)

who is divine Wisdom. Greatly longing to enfold his beloved more
in the depths of his heart, he sought out a secret place, and impelled
by the amazing vehemence of his love, he stripped the upper part of
his body, and taking a sharp knife, he stabbed the bare flesh above
his heart where he could see the vital pulse throbbing most strongly,
piercing himself so forcefully that every stab was followed by a

FIGURE 1.2. The Exemplar (Augsburg: Anton Sorg, 1482). Library of Congress, Rare Book and Special Collections Division (https://www.loc.gov /item/55003630).

flow of blood that ran from his chest and dropped down drop by drop. And he stabbed himself so often and so mercilessly here and there that finally in this way he had cut the famous name of his spouse, which is "IHC," in great capital letters over "the extent of his heart" (3 Kgs 4:29). And when for a while he had carried these recent and bleeding wounds of love, so very sweet to him, in his discolored flesh with a great fire of love, in the end, after many days, they healed, and his flesh perfectly preserved that name, letter by letter, in that place. (C 321)

This is quite sharply reduced in the Middle English: "And for as myche as fleschly loveres vsen to haue in here cloþes summe worde or tokene wrytene in mynde of here veyne flesschelye loue, so schalle þe disciple of wysdame haue wrytene sumwhere pryvelye þe name of his trewe heuenely spowse Ihesus to bringe him þe oftere to his mynde" (SP VII.331–35). Whereas in Latin and German Suso claims a certain level of modesty concerning his badge of scarred tissue, here the translator actually enforces such discretion, refusing to expose the text on Suso's chest to the reader or give details about the moment of its bloody inscription. In the French rendering of the *Horologium*, however, the passage is translated in full; *ferro acuto* is translated as "un coutel agu,"[144] and instead of the three letters of *IHC*, the text specifies that Suso inscribed "cinq lettres," spelling out the name *Jhesu* in full. Despite the constant emphasis in the German manuscripts on the significance of the monogram, rather than the name (and the use of *IHC* as a running header in numerous English devotional manuscripts), the French translator seems not to have thought this a quite integral element of one of Suso's best-known acts of devotion.

In both the *Horologium* and the *Exemplar*, Suso also expresses a desire to have the Holy Name *gilded* onto his heart—a motif that appears in a manuscript illumination of Rolle, despite Rolle's never mentioning this particular medium (see fig. 1.3). There is, however, a common origin for this desire, mentioned in the last letter of Suso's *Little Book of Letters* (given, unsurprisingly, the pericope *Pone me ut signaculum super cor tuum*, and concerned primarily with encouraging devoted attention to both the name and *IHC/S*). It has particular prominence given its placement at the very end of the *Exemplar*. In the letter, Suso recounts that Saint Ignatius of Antioch repeated the name of Jesus during his martyrdom, claiming that the name was written on

FIGURE 1.3. British Library MS Cotton Faustina B.VI (Pt. II), fol. 8v. © The British Library Board.

his heart. The heart was then examined after his martyrdom, and indeed was found to have "golden letters inscribed all over which read 'Jesus, Jesus, Jesus.'"[145]

This repetition of the name in this legend, too, points to the ways in which *IHC* regularly subsumes its representational role and takes on more extralinguistic totemic and apotropaic qualities. Rolle writes, for instance:

> If þou thynk Ihesu continuely, and hold hit stably, hit purgeth þi syn and kyndels thyn hert, hit clarifieth þi soule, hit remoueth anger, hit doth away slownesse, hit woundeth in loue, fulfilleth in charite, hit chaseth þe deuyl and putteth out drede, hit openeth heuyn and maketh a contemplatif man. Haue in memorie Ihesu, for al vices and fantasies hit putteth fro þe louer.[146]

Rolle here combines thinking and "holding" the name of Jesus into one superbly efficacious act of devotion that provides a panoply of benefits, culminating in the overall creation of "a contemplatif man." This passage is echoed in the Latin commentary on the verse *Oleum effusum est nomen tuum* found in his *Super Canticum Canticorum*: "If one holds in mind this name 'Jesus' faithfully, it erases vice, plants virtues, sows charity, pours out the taste of heaven, lays waste to discord, restores peace, issues internal calm, eliminates the most disturbing fleshly desires, changes all earthly things to loathsome, and fills lovers with spiritual joy."[147] Without detailing precisely how the name is to be "held in mind," it nevertheless posits the Holy Name as itself a sufficient cure to most spiritual ailments.

In the commentary on this phrase of the Song of Songs, Rolle expresses a desire—shared, of course, with Suso—to have the Holy Name written on (or in) the heart: "O, tender Jesus, pour this oil deep into our body; write your name in our hearts."[148] The oil of consecration, rather than a stylus or a pen, is here figured as a tool for inscription. Slightly later on in the commentary, the rhetoric of humanity's creation is invoked in the desire to fashion the heart in Christ's image: "and let this name, your image and likeness, be printed in our hearts!"[149] (see fig. 1.4 for a miniature of Jesus's heart in Oxford, Bodleian Library MS Douce 322, wounded and with the monogram written just above it). Just as man is made in the image and likeness of God, so too is the relationship between Christ and the Holy Name intricately linked; the *name* here is used to mediate and shape affective response to the Song of Songs and its fiery erotic language. The image of stamping and sealing was often used to illustrate the relationship between the original (God) and its image

FIGURE 1.4. Bodleian Library MS Douce 322, fol. 78r; first chapter of "Emendatione Peccatoris"

(humanity), while here the image or reproduction of the original (Christ) is the name of Jesus itself.[150]

One critical aspect of devotion to the Holy Name seems to be the way in which it both acts as a signifier for Christ and retains a measure of its ineffability: especially when abbreviated, or simply invoked repeatedly in prayer, it is on the outer horizon of communicative practice. In the Middle English *Verba seniorum*, found in Huntington Library MS HM 148 (along with Rolle's *Prose Psalter*, *Þe holy boke Gracia Dei*, and other "Rollean" texts), noncomprehension of prayer is seen as quite acceptable in fighting thoughts of lechery. When a brother complains he feels "no compunccioune ne deuocioune" in prayer because he does not understand the words, a desert father answers, "Do furth as þou dose. For a charmere of neddyrs sayes mony wordes in his charmyng ande wot not þe menyng of þaim. Ande neuerþeles þe neddyre herys þaim ande fels þe myght of þaim ... ryght so we when we pray or thynkes, þof we knowe not vertue of þe wordes, neuerþeles fendes hers þam ande are ferde, ande þai lose þaire myght ande gose away fro vs thorowe vertue of þe wordes."[151] Although vain or unfeeling prayers are often criticized in late medieval devotion, here the overwhelming importance of the prayer overcomes the possibility that one does not fully understand it (even as fiends may nevertheless suffer from its power).

This phenomenon is not limited to Suso and Rolle in the fourteenth century, of course: scholars of religion and literature south of the Alps often seem to imagine devotion to *IHS* beginning in the fifteenth century with Bernardino of Siena (1380–1444). Bruder Hans in the fourteenth century, for instance, in his devotion to the Annunciation (extreme in its emphasis on the word *Ave* in particular), imagines *Ave* written on his forehead, in a modification of Ezekiel 9:4–6 and its use of *Tau* to mark out those not to be slaughtered for idolatry: "I would love to engrave and print on my forehead, *Ave*, those three letters."[152] And Rolle's *English Psalter* seems largely unconcerned in connecting the fervent devotion to names in the Psalms to his exegesis of the Song of Songs (in the Psalter he tends to skip directly to the thing named, Jesus, whenever the word *name* is used), but when he does link the two, it is through song. His commentary on Psalm 68:31 (*Laudabo nomen dei mei cum cantico et magnificabo eum in laude*) includes a description of the heavenly melody sung internally by the devotee: "he louys the name of ihu with sange— noght formed in notes of men, bot in the sown of heuen, that he rasaifes in his hert."[153] Song is used to love the name "ihu," but only internally received, heavenly notes are treated as adequate praise.

Rolle also points to a synaesthetic understanding of the experience of the Holy Name, blending taste and sound with the other emotional benefits received from repetitively reciting it:

> þis name Iesus, fest hit so faste in þi herte þat hit cum neuer out of þi þoght. And whan þou spekest to hym, and seist "Ihesu" þrogh custume, hit shal be in þyn ere ioy, in þi mouth hony, and in þyn hert melody, for þe shal þynke ioy to hyre þat name be nempned, swetnesse to spek hit, myrth and songe to thynk hit.[154]

Near the end of the *Incendium amoris*, Rolle refers to his being captivated by devotion to the Name, again in terms of song: "O good Jesus, you bound my heart in the thought of your name, and now I can do no other than to sing it!"[155] Singing the name of Christ—and singing it through a form of affective bondage, a fusing of his voice with the Holy Name—will recur in his vernacular works, particularly the climax of the *Ego Dormio*, with the exclamation of "Ihesu, Ihesu, Ihesu!" at lines 285 and 290. Here, however, it is the intersection of *music* and the Holy Name that is especially significant. Both *IHC* and descriptions of *canor* are instances of a language twisted away from typical standards of representation, exceeding their putative role as signifiers even as they draw our attention away from their representational possibility. The use of *IHC* serves to liberate Rolle and Suso from what Vincent Gillespie calls "the linguistic incapacity trap": "the inability of a fallen language to articulate and express an experience of perfection which persistently refuses to allow itself to be categorised in terms of human sense perception as articulated by the limited potential of either Latin or the vernacular."[156] *IHC* and *canor* both draw us toward their opacity as signs themselves—the very letters of the name are themselves individuated and, in their opacity, demand the readers' hermeneutic attention and elicit their most extreme affective responses.

Suso's self-inscription, and its echoes in Rolle, might also be seen as a kind of substitute stigmata: Dominicans and others somewhat jealous of Francis, the charismatic founder of the Franciscans, and his vibrant life story—not to mention the affective power of images of Francis receiving the stigmata—may have welcomed the promotion of a cult that might be seen as, in one way or another, surpassing the stigmata in mimetic identification with Christ. Suso and Rolle may not be depicted as wounded like Christ, but they bear his very name on their flesh. The signification of the abbreviated form of Christ's name also participates in what Michel de Certeau considers the central constitutive feature of the mystic phrase: "It turns the attention away from the thing being represented and focuses it on the way the word is being used, that is, on the sign-as-thing. It therefore opacifies the sign."[157] This opacification can be seen in the manuscript use of the Name and its status as a liminal signifier between image and text. And just as the Holy Name draws us to the signifier itself, into both the letters written on Suso's flesh and the letters sewn on silk and pressed against his body, so too music focuses the reader on the nondiscursiveness of mystical experience and the performance of its impossible representation as both deeply embodied and ineffably transcendent.

MUSIC AND MYSTICISM: SONGS OF EXPERIENCE

Seeing, touching, tasting are in Thee deceived:
How says trusty hearing? that shall be believed.

Visus, tactus, gustus in te fallitur
Sed auditu solo tuto creditur

—Gerard Manley Hopkins, "Godhead here in hiding"
(translation of *Adoro te devote* by Thomas Aquinas)[158]

Whereas the importance of music and aurality in Rolle's account of mystical experience has long been well studied, in part as a result of his emphasis on the tripartite system of mystical ascent (*fervor, dulcor,* and *canor*), which culminates in the canoric experience of divine music, the pivotal role of music and aurality in Suso's mysticism has gone relatively unnoticed.[159] There are major congruences, moreover, between the musical-mystical vocabularies employed in both bodies of work. It is necessary, too, to contest here two critical commonplaces: that Rolle's *fervor-dulcor-canor* schema is unique (that Rolle is asserting *canor* as "a new doctrine and himself as its prophet"[160]) and that a concern with the role of images and vision form the core of Suso's spirituality.[161] The centrality of musical and aural experiences of the divine to both figures helps tilt the ongoing redefinition of medieval aurality and liturgy toward a deeper recognition of the importance of a shared devotional culture in fourteenth-century England and Germany.

It is the illegibility and ineffability of music that most fundamentally appeals to the apophatic predilections of both authors. Beyond simply consisting of an ineffable experience, they also assert that divine music cannot be translated, recorded, written down, or even properly described.[162] Whatever their actual musical literacy may have been (in Suso's case, of course, rather considerable: he describes himself singing hymns and sequences and using a missal), they both claim their experiences of *divine* or mystical music are ineffable and, to use Katherine Zieman's terminology, "extragrammatical."[163] Divine music, somewhat like the treatment of the divine name discussed above, serves to thwart expected linguistic structures of meaning and grammar; it both exceeds and transcends language's typical roles in the transmission of information and the construction of narratives. In heavenly music, one encounters both an excess of meaning and an impossibility of that meaning being translated into or reduced to discourse, whether Latin or vernacular.[164]

Rolle's devotion to music and aurality finds one expression in the prosimetric Middle English epistle *Ego Dormio* (*I Sleep, but My Heart Is Awake*): "When may I cum þe nere / Thi melody for to hire? / Of loue to hyre þe songe þat is lestynge so longe? / Wil thou be my louynge, þat I þi loue may synge?" (208–11). Movement toward God is linked to hearing his sweet melody; the last line, however, then inverts the musical metaphor and states that the Rolle-character himself wishes to sing of God's love even as he longs to hear and transmit God's own loving song. This bidirectional emphasis on the use of aurality is linked not only to the affective potential of the lyric, but also to cognitive and mnemonic theories. McIlroy writes of the link between hearing and imagining, for instance: "The process of hearing a story and envisioning it in one's own mind's eye" was such a common activity that "the medieval writer could move with impunity from verbs of reading and hearing to verbs of seeing and imagining."[165] The orality of these passages, then, and their emphasis on song and melody coincide with a more general focus on the connection between reading texts (or hearing them read) and vividly imagining the scenes described within them. This emphasis is only strengthened by Rolle's attention both to the structure of his treatise and his descriptions of the experience (and production) of heavenly song.[166]

The conclusion of *Ego Dormio* begins with the announcement of a final poem: "Now I write a songe of loue þat þou shalt haue delite in w[hen] þou art louynge Ihesu Criste" (O-T 265–66). This interruption, rather sudden, of another devotional lyric perhaps serves to jolt the reader into a finer, more alert understanding of the text's significance; it also reinforces the orality of the text by refocusing our attention on Rolle's presence as a first-person voice within the text and by reminding us of the inherent musicality of the treatise itself. The opening of the poem serves a similar purpose: "My songe is in seghynge, my lif is in langynge" (O-T 267). Rolle's own despondency about his distance from Christ is highlighted; he also brings the reader's gaze to his own condition and encourages the reader's identification with the speaker of the poem. Nicholas Watson writes, "*Ego Dormio* is not only a treatment of the reader's ascent to union with Christ by means of Rolle, but also to a kind of union with Rolle himself."[167] One's reading of the text, insofar as it is also the performance of the song that is the text, creates a composite voice of reader and writer: the reader joins with Rolle in an amorous duet.

This final poem also features the return of earlier erotic and courtly imagery coupled with an even greater emphasis on the speaker's desire to see God. Rolle concisely sums up the medial and pedagogical role that Christ plays in the reformation of his affect: "Ihesu, both God and man, thi loue þou lered me þan / When I to þe fast ran; forþi now loue I can" (O-T 282–83). He continues in a wonderfully alliterative line that brings his own languishing role in participating in divine song to the fore: "I sit and synge of loue langynge þat in my brest is bred" (284). The importance of aurality returns once again, as Rolle exclaims, "Ihesu, my dere and my drery, delites art þou to synge; / Ihesu, my myrth, my melody, when wil þou cum, my kynge?" (292–93); Christ functions both as subject and source of Rolle's heavenly singing. The poem ends on a similar note, fusing both sight and song in an imagining of heavenly unity with God:

> When wil þou rewe on me, Ihesu, þat I myght with þe be,
> To loue and loke on þe? My sete ordain for me,
> And set þou me þerin, for þan [may] we neuer twyn,
> And I þi loue shal synge þrogh sight in þy shynynge
> In heuyn withouten endynge.
>
> (O-T 308–13)

Ego Dormio thus links the reader to Rolle in an affective bond through the attempt to mimic, textually, the immediacy of the oral and the sung. In part through its mixture of prose and verse, it shows Rolle at his most intimate in an attempt to seduce the treatise's readers, reform their vision, and direct their affect toward Christ. The space of the poem and its interaction with the reader brings to bear the parallel formation of Rolle-as-writer and Rolle-as-text. These dual intermediaries, poem and Rolle, both serve to draw the reader inward to the senses of the heart and mind, and upward toward the ineffable Godhead.

In Suso, a passage from his vernacular *Life* provides perhaps the richest interaction between music, text, and image in his works: as the Suso-character meditates, a young man takes him by the hand to a green heath where he sings a song in Suso's soul.[168] All his senses fly away ("alle sin sinne verflogte" [B 139]) and his heart felt as if it would burst; Suso places his hand on his heart to steady himself in the midst of the rapture. Then,

> it seemed to him that his heart was completely full of passionate love and longing for God, so that his heart started moving and raving madly within his body, as though it almost needed to burst, and he needed to lay his right hand on his heart in order to help himself, and his eyes became so full with tears that they overflowed. When the song was finished, a picture was presented to him so that he could learn the same song and that he might not forget it.[169]

The picture, we are told, represents Mary pressing Eternal Wisdom (as a child) to her heart; above the child's head "the beginning of the song was written . . . with beautiful, well-flowered letters, and the writing was secret, so no human could read it."[170] He sees *bûchstaben* (letters), not notes or neumes; the letters read, simply, *herzentrut* (beloved of my heart).[171]

Although the text—or at least the script—would allegedly be secret, Suso immediately reveals it to his readers; it is the melody itself that alone must remain hidden. The picture is described, the lyrics provided, but the music is unrecorded and untranscribed: it is the only truly ineffable aspect of this intensely moving scene, both present and absent. In the image of this scene from the Einsiedeln manuscript (fig. 1.5), one can see the text-turned-image for the term *herzentrut*: not only do the majuscule red and blue letters take up two lines of writing space within the body of the text, it is also between red lines in the image below, separated between *herz* and *trut* by the image of the Virgin and Child. The illumination itself seems to describe the event *in media res*: the two angels and their instruments imply a contemporaneity with the action descried in the passage above, even as the entire scene is rendered in a gesture of memorialization.

A nearly identical gesture in Rolle's *Incendium amoris* emphasizes the extralinguistic aurality of *canor*, specifically the mysterious, unavoidably experiential soundedness inherent to it: "Lovers of the world, of course, may know the words or music [*carmina*] of our songs, but not the melody [*cantica*] of our songs: for words can be read, but sweet savor of notes and tones cannot be learned."[172] Both words and music are legible

FIGURE 1.5. Einsiedeln, Switzerland: Stiftsbibliothek MS 710 (322), fol. 82v

to all in the world, but there is both a "savor" and a melody that is incomprehensible to those not properly initiated into the contemplative process that culminates in an experience of *canor*. The core experience itself, despite the best efforts of the text, can neither be learned nor read.

Although some critics have seen Rolle's massive alliterative Latin prose *Melody of Love* (*Melos amoris*), and others the English lyrics, as a textual instantiation of *canor*—as a re-creation or a performance of *canor*—Rolle's grappling with the inability of writing *canor* in the *Fire of Love* (*Incendium amoris*) also offers critical commentary on his understanding of the fundamentally extragrammatical ineffability of true divine song. For instance, he writes:

> In fact, if I imagined that that song or roar were hidden to all external ears (and I would dare to report that to be), would that I might find a human author for those melodies, who by no means would use spoken words, yet who would use writing to sing my joy to me, and whose spirit would be bound with the name of the highest, and who would produce singing and sighing such that I would not blush to say in the presence of my love.[173]

In this passage, Rolle appears almost to imagine an alternate authorship: were these sounds hidden (as, in a certain sense, he indicates that they indeed are), he imagines that he would then wish to find a new author who could textually—but not orally, he specifies—sing these joys to him. Is he imagining a hagiographer, or perhaps imagining that he would have need of one were he not himself already an author? It would be an odd twist of fate, given the stress on the necessity of *written* praise in this passage and the performative-liturgical foundation of the main source of biographical information about him, the *Officium*. The desire not to blush when in the presence of this beloved might indeed signal Rolle is concerned about overflattery in the course of this new author's description, potentially hagiographic, of his virtues.

Rolle's image of this shadowy figure (Jacob McDonie refers to the character as the "phantasmal companion")[174] seems to change, however, first into a desire for tutorship, then into something closer to companionship, or perhaps even discipleship. Immediately after the passage above, he imagines the same character teaching him about song and *jubilus*; the following chapter opens with a renewed desire—seeming to go against his otherwise strenuous attempts at solitary life and fleeing even the communal space of the choir—for a companion. "But if only you [God] had showed me a companion along the way, that with his encouragement my heaviness might have been gladdened . . . [and] among the rejoicing in hymns of loving sweetly I might have rested with that companion you would have given me,"[175] a strange wish for a hermit who has even fled his hermitages if they seemed to him to become too noisy or "worldly." This excursus, initiated by Rolle's imagining himself as a nonauthor, prompted by the presumed utter nondiscursiveness and ineffability of *canor*, is a breach in the otherwise carefully cultivated relationship between author and audience.[176] McDonie argues, however, that this novel figure of companionship and friendship instead functions partly as the mystical text itself, partly as an affective substitute for Christ: "The friend becomes sacralized not only as the joint recipient and propagator of mystical experience, but also perhaps even as an end of mystical contemplation itself, much like the angelic choir does elsewhere."[177]

Both here and elsewhere in the *Fire of Love*, Rolle continues to explore the depths of the ineffability of *canor*. At the end of chapter 37, for instance, he writes that "this is spiritual music, which remains unknown by all those concerned with secular things, whether licit or illicit; no-one else may know this unless he has studied solely God alone."[178] Here, any secular study whatsoever renders *canor* inaccessible; constantly undistracted meditation on the divine is a prerequisite for comprehending *canor*. This stands in contrast to an understanding of prayer voiced in the *Mending of Life* (*Emendatio vitae*), which states that "all our desire and accomplishments shall be that we do not 'overrun' [*transcurramus*] words in our prayers, but offer to our God each and every syllable with a strong shout and with desire."[179] This passage indicates a precision of prayer that emphasizes its clarity and intelligibility, distinct from the nearly glossolalic account of *jubilus* one finds elsewhere.[180]

And yet Rolle continues by explaining that "for while beseeching in prayer, ineffable sweetness is poured out, the same prayer is in turn transformed into jubilation."[181] The precision of syllabic prayer is transformed into a more synaesthetic, extralinguistic experience of divine grace. Here he demonstrates what Katherine Zieman refers to as "the isolation of a sense of sacrality in linguistic excess—the production of extragrammatical 'meaning' that becomes . . . the site of affect."[182] The careful attention devoted to avoiding "overrunning" words yields to a wordless *jubilus* of sweetness and praise. Something akin to this combination of sweetness and text is also found in the sixth lesson of Rolle's *Office*, which, as Andrew Albin writes, is saturated with "references to the industrious bee, its honey, and the honeycomb squeezed by the hand made sticky with sugar and beeswax. Yet the stanza melds this imagery of tactile, tooth-some sweetness with sounds, with speech, words, and harmony: the bee's sweetest labor is the pronunciation of words; medicinal teachings drip from the squeezing hand."[183]

Although Suso and Rolle both acknowledge that they cannot ade-quately write, transcribe, or represent the music they hear and produce—and both advertise this lack repeatedly—the fundamentally *experiential* element of it is just as clear in both authors. Suso's metaphor (in which the written vernacular compares to the spoken word just as inadequately as hearing a description of musical performance compares to hearing the music itself) is a particularly apt conjunction of the *experiential* element at the heart of both text (as Suso imagines it) and music. Yet it is this ul-timately necessary failure of representation, and its aftermath, that gener-ates the desire to go beyond both text and music in the attempt to achieve an experience of transcendence, and, ultimately, to communicate this and to attempt to bring one's readers into the same closed circle of contem-plative victors.

This failure of representation is desirable, too, as it serves to em-phasize the stark distance between signifier and signified. Rolle writes in *The Form of Living*, "if þou wil witte what kyn ioy þat songe hath, I say þe þat no man wote bot he or sho þat feleth hit, þat hath hit, and þat prayseth God syngynge þerwith. O thynge tel I the: hit is of heuyn, and God yeueth hit to whom he wil" (O-T 17.579–82). Having, feeling, and praising God in song are the ineluctable, experiential elements of Rolle's *songe*; the gift of song is a function of grace.

Vincent Gillespie writes that Rolle's *Melody of Love* "stands at the head of a hierarchical repertoire of songs and lyrics that offers a linguis-tic ladder towards the ineffable."[184] That is to say, reading or reciting the dense alliterative prose of the *Melody of Love* offers the possibility of in-spiring or creating, in the reader, at least a shadow or faint reflection of *canor* itself; the ineffability of *canor*, however, is yoked to the ineffability of the experience of reading (or hearing read) Rolle's treatise.[185] In Rolle and Suso alike, however, it is crucial to note that one sense is never *overwhelmingly* privileged over any other, in fact: just as all have their particular dangers when misdirected, so too each can bring the contem-plative to another aspect of the overwhelming experience of the transcen-dent. *The Form of Living*, for instance, in listing the numerous "synnes in deede" mentions dancing ("led karolles") before simply listing "syn in syght, in hyrynge, in smellynge, touchynge, handlynge, swelighynge [swallowing, i.e., tasting]" (O-T 12.375–76). It is the synaesthetic aspect of mystical experience that demands further analysis in the attempt to move past the contemporary categorization of Rolle as a prophet of *canor* and Suso as concerned primarily with devotional images and strictly visual revelations.[186]

In Rolle's *Against the Lovers of the World* (*Contra amatores mundi*), for instance, visual apprehension of the divine is singled out as the summit of mystical experience, only to be immediately acknowledged as impossible and unattainable. After detailing the scriptural prohibitions on sight of the divine (in Exodus 33:20 and John 1:18), Rolle addresses visionary experience as a category:

> There are others who say otherwise; namely that they have seen heavenly things clearly. Let them speak thus who have known this phenomenon; I have not experienced it, and I do not expect to experience it as long as I remain in the flesh. Even Paul, who was caught up to the third heaven, did not say that he saw God or those in heaven face to face, but that he heard the secret words of God. . . . And when he was to set forth the occasion of his temptation, he wrote, "Lest the greatness of the revelations (he does not say visions) should exalt me, there was given me a sting of the flesh" (2 Cor. 12:7). Wherefore I make bold to say that a perfect vision of eternal things is granted to none of the saints in this life, unless it be out of some spiritual need, so that someone may be converted.[187]

Although the beatific vision is gestured toward as a pinnacle of sorts, it is such an overwhelmingly unattainable pinnacle that Rolle dismisses its utility for the living altogether.[188] Instead, he begins to gesture toward an understanding of Paul's rapture as predominantly *aural*, explicitly pointing out that Paul does not mention *visions* in his account of his rapture.

Despite this focus on aurality in Rolle, his famous tripartite structure of *fervor*, *dulcor*, and *canor* is not, in fact, nearly as tidy as we would like it to be. Whereas the triadic structure can be easily remembered and is undoubtedly appealing to a present-day desire to systematize theological treatises, it is explicitly referred to rather infrequently. Overlapping interaction between the three, instead, is found far more commonly in Rolle's texts.[189] Additionally, linking heat, sweetness, and song is not unique to Rolle. In the *Horologium*, for instance, we find Suso describing the court of heaven in which "the confessors give a fiery light, the virgins appear 'in snowy brightness' . . . how all the company of heaven abounds in divine sweetness and is filled with rejoicing. These heavenly hosts, all as one, leading the choirs with untellable rejoicing, utter their melodies before the throne."[190] This is not precisely a systematic procession from one level to another (and, as we've noted, this is not always the case in Rolle either), but it is clear that the elements of fiery heat, delightful sweetness, and rapturous music were also incorporated into some of the descriptions of Suso's mystical universe. For instance, when describing praise of the Virgin in the *Horologium*, Suso again involves all three of these elements: "Youths sing with joy to the organ's sound, and every heart grows glad at these happy notes, and I too burn with the fire of a divine love, for I am moved by your sweetest memory, and I long to praise you."[191]

A different tripartite structure of ascending mystical experience is linked to three-part (or three-rhythmed) music in one passage in Suso's *Horologium*. Wisdom tells the Disciple to build a marriage bed within his heart; when Jesus is present, he will sing: "Then let my devout soul make me hear His voice singing to me of the songs of Sion, its melody composed in three parts rendering the sweetest sound, namely: perfectly forgetting everything earthly, fervid passion for everything eternal, and a beginning of the glory of blessed spirits."[192] This song is both *felt* and *tasted* in the heart: "Happy is he who deserves to feel this taste inside and who has known this from true experience rather than from spoken or written words."[193] The description of feeling and tasting a melody, coupled with the emphasis on experience over text, demonstrates a central theme in both Rolle and Suso that may help to account for Suso's popularity within fifteenth-century England: indeed, this comparison helps also to explain the common manuscript companions Suso and Rolle shared and their unique popularity to both clergy and laity.

Similar language appears when Suso invokes David as an ideal lover-musician, a perfect Minnesinger. The Disciple asks Wisdom, "What did that musician of yours—that man after your own heart—do, he who 'naked like one of the buffoons' with handheld instruments 'danced with all his might.'"[194] Inspired in part by Psalm 150, Suso then imagines another attempt to praise the works of God, a polyphonic outburst imagining his own dissolution into a universal music of praise: "For if all of the parts of my body were as innumerable as grains of sand from the sea, and each were a sweet-sounding instrument, and all my powers were jubilant voices, I would long to praise you with all these powers of mine, O author of the universe."[195] Suso's own body becomes both atomized and universalized in an effort simply to imagine an adequate performance of worthy praise of the Godhead.

A detailed vernacular description of song in Rolle's *The Form of Living* likewise emphasizes its position as the pinnacle of mystical experience, achieved after one has passed through a stage of burning love:

> Þan þe sowl is Ihesu louynge, Ihesu thynkynge, Ihesu desyrynge, only in coueitys of hym [ondynge], to hym seghynge, of hym brennynge, in hym restynge. Than þe songe of preisynge and of loue is comen. Þan þi þoght turneth in to songe and in to melody. Þan þe behoueth synge þe psalmes þat þou before said; than þou mow be longe about fewe psalmes. Than þe wil þynke þe swetter þan hony, for þan þou art siker to see hym þat þou louest. (O-T 17.556–63)

The intense, physical feeling of burning is superseded by the soul's focus on Jesus: a string of gerunds in which the soul concentrates all of its energies on Jesus is subsumed into an evocation of song and melody. Rather than passively experience this music, Rolle encourages the singing or reading of the Psalms as the only aural-linguistic possibility appropriate for the devotee. Indeed, in the prologue to the *English Psalter*, Rolle writes that performances of the Psalms "drope swetnes in mannys saule . . . and kyndils thaire willes with the fyre of luf makand thaim hate and brennand withinen"[196] (Bramley 3.3–5). Both of these passages also include a gustatory reference to the sweetness of the experience: the interweaving of the various senses in the experience of sound is as central to Rolle as to Suso.

Suso also describes a sensation of heat and burning associated with a performance of aural praise:

> O "arise, arise" now, my soul, and "utter a canticle"! A canticle of praise indeed "with an exulting voice." Let cymbals crash and hearts jubilate together, all lands resound in praise of the creator! O most beloved Wisdom, eternal goodness, I beg you that at every morning's

sunrise when I rise to you and open my eyes, I might also uncover my heart in your praise, and that from it might then arise the brilliant morning star and an immense flaming torch of ardent praise for you, bearing in it the most intense level of your love which has ever been granted to the human heart from up above. Let it kindle within itself an ardor like that of the spirit which burns most fiercely among the highest rank of the heavenly host, in you and because of you, no less like the burning of that supersubstantial and superessential and ineffable love in which you, O heavenly Father, love most fervently your only-begotten Son in the Holy Spirit.[197]

Echoing the third part of the *Horologium* (in which Suso creates a liturgy with considerable popular success, the *Office of Eternal Wisdom*), he here begins to imagine the possibility of lauds devoted entirely to Eternal Wisdom in vivid, exuberant language. The synaesthetic language grows evermore intense as sounds, scents, and colors interact, and it is the feeling of sweetness that is emphasized (as seen in Rolle, as well):

And I ask that this praise resound in your fatherly heart as sweetly and alluringly as the sweet melody of all the cithara-players and musical instruments is accustomed to sound in delighted hearts during the flowering of our best days. And may there ascend from this torch of praise a perfumed "pillar of smoke" for your praise, as agreeable as if it were made of all "aromatical spices, of myrrh, of frankincense, and of all the powders of the perfumer": as delightful as the flowers of the field blooming in the springtime, beautifully colored, and the trees standing richly adorned with foliage and their beloved fragrances.[198]

Here, Suso's torch seems to be imitating either a thurible or an Old Testament fire-sacrifice, which yet can penetrate with his song into the *fatherly* heart of Eternal Wisdom (a change from the predominantly feminine portrayals of Sapientia). The aural-olfactory focus of this passage is then superseded by Suso's focus on the visual effect the torch will have:

And let the torch of this praise be full of love and delight that your eyes will consider it joyfully, and let the entire hall of heaven rejoice! And let this rise up ceaselessly, constantly, with the most fervid fire

and fastest heat of your love from the heart through devout meditation, from my lips with fervid speech, and from all the works of my
holy and celestial way of life. And may this mighty torch of praise
drive away all enemies, spread grace, obtain a blessed end and acquire the glory of eternal blessedness, that the end of this temporal
praise may be the beginning of eternal praise in the celestial father-
land. Amen.[199]

The intertwined combination of *fervor* and *canor*, then, is not Rolle's
alone; indeed, their language is quite similar in their treatment of the relationship between the experience of heat and the expression of melody.
The equivalent passage in the *LBEW* ends the second book (the third
book is the *Hundred Meditations* on the Passion). It varies enough from
the lusciously rhapsodic Latin to warrant separate consideration:

> Most loving Lord, my beloved Eternal Wisdom, I ask that when my
> eyes first open in the morning that my heart also open, and that from
> it burst a flaming love-torch of your praise with the dearest love of
> the most loving heart in the world—a love that is most like the love
> of the most sublime spirit of the Seraphim in eternity, and the bot-
> tomless love with which you, heavenly Father, love your beloved
> child in the love that flashes out from both of your spirits. Let this
> praise sound in your paternal heart as sweetly as any kind of sweet
> sound of love-filled stringed-song ever sounded in any free spirit be-
> fore. May the torch of love send forth as sweet a scent of praise as
> if all fine herbs and spices and all good medicinal plants of highest
> purity were powdered up together. May its appearance be adorned
> with the beautiful blossoms of grace so that it may be a joy for your
> divine eyes and the whole heavenly host to see. And I ask that this
> torch of love constantly burst out in all my prayer, from my mouth,
> in song, in thoughts, words, and works, that it may drive away all my
> enemies, scatter all my flaws, gain grace and a blessed end, that the
> end of this worldly praise might be the beginning of an everlasting
> eternal praise. Amen.[200]

The emphasis here varies slightly: both herbs and flowers appear more
vividly than in the Latin, even as the general combination of sweetness,

heat, and song, smell, and sight reinforce the centrality of synaesthesia in the quite exuberantly rendered finale.

I have discussed elsewhere Suso's reevaluation of spiritual authorship; Suso claims to favor a kind of musical devotional performance invoking both song and dance ("a new carol and unusual praise [*niuwen reyen und selzenen lobe*]," B 90) over strictly textual production.[201] This leads him to see birdsong, too, as a mode by which creation offers praise (coupled with another attempt at humbling his authorial persona).[202] He writes in the *Horologium*, "Truly, we commonly see that among the beautiful birds of the wood and chirping nightingales there are also cawing crows present that, in their own way, insofar as they are able, serve their creator."[203] This sense of all of creation praising God at various levels and in various ways, each creature according to its ability, also finds expression in Suso's *LBEW*: "Dearest Lord, even the frogs in the ditches praise you, and if they cannot sing, at least they croak."[204] The passage on the crow, however, is followed by Suso's own role in this auditory system, one more pastoral than laudatory: "I, sinner that I am, have a song for sinners at hand, and with it I will praise and glorify my God forever."[205] He then quotes verses of three Psalms afterward claiming: "My soul will sing this charming canticle at all times with a sweet, joyful song among the spiritual race of birds."[206] Although just what this curious *spirituale genus avium* is remains unclear (the extended metaphor of crows and nightingales explored just before pushes us away from thinking these spiritual birds might be angels), the general wish of the mystic author to praise God as a bird appears in Rolle as well.[207]

When this avian imagery is employed by Rolle, however, the link is somewhat more eroticized. Near the end of the *Fire of Love*, he writes, using language also found in the lyrics,[208] "In the beginning of my conversion and my unique way of life, I thought I would like to become a little bird who, because of love, longs for his lover, but whose longing is gladdened by the arrival of the beloved and joyfully sings, singing even as he suffers, but suffering in sweetness and heat. As it is indeed said of the nightingale who grants song and melody the whole night in order to please who she is united with [*copulatur*]."[209] Even as it bears a heightened eroticism—and the conventional imagery of the alternating joy and suffering of the game of love—the displacement of Rolle's desire first to a bird, then even further through a simile of a nightingale, seems much more anthropomorphizing than Suso's own imaginings. Rolle continues,

> How much more might I sing with the greatest sweetness to Christ, my Jesus, who is the bridegroom of my soul through all this life (which is like night compared to the clarity yet to come). I would yearn, that yearning I might die for love. But in dying I will grow stronger and suckle on heat and jubilate and jubilating will sing to the delight of my love with joy and from something like a pipe will blow forth a melody and burning devotion and send forth highest burning odes inside me.[210]

This passage links the erotic musical relationship between bird and beloved with the changing relationship between the soul and Christ before and after death; the very act of loving Christ here seems to hasten the journey to death. The combination of this *Liebestod* and the soul's consequent union with God leads Rolle to ever-more enthusiastically embodied musical expressions of joyous mystical heat and an understanding of the beatific vision in terms ultimately both internal and purely aural.

In *The Form of Living*, the nightingale is again used as an example of the burning desire for melody:

> Bot þe soul þat is in þe þrid degre is as a brennynge fyre, and as þe nyghtgalle, þat loueth songe and melody, and failleth for mykel loue; so þat soul is only conforted in praisynge and louynge of God, and til þe deth cum is syngynge gostly to Ihesu and in Ihesu. And "Ihesu" nat bodily cryinge with þe mouth: of þat maner of syngynge speke I nat of, for þat songe hath both good and il, and þis maner of songe hath none bot if þai be in þis þrid degre of loue, to þe which degree hit is impossibil to cum bot in a greet multitude of loue. (O-T 17.571–78)

This song of praise, then, returns us to the utter ineffability of music: the highest stage of performance is identifiable only by the contemplative state of the mystic, not by the text or melody itself. Any song or prayer—even the simple and pure recitation of the Divine Name expressed by the bodily mouth!—can be tainted by some aspect of worldly involvement.

In this account, it is alone the purification through love required to rise to the third stage of contemplation that can render the devotee's song truly authoritative. Suso seems to indicate that his own authorial production is an instantiation of the "new carol and unusual praise," but Rolle seems more intent not on *writing* canor, but rather using text to create the meditative circumstances under which one can oneself produce and experience this ineffable song that represents the peak of contemplation.

Suso's understanding of earthly music—liturgical, secular, or animal—is constantly invoked in positive terms: even secular music about chivalric love delights him, he reports in the *Vita*, because it helps him think about his divine beloved.[211] Rolle's opinion of secular—and even liturgical—music differs quite drastically. Whereas for Suso it seems that any type of music whatsoever can be converted into a love song, inspiring him to an ever-deeper romantic relationship with Eternal Wisdom, anything less than pure, undiluted *canor* is a dissonant distraction for Rolle. Famously, he flees the liturgy, risking criticism for his distaste even for the Divine Office. And yet this was a crucial point for Rolle. Katherine Zieman writes that "the dissonance of one's heavenly song in relation to liturgical singing was a litmus test of authenticity: the contemplative could be sure of the divine nature of the internal song he heard if, on account of it, 'he cannot bear the noise (*clamor*) of psalmody unless his inner melody can be made to reflect it.'"[212]

Suso's interest in spiritual music was not unnoticed by his English audience: the majority of the passages dealing with Susonian *canor* in the *Horologium* made their way into the *Seven Points*. The term *organa* (which also appears nineteen times in Rolle's *Melos amoris*),[213] is translated straightforwardly as *organes*: "O summa ineffabilis pietas, quam suavissime et peroptime organa haec in aure resonant tristiori" (K 487.24– 25), "O þou souereyne and vnspekable pite, how souereynlye swete and lykynglye þese organes sowne in þe eeres of him þat is sorowfulle!"[214] The breadth of Suso's musical vocabulary is not always rendered exactly into English, however: at times the translator seems to make strategic choices about the terms used, elsewhere there is a straightforward attempt simply to render the Latin accurately.

The sound of the psaltery, for instance, a central feature of Suso's account of spiritual music, is transformed into the human voice in the Middle English: "Te namque sic dulciter psallente, animus tristitia

pressus alleviatur, et tua caelestis modulatio spiritum tristitiae mentem ex-
agitantem saltem ad tempus fugat, ut levius quod patitur ferat" (K 488.1–
4),[215] for instance, becomes, "For while þou singist so swetelye, þe
sperite þat suffriþ sorowe is lihtened, [and] þi heuenlye melodye driueþ
awey for þe tyme þe sperite of sorowe þat diseseþ þe mynde, so þat hit
may be þe lihtere borene" (*SP* III.276–79). Perhaps the repeated references to psaltery music seemed too sublunary for an English readership likely to have encountered Rolle's more strictly transcendental
descriptions of *canor*, infused with ineffability. Vocal music, still undoubtedly material, appears to come closer to the transcendental Rollean ideal than instrumental music.

The cithara, however (a term used emphatically and positively by
Rolle, twenty-seven times in the *Melos amoris* alone), is consistently rendered as "harp" in the *Seven Points*: "Eya age nunc, quod coepisti; quia
se quasi nihil pati existimat, cui tam dulciter aeterna Sapientia in adversis
citharizat" (K 488.6–8), becomes, "Wherefore do now forth wiþ me þat
þou hast begunne; for þat man þinkiþ þat he suffriþ is as nowȝt, to whom
euerlastynge wisdam so swetelye harpiþ in aduersite!" (*SP* III.283–85).
Suso's language in both of these passages refers to the receipt of music
from a divine source, and yet the contrast between the translation of psaltery and cithara points to a careful concern for musical terminology in the
process of translating his work in early fifteenth-century England.

The stretching of the strings of the cithara in order to properly tune
the instrument, commonly linked to Christ's physical torture since antiquity, is also involved in Suso's text. Wisdom responds to Suso's urgent
request for spiritual music in the *Horologium*: "If you want to hear the
cithara—its spiritual music resounding beautifully—rise up! Attend carefully to the precious fruit of temporal adversities. For indeed, just as the
strings of a cithara, when stretched proportionately, render a sweet sound,
so too any one of the elect, while oppressed by adversity, is distended as
if by an external force, and from this is better able to render up a sweet
and heavenly melody."[216]

This motif of the tortured body as well-tuned musical instrument has
a rich history;[217] here, we are fortunate to see its translation into English
by the author of the *Seven Points*:

> Wolt þow now here þe harpe of gostelye musike feyre and swetelye
> sownyng? Sitte vp and take hede besily to þe precious fruyte of

temperele aduersitees! Riht as in an harpe þe strengis in proporcione streynede & (wrastede) ʒiuene a swete sowne to him þat heriþ, riht so euery chosene man, what tyme þat he is ouerleyde wiþ aduersite, he is as in manere by strengþe out of him selfe constreynede and more pleynerlye made able forto ʒelde a swete & heuenlye melodye. (*SP* III.286–94)

This language of transformation—from flesh to song, from torture to beauty—is deployed starkly and emphatically in this passage: the passive phrase *extra se tenditur* is translated as a reference to constraint and enclosure rather than to the stretching language of crucifixion. The strings of the instrument here are more loosely related to the suffering of crucifixion, yet the central metaphor of body-as-instrument is maintained carefully.

In the *Seven Points*, instrumental terminology seems to be modified to fit the expectations of the audience, but compare the careful etymology in the prologue to Rolle's *English Psalter*: "This boke is cald the psautere, the whilk nam it has of an instrument of musyke that in Ebru is 'nablum,' in Grek 'psautry' of 'psallm,' that in Inglis is 'to touche.' And it is of ten cordis, & gifes the soun fra the ouerere thurgh touching of hend" (Bramley 3). An awareness of the history of the term "psalter" and its English etymology gives Rolle a way of acknowledging the historicity of divine music and its (occasional) materiality: surely the exemplar of all musicians, David with his psaltery, would have been engaged in some degree of *canor*. The arch-asceticism of descriptions of *canor* found elsewhere is tempered by the example of the use of music in revealed scripture and the pastoral goals of a particular authorial project, but in this case, of course, the *English Psalter* claims to have been written at the express request of the anchoress Margaret Kirkby.

In terms of ineffability, the representation of mystical experience, the creation of authority, the consolatory power of heavenly music, and the role of human- and animal-generated music in divine praise, the convergence between Rolle and Suso is considerable. Although their particular textual and authorial strategies diverge on some more minute points— the role of "external" music, for instance, in the cultivation of mystical or divine music—the specifically experiential modality of the aural and musical is at the heart of their understanding of the ascent to divine union. The role of the author himself as creator of melody—rather than passive recipient—shapes their own authorial self-presentation, despite their constant awareness of the inherent impossibility of writing about an ultimately transcendent, nonlinguistic experience. Although scholarship has heretofore emphasized the triadic structure of Rolle's thought and the visual aspects of Suso's mysticism, they both resemble something more akin to a synaesthetic account of mystical experience that regularly highlights music as the ineffable route to—and pinnacle of—union with the divine.

CHAPTER 2

Henry Suso in England

Rhineland Mysticism and Middle English Literature

For more than 250 years, Henry Suso proved an authority of enduring significance for English devotional writers in a variety of genres. Given the similar devotional cultures in which Rolle and Suso wrote so successfully, and Rolle's widespread acceptance and popularity in a variety of later English devotional contexts, this is perhaps little surprise. Yet Suso's influence was more significant, longer lasting, and much more diversely expressed than has been previously acknowledged; his typically anonymous translators, too, have yet to receive their due as devotional authors of real theological and literary accomplishment. Translation, as contemporary scholarship increasingly recognizes, is a creative, imaginative process that is of profound literary value (and, quite often, of substantial theological significance). As Ian Johnson argues, for instance, of the Yorkshire Carthusian Nicholas Love (d. ca. 1424), his translation of the Pseudo-Bonaventurean *Meditations on the Life of Christ* "delicately re-sculpts his source into a new, more realized cognitive topography, befitting his portrayal and direction of unsaved souls beset with their own various, contingent challenges. When he does something grammatical he does something imaginative and something theological."[1] Although *Seven Points of True Love and Everlasting Wisdom* is the most substantial witness to Suso's work in Middle English, throughout the fifteenth century Suso's Latin *Horologium* was intricately involved in these imaginative processes, excerpted and translated across the English literary landscape, including by Nicholas Love. Perhaps best known today is Thomas Hoccleve's translation of Suso's chapter on the art of dying well (*Horologium* 2.2, "Learn to Die") in the *Series*.[2] But his thought played an important role in quite a wide range of other works: the morality play *Wisdom*, Simon Winter's *Life of Jerome*, *The Chastising of God's Children*, and the *Mirror for the Devout* (*Speculum devotorum*).

Even in the sixteenth century, Suso's *Ars moriendi* remained a significant participant in the substantial English discourse surrounding the art of dying well; it was translated—or paraphrased—by Saint John Fisher, bishop of Rochester, as he awaited execution in the Tower of London. Suso's influence on liturgical reading material in Latin was also pronounced before and after the split with Rome: one of the last things Thomas More read before his beheading was a simple printed Book of Hours containing Suso's *Hours of Eternal Wisdom*, later translated into English as the *Jesus Matins*. Suso's influence in England did not end during the reign of Henry VIII, however. In 1536 and 1575, two different English translations of Suso's office were published as parts of vernacular Books of Hours. A Catholic English readership of Suso's works is unsurprising, but he was also read by nonrecusants, and continued to be translated into English anew. Richard Brathwaite's wide-ranging devotional anthology, *A Spiritual Spicerie* (1638), nearly unknown today, brought Suso into conversation with a range of spiritual texts in a diverse collection of pious translated material.

These translations offer literary history much more than simply an array of witnesses to the insular reception of an important Continental devotional author, however. In and by their translation and complicated transformations, they are themselves significant works of devotional theology; these texts contribute to an understanding of the crucial role of translation in shaping popular theological discourse in English across the divide of the Reformation, and, even more broadly, to the ways in which literary and theological authors engaged creatively with source-texts in the creation of translated literature. Critics have typically focused on the ways in which insular spirituality was allegedly a pale imitation or inferior dilution of the presumed purity or profundity of Continental thought, but examining these translations on their own terms, and in their context of literary and translational mobility, reveals a devotional landscape in which Suso's work was, in fact, carefully adapted and creatively tailored to local needs (even as these translators worked within a cultural framework that, as we saw in chapter 1, shared considerable commonalities with Suso's own milieu). Translation was, and always had been, part and parcel of literary and devotional activity, both in England and on the Continent.

My main concern in this chapter is to examine some of the theological and literary changes wrought in the ongoing process of Suso's adaptation in English, from its origins to the seventeenth century, and to demonstrate the mutual contributions of translation and theology to several major genres of late medieval and early modern religious literature. The effect of Suso and his translators across the literary and devotional landscape was widespread, but it was not diffuse. I concentrate here on three main streams into which Suso's influence flowed: changing models of authorship (particularly the use of author-characters as exemplary figures), the reworking of gender dynamics and erotic terminology in the discourse of spiritual marriage, and the reshaping of the role of experience in the practice and exercise of contemplative literature.

Suso's role in the creation of fifteenth-century English piety has long been more or less dismissed: his translation into English was a process of reception that may have made Suso broadly accessible to vernacular readers, but at the same time rendered his work a shallow and diluted shell of its former self (these accounts often neglect to mention Suso's own role in the popularization of Meister Eckhart's thought in the vernacular in Germany). Since the 1980s, in particular, this dour tone has seemed rather intractable: Roger Lovatt discounted the potential for future studies of Suso's influence in England, claiming influentially that English translations of Continental spiritual material in general, and Suso in particular, were uniformly insipid, uninspired works of anodyne piety. Lovatt reaches a fever pitch in the discussion of the *Seven Points*: it represented, to him, "integration as dilution, absorption as emasculation"![3] Even in the course of this radical dismissal, he and A. I. Doyle, furthering the work of earlier philologists (especially Carl Horstmann), brought to light a number of relevant Middle English materials, and research into Suso's translation and reception has managed to persist, but large-scale reassessments of Lovatt's dour conclusions, particularly outside of the study of Lollardy, have unfortunately been rather sparse.[4]

New critical work and significant discoveries in recent years, and a different hermeneutic environment concerning literary translation, now call for the critical recalibration of our understanding of Suso's legacy in England.[5] Perhaps most fundamentally, Dirk Schultze has provided, in 2005, a critical edition of the *Seven Points* (based on Aberystwyth, National Library of Wales MS Brogyntyn II.5), which provides detailed and precise commentary on the language of the text and the technique of the translator, also helpfully setting the stage for further study of the text.[6] The recent resurgence of interest in Thomas Hoccleve, too, has allowed for a reassessment of earlier dismissive analysis of Hoccleve's translation.[7] My research has also revealed evidence of Suso's lasting reputation in England into the seventeenth century: his importance continued well past the upheavals of the 1530s, albeit in an attenuated form.

It is true that from his earliest traces in England, Suso was read not principally for the exemplary (and at times extraordinary) authorial persona he took such pains in creating, but rather his ability to provide texts both popular and resolutely orthodox. These texts, in turn, were transformed in the process of creating books aimed at wide vernacular circulation in order to promote orthodoxy, foment piety, and, ultimately, save souls (all goals shared by Suso in Swabia and the wider German-speaking world, it bears mentioning). Insular interest in his text does give us some direct evidence of English engagement with the characters he created, however. Lambeth Palace Library MS 436, for instance (fifteenth-century Witham Carthusian John Blacman's copy of the *Horologium*), has "frater amandus" written in margin of fol. 129v, *Horologium* 2.7, where the new and mystical name given to the "Disciple" is first introduced.[8] Overall, however, the vernacular circulation of Suso's works tends to veer away from pseudo-biographical details of the sort literary critics often seem to crave. Barry Windeatt speculates on the stripping of Suso's name from his English circulation and wonders if "in a market already saturated by the fervid Rolle brand, it was more the insights attained and validated by Suso's fervours that were widely marketable than the fervours themselves."[9] With his impressively constructed textual self diminished, and often distributed in Carthusian circles, his status as a Dominican was nevertheless regularly recorded, however; perhaps in part simply to distinguish him from the hermit Rolle (particularly as several texts, including Suso's, were indeed misattributed to Rolle).

The freedom taken by translators, however, also points to the confident orthodoxy that must have surrounded Suso. Vincent Gillespie remarks, for instance, that the *Seven Points* "finally completed a full decade after Arundel's decrees" does not show any signs of a translator's "anxiety about a radical reconfiguration of the text and wholesale extension of its potential readership."[10] The repeated mention, in Middle English texts, of the author of the *Horologium* as a Dominican, albeit an unnamed one, may also have served to reassure readers of his orthodoxy. Mentioning his roots in Swabia may have been another gesture contributing to a sense of his orthodoxy in the years during and after the Council of Constance (1414–18), some sessions of which would have taken place roughly 500 meters along the shores of Lake Constance from the Dominican house Suso inhabited for decades.[11] Along similar lines, insular awareness of the Joachite heresy of the Spiritual Franciscans may also have made Suso's Dominican identity slightly more trustworthy than the other fraternal orders; in 1330, for instance, four Cambridge Franciscan lectors were arrested.[12]

There are thirty-two extant manuscripts of Suso's Latin *Horologium* of English provenance; some of the insular witnesses to the Latin works of Suso contain the entirety of the *Horologium* (five manuscripts), but far more contain only extracts (nineteen manuscripts). Two more manuscripts contain the first two books of the *Horologium* without the *Cursus*, and three contain the *Cursus* alone. The remaining three manuscripts also appear to bear witness to one of the several Latin translations of the third part of the Middle High German *Büchlein der ewigen Weisheit*, the *One Hundred Meditations on the Passion* (*Centum Meditationes*).[13] English and Latin were not the only languages in which Suso was read in England, however: one manuscript of the French translation of the *Horologium* (Paris, National Library of France MS Fr. 446) can also be confidently associated with England because it belonged to Charles, Duke of Orleans, and was part of his library during his long imprisonment in England.[14]

The earliest securely datable evidence of Suso's textual presence in England is found in the 1393 will of Bristol merchant Henry Wyvelscombe, in which a copy of the *Horologium Sapientiae* is given to the chaplain Henry Inet. Wyvelscombe is also associated through testamentary evidence with donations to the Witham Charterhouse, Somerset, establishing the earliest datable references to Suso in England in both lay and monastic settings in the southwest of England.[15] Another important early witness to Suso's English reception is his brief use in *The Chastising of God's Children*. The dating of *Chastising* is not entirely certain, but it likely predates the main vehicle for the reception of Suso in English, *The Seven Points of True Love and Everlasting Wisdom*, by at least a decade, and may have been completed as early as 1395.[16] *Chastising* was likely produced in the southeast, quite possibly London, between 1395 and 1405, with a possible connection to Sybil Fenton of Barking Abbey; both Barking and the Dominican nuns at Dartford Priory also later owned manuscripts containing Middle English translations of Suso.[17] Besides being printed by Wynkyn de Worde around 1493, *Chastising* was also used as a source for the devotional compilations *Disce Mori* and *Ignorancia Sacerdotum*.[18] The *Ignorancia Sacerdotum* thus indirectly participates in the dissemination of Suso in the vernacular: one section of the *Ignorancia* cites the entire chapter 21 of *Chastising* (save the concluding paragraph), "which, in turn, borrows the second half of this chapter from the seventh book of Suso's *Horologium Sapientiae*."[19] A copy of the *Horologium* was also given to Archbishop Arundel in 1405, cementing its association in England with anti-Lollard orthodoxy.[20] It is from this religious milieu that Nicholas Love would compose the 1409/10 *Mirror of the Blessed Life of Jesus Christ* (a translation of the Pseudo-Bonaventurean *Meditationes Vitae Christi*), ending the text with a prayer to the Eucharist translated from the *Horologium*.

EXCERPTING SUSO IN MIDDLE ENGLISH DEVOTIONAL TEXTS

English Carthusian interest in Suso extends well beyond testamentary evidence. One of the most remarkable vernacular Carthusian productions of the fifteenth century, British Library MS Additional 37049, contains a short lyric on fol. 28r that further attests to a general awareness of Suso as a spiritual author of value and originality.[21] Even if its readers were not encountering specifically Susonian texts elsewhere in the miscellany, his *Horologium* is still cited by name:

Whoso rememors cristes passion deuoutely
To hym profets specially two þinges in hye
Þe t'one is if a man be put in heuynes
It remefes a way his gret distres
Also ane oþer it dos & helps certanly
To relese þe bitter paynes of purgatory
Þis affermes þe boke horologium sapiencie cald
To þaim þat deuoutely cristes passion in mynde wil halde
Also take hede to þis insawmpyl here.

———

Whosoever remembers Christ's passion devoutly, / To him, two things profit him especially on high: / The one is if a man be put in heaviness, / It removes away his great distress. / Also another [thing] it does, and helps certainly: / To release the bitter pains of purgatory. / This affirms the book called *Horologium Sapientiae*— / To them that will devoutly hold Christ's passion in mind, / Also take heed to this example here.

In this short lyric, the enhanced *remembrance* of Christ's passion is cited as the most prominent aspect of the *Horologium*'s effect on the devout reader.[22] Giving the book its full Latin title, the poem suggests that Suso's work was associated in England with the ever-growing practice of Passion meditation. The role of the Carthusian Order in shaping this practice in the fifteenth century, of course, was especially prominent.

It was in another Passion meditation, indeed, that Suso reached his greatest Middle English audience. Among the many Middle English texts drawing on Suso in fairly compact excerpts, the Yorkshire Carthusian Nicholas Love's *Mirror of the Blessed Life of Christ* was easily the most popular (to judge by manuscript witnesses). It survives today in sixty-four manuscripts (including fifty-nine complete or assumed originally to be complete) and was printed nine times before 1535 (by Caxton, Pynson, and Wynkyn de Worde).[23] Nicholas Love's translation of the Pseudo-Bonaventurean *Meditations on the Life of Christ* borrows from Suso in the treatise on the Eucharist that ends Love's text.[24] The importance of this Eucharistic prayer for the structure of the *Mirror* as a whole can be seen as a gesture intended to conclude the reader's experience of the text by reinforcing orthodox Eucharistic doctrine as the centerpiece of its encouragement of the popular practice of Passion meditation. Its placement serves to return the reader's vivid imaginings of the life of Christ back into the present-day world beyond the pages of the book, in which the body of Christ is (still, through the Eucharist) immediate and accessible. Both the book and its promotion of the sacrament of the altar provide the devotee with a renewed sense of the ongoing presence of Christ, accessed via both contemplative reading and sacramental participation. But Michelle Karnes has drawn a sharp distinction between Love's *Mirror* and its source-text, arguing that the latter invited more vivid imaginative interaction with the scenes of the Passion.[25] Nicholas Love steers the reader toward the relationship between the Passion and the Eucharist, introducing the prayer carefully by emphasizing its benefits and its proper use (at the moment of the elevation). It aids the reader in the "wiþstondyng of temptaciones & overcomyng of vices . . . getyng of vertues & encrese of feruent affecciones in þe loue of oure lorde Jesu" (*Mirror* 238.3–5).[26] The position of the treatise and prayer on the Eucharist here, at the end of the *Mirror*, emphasizes Love's clear dependence on this sacrament as the liturgical centerpiece of an orthodox response to Lollards, doubters, and the insufficiently pious.

The translation of the prayer itself bears some similarities to the *Seven Points*; Love likely drew on both the *Seven Points* and the *Horologium* in phrasing the prayer.[27] In considering translation more broadly, Love expresses his concerns about the intellectual abilities of his audience in terms quite similar to those used by the translator of the *Seven Points*: he writes that his main source-text is "more pleyne in certeyne partyes þan is expressed in the gospell of þe foure euangelistes" (*Mirror* 10.8–9).[28] Love follows this justification for an extrabiblical life of Christ (supported by the authoritative example of the putative author, Bonaventure) with the commonplace that beginners in contemplation must be "fedde with mylke of lyȝte doctryne" rather than "sadde mete of grete clargye & of h[ye] contemplacion" (10.15–6). He continues in defending the "deuoute meditacion[s]" (11.9) of his treatise by explaining the importance of likenesses in making a devotee aware of the "gostly inuisible þinges, þat he kyndly knoweþ not" (10.39); he stresses the validity and efficacy of imagining scenes in the life of Christ found in neither the Gospels nor the writings of the church fathers. That is to say, just as Suso and his translators emphasized the allegorical nature of the Disciple's conversations with Eternal Wisdom (the text presents them this way simply to make their teaching more effective), so too Love here makes clear that his vernacular *Vita* "passyng alle þe lifes of alle oþer seyntes" (11.12–13) narrates the life of Jesus "in a maner of liknes as þe ymage of mans face is shewed in þe mirroure" (11.15–16).[29] Through the process of imaginative contemplation enabled by the text, as Katie Bugyis writes, the readers "become actors in the drama of salvation history in the eternal now of their imaginations."[30] The life of Christ—or at least the most soteriologically efficacious parts of it, and its contemporary replication in the Eucharist—is superior to (and thus considered in some way as in competition with) the numerous lives of saints one could read; that life is reflected in Love's *Mirror* just as clearly, he claims, as a human face is reflected in a mirror.

The Carthusians of Sheen (often associated with the Bridgettines across the Thames in Syon Abbey) give us another perspective on early English interest in Suso among Carthusian authors of Passion meditations. The anonymous *Mirror to Devout People* (*Speculum devotorum*) is likely a 1420s product of the Sheen Charterhouse—slightly later than Nicholas Love's *Mirror of the Blessed Life of Jesus Christ*—and seems to have been written initially for the sisters of England's only Bridgettine foundation, Syon Abbey. This text employs Suso once again in the service of Eucharistic orthodoxy. Although the text draws heavily on female Continental authors, particularly to supplement gaps in the Gospel narrative (Bridget of Sweden most prominently, but also Mechthild of Hackeborn and passages from Raymond of Capua's *Life* of Catherine of Siena), the *Mirror*-author initially cites Nicholas of Lyra, "Master of Stories," as his principal source in supplementing and explaining the Gospel:

> Ferthyrmore, gostly syster, ȝe schal vndyrstande that þe grounde of þe boke folowynge ys þe gospel and doctorys goynge thervpon. And specyally I haue folowyd in þys werke tueyne doctorys, of the whyche þat one ys comunely called the Maystyr of Storyis, Nycholas of Lyre, þe whyche was a worthy doctur of dyuynytee and glosyde all the Byble as to the lettural vndyrstandynge of eny doctorys that I haue red.[31]

The author focuses on following the literal-historical meaning of the Gospel, finding Nicholas of Lyra (and the other of the "twain," the unnamed

Peter Comestor) the most dependable of commentators among the many he has consulted.[32] The emphasis on the literal meaning is a bit striking: one might expect a meditation on the life of Christ to focus more heavily on allegorical readings of the events in order to offer a more complete, self-enclosed interpretation for the reader. Perhaps the reaction to Lollardy led to a greater demand for the literal sense of the Bible in the vernacular (like that offered by French historiated Bibles, for instance): the text can offer first and foremost an orthodox counterweight to Wycliffite insistence on the primacy of the literal meaning of the Bible, while also providing a reliable vernacular commentary on central passages of a text that itself was (technically, legally) unavailable to non-Latinate readers in post-Arundel England.[33] It is also significant to compare this emphasis with Nicholas Love's similar concern about presenting the literal history and the "direct" meaning of the life of Christ to his readers. In each case, allegory seems to be downplayed in the attempt to create an imaginative pilgrimage across time and space to the life of Christ as a historical event (one both utterly unique and infinitely repeatable in the minds of devout readers).

The *Mirror*-author continues to justify both his authorship and his citations by minimizing his own authorial profile:

> Notwythstandynge, I haue browgth inne othyr doctorys in diuerse placys, as to the moral vertuys, and also summe reuelacyonys of approuyd wymmen. And I haue put nothynge too of myne owen wytt but that I hope maye trewly be conseyuyd be opyn resun and goode conscyence, for that I holde sykyrest. For thowgth ther mygth haue be put to sum ymagynacyonys þat haply mygth haue be delectable to carnal soulys ȝytt that þat ys doo aftyr conscyence ys sykerest thowgth the medytacyonys þat haply mygth haue be, be sueche ymagynacyonys, haply more confortable to some carnal folke. (*Spec* 6)

"Imaginations," though more revealing and comforting to some devotees, are also more suspicious (susceptible as they are to demonic influence); the *Mirror*-author pointedly excludes any subjective experience from his account. Just as Suso claims that his text is taken "either from the mouth of Eternal Wisdom, who Herself spoke them in the Gospels, or from the highest of spiritual teachers,"[34] so too this author goes to great lengths to emphasize the authoritatively sanctioned, unambiguously orthodox nature of his writing, even when moving from the "letterale vnderstondyng" to "morall vertues." Misinterpretation is possible, but the only novel materials he has introduced to his many sources come through the virtuous, well-intentioned exercise of "open resoun"—he has rejected adding some of his own "ymagynaciouns" to his material, even if it might have aided some readers. All this, however, is in the hope of spurring the reader's own imagination in an affective pilgrimage, as he urges his readers to imagine themselves in the various scenes of the Passion, taking part through contemplative reenactment in the suffering of, especially, Mary.[35]

These authorial anxieties make it all the more significant that the Carthusian *Mirror*-author turns to the once controversial Suso, even though by this time the papal condemnation of Eckhart is nearly a century old, and Suso's own *Little Book of Truth* and its specific concerns about the misuse of Eckhartian mysticism by the putative Heresy of the Free Spirit do not appear to have circulated much beyond the German and Dutch-language regions.[36] If, however, Vincent Gillespie is right in asserting that the *Mirror*-author had "no first-hand knowledge of Love's book, nor does he even seem familiar with it despite its status as a widely circulated and popular text,"[37] then it is particularly surprising that both authors would independently draw upon the same passage in Suso's *Horologium* to emphasize the (orthodox) significance of the Eucharist for lay readers (unless they are both relying on a lost common source, a Latin Carthusian miscellany of some sort, perhaps, which invokes Suso on this topic). Although Suso certainly had some role in popularizing strands of Eucharistic piety, it does not play an overwhelmingly dominant role in his works, nor is he regularly associated with the most strongly Eucharistic modes of piety (or popular Eucharistic miracles) emerging elsewhere in Europe. This makes it especially unexpected that still another independent translation of Suso's treatise on the Eucharist was recently discovered in a manuscript that otherwise contains predominantly Lollard-associated materials.

The chapter of the *Speculum devotorum* describing Maundy Thursday details the importance of the Eucharist for his readers, stressing the importance of the Paschal lamb and the washing of the apostles' feet. Turning to the moment of the Eucharist itself, we read:

For hyt ys the condycyon of some louarys that whenne they be departyd bodyly, they wole desyre summe memoryal or tokene that they maye the bettyr thynke eueryche on othyr by. And so oure louely

Lorde Ihesu Cryste, whenne he knewe þat hys tyme was come be
hys owen ordenaunce, þat he wolde dye for mannys soule and aftyr-
warde gloryusly aryse. (*Spec* 90)

As if to invoke the mixture of courtliness and devotion one finds commonly in Suso and Rolle, the *Mirror*-author emphasizes the role of
the Eucharistic in terms of a worldly lover's use of a token to recall to
memory thoughts of an absent partner. He then turns to Suso, citing the
Horologium by name (in English, in contrast to the Latin title given in the
prayer mentioned above from British Library MS Add. 37049):

> For he seyth to hys dyscypyl in the boke þat ys callyd þe Orlege
> of Wysedome thus: "Sykyrly, trewly, and wythoute eny doute, I am
> conteynyd in thys sacrament, God and man, wyth body and soule,
> fleyisch and blode, as I wente out of my modrys wombe and hynge
> in the crosse and sytte att þe rygth hande of my Fadyr."[38] Loo, gostly
> systyr, how mygth hyt be seyde more opynly? (*Spec* 90)

This translation, scrupulously exact, links the Eucharist to the beginning and ending of Christ's life, his path from womb to cross. Bringing his narrative away from the subject matter of the chapter (the Last
Supper), the *Mirror*-author chooses a passage of Suso that gives the Eucharist relevance to the Nativity (specifically, to Marian devotion), the
Passion, and the Ascension; he emphasizes for his reader the openness
and clearness of Suso's exposition of the same. The chapter continues
by justifying the Transubstantiation in aesthetic terms (Christ appearing as actual flesh, dripping blood, might be unappetizing to the more
squeamish in the congregation) and in moral terms (the very challenge
of belief in transubstantiation gives one a greater opportunity to exercise
one's faith). The author briefly defends the reception of the Eucharist in
the species of bread alone by nonprelates, ending the theoretical discussion of the Eucharist by discouraging further, more general questioning
about its mysteries.

Returning to the prologue, we find an author aware of the preemi-
nence of Bonaventure, the putative author of the *Meditationes Vitae
Christi*, mentioned by name as the author of the "*Vita Cristi*." Here, however, the *Mirror*-author also draws on Suso to reinforce the importance

of meditation on the life of Christ, in particular its pedagogical and sapiential value:

> For Euyrlastynge Wysedom seyt, in the boke þat ys called the *Orlege of Wysedom*, to hys dyscypyl thus: "Be hyt knowe to the that hyt ys not ȝeue to come to the hynesse of the godhede or vnvsyd suetnesse but to folke drawe be a manyr meke affeccyon of feythe and loue be the byttyrnesse of my manhede and Passyon. And þe hyer eny man goeth, thys forsclewde, the lower he falleth. For forsothe þys ys the weye the whyche me goeth; thys ys the gate be the whyche an entrynge ys grauntyd to the desyryd ende." And in anothyr place of the same boke he seyt also thus: "The ofte thynkynge of my Passyon makyth an vnlernyde man a ful lernyd man and vnwyse men and ydyotys hyt makyth [into perfyte] maystrys, not of the sciens that bloweth a man wythinne but of charyte that edyfyeth; hyt ys a maner boke of lyf, in the whyche ben founden all thyngys necessarye to helth." (*Spec* 5)

The English title of the *Horologium Sapientiae*, but not its author, is once again cited: clearly the title and its embedded image of a spiritualized clock had some import among English Carthusians in the fifteenth century, as did invoking the portrayal of Jesus in Suso's text as "Everlasting Wisdom." The danger of overweening spiritual ambition is here yoked to the necessity of contemplating Christ's passion as if it were an enlightening, health-giving book. The comparison of worldly knowledge and spiritual wisdom is, of course, a commonplace, giving particular significance to the *Mirror*-author's choice of Suso (when he could have made a similar point with any number of other quotations). Given the *Mirror*-author's wide range of sources, too, and his emphasis on Continental female visionaries, the use of Suso here indicates a deep affinity for the Dominican and his particular utility in justifying the authorial project of the *Speculum devotorum*.

The quotation of Suso continues with an emphasis on Christ's humanity and suffering, paired with a detachment from the world and an increase in grace:

> And sone aftyr he seyt thus: "Blyssyd ys he or sche that sadly takyth hede to þe studye of hytt, for he schal profyte in the dyspysynge of

the worlde and in þe loue of God and all vertuys, and he schal take the encresyngys of gracys." (*Spec* 5)

This brief third passage from the *Horologium* completes his exposition of the virtues of meditation on the Passion, focusing again on Suso's dismissal of scholastic, bookish learning in favor of the particular affective modality granted through the contemplation of Christ's suffering. He is certainly not as important a source in this text as in Nicholas Love's *Mirror*, but Suso again bolsters the treatise's Eucharistic piety; his text (but not his name) also features prominently in the preface as a source of authority, alongside Bonaventure, the "approved women," and Nicholas of Lyra.[39]

The complex network of sources drawn on by the author of *The Chastising of God's Children* includes Suso; this treatise—written between 1395 and 1405 and associated with Barking Abbey—is likely the earliest English vernacular engagement with Suso's work. The author silently draws on Suso for his descriptions of the "play of love" and the spiritual meaning of tears (the latter also associated in England with Catherine of Siena). In the first of its twenty-seven chapters, the author describes God's performance of a motherly technique of withdrawing succor from us, as a mother leaves her children, so that they "wepe and crie and besili . . . seke hir wiþ sobbynge and wepynge," only to reappear with embraces and kisses to the child's delight (an analogy also found in the *Stimulus amoris* and William Flete's *Remedy against Temptations*).[40] This alternation between love and sorrow is then linked to love more generally, translating directly from Suso's *Horologium*:

Þe pley of loue is ioye and sorwe, þe whiche two comen sundri tymes oon aftir anoþer, bi þe presence and absence of him þat is oure loue. Þis is a propirte of loue, þat whanne we han him presente þat we loue, we knowe nat hou moche þat we loue, but whanne he is awei, þanne we perceyuen bi his absence what matier we han to loue hym.[41]

Here, Suso's text is shifted in context slightly, with the courtly and erotic game of love transformed into a childish game played between mother and child. In discussing the use of tears in spiritual practice, the *Chastising*-author refers to Suso as "þe disciple of loue." This figure is answered inwardly about the many kinds of tears by "þe wisdom of god."[42] In the third use of Suso in the text, the *Chastising*-author draws on Suso for a prayer to God the Father to be used to discourage the devil, immediately after a reference to Saint Bridget's own prayer, taught to her by Mary, for dispersing demons (a gesture not unlike Nicholas Love turning to Suso's *Horologium* for his closing prayer to the Eucharist).[43]

Suso's work appears in one more vernacular English devotional compilation, however. Long-held assumptions about the orthodox reception of Suso in England, as used in devotional compilations, have recently been overturned by the discovery of another translation of his chapter on the Eucharist (*Horologium* 2.4) in Cambridge, St John's College MS G.25. Discovered by Sarah James and edited by Dirk Schultze, the texts directly following the Suso treatise have been described as "emphatically Lollard, and of a particularly strident variety."[44] The Lollard use of this treatise on the Eucharist contributes to the present reappraisal of the role of Suso in English religious culture.[45] The text carefully skirts outright heterodoxy, but it nevertheless silently suppresses aspects of Suso's treatise that are more unseemly to Wycliffite eyes. Sarah James argues that the text performs a delicate masquerade: without adding anything that would immediately jump out as heterodox, the translator simply omits sections of Suso's text he might disagree with. A contemporary reader perhaps might have recognized the (safe, Dominican) source of the treatise, without investigating too closely for matters of interpolation or omission. Meanwhile, a Lollard reader would also find nothing to object to, finding only "a refusal . . . to enter into precisely those contemporary debates about substance and accidents, or about 'material bread,' which divided mainstream and Wycliffite thinkers."[46]

CONTEMPLATING DEATH: SIMON WINTER AND THE ANONYMOUS PROSE "LEARN TO DIE"

Suso's words on preparing oneself for death, imagined as a dialogue between the Disciple and the image of an unprepared dying man, proved especially popular in late medieval English devotional culture. At least three authors, beyond the *Seven Points* author and Thomas Hoccleve, drew on Suso's chapter in creating Middle English devotional prose tracts on dying well. Most directly, Lichfield, Cathedral Library MS 16 contains both a unique translation of Suso's "art of dying" (the chapter of the *Horologium* titled "Learn to Die" [2.2]), along with a Latin copy of *Horologium* 2.2. The Lichfield translation's source-text seems to have been somewhat corrupt (but not all apparent lapses found in the English can be attributed to the copy of the Latin text in the manuscript itself).[47] Another independent prose translation of this *Ars moriendi* is found in two manuscripts: Glasgow, University Library MS Hunter 496, and Oxford, Bodleian Library MS Bodley 789. This version, Elizabeth Westlake writes, removes the Disciple from the narrative, thus casting the reader in the role of interlocutor: the words of the unprepared dying man now directly address the reader of the text.[48]

Simon Winter, a brother at Syon Abbey, cites the *Horologium* in his *Life of Jerome* (written between 1422 and 1440), giving further evidence of the use of Suso in late medieval England in connection with the art of dying well.[49] In Winter's case the chapters dealing specifically with the craft of dying are drawn primarily from letters by Pseudo-Jerome to Cyril, but Winter describes the importance of those chapters in the introduction by citing Suso.[50] The quotation differs significantly enough from its analogue in the *Seven Points* that we can be certain Winter is here translating the *Horologium* into English anew, rather than simply citing the *Seven Points* (or the Lichfield or Bodleian texts): "What ys hit to kon lyue and dye, but to lyue soo that we be always redy to dye, so to haue oure hert and oure soule redy vnto God þat we abyde deeth as the comyng of a loued frende that we desyre to goo wyth from wrecchednes vnto delyces?"[51] Although this is a common enough sentiment in any text of the *ars moriendi* tradition (and a fairly brief quotation within Winter's text as a whole), that Simon Winter turned to Suso as an unacknowledged source further demonstrates Suso's critical role in the fifteenth-century development of the genre. Even when translating spiritual advice on dying from an entirely different Latin text, the material is nevertheless still framed by reference to Suso's terminology.

BECOMING THE SPOUSE OF CHRIST IN MIDDLE ENGLISH

The most important Middle English adaptation of Suso is undoubtedly *The Seven Points of True Love and Everlasting Wisdom*. Very little is known with certainty about its authorship, and it cannot be dated securely, but it seems probable it was composed by a Carthusian over a period of several years. Although Nicholas Love appears to have known its version of the prayer to the Eucharist when writing the *Mirror* (thus placing the composition of its chapter 6 *before* 1410), there are two manuscripts that bear the following colophon: "S*c*ript*us* finalit*er* in Monte gra*c*ie vltimo die Mens*i*s Maij Anno d*o*m*i*ni M°CCCC°XIX°. Deo gra*ci*as. Am*en*" (*SP* VII.578–79), indicating a text not completed until May 31, 1419.[52] The Carthusian house of Mount Grace, home of Nicholas Love in north Yorkshire, would not be a surprising place for its composition (evidence from its dialect sends us significantly mixed messages), but its being completed in 1419 poses significant problems both for its use in Love's *Mirror* and its overall tenor. If this colophon is to be trusted, it seems most likely that *Seven Points* was written gradually, over a period of at least ten years, with Nicholas Love having in-house access to Point VI before 1410, but the complicated text as a whole not considered finished until 1419 (that is, firmly in the aftermath of the Constitutions of Arundel).

The text rearranges and cuts its source in order to transform the twenty-four chapters of Suso's Latin into a seven-chapter treatise; even though the translator claims this is an homage to the seven gifts of the Holy Spirit, it seems quite likely that some degree of competition with the weekly structure of Nicholas Love's *Mirror* also influenced the choice of format. Points I, II, and VI are fairly complicated reorderings of the *Horologium*, whereas Points III, IV, V, and VII are relatively unified translations of, respectively, *Horologium* 1.13 and 2.3; 2.3; 2.2; and 2.5, 7, 8.[53] As Michael Sargent notes of the process of compiling and translating the *Horologium*, we have the work "of a translator whose command of the text of the *Horologium Sapientiae* was thorough enough to allow him to range back and forth, excerpting, deleting, reinserting, and rearranging his material."[54] The *Seven Points* survives complete in six manuscripts: Aberystwyth, National Library of Wales MS Brogyntyn ii.5 (*olim* MS Porkington 19); Cambrai, Municipal Library MS 255; Cambridge, Gonville and Caius College MS 390/610; New York City, Columbia University, Plimpton Library MS 256; Oxford, Bodleian Library MS Douce 114 (alongside a unique Middle English translation of a letter about Catherine of Siena, discussed in chapter 3); and Bodleian Library MS Tanner 398. The *Seven Points* is found without the translator's preface, but otherwise complete, in Bodleian Library MS E Museo 111, and Cambridge, Corpus Christi College MS 268. It was printed by Caxton as a major part of his circa 1491 *Book of Diverse Ghostly Matters* alongside *The Six Masters on the Tribulation*,[55] *The Twelve Profits of Tribulation*,[56] and an English translation of the Rule of Saint Benedict;[57] this incunable survives in at least six copies.[58] Some of the chapters also circulated separately, particularly the popular *Ars moriendi* (chap. 5): it can be found in London, British Library MS Additional 37049 (which also contains chapter 4), BL MS Harley 1706, Cambridge University Library MS Ff.5.45, and Bodleian Library MS Douce 322. Chapter 4 alone (how to persevere in spiritual life and flee temptations) is found in British Library MS Additional 37790 (Amherst); and chapter 6, on the Eucharist, is found in Cambridge University Library MS Hh.1.11.[59]

Most modern-day commentators have found interest in the *Seven Points* only in relation to the *ars moriendi* tradition, Nicholas Love, Lollardy and Arundel, perhaps the morality play *Wisdom*, and so forth. It becomes seen as a source-text for a more interesting text, an instance of translation, perhaps one example of shallow English orthodoxy and piety, but not a work of effective devotional literature or significant vernacular theology in its own right.[60] Yet as devotional theology, its literariness is an essential component of its success. A. C. Spearing, for instance, reflects on his being encouraged by Elizabeth Salter to consider *The Cloud of Unknowing* as *literature* (and seeing book 3 of *Troilus and Criseyde* as theology of sorts): "I read the *Cloud* as a literary text alongside other literary texts; that is, as a text whose meaning is not on the other side of its language, but is created *in* its language."[61] The *Seven Points*, too, might profit from being brought in from the cold of more specifically oriented devotional studies, particularly given the text's popularity and its own engagement with certain facets of chivalric literature not often encountered in English devotion. Here, I focus on the how translation shaped the text's popular devotion, particularly as seen in the categories of experience, gender, images, and love-mysticism. My particular concern will be an exposition of the methods with which the translator transforms and adapts Suso's use of these concepts in the process of preparing the text for a popular, mixed, English audience.

The language of bridal mysticism, absorption in God, and *excessus mentis* used in the *Seven Points* represents a significant expansion and exploration of these themes in the English vernacular. Julian of Norwich is well known for her exposition of the motherhood of Jesus and the soul's marriage to the Trinity, and Margery Kempe's marriage to Jesus has also attracted extensive scholarly commentary, but the final chapter of the much lesser-known *Seven Points* is an intricately constructed description of the marriage of the Soul and Eternal Wisdom, detailing the spiritual benefits of this mystical marriage. Although one might expect a diminishing role of bridal imagery as the *Horologium* was translated from Latin into a vernacular without grammatical gender, we find instead a wide-ranging array of gendered relationships between God and the soul of the devotee.

Saint Augustine's famous command concerning the primacy of love in moral action is another significant addition by the translator to Suso's text. In the prologue, the translator writes: "For seinte Austyn seyþ: 'Loue perfiȝtelye and do what þou wilte'" (*SP* 151–52).[62] Given the significance of mystical marriage in both the *Horologium* and the *Seven Points*, the use of this passage in the preface is especially well suited to illuminate one of the central messages of the treatise. And while this aphorism might have been viewed with some suspicion in Suso's milieu, considering the possible misuse of the text by those sympathetic with, for instance, Marguerite Porete or Free Spiritism, it would seem that English authors concerned with reinforcing orthodoxy among insular devotional readers could safely include it without fear of misinterpretation.[63] The deliberate attribution of the phrase to Augustine (when, more commonly in the text, other sources are quoted without citation) also helps to lend the passage the additional orthodox credence of one of the Four Doctors; the rubrication of *seinte Austyn seyþ* in MS Brongyntyn II.5 similarly adds visual emphasis to the authority of Augustine's aphorism.[64]

The most extended discussion of the mystical marriage of the Disciple to Eternal Wisdom is found in Chapters I and VII, effectively bracketing the rest of the treatise and emphasizing the overall importance of bridal mysticism to the author-translator-compiler. Chapter I discusses the name of "Everlasting Wisdom" as the initial step toward understanding the marriage of the devout Disciple to the Godhead. Sapientia begins the text, addressing the Disciple, explaining that among the many names appropriate to the Godhead, the appellation "Everlasting Wisdom" is "moste conuenient and beste acordynge to myn nobleye" (*SP* I.7–8, translating "quod utique meae congruit peroptime nobilitati") (K 420.13–14). Sapientia goes on to explain how "Wisdom," although belonging to all persons of the Trinity, can be particularly applied to the God-Person, "now as he þat is þe spouse of his chirche, & now as sche þat is þe spowse & wyfe of euery chosen sowle þat may seye of hir, euerlastinge wisdam, in þese wordis of þe boke of wisdom" (*SP* I.15–17). It has been suggested that this passage is indeed a loose translation of the *Horologium* ("Nunc etiam Dei Filium ut devotae animae sponsum inducit; postea eundem tamquam aeternam sapientiam viro iusto desponsatam introducit"), but I believe it is original to the *Seven Points*.[65] Beyond linguistic grounds—it would be a very loose translation, indeed—it would also be a departure from the structural program of the text. Passages from the prologue of the *Horologium* are used in both the "Translator's Preface" and the "Preface," but the main chapters themselves never return to Suso's prologue (Point I itself draws on *Horologium* 1.6, 1.8, and 1.1, for instance)—the author has, by then, quite thoroughly prefaced his work and moved forward in his project. It seems very likely, then, that this does not represent the translator's compression of the entire paragraph in Suso's prologue dealing with the gender dynamics of the *Horologium* (K 366.6–17), but rather the translator's own understanding of the function of the quite labile gender of Christ-as-Wisdom in the text he has produced.

Barbara Newman accounts for some of these differences in Suso's corpus—the *Horologium* focusing on Suso's relationship with Jesus as female Eternal Wisdom, the *Little Book of Eternal Wisdom* (*LBEW*) on the humanity of the male Christ—as a function of different audiences. A predominantly vernacular readership, she argues, would also be largely female, and thus more comfortable with marriage to Jesus than the Latinate, male audience, who in turn need a female spouse in the form of Jesus-as-Sapientia.[66] In English, however, we see some of the potential variance of the gender of Eternal Wisdom within single works, both Latin and vernacular; there does not seem to be as strong a pattern in the gender dynamics of the vernacular translations of the *Horologium*—a remasculinization of Sapientia for a vernacular-female audience.[67]

Although it would be worthwhile to examine the entire vernacular reception of the *Horologium* in this light, the English translations alone already show a range of widely divergent evidence on this matter. The translator's preface to the *Seven Points* confirms the association of vernacularity with femininity, being written for a "derreste loued gostly douȝter" by her "simple trewe chapeleyne."[68] The soul of the Servant, however, loses its (grammatical) femininity in English translation; thus in the initial explanation of the association of Christ with Wisdom we are told that Christ-Wisdom is to be understood "now as god & now as man, now as he þat is þe spouse of his chirch, & now as sche þat is þe spowse & wife of eu*ery* chosen sowle" (*SP* I.14–16). The relationship established in the preface (of learned clerk translating Latin for a high-born female devotee) is overturned in the opening of the first chapter; Eternal Wisdom is now to instruct both a soul and a servant gendered male (his "parts" in the dialogue are marked in the margins of some of the manuscripts as *Discipulus*, hers *Sapiencia*).[69]

As we saw in chapter 1 in Suso's Latin and Middle High German works, it is particularly significant here that the translator-author seems to have little interest in Christ-as-Wisdom's gender oscillations. There is no real ontological weight placed on the distinctions in the passage, only a concern for pedagogical, rhetorical, or pastoral efficacy. Despite the lack of grammatical gender in English, Christ-as-Wisdom remains the bridegroom of *Ecclesia*; the devout soul, however (traditionally female), becomes male in order to serve as the bridegroom of Sapientia. The roughly analogous passage in the *Horologium* explains that the Son of God is the spouse of the devout soul, but when he is portrayed as (the goddess) Eternal Wisdom, it is in order to be betrothed to the "just man." The English masculinizes the soul of the devotee in order to wed it to a feminine Sapientia, but it does so in the context of a sentence that simultaneously uses the Church as an allegorical female character, itself, in turn, wedded to a distinctly male Jesus.

Returning once more to the opening of the *Seven Points*: just after the prefatory material treating the fluctuating gender(s) of Eternal Wisdom, there are six quotations from the books of Wisdom and Proverbs, all translated faithfully, and all maintaining the feminine gender of Sapientia/Wisdom throughout. Wisdom's declaration of her ubiquity in this section also maintains the emphasis of the source-text on the presence of Christ in every space, both religious and secular. For instance, the Latin "praesens in choro, praesens in thoro, in mensa, in via, in claustro, in foro, ita ut non sit locus, ubi non sit praesens caritas Deus" (K 425.12–14) is rendered as "I am p*r*esente in chirche and att þe borde, in þe weie and in þe cloystere & in þe market. So þat þere is no place but þat þer is present charite god" (*SP* I.52–54). The one term omitted here, *t(h)orus* (bed), indicates a certain degree of concern over the use of sexual terminology in the otherwise florid description of the relationship between the Disciple and Sapientia.[70] Later on in Chapter I, Wisdom explicitly cautions against overreliance on secular motifs in understanding divine love. Analogy and allegory, however exuberantly deployed elsewhere, once again have their limits.

Still, it is allegorical reading that Sapientia recommends when the Disciple complains of the difficulty of ever being separate from she who has "so woundit" him "wiþ loue" (*SP* I.169–70)—scripture is described as an "amorous letter" sent to the Disciple to comfort him. Nevertheless, his complaint continues, as he describes how bleak everything seems when Wisdom's presence is withdrawn, and how exceedingly wonderful the world seems when the brightness of Wisdom rises, like the morning star, in the darkness of his heart. She refers to the suffering of lovers as a "turnynge aboute of þe whele of loue" (I.327–28) in a modification of the popular Boethian image, and, after a long speech about the potential suffering lovers undergo, claims that these zeniths and nadirs are all part of the *ludus amoris*, "þe pleie of loue" (I.305). This game of love is, she explains,

> Ioye and sorowe, þe whiche oon aftir anoþer of my presence and of myne absence fallen to þe lovere. For þat is þe propirte of loue, þat in þe presence of þat þinge þat is louede hit is hidde and not knowen, but in þe absence þerof hit schewiþ hit selfe and is more knowyn. (*SP* I.306–10)

The epistemological paradox of courtly love-mysticism, already present in the Latin (and explored in maternal terms translating these words of Suso's in *Chastising of God's Children*), is intensified in the Middle English of the *Seven Points*. The doubling of the Latin's *latere* and *percipere* emphasizes the significance of the phenomenological and cognitive implications of the Latin source-text. Divine Love here is only efficacious insofar as it makes what is *present* hidden and unknown, and precisely what was once *hidden* becomes what is both most easily perceived and most readily understood. The "play of love," properly understood, is certainly grounded in the emotional experience of earthly love (for some authors erotic, for others maternal). But ultimately it requires an utter abandonment of the senses, and a complete reversal of one's sense of the ordinary and the visible. As we have seen already in other reversals of gender in the text, it is this displacement of perception, occasioned by the transformation of gender categories, that brings the reader both further from and closer to the text. We are distanced, perhaps even alienated, from the text by the complicated reversals involved in the genders of the characters in the story of the mystical marriage. But we are brought into a closer communion with the text—particularly the translated text—insofar as these transformations, translations, and transgressions invite us to travel on interpretive journeys in which we become closer readers of rhetorical effects, grammatical genders, and narrative contexts.

Human categories of maternal, erotic, and romantic love initially provide the foundation for a richly detailed and almost extravagant deployment of changing genders to represent mankind's relationship with the divine in Suso's texts, but these are ultimately superseded by a recognition that God's transcendence makes that foundation, at its heart, little more than an extended rhetorical effect. But we might, in the end, see such gestures as the great contribution of mysticism to the history of Christianity—as Michel de Certeau pithily puts it, mysticism "is the Trojan horse of rhetoric within the city of theological science."[71] But in literary study, which prizes paradox and allegory, transgressive narratives and linguistic ambiguity, imaginative journeys and rhetorical exuberance (all characteristics of devotional theology), one might instead do well to argue that these texts are rather more akin to the humble quartet of theological horses in *Piers Plowman*, following behind the mighty team of Evangelical oxen given to Piers to help him till the field of Truth.

The unceasing oscillations of the genders of the figure of the Disciple, "his" soul, the Church, and even Christ-as-Sapientia Herself all serve to reinforce the central message: representations, whether in scripture or in devotional literature, are all ultimately representations only, born from the fundamentally literary impulse to exceed language, to use words to experiment and transform and provoke and astonish. The categories of gender, and the emotions of love, are some of the most powerful we have at our disposal, but the ontological status of the representation of courtly love is of minimal importance for the human bodies created in these texts, and of no significance whatsoever, beyond serving as transitory heuristic tools, when applied to a Godhead that surpasses not only all human categories, but also the very language and thought that constructs those categories.

Suso's *Little Book of Truth*, his first work, draws on the great sixth-century Syrian Greek writer, the patriarch of mysticism, Pseudo-Dionysius, arguing of God's Oneness and Nothingness that "as long as a person understands oneness . . . as something that can be presented in words, he still has to go further within [*inbaz ze gaenne*]."[72] Forms, images, words, gender dynamics—all essential in late medieval mystical discourse—must also be discarded in the pursuit of the truth of the true, hidden God. Along these lines Meister Eckhart, in a well-known German sermon, bluntly criticizes those who would dare to see God with the same eyes they use to see a cow. Even Being itself, let alone its human subset of sexual difference, ultimately cannot be the target of the mystic's quest, however construed; for within mystical theology God does not "exist" in any of our senses of the word. Already in the sixth century, indeed, Pseudo-Dionysius tells us that "God is not a facet of being. Rather, being is a facet of God."[73]

THOMAS HOCCLEVE AS LITERARY THEOLOGIAN: THE POETRY OF DYING WELL

Both English literature and insular vernacular theology were shaped by the translation of Suso's texts in the late Middle Ages; separating the two, of course, is no simple task. Turning from the more straightforwardly devotional to texts traditionally classified as literary, however, one finds that Thomas Hoccleve's "Learn to Die," the morality play *Wisdom*, and Saint John Fisher's prose *Consolation* all participate in refigurings of the *Horologium*, and of the role of Suso's author-character therein. All three authors remove the character of the Suso-Disciple from their narratives in one way or another, but their texts also present, in three quite distinct ways, an enlargement and enhancement of the personal, the individual, and the affective. Their attention to the role of personification and allegory also leads them to careful strategies surrounding the language of resemblance: we are created in God's image and likeness, and care must be exercised in the literary and performative representation of that relationship.[74]

Hoccleve's translation of a chapter of the *Horologium* (often called the "Learn to Die," or *Scire mori*, 2.2) performs a variety of alterations on its source-text in the process of creating this vernacular verse *ars moriendi*, presented at a turning point in the pseudo-autobiographical *Series*.[75] The rehabilitation of Hoccleve in recent decades has also seen a new awareness of the sophistication of Hoccleve's literary technique and theological knowledge. Most emphatically, Sebastian Langdell has recently argued that scholars have overlooked Hoccleve's "sustained interest—*throughout* his career—in the role and function of priesthood, the spiritual health of the institutional church, the treatment of laypeople, and the ability of poetry to act as a conduit for prayer, penance, and reflection."[76] Within this framework, Hoccleve's interest in Suso—and his drawing on Suso's tract on dying well at a pivotal moment in the *Series*—demonstrates both Hoccleve's own theological sophistication and the ready accessibility of Suso among literary laypeople in early fifteenth-century London.

This verse translation of the most popular chapter (in England) from the *Horologium* is part of a larger series of poems aimed at rehabilitating Hoccleve's social "image" after, the poem claims, a long period of acute mental illness and a rural retreat from London. The text opens with a gloomy, autumnal inversion of Chaucer's meditation on April, as the Hoccleve-character sees the falling of the leaves as a reminder that nothing can escape death. Within a pseudo-autobiographical structure that begins with a character named "Hoccleve" staring into a mirror and imagining how his face might give evidence to passersby of his recovery from madness, "the rest of the *Series* can be read as Thomas's account of looking into different kinds of mirrors in order to learn what form his reform should take."[77] Hoccleve's "Learn to Die" demonstrates an intricately patterned attention to the language of images and their central role in helping us comprehend our relationships and resemblances to God, ourselves, and each other.[78] Amy Appleford notes, too, the intense isolation and asceticism inherent in the framing narrative around the "Learn to Die": "Learning to die in Hoccleve's analysis is individualistic, focusing on shaping the soul to be less reliant on the potentially mechanistic economy of purgatorial prayers . . . and on the voicing of a poetic version of ascetic identity."[79]

Hoccleve's self-named character in the *Series* writes, translates, and glosses in order to seek social and theological redemption (even as his unnamed friend argues emphatically that excessive studying and writing was the very cause of his illness); the poetry of texts like his "Learn to Die" confronts the impossibility of the former while seeking, in Suso, the latter. As the Image of Death asks, "Can yee portreye / Your wordes so gayly, and effect noon / Folwith, but al as deed is as a stoon?" (Hoccleve, ed. Roger Ellis, *Series*, 712–14). This, Hoccleve's inventive addition to Suso, contrasts the deadness of beautifully arranged words to the potential redemptiveness of a poem that teaches its readers properly how best to die. When the Image-character dies, he laments: "no lenger Y now see this worldes light. / Myn yen lost han hir office and might" (664–65), considerably expanding Suso's *lucem huius mundi amplius non video* (K 536:23–24) and powerfully amplifying the abjection of Image in the complete failure of his senses.

Even the early twentieth-century critic B. P. Kurtz (otherwise fairly steadfast in his disapproval of Hoccleve's translation) admits that, of Hoccleve's additions to Suso's text, "a few are slightly stronger or more personal than the Latin." He sees this as almost unambiguously detrimental, however, and glumly claims that this "simple and direct-minded poet has again and again brought into the lofty sentences of Suso phrases of personal revelation."[80] But it is exactly this heightened imagery and intimacy, this sense of the personal, and this language of individual revelation that make Hoccleve's dialogue such a powerful affective tool. Suso, in many respects, would have admired Hoccleve's poem—personal revelation was part and parcel of his understanding of spiritual authorship. Just as the Disciple character in Suso's works stands in for the author, representing textually the authority of the historical Henry Suso even as it denies any ironclad link between the two (as the Hermit character does in Rolle), so too is Hoccleve's self-named character in the *Series* experiencing a vision of death in order to play a role somewhere between fictional character and historically verifiable author.[81] The character named as Hoccleve in the poem and the historical author-figure Hoccleve must remain distinct. As A. C. Spearing has written of this character, in words that apply also to Suso and his own author-character, "there may be a danger of reading Hoccleve as a whole self back into a text in which he appears as a fragmented subject."[82] This is especially true when encountering a narrator forced to witness death in the pursuit of an experiential understanding of the horrors of what it means to die.

WISDOM, WHO IS CHRIST: HENRY SUSO
AND THE THEATER OF THE MIXED LIFE

The role of experience, a central category in both Suso's theory of death and its widespread employment in Middle English, also contributes to fifteenth-century English theater. Hoccleve and the anonymous prose treatises translated Suso's chapter on the art of dying properly, but the materiality of Suso's mysticism would find its greatest expression in drama. Nowhere in the story of Suso's reception in England is there a deeper and more persistent engagement with the very material grounds of devotional and mystical experience than in the play *Wisdom*. The play offers a form of materiality embedded in the very text: the dramatic script calls scenes into being, demands specific materials of costuming and staging, and performs on that stage the intricate gendering of Christ as developed more abstractly in Suso's texts themselves. The text of the play *Wisdom* transforms the material *potential* of Suso's text, exploring the puzzling matter of humankind's likeness to God by putting the roles of Christ-as-Wisdom and the Soul on actors, in costume, on stage. Wisdom and Anima, in the performative space generated by *Wisdom*, are both human and both actors, even as each bears an essential likeness to God.

Caroline Walker Bynum has considered physical, primarily churchly, material as "holy matter": she takes into account the materiality of images, relics, the material wonder of nonputrefying bodies, the deceptive appearances of sacramental and Eucharistic matter, and ultimately sees the valences of Christian matter expressed through a "locus of generation and corruption."[83] The paradox of late medieval Christian materiality, she argues, is that the Incarnation demanded the created world be both corruptible and sacred; "miraculous matter," she writes, "was simultaneously—and hence paradoxically—the changeable stuff of not-God and the locus of a God revealed."[84] This account of late medieval Christian materiality illuminates the particular use of materiality in the play *Wisdom*, which presents both the troublesome mutability of matter itself and the redemption of the natural world through its re-creation. Even more to the point, however, in *Wisdom* we have a work of Susonian theater—a text of performance, outward and material, embodying an imaginative theology that calls for the incarnation of its images, and the iterative re-creation of the images it develops. I see in the dramatic text the possibility Bynum sees in medieval sacred art—texts that, like art, can "lift matter toward God and reveal God through matter."[85] Here, however, my focus is on the possibility of the text creating matter, and on the public display of that matter, for the uneasy blend of entertainment and edification that is found in so many morality plays of the late Middle Ages. Public matter, staged matter, and gendered matter are all employed in *Wisdom*, making a complicated case for the imbrication of human and divine.

The morality play *Wisdom* (ca. 1465–75) draws on not only the *Seven Points*, but also Walter Hilton's *Scale of Perfection* and *Epistle on the Mixed Life*.[86] The play's appeal to a mixed life and the suggestion of the involvement, in a stage direction, of female actors have generally pointed to an episcopal or secular audience and performance context, but both extant manuscripts have concrete links to the Benedictines at Bury St. Edmunds, leaving both the original audience and the author of the play in question.[87] This text can be seen as concluding the process begun in its main source-text, *Seven Points*: Suso's Disciple character is sapped of some aspects of his distinctive persona, and the affective power of the text and its deployment of images and personification is heightened and enhanced (accordingly, a distinction between image and likeness also plays a central role in the text's understanding of the uses of imagery). The amplification of the affective we just saw in Hoccleve is even more prevalent in *Wisdom*'s adaptation of Suso, particularly in the vivid onstage personification of Eternal Wisdom—even as the gender dynamics of the spiritual marriage between Wisdom and the Soul, seen in the *Seven Points*, has been reversed.

The play opens in grand, spectacular form, with stage directions specifying the costuming and pomp surrounding the entrance of Wisdom:

Fyrst enteryde Wysdome in a ryche purpull clothe of golde wyth a mantyll of the same ermynnyde wythin, hawynge abowt hys neke a ryall hood furred wyth ermyn, wpon hys hede a cheweler [wig] wyth browys, a berde of golde of sypres [cloth] curlyed, a ryche imperyall crown þerwpon sett wyth precyus stonys and perlys, in hys leyfte honde a balle of golde wyth a cros þerwppon and in hys ryght honde a regall schepter.[88]

Just as the magnificent frontispieces of the French translation of the *Horologium* emphasize the majesty of the regal Sapientia enthroned, here too a theatrical audience experiences supreme splendor and pageantry at the opening of the play. The crucial difference, however, is Christ's gender: Wisdom is now emphatically male, even to the point of being bearded. His first speech is adapted from the opening lines of Point I:

Yff ʒe wyll wet þe propyrte
Ande þe resun of my nayme imperyall,
I am clepyde of hem þat in erthe be
Euerlastynge Wysdom, to my nobley egalle;
Wyche name acordyt best in especyall
And most to me ys convenyent,
Allthow eche persone of þe Trinyte be wysdom eternall
And all thre on euerlastynge wysdome togedyr present.
Neuerþeles, forasmoche as wysdom ys propyrly
Applyede to þe Sune by resune,
And also yt fallyt to hym specyally
Bycause of hys hye generacyon,
Therfor þe belowyde Sone hathe þis sygnyficacyon
Custummaly Wysdom, now Gode, now man,
Spows of þe chyrche and wery patrone,
Wyffe of eche chose sowle. Thus Wysdom begane.[89]

(*Wisdom* 1–16)

Although the text is mostly faithful to the *Seven Points*, the gendering of Wisdom becomes more ambiguous in this passage. He is bearded and emphatically the Son, but she is also "spouse" of the Church and *wife* of the Soul. The borrowed, versified text maintains some of the femininity of Suso's Wisdom, even as the bulk of the gender dynamics of his bridal mysticism have been either reversed or simply excised.[90]

When the soul enters, the stage directions tell us it is "Anima as a mayde," and nearly as richly arrayed as Wisdom. But the gender of Anima is not as stable as the stage directions initially might make one imagine. As Karáth summarizes, her gender identity "becomes nominal, even delusive. Not only are Anima's faculties—Mind, Understanding, and Will—masculine . . . but Anima herself is constantly identified with masculine pronouns or gendered nouns to fit the gender identity Christ/Wisdom attributes to the personified soul in His direct address."[91] Near the end of the play, Wisdom addresses Anima, in the words of the Song of Songs, as "my sister, my wife" (soror mea, sponsa) (*Wisdom* 1083), following the Latin with an English rendering ("syster, spowse dere"; *Wisdom* 1085), even as Anima joyfully proclaims the grace she has received from "my modyr, Holy Chyrche" (1078). But Anima's first lines almost seem to skirt the issue of the gendering of both Wisdom and Soul, and in fact address the other character on stage first as "spouse," then with the second-person pronoun, then "wisdom," before finally using the masculine pronoun:[92]

> Hanc amaui et exquisiui:
> Fro my yougthe thys haue I sowte
> To haue to my spowse most specyally,
> For a louer of yowr schappe am I wrowte.
> Aboue all hele and bewty þat eyer was sowght
> I haue louyde Wysdom as for my lyght,
> For all goodnes wyth hym ys broughte.
> In wysdom I was made all bewty bryghte.
> Off yowr name þe hye felycyte
> No creature knowyt full exposycyon.[93]
>
> (*Wisdom* 17–26)

The playwright skillfully weaves a dialogic aspect of the *Seven Points* into theater in this passage: between Wisdom's speech and Anima's he has omitted "þat may seye of hir, euerlastinge wisdam, in þese wordis of þe boke of wisdam: 'Hanc amaui . . .'" (*SP* I.16–18). In comparison to the *Seven Points*, Anima simply assumes the role of the spouse of Wisdom by reciting these words from the biblical book of Wisdom, not quite as macaronically as in the *Seven Points*, but still beginning her speech in Latin in order to flag the scriptural significance of her lines. The last three lines cited above, however, are unique to the play: an apophatic coloring that might serve to accentuate the gender ambiguity this introduction to Wisdom and Anima generates. Despite the mighty visual and linguistic display in these opening minutes of the performance, the exposition of even something as basic as God's name cannot be completely explored or fully known.

Wisdom, in order to better manifest the characteristics of his name, responds, again in the words of the book of Wisdom:

> Sapiencia specialior est sole.
> I am foundon lyghte wythowt comparyson,
> Off sterrys aboue all þe dysposicyon,
> Forsothe of lyght þe very bryghtnes,
> Merowre of þe dyvyne domynacyon,
> And þe image of hys goodnes.
> Wysdom ys better þan all worldly precyosnes,
> And all þat may dysyryde be
> Ys not in comparyschon to my lyknes.
> The lengthe of þe yerys in my ryght syde be
> Ande in my lefte syde ryches, joy, and prosperyte.
> Lo, þis ys þe worthynes of my name.[94]
>
> (*Wisdom* 27–38)

The primary changes from the *Seven Points* are straightforward enough: a revoicing of the biblical passages from third to first person (which eliminates the feminine pronouns of the *Seven Points*), and an excising of almost all of the Vulgate that the passage translates, save the first line.[95] More importantly, however, Wisdom's explanation of his name depends not only on scriptural passages from Wisdom and Proverbs emphasizing the divinity of the property of the Trinity, but also the (likewise biblical) language of the image and mirror (also a theological concern of Hoccleve's). Anima then responds, in words unique to the play, "A, soueren Wysdom, yff yowur benygnyte / Wold speke of loue, þat wer a game" (39–40)—a possible gesture to the *ludus amoris* of the *Horologium* and *Seven Points* not otherwise mentioned in the play.

Wisdom then responds, again largely in the words of the *Seven Points*, by describing his loveliness, how delightful it is for all souls to embrace and kiss him, how endless his love is, how insignificant woes are in comparison to a drop of his love, the purifying nature of his love, and the rest and tranquility granted to those who take him to spouse. Wisdom's speech goes on to relish the absence of fear of death as a result of divine love, and finally to consider the ultimate unspeakableness of that love. The play cuts significant portions of the *Seven Points* discussion in its versification and adaptation, while still managing to capture most of the main notes of the corresponding passage in the *Seven Points*. Critically, however, the necessity of *experience* is once again stressed as part of the theological program of the play; as Eleanor Johnson has written, its "central challenge . . . is to feel the truth of man's being created in the image of God."[96] In the context of an actual theatrical performance, these words would have had a particularly significant effect: the vivacity of the living word and the experience of God's love would be especially striking in making the claim for the essential *experientiality* of divine love. Wisdom, the God-Man (played by a man and dressed as a regal man), helps Anima and the audience to understand both the preciousness of divine love and its inability to be expressed in conventional language, even as the materiality of the performance, the beard and crown the actor wears, bring the audience into the experience of the affective power of the material over (or alongside) the linguistic.

After this point in the play, only a few lines from the *Seven Points* are incorporated into the otherwise original dialogue between Wisdom and Anima. Immediately after the passage just cited, Anima exclaims, "O worthy spowse and soueren fayer, / O swet amyke, owr joy, owr blys!" (*Wisdom* 69–70), borrowing the term *amyke*, "friend," otherwise unattested in Middle English (coming from Latin *amicus*), directly from the *Seven Points*.[97] This is followed by a slight reworking of the scene in which the Disciple and Wisdom exchange hearts: Anima asks what she could give that would be most pleasing to Wisdom, who responds, "Fili, prebe michi cor tuum" (77). Whereas in the *Horologium* and the *Seven Points* Wisdom speaks more spontaneously, not in response to a question from the Disciple, here it is occasioned as a response to a dialogue with Anima. In the source-texts Wisdom's command stands alone, uttered to the Disciple independent of any glossing and unaccompanied by explanation. Here, it is given heightened attention, glossed by Wisdom: "I aske not ellys of all þi substance. / Thy clene hert, þi meke obeysance, /

Yeue me þat and I am contente" (80–82). The connection between Anima and Wisdom, through heart exchange, is directly flagged as a portion of Anima's "substance" (even as she is now referred to as a son instead of a daughter).

Thematically, however, the play continues to draw on the *Seven Points*: Anima asks Wisdom how she might know the Godhead. Wisdom's response distantly echoes the advice of the *Seven Points*: look inside yourself: "By knowynge of yowrsylff ȝe may haue felynge / Wat Gode ys in yowr sowle sensyble. / The more knowynge of yowr selff passyble, / Þe more veryly ȝe xall God knowe" (*Wisdom* 95–99).[98] The playwright similarly demonstrates an interest in the language of image and similitude used in Hoccleve and Suso to describe the relationship of the soul to the divine: "Wat ys a sowll, wyll ȝe declare? / [Wysdom]: Yt ys þe ymage of Gode þat all began; / And not only ymage, but hys lyknes ȝe are" (102–4). But the play soon goes on to demonstrate an elaborate development of these terms: baptism "reformyt þe sowll in feythe verray / To þe gloryus lyknes of Gode eternall" (127–28), and the character Mind introduces himself by announcing that he is "the veray fygure of þe Deyte" (184). Both terms here are in the realm of similitude and likeness: the temporary, transitory nature thereof is emphasized in the first passage by the comparison to God's eternality (and the utility of baptism in restoring the union between God and humanity); the character of Mind, in turn, will soon be tempted and deformed by the devil. In explaining the Trinitarian nature of the soul (embodied on stage as Mind, Will, and Understanding), Wisdom declares that both the two "things of the soul" are the "symylytude of Gode abowe" (284).

Lucifer describes his jealousy of mankind in terms of human resemblance to God—"Of Gode man ys þe fygure, / Hys symylytude, hys pyctowre" (*Wisdom* 349–50)—and begins his plotting to "dysvygure" this relationship of resemblance and likeness. Before this plan begins, however, he recognizes the difficulty of tempting Will in his current *lyknes*, and so the stage directions (s.d.) specify that he must "dewoydyth and cummyth in ageyn as a goodly galont" (s.d., 126). The audience, having heard of the fragility of the likeness between Anima's faculties and Wisdom, is now given a dramatic, visual enactment of the deceptiveness of material likenesses as Lucifer recostumes himself into a "goodly gallant" in order to better seduce Will into sin.

Twisting Walter Hilton's words to his own design, Lucifer convinces Mind to abandon contemplation. For as Christ's example included both contemplation and action, thus it "was vita mixta þat Gode here began" (*Wisdom* 428). This ultimately convinces Will and Mind, who manage to drag Anima into sin. Again, the audience is given a specific demonstration of the disfiguring of the soul through sin: when Anima next enters, she "apperythe in þe most horrybull wyse, fowlere þan a fende" (s.d., 143); it is this sight—the dirt, the filth of the costume—that causes Mind to repent and realize the gravity of his fall. The similitude is, in this instance, easily corrupted; just as Lucifer recostumes himself, here too Anima's fall is represented by her new dissimilitude to Wisdom, but the experiential and visual effect of this is heightened by having "seven small boys in þe lyknes of dewyllys" run out from under Anima's mantel (s.d., 144). It is only now, and only by Wisdom, that the crucial term, *ymage*, is used:

> What haue I do? why lowyste þou not me?
> Why cherysyste þi enmye? why hatyst þou þi frende?
> Myght I haue don ony more for þe?
> But loue may brynge drede to mynde.
> Þou hast made the a bronde of hell
> Whom I made þe ymage of lyght.
>
> (*Wisdom* 913–17)

After the numerous corruptions and deceptions of likenesses in the play, Wisdom now reminds Anima of the inseverable bond of image. With this, Anima's faculties begin the penitential reformation necessary to restore likeness to this image; in another partial gesture to the source-text, Wisdom then recommends the nine points of contrition and prayer that best link mankind to God. After leaving the stage to confess, Anima and the Faculties reenter, "all in here fyrst clothynge . . . and all hauying on crownys" (s.d., 149)—their divine likenesses restored through the restoration of the initial material of their costumes. A dirty costume removed from the exterior of the actor serves to represent the interior cleaning of the soul-as-character.

From the reference to heart exchange and the use of dirty costuming to represent the spiritual deformity of sin, to the elaborate stage directions calling into being a royal male gendering of Wisdom, the play radically changes the matter imagined by its source-texts, even as it employs the material of stagecraft (and personified aspects of the human mind) to push beyond the potential frictions of material mysticism into a remarkably robust embodiment of Susonian bridal mysticism. For Bynum "medieval objects . . . were labile. In a world increasingly convinced of the possibility of literal (not metaphorical) metamorphoses . . . matter was that which changed,"[99] but here in the world of the play, neither miraculous nor metaphorical metamorphosis is, in fact, needed. Instead, the words on the page create the objects of the stage, bringing Wisdom-as-Christ and the Christian soul into the material world, invoking and creating labile, performed matter in order to re-create Eternal Wisdom and his, her, or their eternal image and frail likeness in the human soul.

THE "E MUSEO PASSION MEDITATION": ORDERING PRAYER IN THE HULL CHARTERHOUSE, CIRCA 1525

One of the least-studied pieces of English Suso to date is a verse translation of his Passion meditation, composed of one hundred meditations and a number of accompanying prayers, found in Oxford, Bodleian Library MS E Museo 160, ff. 116r–136r. It is surprising that this textual tradition only survives in one English manuscript—in the Low Countries it was the single most popular piece of vernacular literature over the course of the fifteenth century. Despite its rarity in England, this verse translation is a significant witness to early sixteenth-century devotional interests among Yorkshire Carthusians, and is a tantalizing glimpse at what elements of Susonian spirituality may have indeed once been present in late medieval England, but are now entirely lost. MS E Museo 160 is a paper manuscript of Middle English verse produced in the Carthusian monastery of Hull in the mid- or late 1520s. Its collation is no longer completely original (nor its binding), and several folios have been significantly damaged by fire, pests, clipping, some intentional defacing, and general deterioration. It was largely copied by one scribe, with significant corrections and additions by the original hand and at least one other (noticeably shakier) contemporary hand, and some later sixteenth-century pen trials and erasures. Acquired by the Bodleian before 1680, it is a miscellany consisting of five texts; some of these have been studied independently of one another, with relatively little attention paid to the overall structure of the miscellany as a complete unit. Its five Middle English verse texts, all unique to the manuscript, are the following:

1. ff. 1r–108v: prosimetric "devotional history" of the world (adaptation-translation of Werner Rolewinck's [Latin, prose] *Fasciculus Temporum*), IMEV 217-1 and 3489-1
2. ff. 109r–115r: dialogue between Marco Polo and John Mandeville, IMEV 4866-1
3. ff. 116r–136r: "Hundred Meditations on the Passion" (translation of Henry Suso *Hundert Betrachtungen*, Part III of the *Büchlein der ewigen Weisheit* [1340s], via Willem Jordaens's Latin translation, the *Centum Meditationes*), IMEV 1696-1
4. ff. 136v–139r: "Fifteen Articles of the Passion," IMEV 2847-1
5. ff. 140r–176v: the *Bodley Burial* and *Bodley Resurrection* plays (mistakenly identified as Digby plays by Furnivall in EETS e.s. 70 [1896]), IMEV 163-1

The manuscript begins with a prosimetric "devotional history" of the world (ff. 1–108), a large portion of which is a fairly loose translation of the Cologne Carthusian Werner Rolewinck's (Latin prose) *Little Bundle of Times* (*Fasciculus Temporum*); first published in 1474, the *Fasciculus Temporum omnes antiquorum cronicas complectens* would be published in more than fifty editions and was also translated into Dutch, German, French, and Welsh.[100] The E Museo-author, however, not only versifies his Latin source-text (which he acknowledges by name twice), but also adds significant material on English and Carthusian history, and updates Rolewinck's text to the year 1518.[101] The page layout indicates an initial goal of illustrating many of the scenes of world history, although spaces for pictures are absent after the treatment of a few Old Testament figures.[102] The author, though a devoted Carthusian, was well versed in secular literature: in his treatment of the battle of Roncesvalles, for instance, he includes the story of Roland (a detail missing in Rolewinck). Throughout the text, numerous English miracles, saints, and disasters (particularly northern English and Yorkshire ones) are also added; at the end of most centuries, space is also left for the addition of more saints if later readers come across them and wish to add to the text (see fig. 2.1).

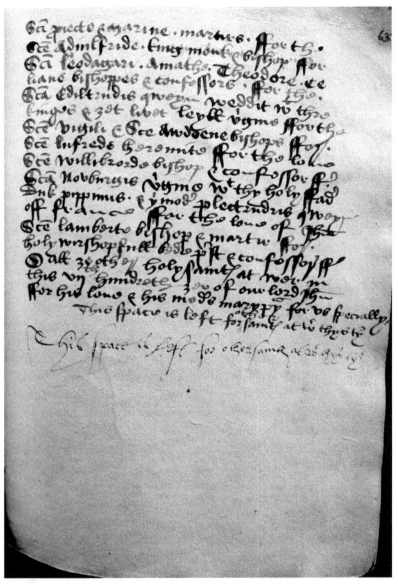

FIGURE 2.1. Oxford, Bodleian Library MS E Museo 160, fol.63r

Perhaps most intriguing in this text is the translator's mention of Arthur's court, something only briefly touched upon in his source-text; this scene also offers another instance of the interaction readers clearly had with the manuscript in the process of using it. In the course of his treatment of each century after the Incarnation, the author concludes with a plea for prayers from the saints of that century. The fifth century's litany includes these: "O Merline, begeten apon a woman by a fend, ȝit thou was of holy life & had spirit of prophecy, & stirrit Wortigonus king of Briton [added marginally in red: '& Vter pendragon & Arthur'] to many gud warkis & incresinge of the cristen faith. Yf thou be a saint in hevyn, for the l[ove].o[f]. Ihesu [pray for vs specially/hertely]" (fol. 47r). The participatory nature of the text in this section is noteworthy, too: only Vortigern has been mentioned in the initial copying, and another reader-scribe has been moved to add in Uther Pendragon and Arthur marginally (see fig. 2.2).

The manuscript later continues to explore historical memory by returning to a moment already considered in its translation of the *Fasciculus*: the Passion. This verse translation of Suso is an important witness to early sixteenth-century devotional interests among Yorkshire Carthusians, particularly those beyond the much better-known house of Mount Grace. It is unclear when in the fifteenth century the poem was originally composed, but this sole witness of the text is certainly not an autograph copy; the dialect does appear to place it in the environs of Hull. Turning to the source-text of this Passion meditation, it is the Latin translation, by the Groenendaal Augustinian Canon Willem Jordaens (ca. 1321–72), of the south Netherlandish translation of Suso's Middle High German original.[103]

This text, quite popular in Germany and incomparably popular in the Low Countries, consists of one hundred short phrases—ranging from just a couple lines to larger, multisentence paragraphs—addressing Jesus and "representing" to him various of his sufferings and those of his mother between the Last Supper and the Deposition. The phrasing and language of the meditations is directed from the reader to Jesus and Mary: in addition to wishing to join in the suffering of Christ and Mary, the reader is also constantly claiming to "present" these sufferings. Re-creation of scenes of the Passion in the mind of the reader is intended here to create an intersection between past history and present readerly experience, as if the intersection between past and present occasioned by the text in the

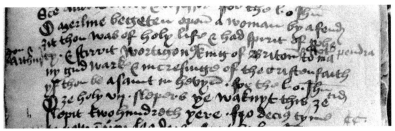

FIGURE 2.2. Oxford, Bodleian Library MS E Museo 160, fol.47r

imaginative faculties of the reader both renews the pain of Christ and Mary and concomitantly joins the reader to these figures through his or her own, newly inflicted emotional pain. Interspersed every five or ten lines are more detailed prayers and petitions for mercy and sympathy to Christ and Mary, bringing the reader out of the space of the imagined Passion and reminding him or her of the practical moral benefits to be gained through the performance of the text.

The first ten meditations (or articles) concern Jesus's arrest in Gethsemane and his judgment and sentencing before Pilate and Herod. Articles 11–35 have the reader directly addressing Jesus concerning all of the particular sufferings of the process of crucifixion itself and Jesus's pain while hanging on the cross. Articles 36–55 detail the circumstances of the first three words on the cross. Articles 56–65 have the readers meditate on Mary's incomparable suffering. The text then returns to Jesus's final four words on the cross in articles 66–75. After Jesus's death in article 75, the reader continues to address him, thinking on the piercing of his side for five meditations. The petition after each meditation now changes to a Hail Mary; articles 81–90 consider Mary's own suffering; the text then skips straight to a pietà scene at the foot of the cross in article 91 (without describing the Deposition). Descriptions of the utter deadness of Jesus's body and the further sorrows of Mary compose the last ten meditations of the text.

As might be expected from the transition from Latin prose to English verse, significant changes are made to nearly every aspect of the source-text. Some phrases from the Latin are omitted, new phrases added, expansions and compressions are made, and word order is significantly altered to fit English syntactical conventions. Some straight Latinizations are made of challenging terms in the original, and at other times a much freer approach to the Latin is pronounced. Suso's introduction is translated faithfully; it describes the visionary source of the meditations, the burning devotion he experienced from their daily exercise, and practical instructions to the reader for their use. There is a particular emphasis on controlling the bodily gestures of the readers (whether they were originally Carthusians or otherwise): the articles are to be read standing, the prayers kneeling, except for the prayer after article 75, which should be said while completely prostrate (a supplemental instruction here in the introduction, found neither in Suso nor Jordaens).

The text begins with a rubricated divine monogram (*Ihc*); following this rather Susonian "title," the translator renders the preface of Jordaens's translation, in prose, beginning, "The wurshipfull discipull of goddis son, Eternall sapience incarnate, The most Crafty maker of that swetly buke callit 'The cloke of eteranall wisdom' compilete & made The .c. articles or the .c. meditacions to be said or thought abuout thee passions of the said Eternall sapience, the sone of god crucifiede" (fol. 116r, 1–8).[104] The prologue continues by explaining that the original meditations were made in the vernacular for the "common pepull of Swenyce or Teutonye" (fol.116r, 13) and detailing the use of the meditations: each must be followed by a petition in their use; this is clear in this particular manuscript, with an abbreviated petition following each meditation, but these are lacking in some copies in other languages.

Next comes the English translator's brief introduction, followed by Suso's own. The English translator's preface is extremely concise, but it provides one useful piece of information for our consideration of the text's audience: despite this text's sole attestation in a Carthusian manuscript, the translator claims that it has been rendered into English meter "so simpely oss is for the commoun lay pepill" (fol. 116v). The text is certainly written in a Hull-environs dialect, but one can only speculate if the author was a Carthusian aiming at some lay outreach, or if the Charterhouse had imported the text from another order—or perhaps even a parish priest or layperson. In any case, this meditation seems to have found readers both inside and outside the cloister.

One of the central concerns of the Jordaens source-text is the emphasis on the cognitive and mnemonic power of the meditations, and certain of the E Museo author's additions further strengthen this emphasis. For instance, the prayer after article 10 contains these lines: "tech me to heyll with thy woundis smarte / *By deuowte remembrance of harte*" (fol. 119v; my italics indicate material added to the source-text)—the heart's remembrance of Jesus's wounds can be used to heal the practitioner's own "gastly woundis that synnys bee" (fol. 119v). Later in the same prayer, "with wepinge eyn" (fol. 119v) is added to the petition "da autem michi, domine, dolorum tuorum amatoria semper memoria recordari," even as the doxology in the Latin text is omitted. In a similar vein, article 21 renders "O amator hominum, benignissime Ihesu Christe" as "Cryste Ihu louere of mankinde. / Thy crucifyinge I call to mynde" (fol. 121v). Whereas the cognitive creation of these pains in the process of praying the meditations is already prominent in Suso's original text, here the translator further emphasizes that experiential element of the meditation, even while omitting "benignissime."

Articles 21 through 26 are particularly notable for their large number of additions; the remainder of these, adding some affective detail, do seem mainly intended to complete both rhyme and couplet: "as it suld not fayll" (fol. 121v), "þat blude owt birlyte" (16), "syn, uayne, & brawn" (19), "far owt of syse" (21), "and suld not stinte" (27), for instance. There are several other instances in which the additions seem principally inspired by the need to have each meditation complete an entire couplet: article 13, "Odoratus tuus nobilissimus putorem fetentissimum respirauit," for instance, is rendered as "Thy moste nobill smell with stinke was fillit / Of dede men that on the mownt war spillit" (fol. 120r).

Other additions seem primarily intended to increase the affective power of the text by including longer and more detailed descriptions of Christ's suffering. Article 16, for instance, adds "with hiddouse payn of thornys thriste" (fol. 120v) to a description of Christ hanging on the cross. Article 76, immediately after the reader prostrates him- or herself, addresses the dead Jesus: "O piarum flebile spectaculum animarum, Ihesu domine crucifixe, momento quomodo te mortuo in cruce pendente unus militum acuta lancea latus tuum sacratissimum perforauit." The English translator expands this slightly, giving us the chance to begin to meditate on both the sacred wound and the sacred heart: "O pitefull sight of sawlis meke. / Lorde Ihu crucified ȝit hau mynd eke / On the crosse dede os thow did hinge / With a sharpe spere a knyght dyd thringe / And thyrlit thy most holy side. / Unto thy harte the wound was wide" (fol. 130r). Although the source-text will quickly move to worship of the side wound, it does not mention the connection between that wound and the heart at any point; the English author was eager to emphasize both this connection and the side-wound more generally as an important focus of the text's project of affective meditation. In other places, more general tags such as "but was withowt comfurth for cristes sake" (fol. 131v) are added in the process of translation and versification.

Similarly, shortly after this passage, the English text invokes the image of Christ as a "bludy buke," a common enough image, but one certainly lacking in the original. Near the end of the text, we once again find a heightened attention to Christ's wounds: Jordaens's "Heu mater amabilis, uirgo beata, quam dolorosa sub cruce sedisti, iacente in gremio tuo uirgeneo dilecto filio mortuo et extincto" becomes "A, louabill modere & blesside maide, / In thy lappe when thy son was layde / How doolfully sat þu under the rude / Seying his woundis all roun with blude" (fol. 133v). The reciprocal effect of Mary's suffering on Jesus is also expanded in the E Museo text: "Tristissima eius anima et gestus nimium lugubundus tuum tibi, domine, martyrium duplicabant" is translated as "O lorde hir most sorowfulle saulle / Weping & heuy cowntnance all / Thy marterdom dowblite to thee. / *To se that virgyne so soree*" (fol. 126r; italics indicate added material). One can find a similar desire to use proper names when the character is simply alluded to in the source-text in another passage, where references to John as the "beloved disciple" are twice expanded to also include his proper name (fol. 126v). There is also a stronger emphasis on the practical need to switch the petitionary prayers from the invocation of Jesus to the Ave Maria after article 55; absent in the Jordaens text is the detailed instruction to be found in the E Museo text: the rubrication, two-thirds down the page, reads, "The salutacion of our lady be said after euery article / here & in places after wher it is notid after þis form" (fol. 127r), followed by a verse rendering of the Ave: "Hayle maree full of grace / God is with the in euery place. / Abofe all womene blessit þu bee / And blessid be the frute of thy bodee, Ihc crist. / Amen" (fol. 127r).

This is not the only occasion where the E Museo text adds supplementary practical instructions on its own proper use: although the reader is instructed to prostrate him- or herself after article 75, in the prologue to the *One Hundred Meditations*, the E Museo text also marks the spot with a large cross and adds, "here fall down flatt to the grounde & saye in remembranc of þe dethe of crist ihu: Ihu criste we wirship the / And the louis for certanlee / By thy deth & holy crosse / Thow bowghte hasse all þe warld fro losse" (fol. 129r). This folio has one more instruction for the reader, however, indicating a scribal error when the text was first copied. In the same hand, following this instruction, we find: "her afor this rubrike as tellis of fallinge flate to þe ground lakkis þe prayer or peticion of þe u. articles next afore. & also þer lakkis her .u articles to be said afor this rubrike. Seke thes sade prayer & articles her wanting at þe end of þes mediacouns" (fol. 129r). Luckily, the numbering of the articles is in roman numerals, into each of which following the scribe inserts the appropriate "u," except in the few occasions where an entirely new number is needed (in which case the mistaken number is simply struck through). The final prayer of the E Museo meditations also includes an implicit physical response within the very recitation of the prayer, another feature of practical performance instruction not present in the source-text. The prayer opens: "O Ihu criste uerrey sapience, / Now crucyfyed for our offence, / I haylle the kneling on my knee / Besekinge thy largenesse of mercee / ffor all tham as prayes in gudlie fassioun / thes .c. articles of þin passioun" (fol. 135r).

Other deviations from the source-text can be considered as more general changes of direction, emphasis, or style. In one instance, for example, "O misericordie inscrutabilis altitudo" is translated as "O Depnese of mercy withowtyn mesure / Gud Ihu crist my saulis tresure" (fol. 122r, even though the same term, "depnesse," is used to translate "abisse" one folio later). In other cases the expansion simply seems to provide further details, more or less easily extrapolated from the source-text, as when "O candor incomprehensibilis lucis eterne" is translated "O Whitnesse of ay lastand lighte / Uncomprehensibill fore grete myght" (fol. 133r). At times an entire line can be added, as when "Et tibi, Ihesu bone, cor meum derisionem illam opprobriosam, qua a Pilato ad Herodem missus, illusus et in ueste alba pro fatuo derisus fuisti" is translated as "Gude Ihu my hart offers to thee / That heythinge thoue hadde repreueablee / When þat prowde Pilate the furth sente / To Herode, & hee in whitte vestment / Sent the agayn lik a founnyd foole / *Thus was thain combert in scorns scole* (fol. 119r; italics indicate added material). Here, the new detail emphasizes Christ's public suffering and humiliation and his dress, perhaps something especially shocking to strictly cloistered Carthusians in their habits.

Although the critic's tendency in studying Latin-to-English verse translations has often been to point out any flaws, infelicities, and stylistic shortcomings of the verse, this scarcely known Passion meditation contains many instances in which the language used is especially vivid and well constructed. The translator is able to latch onto a particular image or detail of the source-text and expand it quite elegantly. For instance, the fairly simple "errantium portus et iustorum speculum deiforme" is especially well rendered as "the havyn of us erringe on þe see / The godle glasse of rightwese men" (fol. 130v). Stylistic changes such as these, perhaps the hardest to identify and classify securely—depending, as they do, on a certain level of subjective aesthetic judgment—nevertheless can, I believe, bring a good deal of pleasure even to the present-day reader of this Passion meditation.

The anonymous E Museo Passion meditation, long neglected and unedited, deserves a degree of praise for its many felicities in rendering an extremely popular strand of Continental Passion devotion into well-wrought verse for a northern English audience of the later Middle Ages. Employing the naturalism of counting by ten, and ten times that ten, the English author (translating a Latin text derived from a Dutch translation of a German original) creates memorable schemata to order both history (in centuries) and the Crucifixion. The grouping of the past into centuries has proved enduring, but the one hundred meditations on the Passion are now, of course, less familiar. It is all too easy to see this single worka-day, damaged, paper manuscript as simply an instance of historiography and Passion piety a decade before the Reformation or subjugating it to the changes that we, five centuries later, know are shortly due to come to Yorkshire's Carthusian houses, but it is definitely worth stepping back momentarily and trying to see the manuscript with the eyes of the scribe and the authors. This community of authors and scribes, around 1520, in Hull, in a Charterhouse, used fourteenth-century Latin source-texts from the Low Countries and the Rhineland in an attempt to order charity—the charity of the Passion and the charity inherent in the saints of global history—in the hearts of its early Tudor Carthusian readers.

BISHOP FISHER LEARNS TO DIE

Written in the winter of 1535 in the Tower of London as John Fisher awaited execution for his failure to swear the Oath of Succession, the bishop of Rochester's *Spiritual Consolation* loosely adapts portions of Suso's *Ars moriendi*.[105] As the source-text for one of the last things he wrote (addressed to his half sister Elizabeth), the *Horologium* (or at least one chapter thereof) was a prized piece of devotional writing to which Fisher turned as he prepared for his death. Most significant in his contribution to the *ars moriendi* genre is that he himself becomes the "unprepared dying man" encountered in other versions of Suso's text: when adding to the basic framework of Suso's *Ars moriendi*, "much of Fisher's original material suggests deeply felt personal regrets."[106] His text also gains particular affective power in the awareness that he was, indeed, preparing for death and martyrdom as he wrote in the voice of the death-character: the historical author and bishop has also become the central character in his treatise on learning to die well.[107]

Fisher begins, however, by assuming the persona of the dying man, describing the present work as "a maner of lamentacion and sorowfull complaynyng made in the person of one that was hastily preuented by death (as I assure you euery creature may be)."[108] Even as the claim is being made to write "in the person" of someone surprised by death, the parenthetical aside reinforces the very personal circumstances of composition. The text also departs from the other adaptations of Suso's art of dying by giving the addressee specific instructions for its use:

First when you shall read this meditation, deuise in your mynde as nigh as you can, all the conditions of a man or woman sodaynlye taken and rauyshed by death: and thynke wyth your self that yee were in the same condition so hastily taken, and that incontinent you must needes dye, and your soule depart hence, and leaue your mortall bodie, neuer to returne again for to make any amendes, or to doe any release to your soule after this houre. Secondly, that yee neuer read thys meditation but alone by your selfe in secrete maner, where you maye be most attentyue therevnto. And when ye haue the best leasure without any let of other thoughtes or buzinesse. For if you otherwyse behaue your selfe in the reading of it, it shall anon lose the vertue and quicknesse in stirring and mouing of your soule when you woulde ratherest haue it sturred. Thirdly, that when you intende to read it, you must afore lifte vp your minde to almightie God, and beseech him that by the helpe and succour of his grace the readyng thereof may fruitfully worke in your soule a good and vertuous life, according to hys pleasure and say, *Deus in adiutorium meum intende, Domine adiuvandum me festina. Gloria patri. etc. Laus tibi domine rex eternae gloriae. Amen.* (*Spiritual Consolation* 368–69)

These directions first encourage a deep imaginative and affective identification with the speaker of the text to follow: in order for the narrative to work, the reader must, from the beginning, be imagining him- or herself as just as close to experiencing death as the narrator is (and as Fisher knew he was). The next two instructions combine to form the text as a type of private liturgy: first, secret and solitary reading will allow for the best focus. The reader is then told to begin the reading as though it were part of the Divine Office, with the well-known words from Psalm 70 followed by the prompt for the *Gloria* and the replacement for the *Alleluia* during Lenten and funeral masses.

After preparing the reader for fruitful contemplative reading, the narrative begins in the first person, eliminating the conversational format that dominates Suso's text. There, Wisdom has the Disciple meditate on the inevitability of death; as he withdraws into himself, he meets the vision of the "ymago mortis," the unprepared dying man. Instead, Fisher's preface has effectively served as the voice of Wisdom beginning the dialogue. By urging the reader in the second person to quiet, interior meditation, the reader has become the Disciple; Fisher's first-person voice then becomes the apparition of the dying man.

By and large, the narrative borrows only loosely from Suso, raising the possibility that Fisher did not have access to books for the composition of the *Consolation*, or for only a limited time during its composition. It also points to the significance the text had in Fisher's life: perhaps only able to request a certain number of books, or perhaps relying on memory alone, it was Suso he turned to. After two opening sentences lamenting the approach of death, for instance, Fisher writes, "But whether I shall goe, or where I shall become, or what lodgyng I shall haue thys night, or in what company I shal fal, or in what countrey I shal be receiued, or in what maner I shall be entreated, God knoweth for I knowe not" (*Spiritual Consolation* 369)—capturing the spirit and some of the phrasing of the *Seven Points* "Where, trowist þou, schalle abide þis nihte my sperite? Who schalle take myne wrecchid sowle? And where schal hit be herborowid at niʒte in þat vnknowen cuntre?" (*SP* V.276–78). The emphasis on image and appearance, so pronounced in Hoccleve and *Wisdom*, also appears here: Fisher considers all the admirable elements of the body and its senses: "All these thou hast not of thy self, they were but lent vnto thee for a season, euen as a wall of earth that is fayre painted without for a season with freshe and goodly colours, and also gylted with golde." Just as that "gilting falleth away" and it appears "in hys owne lykenesse," so too the body's "bewtie is faded" (*Spiritual Consolation* 371).

Where Suso and the *Seven Points* consider the ephemerality of worldly riches by the simile "Alle þoo bene passede as a schadewe and as þe mynde of a geste of one day passinge forth" (*SP* V.94–95), Fisher uses the bleaker "my pleasures be vanyshed away as the smoke" (*Spiritual Consolation* 373). In general, the rhetorical flourishes Fisher employs, along with the repeated second-person address, gives the text an undeniable emotive force in urging the reader to consider the inevitability of death and the dangers of being caught unaware by one's own death. The tone of urgency and immediacy performed in the text is only intensified by one's imagining the bleakest of possible historical circumstances under which it was written. In essence, by becoming himself the character of the dying man by means of his impending execution, Fisher provides the fullest instantiation of the principle that dominated the reception of Suso in England. Fisher continued the removal of Suso and Suso's characters from the text, while at the same time inserting still more vivid personification into the narrative. Fisher's himself becoming the *ymago mortis* is but the most intense, almost macabre variation on this theme. But Bishop Fisher was not alone in thinking of Suso while awaiting death in the Tower. Thomas More had with him a simple Book of Hours of the Sarum Use (printed in Paris, 1530, RSTC 15963), which contained, under the name *Hore de nomini Jesu*, Suso's *Cursus de Aeterna Sapientiae* (the third section of the *Horologium Sapientiae*), known as the *Hours of Eternal Wisdom* (ff. 187v–200v).[109] Indeed, it was with this liturgical text, the *Hours of Eternal Wisdom*, that Suso would reach his widest sixteenth-century readership.

BEYOND THE REFORMATION

Textual longevity is one of the hallmarks of vernacular books of devotion in England.

—Vincent Gillespie, "Religious Writing"[110]

Suso's *Hours*, exceedingly popular on the Continent in vernacular translation as part of Dutch Books of Hours, also had a considerable presence in England and in English. By the middle of the fifteenth century, the text can be found in Suso's original Latin in at least three English manuscript Books of Hours—and in a printed quaternion appended, after the table of contents, to a Sarum Book of Hours printed by Wynkyn de Worde in 1503 (RSTC 15899) and given the macaronic title "The matyns of the name of Ihesu" and "hore dulcissimi nominis Iesu."[111] Suso's *Hours/Jesus Matins* begins in this printing without attribution, but when the de Worde text reaches Vespers it suddenly specifies, "Uespere in veneratione nominis Jesu edite a deuoto Ricardo de hampole," before continuing to reproduce Suso's text: another case of the ongoing tendency in insular devotional culture to assume Rolle was the author of Susonian material.[112] In addition to the 1503 print, a 1531 Paris printing of the Sarum Hours also contains the *Cursus* (RSTC 15973).[113] A 1536 Antwerp print of the Sarum *Hours* (RSTC 15992) includes the *Jesus Matins*, this time in English translation (without accompanying Latin in the margins, as it has for the preceding Psalter and Hours of the Virgin), from fol. 141r to fol. 152r, followed by an English translation of Albert the Great's treatise *The Paradise of the Soul*.[114]

Between 1575 and 1578, Suso's name was finally undeniably known among English readers. An unlocalizable translation (presumably the product of a secret press) of the Hours dated to these years (and different from that found in the Antwerp print) was published with the title: "Certayne sweete Prayers of the glorious name of Iesus, commonly called, *Iesus Mattens*, with the howers therto belonging: written in Latin aboue two hundred yeres agoe, by H. Susonne" (RSTC 23443.5). This is likely drawn from a Venetian print of the Latin text, judging from the Italianate *Susonne*, and may well have been produced for recusants, who also continued to read more of Suso than the Hours alone (particularly on the Continent, as far as the evidence reveals).

The interest in medieval mysticism among the Benedictine communities in exile on the Continent reveals an ongoing interest in Suso (and Tauler), now via the Latin translations of the German works produced by the Cologne Carthusian Laurence Surius (1522–78).[115] Gertrude More (1606–33), for instance, mentions Suso as recommended reading material in her *Holy Practices of a Divine Lover, or, The Saintly Idiot's Devotion*, referring to not only a single text but "his life and workes" in her table of texts "as maye much helpe, comfort, and encrease the Devotion of Contemplative spirits."[116] Augustine Baker (1575–1641), confessor to the English Benedictine nuns at Cambrai from 1624 and author of a life of Gertrude More, had an interest in both Suso and Johannes Tauler. In *Holy Wisdom*, a compilation and synthesis of his unpublished writings and translations published after Baker's death by Serenus Cressy (1605–74) in 1657, Baker refers to Suso's recommendation to limit extreme tendencies in ascetic practice; particularly, Suso's reminder that "the dear Jesus did not say, Take my cross upon you; but he said to each, Take up thy cross."[117] Both the worship of Jesus as Wisdom in Suso's enduring liturgy and wider reading of his life and works continued among a variety of English readers well into the seventeenth century.

Previous studies of Suso's readership in England have tended to conclude with either the Reformation (and John Fisher's translation and martyrdom) or perhaps with brief reference to the *Jesus Matins* (dealing with this text's liturgical roots patchily at best). There is no "revolutionary moment" in the reception of Suso in England, however: the story continues into the seventeenth century.[118] Richard Brathwaite (1588–1673), an author prolific in nearly every genre (he produced roughly fifty books), was best known for his macaronic burlesque poem (published anonymously until after his death) *Barnabæ Itinerarium or Barnabees Iournall*, a playful account in Latin and English of a fictional character's drinking adventures across the towns of the north of England that had some popularity into the nineteenth century.[119] His conduct books, *The English Gentleman* and *The English Gentlewoman*, also had some currency in the seventeenth century.[120] In 1617, his apparent interest in medieval literature (he also published a commentary on the "Miller's Tale" and the "Wife of Bath's Tale")[121] led him to append "Chaucer's Ghost Incensed" to his treatise *The Smoking Age*, in which he imagines an angry ghost of Chaucer condemning the early seventeenth century for its interest in poetry praising tobacco.[122]

In 1638, however, he published a lengthy devotional miscellany, *A Spiritual Spicerie: Containing Sundrie sweet Tractates of Devotion and Piety*. This draws together a number of patristic and late medieval religious texts, beginning with a dialogue between Christ and a sinner by the Dutch Carthusian Jacobus van Gruitrode (d. 1475),[123] and encompassing both Brathwaite's own texts and his translations of authors such as the German Carthusian Lanspergius (1489–1539), Augustine, Aquinas, and Bonaventure (all identified marginally in the table of contents).[124] The miscellany ends with a ten-part spiritual pseudo-autobiography by

Brathwaite, the *Holy Memorials*; this begins with an account of his conception (and its sinfulness) and ends with a meditation on his future death
("I enter'd this world with a *Shrique*, and I leave it with a *Sigh*"; *Spiritual Spicerie*, 469). Overall, the wide-ranging sources he employs, on the
eve of civil war, demonstrate a different facet of a religious literature encompassing texts that "are neither Puritan nor Laudian nor Calvinist nor
Arminian, but rather seem to speak from a moment before it became necessary to take sides, a moment when it was still conceivable that the centre might hold."[125] *Spiritual Spicerie* also includes (304–22) a translation
from Suso's *LBEW* (via a Latin translation of the German), providing
the first appearance of the *LBEW* in English translation. As in the *Jesus
Matins*, Suso is here identified as the author as part of the initial title of
the work, the name appearing in its Latinate form (rather than German
or Italianized): "Certain choyce or select sayings of *D. Henricus Suso*"
(*Spiritual Spicerie*, 304).

This subsection of *Spiritual Spicerie* begins with Suso's lament for
those "beautifull soules stamped with Gods image" who turn away from
the "spirituall wedlock" (*Spiritual Spicerie*, 305) God offers for the sake
of transitory, earthly love. Brathwaite then translates a passage on the
Passion, prefacing the monologue with an explanation of the place of the
passage in the work as a whole: "The same *Suso* in a Dialogue bringeth
in the eternall wisdome, that is Christ Jesus, talking with this Minister
of his *Passion*, after this manner" (*Spiritual Spicerie*, 309). Again, the
emphasis on Suso's name is a new development in his English reception, while the following dialogue takes place emphatically with Eternal
Wisdom as the *male* Jesus. The passage Brathwaite chooses to translate
deals primarily with the proper affective response to the Passion: how
emotional aridity in Passion contemplation should be ignored in order to
be overcome. There follows a passage on the Eucharist: how its splendor surpasses that of the sun, the impossibility of being worthy to receive the sacrament, and the miseries occasioned by receiving it while in
mortal sin (*Spiritual Spicerie*, 313–16). The final, and longest, passage
deals with detachment, self-mortification, and the resignation of one's
will to the will of God (*Spiritual Spicerie*, 316–22). Brathwaite's interest
in late medieval spiritual literature is not entirely unique in the 1630s, but
this seventeenth-century nonrecusant English use of Suso does seem to
stand alone, at least in its citing him by name. As late as 1648, however,

a short text about fellow Dominican Rhineland mystic John Tauler was published in English in London (via a Latin intermediary), alongside the *Theologica Germanica*. The continued use of Catholic religious texts by non-Catholic English readers in the seventeenth century has, as will be seen in further detail in chapter 3, an elaborate and complicated history.[126]

With these seventeenth-century witnesses, particularly the translation by a prolific, popular—if widely overlooked—author, Suso's early modern reception in English appears to draw to a close; in 1887, for instance, an English translation of Suso's *LBEW* printed in Boston claims, on its title page, to be the first American edition of Suso's work. There is no evidence of fervid denunciation of his work by Puritans or Anglicans, as we will see in chapter 3 in the case of Catherine of Siena. Nor is there any widespread appropriation of his work by later generations of religious translators, as in the case of the *Imitation of Christ*. In any case, however, the general anonymity with which he was read in English may simply have made his influence past Brathwaite largely invisible. Although Suso was widely read by pious devotees both lay and religious for centuries, it is the sapiential-devotional project of the *Imitatio* that would prove far more enduring in the centuries to follow, even as the nineteenth century's philological predilections would see some renewed interest in Suso as part of a national-linguistic canon (alongside Eckhart and Tauler). Twentieth-century literary and historical scholarship has brought Suso some new readers, but his works still tend to be situated somewhat unsteadily between the stylistic glamor and metaphysical profundities of Meister Eckhart (or, in the English-speaking world, Julian of Norwich) and the Christocentric piety and sapiential tone of Thomas à Kempis (particularly among the popular public for devotional literature).[127] Suso is overshadowed in some regards by these other authors today, but there is considerable potential for a new readership across disciplines. Suso's exuberant devotion to a feminine Eternal Wisdom, his complex deployment of the oscillating gender dynamics of the soul's marriage to Wisdom, and his perceptive and detailed treatment of visionary and aural experience once captured the imaginations of vast numbers of readers and writers across England and Germany, and, indeed, across Europe.

By beginning to recognize some of the literary power and cultural importance of late medieval translations of Suso's works—and their ongoing adaptation into the seventeenth century—in both literary and devotional traditions, we may yet see him as an integral part of a trans-Reformation English canon both literary and religious. While Suso's investment in the femininity of Wisdom is an alluring aspect of his theology for many readers today, among the Continental visionary women read in trans-Reformation England, his fellow fourteenth-century Dominican, Catherine of Siena, plays a particularly prominent role.

CHAPTER 3

Catherine of Siena in Trans-Reformation England

Translations of Female Visionary Authority and Changing Structures of Sanctity

Behold, I see some people wounded, others bound, others languid, others growing faint—and all from love. . . . Love makes one weak; it leads to languor. Love has chains; love inflicts wounds.

—Richard of St. Victor, *The Four Degrees of Violent Love*
(trans. Andrew B. Kraebel)

What would the world look like without saints? For both medieval worshippers and modern readers of any stripe, the ideas generated by this thought experiment might take the imagination down any number of forking pathways. For even the most tepidly devout late medieval layperson, personal names, landmarks, local and international travel networks built around pilgrimage, and even the rhythms of time itself would be quite unrecognizably transformed.[1] In the Americas, setting aside the obvious swarm of religious and art-historical changes, without the saints the very geography of much of the continent would be profoundly altered: most of California, cities from San Antonio and San Juan to Saint Louis and Saint Paul, and entire nations named for Saint Dominic and Saint Lucy would, at the very least, need renaming.[2] Germans would need a new mnemonic device for the end of asparagus season (June 24, the feast of John the Baptist); universities from Scotland's Saint Andrews to a whole host of Loyolas would need substantial rebranding.

But even more importantly, of course, the ideals of sanctity transmitted by widely shared tales of the holy lives of saints both reflect and shape the cultures in which they circulate, including our own. Even today, for those to whom medieval saints might seem little more than a faint reflection of a vastly different era (let alone for the hundreds of millions who *do* venerate them, of course), some of the fundamental structures and concepts surrounding sainthood, both institutionally and thematically, continue to inform contemporary lives. We still travel to the relics, homes, and shrines of famous artists, authors, and musicians (perhaps decorating our own homes with their icons; wealthier devotees buy contact relics at auction), celebrate the feast days of secular saints (often those tied to national origins), and valorize athletic and professional ideals of asceticism and self-sacrifice (with the annual civic festival of the marathon in many cities now taking the place of urban processions of patron saints or Corpus Christi).[3]

For the modern secular reader or teacher, inspiring tales of both heroism and superheroism also remain a powerful component of ethical formation and an ever-growing element of popular culture; a significant portion of contemporary media is involved in the ongoing promotion of cults of both heroic historical figures (national founders, military martyrs) and legendary ones (most notably in recent decades perhaps the superheroes of comic book and film).[4] Simon Yarrow, for instance, begins his introduction to saints by drawing the sharpest possible line between the medieval saint and the modern superhero: "Let's begin with Kal-El, better known as Superman. Everyone knows his story."[5] Just as for medieval cults of saints or for contemporary veneration of Moses (paralleled in the story of Superman), it is the common, participatory nature of the narrative enshrined in myth that is an integral part of its potency: there is no such thing as a private saint, to paraphrase Wittgenstein. Other writers, indeed, have examined the philosophical and theological valences of contemporary cults of superheroism and their intersection with the intricacies of received Christian notions of sanctity.[6] Through the sense of a communal, popular mythology infusing these works, we might better understand the ongoing significance of the cult of saints and the rich network of ways in which saints created shared meaning for medieval audiences.[7] For post-Reformation religion, too, the attempt to build a religious system on scripture alone nevertheless quite quickly incorporated extrabiblical saintly figures; the new religion called upon recent martyrs who acquired sanctity through their persecution, creating images and narratives often akin to those of medieval sainthood. In England, of course, Foxe's *Acts and Monuments* provided the most popular and enduring source of neohagiography to fulfill these devotional needs.[8]

Catherine of Siena (1347–80, canonized in 1461) was one of the most important of fourteenth-century saints, but a contemporary Britain or North America without her would, admittedly, be much less altered than one without Thomas à Becket, Catherine of Alexandria, or Thomas More; insular textual and material culture alike testify to wider-established cults of many saints, English and otherwise, from previous centuries.[9] Noncanonized devotional authors, such as Henry Suso, also found a wider audience in the later Middle Ages than Catherine (but his postmedieval cult was largely localized around Lake Constance). Yet her most important text, typically called the *Dialogue* today, a work of visionary theology bridging mystical and devotional discourses, was read in English within decades of her death, alongside a number of biographical works and extracts of her spiritual teaching. Despite the popularity of other forms of devotional theology, works by and about saints have always managed to claim a special cachet. Medieval English interest in the particularities of Saint Catherine's devotional life, indeed, demonstrated an interest in her as both author and saint that vastly exceeded Suso's more depersonalized insular popularity. Readers encountering Catherine during much of the fifteenth century could have found a wealth of information about both her life story and her teaching, interpreted through the Middle English translation of her *Dialogue* (which she referred to in correspondence simply as her *Book*), the *Orchard of Syon*, and through translated texts written by male hagiographers (some of which aim to preserve her words by quoting from her letters or claiming to recall conversations with her). Her identities as woman writer and as a woman written about were closely connected: her range of individual identities (as female visionary, charismatic ascetic, holy woman, and eventually saint) was always a significant component of her reception, in England and elsewhere. As with Suso and Rolle, separating her from the texts surrounding her is impossible; her life and her *Life* have been intertwining ever since her death. But in examining the holy persona created in and through Catherine's texts, we are given the opportunity to see her from at least two distinct perspectives: in her own authorial self-fashioning as a soul in conversation with God and in the work of several other authors in constructing her life story as a saintly text to be emulated (in the first eighty years after her death, often also aimed toward the goal of promoting her canonization).

The vernacular texts by and surrounding her in England, Jennifer Brown has shown, "form a node of dense connection among other devotional texts" while also residing "between oral and the written, Latin and the vernacular, the public and the private in a way not frequently seen in one discrete set of English texts."[10] Catherine of Siena had an especially long and complicated reception in English, beginning not long after her death and extending well into the seventeenth century. Institutionally, Edinburgh in 1517 saw a Dominican convent dedicated to her (named Sciennes, after her hometown), but it was, of course, soon dissolved.[11] She was often linked with Bridget of Sweden (ca. 1303–73, canonized 1391), and indeed the Bridgettine house of Syon Abbey, founded in 1415, was the most prominent site of English translation and promotion of Catherine's work. Someone close to this community, perhaps from the neighboring Carthusian monastery of Sheen, translated her *Dialogue* in full from a Latin intermediary into Middle English; passages from her *Life* were also excerpted in vernacular texts with Syon connections.[12] Several other manuscripts contain pieces of material from hagiographical texts by male clerics testifying to her sanctity or explaining her theory of discernment. Due in part to the influence of her English confessor, the Augustinian hermit William Flete, her reputation in England was closely linked to her teaching on the discretion of spirits and resisting spiritual temptation.[13] In the *Miracoli*, a short collection of Catherine's miracles written by an anonymous follower during her lifetime (around 1375), she is already connected to Flete, who is in turn identified as English, even in this quite early textual witness to her growing holy reputation.[14] As late as the 1609 translation of the *Life*, Flete is mentioned as her English confessor: "a certaine holie Heremite of S. *Augustines* order, called brother *William*, an English man."[15]

This proliferation of texts in late medieval England offers a range of evidence for insular interest in the Sienese saint—far more interest, in many ways, than was the case for Suso, as we examined in chapter 2.[16] One might expect Catherine's name to be found in fifteenth-century England almost as infrequently as Suso's, the Swabian Dominican—most particularly before her canonization—but insular texts quite regularly identify her: not only by name, but also by place of origin, status as virgin, and association with the Dominican Order. For a female author such as Mechthild of Magdeburg among the Dominicans of fourteenth-century Germany (or Marguerite Porete in medieval England),[17] a wider readership and greater theological authority often seemed to require anonymity and a pronounced distancing of text from author (stemming from, in Sara Poor's words, both "the ideological problem of female authorship" and "the lively participation of [Mechthild's] writings in a religious textual practice that valued the conversation with God more than authors' names"),[18] but Catherine was well known and widely accepted by name as a spiritual authority in England, Germany, and France within just a few decades of her death. The only female author of equivalent spiritual authority is Bridget of Sweden, who had the considerable advantages of both a speedy canonization and a wealthy aristocratic family.[19] After Catherine's canonization in 1461, of course, this prestige would not be especially unusual, but insular awareness of—and reverence for—her name and life significantly precedes this official recognition of her sainthood. Her treatment in pre-Reformation print similarly addresses the wide array of her spiritual identities: as the named author of a revelatory book, the subject of lengthy (and at times controversial) hagiography, and the source of excerpted passages of devotional wisdom.

Her corpus clearly maintained its significance in the sixteenth and seventeenth centuries: a new translation of her *Life* was produced by exiled English Catholics in Douai in 1609, and her works were vehemently denounced by Protestant clerics throughout the seventeenth century (partly in reaction to her ongoing use among recusant English communities on the Continent, especially female religious).[20] She offers us a particularly vivid illustration of the ways in which the lives and texts of medieval holy women from Continental Europe profoundly shaped insular spiritual literature and devotional culture, and she shows the ways in which translation itself can be a theological and creative and literary enterprise. Texts by Bridget of Sweden, Elizabeth of Hungary/Töss, Mechthild of Hackeborn, Marie of Oisterwijk (or Maria van Hout, fl. 1530–47), and Marguerite Porete were all translated into English (Hildegard von Bingen and Elizabeth of Schönau also survive in several insular Latin manuscripts)—and Elizabeth of Schönau's *Book of the Ways of God* was even published in dual-column Latin and English around 1557[21]—but Catherine of Siena's reception was markedly different, both before and after the Reformation.[22]

CATHERINE OF SIENA: VIRGIN NONMARTYR, PROPHET, AND LAY ACTIVIST

Very little about Catherine *was* typical, however. From a prosperous but decidedly mercantile family, Catherine of Siena (born Benincasa, the twenty-fourth of twenty-five children and daughter of a dyer) was a lay-woman associated with an unofficial group of devout women penitents, mainly widows, who admired and emulated aspects of Dominican piety informally. They were known at the time as *mantellate* for their distinctive habit. She was *not*, as is very commonly claimed, a Dominican tertiary (but one could perhaps see the *mantellate* as a kind of proto–Third Order): a rule for what are now called Dominican tertiaries would not be promulgated until 1405, well after her death.[23] After a vow of virginity, following a vision of Christ at age six or seven, she lived a semianchoritic life in her father's house for several years. In 1374 she began an "itinerant apostolate" in which she wrote hundreds of letters, cared for the sick, gave spiritual counsel, and traveled to Florence, Avignon, and Rome in her attempt to promote peace and reform, seek martyrdom, and return the papacy to Rome.[24] She traveled surrounded by a cadre of both clerics and laypeople (many of whom also served as her scribes), who called her their mother and to whom she referred as her "family"; beyond her vow of virginity and her lack of a fixed religious community, her desire to place herself at the head of a more flexibly defined surrogate family may have been especially crucial to her emotional well-being, in part given her status as "twinless twin" (her twin sister, Giovanna, having died at age two).[25]

Born shortly before the first appearance of the horrors of the Black Death in Tuscany, she died on April 29, 1380, in Rome, after long periods of self-inflicted starvation. She yearned for a bloody martyrdom (and nearly achieved it while intervening in political disputes in Florence), but her death instead followed long periods of consuming only the Eucharist; her practice of inducing vomiting immediately after meager meals as a form of asceticism was also widely reported. Both her life and works have left us one of the most complex and challenging legacies of any late medieval saint; like Suso in Germany or Rolle in England, she is a figure "remarkable both from the perspective of the history of Italian literature and from that of theology."[26] Despite Catherine's short and uncloistered life, her revelatory vernacular *Dialogue* and her wide-ranging correspondence—more than three hundred of her letters survive—established her as both a prominent theological voice and an important force in key political struggles of her day.

Her cult grew quickly after her death, fostered by both Dominicans and Carthusians (among others)—inspired in part by her own letters and revelatory writings, in part by a variety of hagiographical texts—and she remains a significant ecclesiastical figure to this day. Catherine's status has steadily grown over the centuries as a Sienese and Italian saint, as a patroness of Europe, and as a global doctor of the Church.[27] Among a wide range of scholarly, devotional, and popular texts written about her in the twentieth century, the Nobel Prize–winning Norwegian novelist Sigrid Undset (most famous for her vast trilogy of historical novels, *Kristin Lavransdatter*), wrote a posthumously published biography of Catherine in the 1940s.[28] Catherine's role in contemporary English-language spirituality extends beyond spiritual literature about her and numerous churches dedicated to her; among many other widespread instances of her contemporary cult, particularly among Dominicans, a popular one-woman show by Sister Nancy Murray, O.P., has introduced Catherine of Siena to audiences in recent years as "A Woman for Our Times."[29]

Catherine's work engages with key issues in late medieval religious and literary discourse: in different registers than we've seen in chapters 1 and 2, her works (and their later reception) interrogate the role of visionary authority and the resonances of authorial collaboration, while also complicating the interface between communal interpretation and individual authorship. Paralleling the processes already seen in the works of Suso and Rolle, her texts also offer complicated models for exemplarity, drawing the reader into a dialectical relationship between the imitation of the character in the text and the imitation of that character's own relationship with Christ.[30] The knowledge of one's self and one's relationship to God (and the role of this knowledge in the process of discernment) is at the core of her theological system—a spirituality that "has been defined as the doctrine of twofold knowledge: knowledge of God—the absolute Being, the first sweet Truth and infinite Love—together with knowledge of oneself, one's nothingness and one's sin and disordered self-love."[31]

Attention to Catherine's female and saintly body was intimately connected with the regard paid to her textual corpus and her developing reputation for healing, piety, and advocacy for reform. From detailed accounts of her self-inflicted food deprivation (and other forms of extreme asceticism) to Jesus's dual gifts to her of invisible stigmata and fleshy wedding ring, the language of the body permeates the constellation of texts by and about her. In particular, metaphorical uses of blood saturate her work. McGinn summarizes: "Blood is life, blood is food and drink, blood is bath, blood is bond and mortar, blood is ransom, blood is key, blood is door, blood is clothing, blood is reproach, blood is witness, blood is even grace, and more."[32] This combination of blood and body in both her theology and her metaphorical world yields a surprisingly rich range of personal transformations in the self she creates in that work. The malleability of blood as both symbol and fluid substance also contributes to the rich representations of the flexibility of her body's own gender. Her early confessor and hagiographer Raymond of Capua (ca. 1330–99), for instance, recounts her vigorous use of Galatians 3:28 ("there is no longer male and female") to argue for the insignificance of her gender when considering her mission; she is described as cutting her hair short and yearning to wear the habit of male Dominicans from her childhood.[33]

CATHERINE AS AUTHORITY AND WRITER
OF HOLY SELF-KNOWLEDGE

Exploring Catherine today, as both female author and subject of multiple male authors, is further complicated by discussions (both medieval and contemporary) surrounding Catherine's own relationship to written words and the pages on which they appeared. How she was perceived as a producer of texts shaped how her works and her life were understood, both in Italy and abroad, then and now. Nancy Bradley Warren astutely writes of Catherine (alongside Bridget of Sweden and Julian of Norwich) that "bodies produce texts, and texts are themselves in some respects living bodies."[34] Nearly every aspect of her body's ascetic and literate practice was debated quite intensely in the years following her death (as was the other main dispute surrounding her legacy: her invisible stigmata and how to depict them posthumously). Questions and legends surrounding the possibility of her literacy—and the degrees of her vernacular and Latin literacy—are legion. It is clear, on the one hand, that in many instances texts ascribed to her, especially letters, were dictated (often to female scribes); she herself often refers to the linguistic portion of her mission as a predominantly oral one.[35]

But she also claims in one letter, sent sometime in October 1377, to have been given the ability to write miraculously. The gift of literacy, with John the Evangelist and Thomas Aquinas, the Angelic Doctor, as tutors, is described as itself both visionary experience and rapturous event; the new act of writing is seen as aligning parts of her body (those involved with both oral and written language) with her heart, source of the overflowing emotions she desires to transmit.[36] Troublingly, however, the recipient of the letter, her confessor and later hagiographer Raymond of Capua, never seems to have mentioned this vivid miracle in his lengthy account of her life, nor her ability to write more generally: "Through her prayers did she learn miraculously how to read," and reports that she could not speak Latin with fluency, but could read and pronounce the Latin of the Psalter.[37] Raymond's *Legenda Maior* itself, however, has quite significant variants in the manuscript record—in brief, a stricter Carthusian tradition and a more interventionist Dominican tradition that is unafraid to tamper with Raymond's text to further the cause of Catherine's potential canonization.[38] The Carthusian chain of transmission of the *Legenda* entirely omitted her writing ability, but Dominican Tommasso Caffarini (or Tomasso of Siena, ca. 1350–1434), eager to spread Catherine's saintly fame (and quite willing to alter Raymond for this cause), added writing to her collection of miraculously granted talents in both the Dominican recension of the *Legenda Maior* and his own *Legenda Minor*.[39]

No writing definitively in Catherine's hand survives today (but her head does survive, and is displayed prominently in the Dominican church in Siena), but Tommaso Caffarini's description (or fabrication) of her literate activities was much more vividly rendered than simply an account of her Psalmic literacy or her moments of letter-writing. In his *Libellus de supplemento* he describes a scene in which Catherine takes a jar of red ink and a quill, despite her lack of substantial training in writing at this stage in her life (yet he does mention that she had received only "minimal" training at this point, whatever we might imagine that entails), and writes a prayer to the Trinity on a sheet of parchment. He then engages in a form of hagiographic paleography, reporting that "the style and the form of the text above were such that they produced a clear sign of a miracle. Similar results are normally produced only after long practice in spelling, calligraphy, and writing."[40] From this close attention to the text her hand has produced, he moves to a similarly careful attention to the path the miraculous sheet of parchment itself took, tracing the lineage of the prayer after Catherine's death from one holy man to another until it reached Tommaso in Venice (the site of the most substantial early cult of Catherine); he also notes that some letters in her own hand were preserved—and were being venerated—in a Carthusian monastery near Siena. This interest in her literate practices did not appear to influence her canonization, however: as Catherine Mooney and others have noted, Pius II did not mention her textual production in the bull announcing her canonization.[41]

Catherine herself also employs numerous metaphors involving writing, the power and vividness of which at times threaten to overwhelm critical attention to what her connection to literacy as a historical figure may have been.[42] Jane Tylus has examined a range of manuscript illuminations displaying the marks of the stigmata (or lack thereof) on representations of Catherine's body, and argues that in the context of late medieval Dominican female spirituality, "writing and the bearing of the stigmata . . . are equivalent and active processes" in depictions of holy women.[43] Significantly, text and body are worshipped together in contemporary Siena: the original manuscript of the *Processo Castellano* "is kept as a venerated object in the chapel dedicated to St Catherine. There, in a reliquary, it rests in a steel box directly underneath the holy woman's head."[44] This continued interest in marks and signs, in linking her texts and her body, also joins in giving Catherine a prominent place in the annals of typography: the first use of an italic typeface in history is found in the frontispiece of an edition of her letters printed in Venice by Aldus Manutius in 1500, appearing on a book she holds in one hand (reading *iesu dolce iesu amore*) and on a heart she holds in her other hand (bearing the word *iesus*).[45] The link between textual and bodily devotion to Christ—and between the codex and the heart—is indivisible in both her work and its reception.

FEMALE VISIONARIES IN MEDIEVAL ENGLAND: CATHERINE AND HER CONTEXT

Works by and about Continental female visionaries were translated and read widely in late medieval England, from texts written by Bridget of Sweden and Elizabeth of Hungary to the lives of charismatic holy women such as Elizabeth of Spalbeek and Christina the Astonishing.[46] Catherine benefited, in England, from promotion by members of a variety of religious orders: the Carthusians (especially Stephen Maconi), the Dominicans, and Augustinian connections via her English confessor, William Flete. The *Speculum devotorum*, which we discussed in chapter 2, demonstrates that some English Carthusian authors had a clear sense of a canon of recent female authors from the Continent; Catherine was counted among them (authors, indeed, whose visionary authority was substantial enough to allow them to contribute extrabiblical material to Episcopally approved accounts of the Passion).[47] Catherine was also read in pious lay circles at the very height of English aristocracy: she is mentioned, for instance (alongside Bridget of Sweden and Mechthild of Hackeborn), as prelection material at the dinner table of Cecily, Duchess of York (1415–95, mother of Edward IV and Richard III), after she was widowed in 1460.[48] Lady Margaret Beaufort (1443–1509, mother of Henry VII), translator of one book of the *Imitation of Christ* and the *Mirror of Gold for the Sinful Soul*, willed a copy of the *Life* of Catherine to her granddaughter.[49] The fall from grace was swift, however: female visionaries would become the most harshly criticized of medieval texts in late sixteenth- and seventeenth-century anti-Catholic polemic, serving as examples of exactly what the new religion most robustly repudiated in

Christianity's medieval past (even as female visionaries and their texts continued to attract considerable interest among recusant communities); Catherine's fervent activism in support of the primacy of Rome also made her a prime target.[50]

Just as Caxton saw Suso's *Seven Points* as an integral component of his *Book of Diverse Ghostly Matters* in the early 1490s, so too did his successors in the pre-Reformation printing industry envision a profitable commercial audience for printed works by and about Continental holy women, including Catherine.[51] Bolstered by her 1461 canonization (and perhaps encouraged by the rapid printing of her work and her *Life* in Italy), Wynkyn de Worde printed Raymond of Capua's *Life* of Catherine in English translation around 1493; the volume also contained a translation of the putative *Revelations* of Elizabeth of Hungary (in actuality, the text is by Elizabeth of Töss, Switzerland, a Dominican written about in the Töss Sisterbook composed by Henry Suso's spiritual daughter, Elsbeth Stagel).[52] The *Orchard of Syon* was printed in 1519 also, with a colophon mentioning that a Syon brother found it lying neglected in a corner of the monastery library.[53] The exclamatory prayers known as the *Fifteen Oes*, attributed to Bridget of Sweden, were printed several times between 1491 and 1540, and both the Middle English translation of and commentary on her Rule, *The Mirror of Our Lady*, and an extract of her revelations (*The Four Revelations of Saint Bridget*) were printed in the early sixteenth century.[54] In 1521, Henry Pepwell published a wide-ranging devotional miscellany of seven treatises (sometimes called the *Cell of Self-Knowledge*, RSTC 20972, and perhaps best known for containing a brief, pious extract of Margery Kempe), including "Diverse Doctrines, Devout and Fruitful, Taken out of the Life of that Glorious Virgin and Spouse of our Lord, Saint Catherine of Siena."[55]

Compilations of this sort were not uncommon before Pepwell's time either. A concise summary of Catherinian thought is found in London, British Library MS Harley 2409, which Jennifer Brown has recently demonstrated is a diverse collection of texts about Catherine by William Flete and Raymond of Capua.[56] Vernacular extracts of Latin Catherinian texts of this kind were fairly widespread: one, based on a passage in William Flete's *Documento spirituale* and known as *Cleanness of Soul*, is found in three versions in a total of nine manuscript assemblages (in three manuscripts—Oxford, Bodleian Library MS Bodley 131; British

Library MS Royal 18.A.x; and Harley 2409—*Cleanness of Soul* appears alongside Middle English translations of Flete's *Remedy against Temptations*).[57]

The Middle English text in Harley 2409, which Dirk Schultze's recent edition has christened "Spiritual Teachings by Catherine of Siena," presents four separate passages, condensing aspects of Catherine's teachings, as interpreted by William Flete and Raymond of Capua: "Cleanness of Soul" (version C, following Joliffe), "The Discernment of Spirits," "Self-Knowledge," and "Mystical Marriage."[58] The text begins by citing Catherine by name and emphasizing the date of the revelation: the rubricated incipit tells the reader: "Here folowes how þe holy mayden Kateryne of Seen first began to sette hyr hert fully to godwarde. In þe yere of oure lorde Criste a thousand thre hundreth foure score and sex, þe .viij. day of Januer, þe holy mayden Kateryne of Seen" (the text then goes on to explain the role of self-knowledge and inner illumination in her spiritual development).[59] In this temporal, geographic, and onomastic specificity, we can see the need for readers of Harley 2409 to be assured of the trustworthiness and inherent historicity of Catherine's revelations.

Other readers and translators tended to seek far more information about and texts by Catherine, but this brief compilation demonstrates some of the central spiritual concerns on which she was considered particularly authoritative (as, indeed, the *Speculum devotorum* and the other variants of the "Cleanness of Soul" text also bear witness). And although her role in the extensive late medieval literature of dying well was not nearly as pronounced as Suso's, it bears mentioning that Richard Whitford's 1537 *Daily Exercise and Experience of Death* (RSTC 25415), appended to an edition of his *A Work for Householders*, makes brief reference to Catherine: the treatise focuses momentarily on Catherine's body and its imperviousness to physical distraction during prayer, even when skeptical women prick her feet with needles.[60]

Out of this intricate matrix of readers and interpreters, across the fifteenth and early sixteenth centuries, we find translation and transmission again playing a crucial—if often undervalued—role in the late medieval reception of Catherine. In a network of English textual transformations even more complex than that of the Middle English Suso, Catherine of Siena demonstrates the powerful variety of theological and literary forces at work in the translation and compilation of works by and about a major

Continental visionary figure. This process, as seen in chapter 2 in the case of Suso, is decidedly not one simply of impoverishment and degradation. Jennifer Brown writes, for instance, that "Catherine was transformed, shaped, and reshaped by her interpreters in order to satisfy the various audiences of her texts in late medieval England. In the process she became a symbol of female mystical devotion, a mother figure, the image of a literate and learned religious woman, and ultimately a symbol of Catholic resistance to the Reformation."[61] Scholarship has often focused on a variety of putatively negative changes this process inflicts on its source-texts, but I argue that the extant textual evidence shows instead a vibrant and widespread culture of Catherinian translation, offering a robust array of encounters the careful reader of late medieval English spiritual literature might have had with Catherine and her program of contemplative self-knowledge.

THE *ORCHARD OF SYON*: VISIONARY LITERATURE AND THE ALLEGORICAL IMAGINATION IN MIDDLE ENGLISH LITERATURE

One of the most intricate literary and theological products of fifteenth century England—and perhaps the most remarkable female-authored Middle English text of the period between Kempe and Beaufort—the *Orchard of Syon* is often overlooked or undervalued in general studies of medieval English female authorship.[62] Margery Kempe and Julian of Norwich certainly deserve the considerable critical attention they have earned in recent decades (and earned their prominent position in most current anthologies of medieval literature), but the *Orchard*, too, is essential to our understanding of the English reception of female visionary authorship and the vernacular development of the central motifs of European mystical discourse.[63] There is much more to any medieval text than simply its contemporary canonicity, but the *Orchard* does richly deserve a much more prominent position in medieval literary studies. Perhaps the most noteworthy aspect of the *Orchard* (in evaluating its greater relevance to literary history, conventionally understood) resides in its ornate, robust creation of an extraordinarily complex imaginative text deeply invested in its own status as the product of conversations between the soul and God; the text's own journeying from Italian to Latin to English warrants much fuller consideration (just as the full process of translation from German to Latin to English in Suso is rarely examined).

Some of the text's supple virtues might perhaps be rather subtle to the modern-day reader; its mode of argumentation is quite allusive and layered; its visionary universe is richly populated with a complicated network of unfurling allegorical narratives and divinely revealed characters. From a purely pedagogical standpoint, inclusion in an anthology would pose considerable challenges in attempting to summarize or excerpt it (in all of this, indeed, I find it rather akin to *Piers Plowman*). The *Orchard* presents itself as a collection of chapters that can be sampled freely, as casually as strolling in different alleys of a garden, but the argument of the text is far more intricate than this might imply. It is laced with moments of narrative layering and allegorical interactions, connecting passages across hundreds of pages with tags such as "bycause I haue schewid þe in party þis in anoþir place, þerfore a lytil moore schal I telle þee þerof now."[64] Other medieval visionary works (from the *Divine Comedy* to *The Romance of the Rose*) have long been studied intensively, and admired, for their effective creation of elaborate imaginative universes and their blending of poetry with theology; even Christine de Pisan's relatively unwieldy prose *Book of the City of Ladies* and its English translation have achieved greater canonicity in contemporary literary studies than Catherine of Siena's *Dialogue* and its extraordinary Middle English rendering.[65]

Critics acknowledge its significance as a substantial work of original, complex female-authored mystical writing, but they have too often seen its translation into Middle English (as we have seen with Suso) through the unfortunate, reductive perspectives of either, on the one hand, insular dullness and the steady dilution of Continental thought, or, on the other, as a straightforwardly post-Arundelian project in the taming of female mysticism and the reinforcing of visionary orthodoxy. Pushing the text outside the somewhat narrow horizons of fifteenth-century English devotional and Lollard studies, however, can help us resist the temptation to see the *Orchard of Syon* as only a partially successful experiment in the late medieval translation of Continental mystical literature. The text has often been read as partially defused of its visionary authority as a result of its potential to threaten "priestly prerogatives," and its attempt to introduce a spirituality of visionary asceticism too foreign for English imitation (the vein of criticism still acknowledges the significance of the text's role in the transmission of the "visible success in joining the active with the contemplative paths" that distinguished both Catherine and Suso).[66] I would not discount these claims entirely; rather, I find that interpreting both the *Dialogue* and the *Orchard* together as jointly ambitious projects in imaginative theological literature leads to a new understanding of the text's significant literary qualities, akin to the inherent narrativity characteristic of Hamm's formulation of devotional theology, and thus its appropriately prominent place in both English and European literature.[67]

Something of the spirit of this approach can be found in Dirk Schultze's recent study of the "Cleanness of Soul" Middle English Catherinian texts. Schultze writes in his study of Catherine in England that "it may occasionally be helpful to place overt Christian references in the background, where they form a solid foundation for all else, and look at what is placed in the foreground by the respective author." The theological framework of Catherine's work has been richly studied in the past, but taking this approach shows us that "in Catherine's case, soul-searching and self-knowledge, the possibility to exercise control over one's drives and stimuli is an important theme, and one that attracted English readers." This methodology leads him to explore, to great effect, the psychologico-literary dimensions of the short Middle English Catherinian texts in Harley 2409.[68]

This perspective, in turn, can be usefully employed in connecting the appeal of Catherine's *Dialogue* and the Middle English *Orchard* to what Stephen Kelly and Ryan Perry have called the "devotional cosmopolitanism" that typifies fifteenth-century English devotional reading, namely, "a radical openness to the suggestions of antithetical theologies which produces among readers a form of 'hospitable reading' in which difference is tolerated, re-thought, adapted and appropriated in the interests of reimagining Christian community in England."[69] In both the widespread reception of Suso already seen and the detailed translation history of Catherine and works about her, this model of a cosmopolitan, hospitable reading of international texts is especially apt; indeed, parts of late medieval England may show far greater devotional cosmopolitanism than a significant range of Continental nodes of intellectual production. Even though both Suso and Catherine were not particularly controversial in the fifteenth century, they are also *not* the most straightforward or unproblematic authors available to a translator or copyist. Particularly given the wide range of devotional and biblical material available to a fifteenth-century Bridgettine, what exactly did the *Orchard* in Middle English contribute to their library (and libraries beyond Syon)?[70] Why not read—or copy, or print—Bridget herself? Or the more typical devotional fare of the Pseudo-Bonaventurean *Meditations on the Life of Christ*, the *Golden Legend*, the *Prick of Conscience*, or a Middle English sermon cycle, for instance?

LANGUAGE AND SOUND

The person you read about in The Lives of the Fathers . . . *was just beginning to write the letter "O," no great thing, when his superior gave him a command. He did not so much as give himself time to finish that letter, but ran at once to obey. So to show how pleased I was I gave you a sign: My mercy completed the other half in gold.*

—*Dialogue*, chap. 165

The text's recurrent considerations of language itself, to begin with, might draw a careful contemplative reader's attention to the possibilities of the words encountered on the devotional page: their potential danger, their relationship to heavenly joy, their effective use in prayer, and even their ultimate limitations in theological discourse. God mentions, for instance, that "finite works" (those not truly grounded in love) are as temporally insubstantial and ineffective as "a word that comes out of the mouth and then ceases to exist."[71] The relative permanence of the very written text in which God declares this, then, is implicitly linked with the fruitfulness of works properly grounded in God's love—and with the writtenness of God's words in Catherine's book. The potential emptiness of vain words in comparison to the primacy of appropriate works is also addressed; God tells the Soul: "I seyde to þee þat I louede fewe wordis and manye werkis. Whanne a man seiþ manye wordis oonly, I noumbre hem not. . . . And ȝit I dispise not wordis vttirly."[72] An excess of good words, particularly if out of proportion with corresponding good works, is ultimately worthless (despite the caveat that language is not *entirely* to be rejected or despised). Vocal prayer used to battle temptations of the fiend, too, can be efficacious if said with proper intent and charity, or can be "unsavory" if the tongue of the one praying is "looth and dulle to seye."[73] Similarly, in a description of the spiritual drunkenness granted by the Eucharist,

God dismisses the weight superficially put on the performance of specific numbers of orally performed prayers.

Catherine also criticizes the "vnkunnynge proude clerkis" who misconstrue scripture: they "vndirstonde raþir holy writt aftir þe lettir, or aftir her owne feelyng, þan aftir þe verry vndirstondyng. And so by taastynge oonli of þe lettir þei maken manye bookis, but þei taasten not þe pith and þe mary [marrow] of þe same lettre, for þei lacken þe liȝt þat I spak of."[74] A literal understanding of scripture—associated with the subjective or the superficial—without a true understanding of the nourishing, allegorical "pith and marrow" within it then leads clerics to the self-promoting (but fruitless) overproduction of lackluster books, as devoid of nourishment as long-dead bones, dried and marrowless. Given Catherine's own relationship with the production of texts (prayers, letters, and the *Dialogue* itself), and the degree to which she was scrutinized as both writer and prophet, God's suspicion of empty words here gestures toward his implicit approval of the marrow of Catherine's own words.

Warning against the powerful damage wrought by "mischievous speaking," however, God tells Catherine's soul that "bycause of wordis, ȝe han seen and herd manye chaungynges of staatis, desolaciouns of cytees, and myche manslauȝtir, and manye oþire yuelis, for a wrecchid word entreþ into þe myddis of þe herte of hym þat it is seid to, where a swerd schulde not entre."[75] Language is seen as a powerful, violent weapon, on both a personal and explicitly political level: words destroy polities, and a single word pierces deep into hearts, shaping the emotional life of the individual in a way that swords cannot. Raymond of Capua's hagiography, too, describes the violent material power of Catherine's own spoken words—a listener "was caried awaie, with the efficacie & strength of her wordes; which pearsed his hart, like sharpe dartes."[76]

Misused language has the power to lead to the destruction of cities, and especially efficacious words can suddenly pierce the very heart of the hearer, but the *excess* of language, which can take the shape of an overflowing in wordless song, is also depicted as a hallmark of the aural landscape of heaven. A prominent interest of Suso and Rolle, as well, the depiction of extralinguistic heavenly joy, imagined as music, brings the text itself into conversation with the reader's hope for future reward. The joy of souls in heaven, for instance, "is clepid *iubilus*, þat is to seye, a sown of a glad song, which may not be toold by word ne schewid by sown of voice."[77] This ineffable, celestial sound—nonvocal, and

somehow both song and not-song—is a commonplace of many late medieval affective accounts of the aurality of heavenly bliss. More unusually, however, the spiritual musicality of the *Dialogue* and *Orchard* is
developed in considerable detail over the course of a chapter that links
the fishing nets (and hooks) of the apostles to the harmonious, enchant-
ing sound emitting from a well-ordered soul in proper tuning with the
body—a music considered to be instrumental, rather than vocal (elsewhere, God likens the harrowing of hell to an elaborate, deceptive fishing
expedition in which he tricked the devil using "þe mete of ȝoure man-
hood and þe hook of my godheed").[78]

The passage continues, God explaining to the Soul that when the
proper gates of the "city of the soul" are opened and other gates closed
(perhaps imagining the pipes of an organ), then "þe affeccioun of þe
soule makeþ a ioye & a sown, temperynge þe stringes & coordis of
þe herte wiþ prudence & liȝt, makynge hem to acoorde in oon, þat is, to
þe ioye & preisyng of my name (affectus quidem anime tunc facit unum
iubilum ac sonum temperatis etiam cordibus cordis cum prudentia et lu-
mine, omnis ad unum sonum eas concordans, id est, ad gloriam et laudem mei nominis)" (MS 87, fol. 249v).[79] This aural environment itself,
in which "the great chords of the soul's powers are harmonized (þe grete
stringes & myȝtis of þe soule ben accordid)" and "the small chords of
the body's senses and organs are blended (þe smale stringis & coordis
of þe bodily wittis ben also accoordid)," was, God reveals, first created
by Jesus on the cross. This instrument and its sweet sound (never given
any content or greater specificity in this passage) is then imitated by martyrs, confessors, doctors, and virgins as a mysterious, powerful tool in
their evangelization.[80] The description of this elaborate transformation of
properly tuned bodies into instrumental sound is embedded, however, in
a detailed allegory concerning the apostles' fishing nets and hooks used
to catch souls (she does not, however, consider the stringed material of
fishing line and net as potentially pluckable); the sweet sound itself, then,
is somehow also used to captivate others in fishing for souls. Cologne's
Saint Ursula is singled out and lauded as a particularly powerful practitioner: she "sownede so swete her instrument þat sche cauȝte first wiþalle
xi þousinde virgyns."[81]

Both the language of prayer and the language of scripture are intimately connected with nutritive value for Catherine. In describing the
third step of the bridge, for instance, Jesus links his mouth to Catherine's

own spiritual mission; the mouth serves as site of both language and ingestion. Just as the mouth uses its tongue to speak and its teeth to chew food,

> riȝt so a soule spekeþ wiþ þe tonge of holy contynuel preyer. Sich a
> tonge ȝeldeth to me boþe actualy and mentaly: [mentaly,] for heelþe
> of soulis, riȝt swete, goostle desirys and myrye; actualy it spekeþ
> in schewynge, admoneschinge, counceilynge, and knowlechinge þe
> doctryne of my verry truþe wiþoute ony fere of peyne, what peyne
> þat euere þe world ȝeueþ, but booldly and hardily afore euery crea-
> ture sche knowlecheþ þe truþe afore alle creaturis, and to euery crea-
> ture aftir his estaat, in dyuerse wises.[82]

Prayer serves two purposes, actual and mental, and the language of
prayer and spiritual digestion—the orifice as conduit for both language
and food—are fused in her account of the sacred mouth to be emulated.
Just as the mouth, tongue, and teeth work together to prepare food for digestion, so too the spiritual mouth "eteþ þe mete of þe heelþe of soulis,
takinge þat same mete upon þe riȝt blessid table of þe cros."[83] This food
for souls, and of souls, is eaten from the table of the cross; the "mouth
of holy desire" then uses its two rows of teeth, hate and love, to chew
(one row is "haate of hersilf," the other "loue of vertu").[84] The food then
comes to the stomach, and the soul is itself fattened by the nourishing
virtues of this meal, providing a spiritual contrast to the extreme deprivation of material food she is often represented as inflicting on herself. This
is joined to a Trinitarian depiction, unique to Catherine, of a holy meal
in which the Father is a table, the Son the food, and the Holy Spirit the
waiter or servant: "I am a mete table, and my sone is to hem mete, and þe
holy gost is to hem a seruitour, þe which cometh boþe fro me, þe fadir,
& also my sone."[85] The words on the page and the Word of the Incarnation are allegorized as healing, life-giving food in an elaborate narrative
returned to several times over the course of the text.

The *Dialogue* and *Orchard* also press at the limits of language in exploring the ultimate ineffability of God and the ways in which human languages fail in the attempt to create theological discourse. Catherine writes,
for instance, following Jeremiah: "O good lord, what schal I seye? What
schal I speke? Al my spekyng is to þee no spekyng. Þerfore I schal seye þus
as a child dooþ: A, A, A, for I can noon oþire speke. Þe tonge of my body
is sich þat it schal haue eende, & þerfore it cannot expresse þe affeccioun

of þe soule which desireþ infinytly" (*Orchard* 376). Here, a child's prelin-
guistic open vowel, repeated three times, represents the dumbfounded response of the finite soul to the infinite God: the use of language to express
a soul taken beyond the linguistic in a reference to the opening chapter of
Jeremiah ("et dixi 'a a a' Domine Deus ecce nescio loqui, quia puer ego
sum," Jer. 1:6).[86] The words on the page draw attention, jointly, to the inadequacy of both the body and its tongue, drawing on the prophetic tradition of the mouth's inability to speak with or for God until opened by
God.[87] The soul's infinite desire cannot be matched by the limited physi-
cality of the tongue; the grammatical discourse of the single-syllable
prayer of the *Cloud of Unknowing* and other texts examining the ultimate
limitations of human language in the act of prayer is also relevant.[88]

This Middle English passage, in fact, is a significant expansion of the
Latin and the Italian (which both, in turn, stray further from the Vulgate
Jeremiah): the Latin source-text of the *Orchard* reads "Et quid dicam?
Faciam tamquam balbuciens, dicens 'A. a.' Quia nescio quid aliud dicem,
qui lingua finita affectum anime non valet exprimere que infinite desi-
derat" (MS 87, fol. 263v).[89] Here, as in Catherine's Italian, the tongue's
twice-repeated vowel is instead figured as stuttering: the impaired speech
of an anxious and tongue-tied adult, overwhelmed in awe, rather than the
confused babbling of a less theologically minded child. The Middle English returns the text closer to Jeremiah's own claim to be a speechless
child (and restores the Vulgate's threefold "a"), but it also emphasizes a
childlike inability, perhaps prior to linguistic ability, to express oneself
before a parental God. Catherine's Italian and the Latin source-text of the
Orchard instead liken the soul's inability to speak to the more permanent
condition of adult speech impairment, distancing the trope from its origin
in Jeremiah.[90] The translation of a stutterer to a child may also provide the
extralinguistic "A, a, a" with a pair of overlapping meanings: it represents
both the sound of stumbling over one's tongue in fear and awe and the
wailing or crying of a confused child. This, in turn, might reflect the evi-
dent insular interest in Catherine's theology of tears: as Catherine Grisé
has argued recently, the *Orchard* "provided the fullest theoretical model
of holy weeping in late medieval England, integrating the physiological
and spiritual functions of tears to make the act of crying into a devotional
practice accessible to all."[91]

In the Italian text, this passage of sublinguistic stuttering—Catherine's
oblique insertion of herself into the long prophetic tradition of the Hebrew

scriptures—is followed by one of only a few instances of Latin in the *Dialogue*. She assumes, for a moment, the voice of Paul in his account of the mystical ascent in which he learns inexpressible divine secrets ("vidi archana Dei," cf. 2 Cor. 12:4).[92] The Middle English *Orchard*, however, is far more Latinate than the *Dialogue*. The preface, following its Latin source, emphasizes the vernacularity of the original composition from Catherine's dictation (the text "was write as sche endited in her moder tunge"),[93] but it also almost inexorably draws in Latin passages of scripture from the Latin source-text. Indeed, in comparison to other visionary and devotional works of the period, it provides a vivid image of what an educated audience in the Sheen/Syon mid-fifteenth-century circle might have *expected* a vernacular visionary female-authored text to look like. In rendering the Latin translation of Catherine's mother tongue into the English vernacular, the expectations of the translator of the *Orchard* of what Latin she may have known (or ought to have known) color the macaronic text. Rather than Catherine's quite sparing use of Latin in the *Dialogue*, the *Orchard* offers dozens of instances: numerous citations of Christ's own words in the New Testament (usually then translated, but he does speak in Middle English alone at times), several quotations of Paul, "nolo mortem *et cetera*" (Ezekiel 33:11), Saint Peter Martyr's dying confession written in his own blood (*Credo in Deum*, also rendered in Latin in the *Dialogue*), a book title (the *Vitae Patrum*, mentioned four times), and a pious explicit. Catherine's text, almost entirely in Italian, is given a degree of Latinity in its Middle English rendition that parallels the use of Latin found in similar insular vernacular revelatory texts of the period.

THE BODY AND THE WORLD

All of you together make up one common vineyard, the whole Christian assembly, and you are all united in the vineyard of the mystic body of holy Church.

—*Dialogue*, chap. 24

The extensive visionary landscape of the *Dialogue* and *Orchard* is shaped not only by its careful attention to language and aurality but also by the acute materiality of Catherine's mysticism and the vividness of her unique metaphors of the human body and the body of Christ.[94] These intersect in the most crucial component of Catherine's visionary world: the elaborate allegory of Jesus as a bridge composed of three steps that are both architectural and corporeal (feet, side-wound, and mouth). The bridge serves as a tremendously flexible motif over the course of the *Orchard*: Christ offers refreshments to pilgrims in a tavern on the bridge, even as the Church fights vicious battles against fiends on it. Hetta Howes writes that the overall motif depicts a spiritual journey in which "Christ's body offers a bridge from the tempestuous, filthy sea of earthly life to the peaceable sea of God"[95]—yet both Christ's body and the bridge itself each have a wealth of other symbolic meanings. The heart is also, unsurprisingly, central to her text: in God's words to Catherine, the heart is like an empty vessel that must be filled with *something*, and when it is properly emptied of vain thoughts and worldly love, it can then be filled with the air of divine love. This in turn leads the soul to the "watir of grace. And þanne . . . sche passeþ and gooþ forþ by þe gate of Crist crucified, and so taasteþ þe watir of liifly grace, rennynge as a ryuer qwikly in me, þat am þe pesable see."[96] The water of the soul and the water of the divine sea are yoked together, even as the image of the empty vessel fades.

Over the course of the text, this passage through the gate and over the bridge of Christ leads to a soul reformed not only through its long conversations with God, but also through a variety of journeys over (and up) the bridge of Christ's body. Howes writes, "Where the earthly flood is polluted, the sea of God is pure; where it clouds sight and is equated with blindness, the sea of God is clear."[97] The clear water of the Godhead also serves, in the final chapter of the *Dialogue*, as "a mirror in which you, eternal Trinity, grant me knowledge; for when I look into this mirror, holding it in the hand of love, it shows me myself"—even the relationship between God and humankind is described in terms of a pool of mirrorlike water.[98] The expansive oceanic imagery is one of the metaphorical centers of gravity of the text—and drinking from the clear well of God's love is also invoked—but Jane Chance has also linked some of the material imagery in the *Dialogue* and the *Orchard* to the physical worlds of trade, craft, and labor in which Catherine lived and ministered: these range from the spiritual anvil on which Christ was forged to the hound of conscience doggedly chasing the soul.[99] Phyllis Hodgson points out the surprising degree to which Catherine's spirituality, particularly when compared to a variety of contemporary English texts, gives relatively sparse attention to the details of the Passion; she also likens the complicated, malleable image of the bridge and its associated figures to the wide-ranging allegorical imagination of *Piers Plowman*, and also draws theological connections to the work of Walter Hilton and Julian of Norwich (Catherine, for example, also sees how God the Father "in his fist al þe world encloside").[100]

Built and human environments—of bridges, fishhooks, teeth, and tables—abound in the text, but the natural world also plays a prominent role in Catherine's visionary universe (even setting aside the ordering motif of the orchard or vineyard). The four winds of this world, for instance, variously smite the tree of "propre sensualyte" (*Orchard* 207) and its rotten root; waves disturb the disordered soul, making her unable to see her descent to hell, blinded as she is by the "cloude . . . of her owne mysrulid and disordynat loue" (115). Damned souls at judgment will find to their dismay that "þanne þe worm of conscience freteþ þe marowȝ of þe tre, þat is þe soule, and þe vttir rynde of þe tre, þat is þe body" (96). The process here, of Conscience as worm devouring both Body and Soul as tree, helps to demonstrate the permeability between allegorical categories in Catherine: rather than seeing only bodily decay through the image of worms, the punishment instead imagines both body and soul joined together in one experience of posthumous horror. Taken as a whole, however, the permeability between human, natural, and celestial categories is perhaps best represented by the dominant, recurring symbol, the bridge of Christ. It connects heaven to earth, God tells the soul, "by þe vnyoun which I haue maad in man, whom I foormede of þe grutty moisture of þe erþe."[101] The union of God and man is likened to the mixture of earth and dust, moistened and used in both bridge-building and human-forming; both unions serve to link the heavens with the material world below, even as Christ's own incarnation serves as model for Catherine's creation of the allegorical characters in her intricate, textual world.

LOVE AND COMMUNITY

Just as the fish is in the sea and the sea in the fish, so am I in the soul and the soul in me, the sea of peace.

—*Dialogue*, chap. 112

While Catherine's text is a dialogue between the devout Soul and God, their wide-ranging discussion encompasses a community richly populated by allegorical and historical figures; the commandment to love God is, of course, regularly paired with the commandment to love neighbors. But her text demonstrates that a fixed "self" capable of loving an equally circumscribed God and neighbor is impossible: both the soul commanded to this love and the intended objects of that love are embedded in an intricate web of textual, allegorical, and social relationships. Even the "Soul" communicating with God in the text is, indeed, a moving target, reflecting God's image in humankind while also representing the Church entire. An important ethical facet of Catherine's text, then, relies on seeing how the putatively individual soul only exists through and in a network of loving relationships to God and neighbor; this rich enmeshment (both theologically and socially) is also found throughout the Catherinian hagiographical texts. God tells the Soul, for instance, that the need for mutual charity is an inherent part of how the world was designed. Each human could have been made to be entirely self-sustaining. God explains, "I wanted to make you dependent on one another so that each of you would be my minister. . . . So whether you will it or not, you cannot escape the exercise of charity!"[102]

Her intertwining circles of ever-adapting allegory in the *Dialogue* and *Orchard* force us to recognize, too, the extreme *permeability* of identity inherent to her text, and the concomitant complications that places on her theology of love. If Jesus is the stone-and-flesh bridge between human and divine realms, the true vine onto which believers are grafted, and a refreshing meal served on the dining table of the Father; if the soul is a mirror of the divine image, a gated city, and a sweet-sounding musical instrument ennobled by marriage to Queen Poverty, then the commandment to love God and neighbor is as impossibly tangled and multifaceted as the intersecting characters of her mystical text itself. Her theology of love depends on an intrinsically permeable definition of personhood. Followed to its limits, this leads us to a sense of social justice in which, Regina Schwartz writes, "our model of the human person is not that of the individual bounded by his body, his soul, his conscience, his consciousness, but of a person embedded in a deep network of association from which he would cease to be if he were cut off from his past, his future, his present, as well as his neighbors, [and] his strangers."[103] Love, in this redefinition of personhood, becomes for Catherine the affective axle around which the intricate, complicated wheel of justice turns.

Traditional bridal mysticism, meanwhile, would understand the loving relationship between God and the soul reflected in the Song of Songs as a relatively binary proposition: one bride and one bridegroom. Bridal mysticism in the Catherinian sense, however, includes not only the lovesickness a soul feels for God, but also exemplary spiritual marriages between multiple historical and allegorical figures. Saint Francis's bride, Lady Poverty, perhaps most notably, is upgraded to a royal figure in the *Dialogue*.[104] After a short depiction of the Nativity (in which Jesus is said to have given us an example by himself wedding poverty in the manger), Jesus is described as being so "drunke wiþ loue" that "he made to ȝou a baþ in his blood" (*Orchard* 370). This, in turn, leads to the revelation of the "rule of love": a rule of poverty that (citing Christ's claim that the Son of Man has no place to lay his head; Luke 9:58, Matt. 8:20) establishes an exemplary form of Christian poverty best realized by the soul's own marriage to the "qweene of pouert."[105] The scene continues by describing the peacefulness of the queen's realm, its foundation on the stone of Christ, and its illumination by the mother of the queen, God's charity.

This relationship of the soul as both subject to and bride of a queen is also described in richly universal and communal terms: the spiritual riches of material poverty are granted to the "soule þat is weddid to þis riȝt swete qwene . . . & sche may not be lady of oon but sche be lady of alle" (*Orchard* 371). Communal marriage to Queen Poverty does not, here, arouse the same tensions as the idea of a polyandrous Sapientia seems to have done in Suso's *Horologium*.[106] The communal foundation of her spiritual marriage leads to a series of metaphors for the spiritual perfection Queen Poverty gives to her spouses: she draws out bitterness from the soul, leaving only sweetness in her. She cuts thorns away, leaving her only the rose. She "dischargeþ þe stomak of þe soule fro þe corrupte humours of vnordynat loue, & makeþ it liȝt. & aftir tyme it is so voidid, sche filliþ it wiþ mete of vertu, which ȝeuen greet swetnes" (371). The elegant, courtly world of the peaceful city of Queen Poverty is sharply juxtaposed with a harshly ascetic world in which the stomach of the soul is allegorically purged, then refreshed with virtuous food.

Whereas in Suso we saw that spiritual marriage to the Goddess Wisdom seemed to require a masculinization of the otherwise feminine Soul, Catherine's text, in both Italian and Middle English, does not always succumb to this degree of heteronormativity. The pronouns for the Soul/

Spouse and Queen Poverty throughout this passage on Queen Poverty both remain feminine in the *Orchard*: "Alle gracis, all plesaunces, & alle delices þat sich a soule þat haþ weddid þe qweene pouert can þanne desire, sche fyndiþ," for example.[107] These figures in the Middle English largely parallel the gender of the Italian (and the Middle English *spouse*, helpfully, can be either masculine or feminine), but there is slightly more variation in the gender of the characters in Catherine's original text, as when "questa sposa riveste lo sposo suo di purità" (this bride clothes her spouse [masc.] anew in purity).[108] In the *Orchard*, the equivalent passage has the "qweene, pouert, araieþ a soule wiþ greet purite" (371). The *sposo* of the Italian is rendered as *a soule*: ungendered as it stands here, but always given a feminine pronoun elsewhere in the Middle English text.

Queen Poverty later reappears in a discussion of the Ship of Religion—which soon becomes multiple ships, representing religious orders—and the virtues of its leaders. The ship, bringing souls to the port of salvation, is captained by the Holy Spirit, but initially piloted by three figures. Benedict is first given the briefest imaginable mention ("Consider the great order with which Benedict governed his ship"), before a long comparison of the ways Francis and Dominic equipped and steered their ships.[109] Francis's asceticism and rejection of wealth is noted: he gave those who entered his order "verry & holy pouert for þeir spouse, which pouert he took also for his owne spouse wiþ her sustir vilite" (*Orchard* 388). He is praised for slaying his will and being nailed on the cross with the Lamb, but the mention of his stigmata is rather subdued: "by special & synguler grace in his body apperide þe woundis of myn oonly soþfast sone, Ihesu Crist, crucified, & so was schewid in þe vessel of þe body þat which was in affecioun of þe soule. Thus he made a way himsilf to hise sogettis."[110] The Middle English is slightly more emphatic in its naming of Jesus as the model of the stigmata (where the Italian refers to him only as "mia Verità," "my Truth"), but in either language the measured praise of Francis as the first mendicant seems partly designed to prepare the reader for the even more lavish praise of Dominic to come.

That Dominic is given more elaborate honor by Catherine's God than Francis is certainly unsurprising; the terms she uses to do so are, however, revealing. Where Francis offers his followers poverty as a spouse, father Dominic is described as yoking poverty *and* learning together in a "parfiȝt ordir." Poverty is depicted as his spouse only after a passage describing the importance of learning to the order and claiming that he left his curse (and God's) on any of his followers who abandon poverty, in order all the better to prove that "he chees to his spouse þe qweene of pouert. But for his principal vertu þat he sette his religioun vpon, was þe liȝt of kunnyng."[111] The spiritual espousal of poverty, though central to the identity of his order, is overshadowed by the repeated emphasis on the "light of knowledge."

The ship is given further elaboration: Dominic rigged the ship with three strong ropes ("obedience, continence, and true poverty") and was himself "vertuously al large, al myrye, & iocunde, & al swete in vertu, as a delytable viridarie" (*Orchard* 390). The rare Middle English term *viridarie*, "gardener" or "forester" (apparently unique, in Middle English, to the *Orchard*), points to the Italian text's different depiction, in which it is the *ship* of the Dominican Order that is "very spacious, gladsome, and fragrant, a most delightful garden."[112] The translator, sharing Catherine's allegorical inventiveness, however, sees nothing amiss in imagining a ship helmed by Dominic as an enormous, joyful forester. Indeed, Christ's role as gardener is also explored in detail by her hagiographer, and God the Father describes himself as a gardener tending to the true vine in chapter 23 of the *Dialogue*.

Catherine then details the glories of two Dominican saints, Thomas Aquinas and Peter Martyr, praising the former for the burning light of his intellect and the latter for his emphatic preaching against heresy and, most especially, his fearless, bloody martyrdom (particularly delighting in his use of his own blood to write *Credo in Deum* on the ground as he died). Catherine praises Peter Martyr for being "a verry knyȝt wiþoute ony seruyle drede" as he stood "in þe feeld of batel," but she also acknowledges that Dominic himself and others "suffriden no martirdom actualy, ȝit þei suffriden mentaly."[113] As she herself actively sought martyrdom, she allies her own mental suffering with that of the founder of the Dominicans, the pilot of the finest ship of religion; the Italian text, meanwhile, claims only that Dominic and others suffered a kind of spiritual or mental martyrdom.[114] The passage on the mendicant orders largely concludes after this, with Benedict long neglected by this point, and the two mendicants transformed once again: "Domynyk & Fraunceis weren tweye pyleris in holy chirche; Fraunceys wiþ his pouert."[115] The reader then learns of the allegorical family one needs to enter into these ships of religion: "þe spouse of verri obediens wiþ her sustir of paciens, & wiþ þe norse of mekenes" (*Orchard* 392).

The numerous interactions between allegorical characters also play a critical role in Catherine's understanding of the just foundations of civic community. The *Dialogue* and *Orchard* develop a complicated system of metaphors that fuse love and social justice, participating in a theology that connects love of God to love of one's community. The forms of proper love and improper self-love depicted in the text hinge on Catherine's belief that the soul itself is made of love: "a soule may in no wyse lyue wiþoute loue, but euere it moste loue somþing, for of loue it is maad" (*Orchard* 120). Combining the erotics of the mystical Song of Songs tradition with her own active involvement in works of charity in the world, Catherine's theology is, Christopher Roman writes, "embodying the spirit of God's charity by opening and emptying the self to commit to a charity without borders or limits."[116] A theology, indeed, in which love is seen as the very cause of the border-crossing incarnation in which God was made man: the Soul describes the Incarnation, to God, as "hidynge and koueringe þin eendelees godheed wiþ þe wrecchidful matere of corrupcioun of Adam," and asks, "Lord, what was þe cause of þis? Truly loue was cause. Thou, God, art maad man, and man is maad as God. Of þis holy loue and for þis holy loue, Lord, I biseche þee þat þou ȝeue mercy to þi synful creaturis" (49). The classical chiastic structure of incarnation and divinization is yoked, as in Julian of Norwich, to divine love (elsewhere, too, God quotes Jesus as saying, "Whoso loueþ me, he schal be oon wiþ me"): the love of the Lord for the Servant in Julian's parable, she writes, yokes together Christ and humankind.[117] In another instance, kenosis is seen as an inherent part of God's love. The Soul, described as "al brennynge in loue and goostly drunke," praises God and rhetorically asks what the cause of the Incarnation was, answering herself: "Certeyn, loue. For þou louedist us first eer þan we were. O good God and euerlastynge in magnificence, þou madist þisilf low and litil to make us mychil" (317). This preexistence of divine love occurs elsewhere in the *Orchard*: "I haue maad ȝou wiþoute ȝou, but withoute ȝou I may not saue ȝou. I louede ȝou first eer þan ȝe were" (268–69).[118]

Divine love is not given precise taxonomic gradations to the degree we find in, for instance, Richard of Saint Victor, but Catherine is particularly interested in the diverse ways in which divine love can join people together and is made manifest in communities.[119] Deploying the image of the Church as sacred vineyard, she explores the "endlessly permeable boundaries among self, others, and God,"[120] writing of the individual soul's relationship to its neighbors:

> Thynke wel and haue in mynde þat alle resonable creaturis haue her owne vyneȝeerd by hemsilf, which is ooned to her neiȝbore wiþoute ony oþir mene; that is to seye, oon so ioyned with anoþir þat no man may do good to hymsilf, ne harme, but þat he moste ȝeelde þe same to his neiȝbore. Of Ȝou alle, þat is to seye, of al þe hool cristen religyoun, a general vyneȝeerd is gaderid togyderis, which ȝe alle ben knytt togyders in þe vyneȝeerd of þe goostly body of holy chirch.[121]

Here, the vineyard is both Church and individual soul, each individual vineyard connecting to a larger one without any intermediary; indeed, each vineyard in some sense constitutes the whole, as good and harm are said to have an equivalent effect on the entire Church (even as the dominant metaphor for the book as a whole imagines it as a well-ordered orchard through which the reader strolls). The vineyard as the source of agent of intoxication is also relevant, as love is expressed as a state of spiritual drunkenness time and time again (and wine springs directly from the vine on occasion); the whole of Catherine's *Dialogue* itself ends with the Soul's final paean to the Trinity, concluding rapturously, from being clothed in the light of holy faith, "with that light I sense my soul once again becoming drunk!" (me semeþ þou hast maad me now late goostly drunke!).[122]

Not as deeply invested in the specifically courtly modes of eroticism that so beguiled Suso in his long quest for Eternal Wisdom, Catherine does refer to the motif of the game of love: after devout souls "ben ful come to perfeccioun," God reports, "I wiþdrawȝ fro hem þe game of loue in goynge and comynge. The which may wel be callid þe game of loue, for by loue I go fro hem, and by loue I come aȝein to hem: not propirly I, for I am ȝoure Lord which is vnmouable . . . but þe feelyng which my charite ȝeueþ to a soule, which gooþ and cometh."[123] Similarly, the language of love-longing and love-woundedness is applied to both the Soul *and* God: God's pity for the weeping soul causes God "to be constreyned and to be bounde wiþ þe chaynes of her holy desier."[124] Similarly, a long address to the "eendlees fadir" concludes by addressing him as "al wounded in loue";[125] the *Dialogue*'s description of God as "like one drunk with love for our good" (Noffke 55), immediately preceding the ineffability passage discussed above, does not appear in the *Orchard*, however. Nevertheless, in these complicated, intertwining images, metaphors, and allegories, the richness of Catherine of Siena's theological and literary imagination, and her unique language of the responsibilities love places on a community, reached their fifteenth-century English audience (beginning with the Bridgettines of Syon Abbey and their milieu) and, in 1521, an even wider insular audience in print.[126]

STEFANO MACONI (STEPHEN OF SIENA) AND MS DOUCE 114

Oxford, Bodleian Library MS Douce 114 is an unusually vivid witness to early fifteenth-century English vernacular interest in the authors of Continental spiritual literature, including Catherine of Siena. A Middle English devotional prose miscellany produced between 1415 and 1425, it was owned by the Carthusians of Beauvale (Nottinghamshire), but may have been produced elsewhere in the general vicinity (perhaps Thurgarton, sixteen miles away).[127] Four of its texts are not attested to elsewhere in Middle English. The manuscript begins with three lives, translations unique in English, of holy women from the Low Countries (none canonized): Elizabeth of Spalbeek, Christina the Astonishing, and Marie d'Oignies.[128] The final section of the manuscript contains the complete text of the *Seven Points of True Love and Everlasting Wisdom*. Between these materials is the fourth unique text: a substantial biographical letter written by the former prior general of the Carthusian Order (from 1398 to 1410), Stefano Maconi (1350–1424). Written in 1411, the letter testifies to the sanctity of Catherine of Siena, and records some of Maconi's conversations and interactions with her.

The manuscript as a whole has received significant attention of late: Sarah Macmillan has argued, for instance, that as a spiritual anthology, its ordering aims to regulate modes of asceticism for its readers as they read sequentially, beginning with the life of Elizabeth of Spalbeek. Such a reader would progress, then, from corporeal to spiritual ideals of asceticism (the latter represented by the manuscript's final text, Henry Suso's *Seven Points*).[129] Brian Vander Veen, however, sees the Douce *Lives* as "constructed in such a way as to discourage the possibility of imitation" in an ecclesiastical and Carthusian effort both to temper female religious enthusiasm and to reinforce Eucharistic orthodoxy.[130] The manuscript's first three lives, Jennifer Brown has argued, offer a progression of increasing fame and decreasing "suspect behavior" (with a corresponding emphasis on "confession and clerical obedience").[131] The relationship between the revelatory and pastoral worlds explored in the miscellany, Vincent Gillespie writes, serves to provide "both models for emulation for aspirant contemplatives and also cautionary tales of the need for clerical support and spiritual guidance"[132]—the careful interface between these two spheres was certainly an abiding concern for both Catherine of Siena and Henry Suso, amply demonstrated in their reception in other English manuscripts.

The Middle English Maconi letter, following the *Lives* of the three Beguines, testifies to interest in rich documentary detail about Catherine in England, from a variety of sources, decades before her canonization. The letter carefully emphasizes Catherine's works of charity, her intellectual and ascetic activities (and the controversy surrounding them), and the approbation she received from prominent clergy (including the papal court in Avignon). Jennifer Brown sees the letter, in its emphasis on Catherine's role as spiritual second mother to Stefano (with Jesus, as her spouse, the implied father) and her insistence that he join the Carthusian Order, as offering a kind of textual-spiritual mother figure to the Beauvale Carthusians (perhaps with the vernacular used for a young postulant weak in Latin and especially in need of spiritual motherhood).[133] The intimacy a personal letter provides and the translator's use of the mother tongue—with its standard connotations as the language of the domestic, the familial, and the nonprofessional, in contrast to Latin—serve to reinforce the choice of text, genre, and language.

The letter is also significant for its careful consideration of translation techniques and its recognition of the variety of English dialects. The letter is followed by a postscript, written by the translator of both the letter and the three *Lives*, titled "A shorte apologetik of þis englissh compylour":

Seynt James þe Apostil seiþ þat whoso synneþ not in tunge, hee is a perfite man. Wherfore þe turner of þis englysshe, þat is not but symply vndirstandynge as here þe soþ preueþ lowely and mekely, [besecheþ] alle men and wymmen þat in happe rediþ or heriþ þis en-glysh, þat þey be not ouer capcyous, ne curyous in ful many clauses & variauns of stile & allso vnsuynge of englyshe as vmwhile soþeren, oþere while norþen. But þe cause why nediþ not to be tolde. And spe-cially, he becheþ lettird men & clerkes, if þey endeyne to see þes bokes, þat þey wol be fauorabil and benigne reders or herers of þis englysche, and forgif hym alle defautes þat he haþ made in compi-lynge þereof (raþer arettynge his lewdnesse to symple ignorauns and obedyens, þanne to pryde or presumpcyon). Ffor wite all men þat he þe which drewe þis englysche, so as is oute of latyne, knowynge his own sympilnesse and vnkonynge, durst not haue presumed to take siche a labour on hand but if his souereyn hadde bidden hym (whome he myghte not ageyne seye).[134]

The performance of humility is especially prominent here, but the de-tails lurking among the lavish protestations of being humble and unedu-cated are quite revealing: men or women and even educated clerks are imagined reading or hearing the text. The assumption that a mixed dialect of northern and southern elements would be both noticed, and deemed not worthy of explanation, may point to dialectal diversity among the original reading community in Nottinghamshire, whether Carthusian or otherwise. This paratext also assumes a readership interested in issues surrounding the rendering of the source-text, or at least some curiosity about the relationship between the source-text and the vernacular treat-ment of the letter. It goes on to explain: "Nota: pro 'ancilla xpi,' verti 'cristes mayden' & pro superlativo gradu, 'vt optimus,' verti 'ful gode' & sic in similibus" (fol. 87v). As Dirk Schultze points out, this also cements that the first four texts were originally translated as one cohesive unit, as *ancilla christi* does not appear in the Maconi letter, but rather in the three Beguine *Lives*.[135]

Maconi's letter about Catherine is itself preceded with this incipit: "Here bigynneþ þe copy of a letter touchynge þe lyfe of Seint Kateryn of Senys, þe whiche lettir endyted in Latyn Dan Stephen of Senys (sum-tyme pryour of þe hede Charteus in tyme of scisme, after pryour of Papy [Pavia]), vnto frere Thomas Anthonij of Senys, of þe ordyr of prechours, as hit is playnly contenyd in þe lettir" (fol. 76v). The careful emphasis on location and monastic order again shows the degree to which English and Venetian readers shortly after Catherine's death were interested in the ecclesiastical and geographical landscapes through which she moved (and the prominence, in the Carthusian Order, of the author). Following this, the text begins in standard epistolary form, focusing on the names and places associated with the request for the letter and the general desire for more testimony to her sanctity: "I haue received affectuosly ȝoure lettirs and haue redde hem bisily, by þe whiche ȝee gretly require and pray me þat I shulde sende to ȝoure charite in open forme trewe informacyone of þe dedys, maners, vertues, and doctrines of famos holynesse of þe virgyn blyssed Kateryn of Senys (whos conuersacyone sumtyme I deserued while she lyued, as ȝee sey)" (fol. 76v). The letter, in contrast to the *Lives* preceding it and the Suso text following it, is depicted as part of an ongoing discourse concerning the nature of Catherine sanctity, and saintliness more broadly. The dispute in Venice (the center of her early fifteenth-century cult), and clarifications needed for worshippers and skeptics there, is given as the ostensible purpose for the letter. The text quickly shifts, however, to detailing her asceticism and her eating habits. He writes in detail, for instance:

> In Rome sumtyme, she toke þe sacrament of þe auter all only. Neuerþeles þe maner of buriynge þat she kepte longe tyme as I sawe many ȝeerys is þis: fflesche, wyne, confeccunes, and egges she loþed gretly. But wymmen þat were wiþ hir dighte vnto hir communly grene erbes whan þey myghte any gette, or ellis oþere while a mece of wortys wiþ oyle. Of an ele she eet allonly þe hede and þe tayle, but chese ete she noon (but if hit wel olde and corrupte), & on same maner grapes and siche oþere. Neuerþeles she ete not þese, but chewyd hem with hir teeþ. Oþer while wiþ brede oþere while withoute brede, soukynge þe iuse, and spittyd oute euery morsel of þe gres mater, soupynge ful often clere watir by hit selfe. And she abode so longe tyme to do so as longe as hir felowes þat were wymmen stode etynge atte borde. Afterwarde she roos & seyde "Go we to þe rightwisenesse of þis wrecchyd synner." And wiþ a stalke of fynel or anoþer þinge þat she put into hir stomake, she broghte oute violently by þe same weye þat iuse & þe watir þat sche hadde taken. And some tyme she soffred so grete vyolens in þat dede þat quykke blode come out of hir mouþ.[136]

The text here focuses on the specifics of her diet (down to the parts of the eel and the age of the cheese), the details of the self-induced vomiting, and the oral or intestinal bleeding that she endured. This careful attention to Catherine's body and its sustenance parallels other aspects of her reception in hagiography, even as her own words in the *Dialogue* and the letters made relatively little reference to these precise details of her asceticism. In the context of the other texts in the manuscript, too, Catherine's asceticism is described in terms of food restriction rather than more active forms of self-inflicted pain. The bloody self-induced vomiting is certainly actively inflicted, but it differs from the corporeal self-punishment of the other women in the manuscript, instead again focusing the reader's attention on her dietary habits.

As we've seen, Catherine's literacy seemed to be almost inevitably commented on and discussed by the many men who wrote about her. So too, Maconi writes:

> I haue hadde summe ȝeeres more þanne many oþer men ful homely conuersacyon of hir in writynge lettirs & hir priuetis. And parte of hir boke þe which I wrote after hir own maydenly mouþe. For abouen my deseruynge, she loued me ful affectuosly with moderly charyte, so þat many of hir sones bare hit heuy and hadde a maner of envye. (fol. 79r)

Here, Maconi emphasizes the collaborative nature of authorship in Catherine's circle: both letter-writing and the composition of the *Dialogue* are portrayed as acts of transcription from Catherine's oral composition of text. Later on, her ability to interpret scripture orally in the presence of two popes helps to prove her sanctity and testify to the divine source of her authorial inspiration:

> Soþely wiþouten þees, þis ful holy virgyne hadde so mykel wysdome of hir soule infused of god þat all þat herde hir were astonyed! She delyuerid and expounyd all holy writte so cleerly and so openly þat alle men (were þey neuer so leryd, or maistirs) as astonyed hadde wonder. . . . Many tymes she made ful quykke and spedful sermons wiþ a wondirful stille & enditynge. Firste in the presens of oure lorde Pope Gregor Elleuenþe, after in þe presens of oure lorde Pope Vrban Sexte & of Cardynals all wiþ grete meruel, seiynge þat neuere man

spake so. And wiþouten doute þis is no woman þat spekes, but þe holy goste. (fol. 84r)

The letter here aims to demonstrate the astonishing miraculousness of her knowledge: she is able to impress scholars and popes alike with her interpretations of scripture and her sermons. The understanding that the Holy Spirit, rather than the woman Catherine, is speaking to the cardinals helps temper the potential violation of the Pauline proscription of female preaching.

Maconi also refers to her nascent cult, detailing both her miracles and the commemoration of these miracles at her tomb:

> Who myghte telle hir most brennynge charite, þurgh þe whiche she gaf to þe worshyp of god and profet for hir neyghbores, not oonly temporel godes while she was in hir fadir hous, but also hir own selfe? . . . Sumtyme she gaf to a pore man hir own cote. Afterwarde oure lorde shewyd hit to hir arayed in þe bakke with ful shinynge precyous stones (as þis dede is figured atte Rome bisyde hir tumbe). (fol. 85v)

The narrative demonstrates a straightforward act of charity, the gift of a coat, then recounts the miracle of its transformation into a bejeweled token of God's favor of this charity. The commemoration of it by her tomb, too, helps the reader to connect the contemporary worship of Catherine in anticipation of her canonization to the historical act of charity and resulting miracle Maconi relates.

The letter also promotes its author's own close connection to Catherine, repeatedly stressing Maconi's personal feelings at first being introduced to Catherine, his devotion as he travels with her, and his presence decades before the letter's composition at her death in 1380. The deathbed scene Maconi recounts also includes her command that he join the Carthusians, and his role in her burial:

> sche closed þe laste daye in my presens. Whan I bare wiþ myne owne handes to | sepulture, þat is to þe chirche of Frere prechours to be beryed, ȝe, raþer to be kepte in a cofer of cypresse & worshypfull toumbe. Sooþly, while she labored in hir laste ende, she ordeyned

wiþ summe men what þey shulde do after hir passynge. Afterward turnynge hir visage to me, she seyde (& strecchyng forþ hir fyngyr): "Forsoþe I bydde the, on goddes byhalue and in vertue of obedyens, þat on all maner wyse þou go to þe Charteus ordyr. He haþ called & chosen þe!" þan she, seynge vs bisyde hir wepynge, seyde: "Ful dere childir, ȝee schulde not wepe no wise, but raþer ioye in oure lorde and make a mery daye! For I am delyuered oute of þis pryson, goyng þis daye to þe most specyall spouse of my soule."[137]

The careful construction of the deathbed scene details Catherine's own empathetic response to the sorrow of her disciples, bringing both her voice and her bodily gestures into the text. The maternal role she plays in determining the spiritual paths her followers should take after her death transitions into a celebration of her soul's journey to its spouse in the ful-fillment of the mystical marriage.

RAYMOND OF CAPUA'S *LIFE* IN 1493 AND 1609: HAGIOGRAPHY AND IMITATION

Any given saint's life or miracle story of that saint . . . is connected to the larger system of hagiographical writing, even as it has a relationship to the written and oral sources on which it is based, the liturgical or devotional rituals that it supports, the theological ideas that it represents, the historical and political events surrounding its production, the religious and lay com-munities that it addresses, or the audiences who experience it.

—Virginia Blanton[138]

Raymond of Capua played one of the most important roles in promoting Catherine's cult—both as master general of the Dominican Order and as author of a *Life* of Catherine (the *Legenda Maior*).[139] This *Life*, though a detailed, richly "protonovelistic" account of numerous holy moments over the course of Catherine's entire life, also emphasizes Raymond's own spiritual relationship with her quite heavily.[140] Like Suso in his *Vita*, Raymond makes himself a key character in this hagiography, emphasiz-ing both his eyewitness accounts of her miracles and his own spiritual relationship with her. John Coakley writes, for instance, that Raymond "inserts himself continually as a figure in the narrative, placing himself at her side as much as possible, connecting himself with events in her life, telling the reader what he was thinking as he interacted with her."[141] The text offers a provocative counterpoint to Catherine's own writing, detailing the ways in which Catherine's relationship with God left "tangible effects . . . on this unusual female mystic's body" (particularly through rigorous asceticism), gave her an apostolic mission, and led her to create a family of followers.[142]

The Middle English *Orchard of Syon* would reach Wynkyn de Worde's press in 1519, and Maconi's letter was copied in Bodleian MS Douce 114. But Raymond's *Life* reached an even broader late medieval English audience, printed first by de Worde in Westminster in English in 1492/93 (also notable as the first printing of a Catherinian text outside of Italy) and again in 1500.[143] Despite the enormity of the theological and political ruptures that took place during the Reformation and as a result of England's split with Rome, the cultural significance of texts by and about medieval holy women did not suddenly disappear in the mid-sixteenth century; some of these were translated into English in order to serve growing communities of vernacular readers both inside and out-side recusant cloisters.[144] In 1609, John Fenn (1535–1615) translated Raymond's *Life* anew. Fenn, a talented Latinist whose two brothers also became priests (his younger brother, James, was martyred in London in 1584), left England in 1562, spending most of the rest of his life in Leuven ministering to English convents; in 1609 he became the chap-lain to a newly established community of Augustinian canonesses.[145] His source-text for the life of Catherine was quite different from Wynkyn de Worde's: Fenn turned to Lancellotto Politi (1484–1553, who in reli-gion took the name Ambrogio Caterino), whose 1524 Italian translation of Raymond of Capua's Latin made significant additions and deletions to Raymond's text.[146] These two early English versions of the *Life of Cath-erine of Siena*—one published before, one after the Reformation—have rarely been studied in tandem. Rather than considering the translation strategies per se of the two versions and their relationship to their source-texts, my focus here is instead on how contemporary communities of readers of each text encountered her life, and the unique commemoration of Catherine each text instantiates.

The examination of key moments in the narrative of her life (and, in some cases, the changes between the late medieval and early modern versions) reveals how some of the narratives in the hagiography took on new significance to their seventeenth-century audience of English Catholics abroad (even as Syon Abbey's continued survival in Belgium and Portugal would provide a focal point for English criticism of or veneration for Bridget of Sweden).[147] Catherine of Siena's reception history in England (as both an author of visionary literature and pious subject of hagiography) also contributed to her central position in post-Reformation debates around visionary authority, discretion, and female sanctity. Catherine, seen by the late 1500s as a champion of both the Dominican Order and a unified, Roman papacy, provided an ideal target for anti-Catholic polemic, even as in the early 1600s her *Life* and its depiction of the saint was published for the ongoing edification and inspiration of recusant readers. The changing representations of Catherine accord well with Virginia Blanton's study of the malleability of the hagiographic tradition, particularly regarding descriptions of a virgin saint's body: she examines the "collection of vitae, miracle stories, liturgical texts, and visual representations that illustrate the multivalency of the saint's story and the plasticity of the saint's body as signifier"[148] over the course of 1,000 years of the cult (or cults) of St. Æthelthryth (Ethelred, Audreé). In these two lengthy English Catherinian *Lives*—among many other potential sources—we can see both the enduring themes that devotion to Catherine of Siena offered to an English audience and some of the most significant narrative changes her cult underwent between the end of the fifteenth century and the beginning of the seventeenth.

Origins

Catherine's pious childhood, for instance, already demonstrates some of the differences in style and content between the two texts. The Wynkyn de Worde *Life* describes an interaction she had with her brother Steven early in her visionary career.[149] At the age of six she was walking past the Sienese church of Saint Dominic, and, looking at the church, saw Jesus on an imperial chair, clad in pontifical garb with a miter on his head, with Peter, Paul, and John the Evangelist alongside him. She stands ravished by this sight while Christ (triumphant rather than suffering) blesses her; the narrative's attention turns to her brother. He notices she is not with him anymore, and turns around:

Thenne he wente nere, cryeng after her; but his voys helped not. He woundred and wente thenne and drewe her by the honde and sayde "what doost thou here? why comest thou not forthe?" She anon cast doune a lytyll her eyen, as she hadde awaked of an heuy slepe, and sayde: "A, yf thou sawe that I sawe, thou woldest not haue lette me from this holy vysyon." And anone as she had said tho wordes, she lyft vp her eyen agayne to beholde more vp that she hadde seen; but the vysyon was alle wythdrawe and cesyd, as his wyll was whiche aperyd to-fore. And that myght she not bere wythout a sharpe stroke of sorowe and anone she vengyd her on her-self wyth sore wepynge, for sorowe that she (had) caste doune her eyen.[150]

Steven's distracting voice and touch interfere with her holy vision; simply moving the direction of her gaze seems to play some kind of role too (and it is this she focuses on in her emotional response to the lost rapture). Here, however, is the 1609 translation of the same moment in Catherine's spiritual development:

But all was to no purpose, until he came at length to the verie place, where she stood, & tooke her by the hand, saying. What doest thou here: whie comest thou not awaie? At the which wordes and pulling of her hand, she cast downe her eyes a litle, like one that had ben awaked out of a dead sleepe, and said. Oh, said she, if thou haddest seene that goodlie sight, that I sawe, thou wouldest never have done so to me. And when she had said those wordes, she cast up her eyes againe, thinking to have seene it, as she did before. But when she sawe that it was vanished awaie, she revenged the iniurie done unto her by her brother, as children are wont to doe, with weping. And it grieved her so much the more, bicause she perswaded her selfe, that by the casting downe of her eyes, she had deserved to leese the blisful fruition of that glorious sight.[151]

The later text maintains the general shape of the narrative, the relationship between Jesus and Catherine that interferes with the relationship between brother and sister, and the emotional details emphasized in the de Worde text. The scene in de Worde's text continues to detail her continued spiritual growth, including her miraculous education:

And from that tyme and houre this yonge mayde and vyrgyn saint Katheryn began to waxe olde in vertues and sadnesse of maners and to have a wonderfull witte and a felyng body bothe by grace and by nature. In soo moche that her dedes were nother chyldysshe ne as a yonge woman, but they semed rather to alle men that they came of the wysedom of a greate worshypfull age. Soo that anone was shewed that the fyre of dyuyne loue was kyndeled in her herte, by the whiche vertu her intellection was made clere, her wyll was feruent, her memorye was comforted, and alle her outward werkyng shewed in alle thynges the rewle of goddes lawe. And, as she sayd in confessyon to hyr confessour full mekely and lowely, she lerned and knewe at that tyme, wythout techyng of ony body or ony redynge or heryng, onely by the Infusyon of the holy ghoost, the leuyng and the maners of the holy faders of Egypte and the lyuyng of many other Sayntes, and specyally the lyfe of Saynt Domynyk.[152]

The spiritual gift of learning to a woman, miraculously bypassing human learning, is a common enough hagiographical trope, but the text emphasizes her youthfulness at the time of receiving it. Her infused knowledge is noteworthy, too, for what it leaves out: there are no female saints specifically named, nor is the Passion of Christ mentioned. She learns "living and manners" rather than more emotionally fraught hagiographical content (martyrdom, crucifixion, severe asceticism). The sudden "maturity" imputed to her by this vision also serves to place a sad emphasis on her early death, even as it brings to mind the perfection of a life matching in years that of Jesus.

In the 1609 version, however, this scene is expanded considerably; both deification and garden imagery are added:

Now when our Lord had after this maner watered the roote of his litle plant with the dewe of his sweet blessing, she began foorthwith to yeald, not only buddes & blossomes of great matters in expectation, but also ripe frutes of diverse and sundrie excellent and perfecte vertues: in so much that in all her behaviour she shewed her selfe to all those, that God vowchsafed to converse with her, not like an infant, as her yeares required; nor yet like a young woman, (which not withstanding in that age had ben a verie strange matter) but like a grave and sad matrone. This heavenlie fyer of Gods holie love had wrought such an alteration in her hart, such a light in her understanding, such a fervour in her will, such a plyantnes in all her powers, both of bodie and sowle, to folowe the instincte of his holie Spirite, that to them, that sawe her behaviour, and tooke good heed to her wordes and deedes, it seemed that she was wholly transformed into IESVS-CHRIST, her sweet spowse and Saviour.[153]

The heightened intensity of the passage for the Continental English recusants of 1609 draws our attention to God's conversation with the young Catherine as a mature adult, the mystical marriage that not only wed her to Christ but also transformed her *into* Christ; God is depicted as a gardener who brings buds, blossoms, and ripe fruit out of the root of his "little plant."[154]

Fenn's description of her early life also introduces the individual asceticism Catherine practices in terms that may have been particularly resonant to recusant readers. Her parents, disapproving of her decision not to marry and her cutting of her hair to discourage suitors, deny her the opportunity to pray privately. But Christ, "her chosen spowse," taught her "how she should buyld a secret chamber, or oratorie in her owne hart."[155] The lesson she learns from this, that the kingdom of God is inside her, she later teaches to the Raymond character in the same chapter: she warns him "that he should buyld a secret cell, or closet, in his sowle."[156] He sees, after some reflection, "what a goodlie thing it was, for a man to buyld a temple in his hart."[157] Readers either living in exile or worshipping in secret may well have found particular comfort in this pre-Reformation instance of successfully balancing exterior persecution and interior worship.

Catherine's Body and Mystical Gender

The importance of Catherine's marriage to Jesus is already clear in the early passages of the hagiography; indeed, her mystical marriage became one of the preferred moments in her life for iconographers. The *Life* regularly refers to her as Jesus's spouse, but the marriage scene itself is relatively brief, and even though in her letters Catherine famously claimed that Jesus uses his circumcised foreskin as a bloody wedding ring for us all, Raymond of Capua's version offers us a much more conventional choice of ring.[158] John the Evangelist and Saint Dominic arrive as witnesses; King David brings his psaltery to play "a heavenlie song of inestimable sweetnes." Beyond this emphasis on the approval of figures from the Hebrew Bible, the Gospels, and the mendicant movement, the setting also revels in the physical splendor of the wedding: Jesus himself places on her finger, for instance, "a ring, that was set about with fower precious pearles, and had in the other part, a mervelous ritch diamant."[159]

Whereas in Suso mystical marriage often is depicted as taking place between a male suitor and the female Jesus, Eternal Wisdom, the potential stability of the Catherinian marriage within a demonstrably heterosexual framework, however, is complicated considerably by several instances of gender fluidity—or what Richard Rambuss has called "gender undecidability"—in Catherine's *Life*.[160] The repeated emphasis on her vow of virginity and her association with pious widows might seem to enable a reading of Catherine as a stable site of fourteenth-century devout female gender norms—to be read forward as operative into the fifteenth and seventeenth centuries—but Catherine's gender is, in fact, rather flexible in different versions of the *Life* and other Catherinian texts. Jesus reminds her that even in her infancy, for instance, "thou haddest a desire to change thyne habite, and to clad thy selfe like a man, that thou mightest be received into the order of the Fryars Preachers" (Fenn 114). This process of gender fluidity and the masculinization of Catherine reaches a fever pitch in her letters, in which she describes the permanent, invisible wedding ring of Christ's foreskin: a physical unification of male and female flesh in a motif unique to Catherine.[161] Her body is joined with New Testament bodies in several other ways, as she becomes both a female apostle and, at times, a female Christ.

Miraculous transformations of Catherine's face occur in the *Life*. In the Fenn *Life*, the transformation of her gender is, in one instance, quite radical: she briefly *becomes* the male Christ. Raymond attends Catherine at her sickbed. As she discourses about her revelations, Raymond wonders to himself if it is all really true. "And with that, looking stedfastly vpon her, he sawe her face sodainly transfourmed into the face of a man: who likewise set his eyes stedfastly vpon him, and gaue him a meruelous dreadful looke. The face, that he sawe, was somewhat long: he shewed like a man of middle age: his beard was of the colour of ripe wheat, that is, betweene red and yallowe: his countenance was verie comelie, reuerend, & full of maiestie." Raymond is terrified, and cries out, wondering who it is that looks at him like this. "It is he (said she) that is. And with that she came againe to her owne fourme."[162] This dramatic moment (which concludes part 1 of the 1609 *Life*) displays a Catherine far more Christlike than is typically seen—even the stigmata she and Francis share in imitating Christ's suffering seem relatively tame in comparison.

This attitude toward gender is in part justified, however, by the text's emphasis on *God's* acknowledgement of God's own ultimate responsibility for whatever gender differences Catherine might imagine exist. Catherine questions her role in the Church, particularly how she "being a simple woman, be able to instructe wise and learned men" (Fenn 115). Jesus emphatically responds: "Who is he that created man & woman? Was it not I? . . . Can my power be limited, that I shall not dispose of man and woman, of learned and vnlearned, of noble and base according to my will?" (Fenn 115). Her own intensive fasting may well have led to amenorrhea, cementing the link between fasting and chastity while also emphasizing the possible disruptions of the putatively "natural" biological functions of gender: both God and humankind can alter aspects of their gender presentation. Gender reversal also appears in a famous letter recounting the execution of Niccolò: "Each principal in the letter undergoes a gender reversal: Christ becomes temporarily female and then male again, and Raymond and Niccolò are feminized for marriage to a male Christ."[163]

The fluidity of gender emphasized here finds a certain parallel in the bodily fluids exchanged between Catherine, God, and those in Catherine's care. Some of the most affectively intense passages of the *Life* demonstrate an understanding of bodies, human and divine, as interacting with one another via the ingestion of fluids, a liminal part of the body, both flesh and not-flesh. Catherine's care of the sick is treated at length in the *Life*, for instance; her attempts to overcome squeamishness around the stench of the severely ill is treated as a significant stumbling block in her path to the exercise of charity. In dressing an old woman's breast, oozing from a sore, and nearly vomiting from the smell of the pus, she castigates her flesh (in Fenn's version): "'Ah, wretched and caraine flesh, dost thou loath thyne even Christian? I shall make thee, not only to endure the savour of it, but also to receive it within thee.' With that she tooke all the washing of the sore, together with the corrupt matter and filth; and going aside put it all into cup, and drancke it up lustely. And in so doing, she overcame at one tyme, both the skeymishnes of her owne stomake, and malice of the Devel."[164] The passage in Wynkyn de Worde is quite similar, but changes the emphasis of her drinking slightly: instead of drinking it *lustely*, de Worde reports "she toke all the wesshyng of that wounde, with the matter and fylthe, and went asyde and dranke it of preuely. Whanne she hadde so do, all hir temptacyon of abhominacion cessyd."[165] The distinct furtiveness of the act in the de Worde text stands in contrast to the emphatic Fenn (even as, for both, the very gruesomeness of this scene's appearance in the narrative certainly must draw attention to the scene).

The very next night, this chapter reports, Jesus appears to her, pleased with her behavior, and repays her in an erotically charged scene: "he reached out his arme, and tooke her about the necke, and brought her mouth softely to the sacred wound of his side, and said unto her: 'Drincke daughter, drincke thy fill at the verie founteine of life.' . . . Then the holie maid set her mouth to, with great greedines, and drewe out of that founteine of everlasting salvation the licour of life. And so she continued sucking a good while, not only with the mouth of her bodie, but also (and that much more) with the mouth of her soule."[166] In the de Worde translation, the scene reads: "he helde hys arme of hyr necke and brought hyr mouth to hys blessyd wounde in hys syde and sayd to hir thus: 'Drynke, doughter, out of my syde the drynke of helthe.' . . . Thenne thys holy mayde sowked out of the pype of lyf comyng out of hys blessyd wounde wyth the mouth of hyr bodye, but moche more wyth the mouth of her sowle" (WdW 105). This exchange of fluids—diseased pus repaid with Jesus's delicious blood, straight from the source—heightens Jesus's femininity, as the side-wound becomes both surrogate breast, nursing Catherine, and a proxy for female genitals (medieval images of the birth of Ecclesia from the side wound make the connection most explicitly, but devotional images of the side-wound are also popular).[167] This moment of imbibing also gestures toward a scene in the *Orchard* and *Dialogue* in which the Soul drinks from a well that represents both love of God and love of neighbor; remaining in the well, the bucket holding this water-love does not empty. In that text the emphasis is on the interaction between social and divine love, but here in the *Life* the ingestion of these two liquids links service to others with an erotic divine reward even more definitively.

Even though Jesus's foreskin does not appear in the *Life*, the barriers between the bodies of Catherine and her divine spouse are nevertheless quite permeable. In the most emphatic demonstration of this, Jesus exchanges his heart with Catherine.[168] She prays in the words of David, "O God, create in me a cleane hart, and renue a right spirite in my bowels." Jesus then appears to her "and opened her lefte side sensible with this hand, and tooke out her hart, and so going his waie lefte her in deed without a hart."[169] She tells her confessor she no longer has a heart, and he laughs at her. After a few days, praying in a Dominican chapel, Christ appears to her again "holding in his handes a redde shinyng hart. . . . Then came our Lord vnto her, and openyng her side, put the hart, that he held in his hand into her bodie." The scar resulting from this surgery remains, and "manie of her sisters sawe it with their eyes"; the chapter ends with her changing the wording of a prayer from "Lord, I beseech thee, keepe *my* hart" to "Lord, I beseech thee, keepe *thy* hart."[170] Despite the new degree of interpenetration of Christ's body and Catherine's, her prayers to him change only a pronoun.

Along with the marital relationship between Jesus and Catherine (and Mary's concomitant role as mother-in-law), other familial relations with visionary characters also shape the depiction of Catherine's spiritual family. Mary Magdalene, for instance, becomes her mother.[171] In Fenn, we also find a detailed vision of Saint Dominic as God's Son, in a dual begetting of Jesus and Saint Dominic. She sees "how almightie God the Father brought foorth his coequal true Sonne (as it seemed to her) by his mouth. . . . She sawe likewise, how almightie God brought foorth the glorious patriarke Saint Dominicke, not out of his mouth, but out of his brest, environed round about with a mervelous goodlie light and brightnes."[172] A voice from God's mouth then tells her: "I have brought forth (as thou seest) these two sonnes, the one naturally, and the other by adoption. She was much amazed at the strangenes of that comparison, made betweene the Sonne of God and Saint Dominicke."[173] The comparison between natural and adopted son continues at length, emphasizing the equal importance of both sons to their divine Father.

Ultimately, Fenn's interest in Politi's early sixteenth-century rewriting of Catherine, and his production of the text for the nuns of Leuven, reveals a hagiographic aspect to English literary history that prizes the ongoing process of translating and adapting late medieval and early modern representations of holy women and their visions. Fenn's *Life* participates in the dialect between, as Jenna Lay puts it, "two literary histories:

One centered on a Protestant Queen as the principal maker within a nonetheless masculine poetic culture, and the other written through, against, and by women whose religious beliefs, geographical positions, and social standing have relegated them to the footnotes of literary criticism."[174] Fenn's *Life*, giving Catherine of Siena a voice, a substantial narrative, and a readerly community of early seventeenth-century English women, is a compelling part of this alternative literary history, connecting recusant readers to the spirituality of both late fifteenth-century London and fourteenth-century Tuscany.

POST-REFORMATION FATES:
APPROVED AND CONDEMNED

Catherine's life continued to provide visionary authority to post-Reformation Catholics, but in the works of some seventeenth-century Protestant polemicists she was represented as one of the most mistaken of the medieval mystics (along with Bridget of Sweden). Most famously, the vehement, almost hysterical denunciation of her visions in Edward Stillingfleet's *A Discourse Concerning the Idolatry Practised in the Church of Rome and the danger of Salvation in the Communion of it*, printed in London in 1671, singles her out for particular, repeated opprobrium. Bridget was attacked even more heavily, as Nancy Bradley Warren has shown, in part because of insular awareness of the continuing English Bridgettine community in Lisbon. In Thomas Robinson's salacious *The Anatomie of the English Nunnery in Portugal* (1622, and reprinted three times over the course of the following four decades), for instance, he hyperbolically claims "that Syon [Abbey] is characterized by female carnality, sexual corruption, and a tainted inheritance when he reports his discovery of the bones of nuns' illegitimate children enclosed within the nunnery walls."[175]

Warren also points out, however, that John Foxe's 1570 *Acts and Monuments* approvingly uses Bridget's criticism of clerical misbehavior to help demonstrate medieval awareness of the corruption of their own medieval Church.[176] This edition of Foxe, with heightened antipapal passages in the wake of Elizabeth I's excommunication, approvingly links Catherine to Bridget in their joint criticism of papal corruption.[177]

Decades earlier, Catherine and Bridget had been denounced for their political prophecies, as the dangers of political prophecy had been especially pressing in the 1530s. The Benedictine Elizabeth Barton's execution in 1534 (after time spent at Syon) for prophecies concerning Henry VIII's first remarriage demonstrates this, of course, most acutely.[178]

Attacks on Catherine of Siena recur regularly from a variety of Protestant authors, but perhaps her most ardent—yet conflicted—detractor was the dean of Exeter, Matthew Sutcliffe (1550?–1629). Jennifer Brown notes his approving use of Catherine as a fervid denouncer of clerical abuses; he also, however, points to her mystical marriage as a demonstration that any church that can support such a concept is "no mistress of truth, but of lies."[179] His approval of her criticism of corrupt medieval clergy continues in Sutcliffe's circa 1625 *The Blessings on Mount Gerizzim, and the Curses on Mount Ebal*: "Catherine of Siena (cap. 125) saith, that religious men, pretend Angels life, but for the most part are worse then diuels. . . . And againe: religious men are made the diuels instruments corrupting religion within themselues, and among their brethren, and without among lay men."[180] In the same work, he also catalogues secular authors alongside Bridget and Catherine, demonstrating the wide variety of pre-Lutheran authors he identified as rightly attacking corruption in the Church: "For the times before the yeare of our Lord 1500, I haue already alleaged the testimonies of Brigit, Petrarch, Catherine of Siena, Boccace, Breidenbach, Hugetin, Robertus Gallus, Math. Paris, and diuers others."[181] Where contemporary scholarship is often all too swift to separate literary from religious, Petrarch and Boccaccio from Catherine of Siena and Bridget of Sweden, Sutcliffe's scouring of Continental authors in search of any and all criticism of pre-Reformation clerical abuses recognized no such divisions.

In the final year of his life, Sutcliffe published another critique of Catholicism using a different passage from Catherine's *Dialogue*. Bishops, he writes, "should build the Church of God, but as Brigit saith, they build the diuel two cities. Catherine of Siena cap. 129 saith, that vnprofitable pastors do not driue the woolues from the sheepe: for that they want the dog of conscience, and staffe of iustice. She saith also, that they feed not their sheepe in the pastures of saluation, nor leade them the way of truth."[182] The "hound of conscience" motif, not found in other early modern English appropriations of Catherine, demonstrates ongoing readerly engagement with her texts: not content to simply draw

on extracts of her work, nor look to Foxe or other sixteenth-century Protestant uses of Catherine, Sutcliffe's reading in Catherine's *Dialogue* is
thorough and ongoing.

Beyond the weighty influence of the 1609 *Life* in promoting Catherine's life to recusants, brief references in support of various Catherinian
narratives are found elsewhere in recusant literature. Saint John of Ávila's
(ca. 1499–1569) main work, for instance, was translated into English and
published in Saint-Omer in 1620. *The Audi Filia, or A Rich Cabinet Full
of Spirituall Jewells* discusses her early home life:

> And remember that holy woman, *S. Catherine of Siena*, who was
> instructed by God; and whose life I desire that thou shouldst read;
> not to make thee couet her *reuelations*, but to breed in thee an imi-
> tation of her *vertues*. For although her parents, did hinder her in the
> way which she had taken, towards the seruice of God; she did neither
> trouble her selfe, nor abandon them. They cast her out of her little
> *Oratory*, where she vsed to performe her deuotions; and they ap-
> pointed her to serue in the Kitchin. But because she humbled her
> selfe, and obeyed them, she found God in the Kitchin, as well, or
> better, then in her Oratory."[183]

Her virtue is to be imitated, even if her status as a visionary authority is
treated more skeptically. Catherine's fame had reached the New World by
the middle of the sixteenth century: the hermit Gregorio López (1542–
96), born in Madrid, moved to Mexico and cultivated a life of piety and
seclusion. The life written about him by Francisco de Losa (1536–1624)
was translated into English and printed in Paris in 1638. It includes a
single mention of Catherine of Siena's theology of prayer: López "did
pray very earnestly for those that were in sin, and he said that this prayer
was very pleasing unto God, relating upon this occasion that which had
passed betwixt our Sauiour and saint Catherine of Siena, who praying
unto him instantly for those that are in mortall sin, heard from his divine
mouth: I intreat thee to pray unto me for them; and he was wont to repeate
those wordes with much tendernes and commiseration, when there was
occasion to talke of those that are in sin."[184]

Finally, the English Franciscan Benoît (or Benet) Canfield (1562–
1610, born William Fitch, in Essex), particularly significant for the early
modern reception of *The Cloud of Unknowing*, mentions Catherine of

Siena quite briefly in considering the limits of individual imitation of saints. *The Rule of Perfection* was printed in Rouen in 1609 (RSTC 10928.3) and reprinted, again in Rouen, in 1635 (RSTC 10928.6).[185] In a discussion of Saint Francis's care of lepers, he writes, "wee reade also of diuers Saints of both sexes, which did kisse and licke the sores and vlcers of poor men, though (perhaps) these examples be left vs rather to be admired then imitated except it be by like particular diuine inspiration: but although they doe not serue vs for imitation, yet at least may they suffice for condemnation of the delicat nicenesse, and also of the disdaine and hard heartednesse of those of this tyme, whoe can not abide to see them, much lesse assist them."[186] Although this male example of leper-kissing is the main instance Canfield refers to within the text, Catherine of Siena's name is printed in the margin as another significant and exemplary instance of this behavior.

Whereas in Suso we saw his appropriation by liturgists, and his diminished seventeenth-century afterlife (without any noticeable controversy) in the curious instance of Brathwaite's *A Spiritual Spicerie*, Catherine of Siena instead remained a potent symbol for both Catholic and Protestant writers of the virtues or fallacies of medieval visionary writing by women. Catherine's complex range of visionary authority, established with painstaking detail in the fifteenth-century in both Italy and, later, England, became instead a simplified symbol of fourteenth-century prophecy or clerical criticism. The Church and papal reform she so stridently fought for instead devolved into the type of bloodshed she had opposed in her letters to John Hawkwood, among others.[187] This sectarian fate befell both Catherine and Bridget of Sweden, but some late medieval works of devotion fared quite differently. In chapter 4, we will see the one work of late medieval piety that proved to have an unstinting afterlife of popularity among a wide variety of confessional audiences.

CHAPTER FOUR

Thomas à Kempis and
The Imitation of Christ

The Devotion of the Fifteenth-Century Low Countries and the Birth of Confessional Textual Criticism

The late medieval Low Countries play a far more prominent role in the history of trans-Reformation English literature than is often acknowledged. Often overshadowed by Francophone neighbors, the Netherlandish influence on English culture in many ways exceeded that of Germany or Italy. The fifteenth century was, in particular, deeply shaped by English connections to the Dutch literary world: important English texts from Caxton's translation of *Reynard the Fox* to the anonymous translation of the morality play *Everyman* were taken from the Dutch.[1] Jonathan Hsy's work on multilingualism and commerce in literature, too, has pointed out the significant Netherlandish and Hanseatic community living in late medieval London, finding the multilingualism of the poem "London Lickpenny" an especially illuminating example of the literary use of Dutch phrases in an otherwise Middle English poem.[2] England's trade relationship, particularly in wool and especially to Flanders and Brabant, made cities such as Bruges, Ypres, and Ghent part of a tightly knit, interdependent mercantile community;[3] English control of Calais from 1347 to 1558, indeed, made Flanders border English territory for centuries.[4] Intellectual and literary connections were numerous: one of the first datable instances of an English reader purchasing a printed book, for instance, took place in Bruges—John Russell (ca. 1430–94, lord chancellor 1483–85) bought a copy of Cicero's *De officiis*, printed in Mainz, on April 17, 1467.[5] Numerous post-Reformation recusant communities in the Low Countries would, beginning in the sixteenth century, lead to a significant presence of English religious well into the eighteenth century.[6]

The spiritual literature of the Low Countries proved especially significant over the course of the fifteenth and sixteenth centuries. The sole extant Middle English version of Suso's *Hundred Meditations on the Passion* was made from a Latin translation of Suso's German by Willem Jordaens (ca. 1321–81), Augustinian canon at Groenendaal, via a Dutch-language intermediary. *The Chastising of God's Children*, noteworthy for its use of both Henry Suso and Catherine of Siena, draws most heavily on Geert Groote's Latin translation of Jan van Ruusbroec's (1293–1381) Middle Dutch work of bridal mysticism, *The Spiritual Espousals*.[7] Similarly the *Treatise of Perfection of the Sons of God*, found uniquely in the Amherst manuscript (immediately following Julian of Norwich's short text), demonstrates an even keener English Carthusian interest in the varieties of Netherlandish mysticism: it renders, in Middle English, Jordaens's Latin translation of Ruusbroec's short Dutch treatise, *The Sparkling Stone*.[8] Nor were patterns of cultural transmission solely a process of English importation from the Continent. The German singer and composer Johannes von Soest (1448–1506), for instance, had a transformative artistic experience while working at the court of Cleves: after hearing English musicians performing for the first time, he follows them in awe to Bruges to study their distinctive vocal art.[9] Bruder Hans (fl. 1390–1400) also appears to have been associated with the court of Cleves some decades earlier, and employed a half-remembered London dialect of Middle English (alongside Latin, French, and German) in composing an intricate quadrilingual poetic expansion of the *Ave Maria*.[10]

From the perspective of the history of popular literature, however, the devotional culture of the Low Countries would prove to shape England most profoundly with the early fifteenth-century book of meditative exempla (more a work of wisdom literature than a guide to contemplation or Passion meditation), *The Imitation of Christ*, by the Zwolle Augustinian canon Thomas à Kempis (or Thomas van Kempen, ca. 1380–1471, originally Thomas Hemerken, from the small Westphalian town of Kempen).[11] The text was first translated into English anonymously in the middle of the fifteenth century, and although it had a limited manuscript circulation in England, in print it achieved rapid, unstinting success. It had early support at the highest levels of the aristocracy: Lady Margaret Beaufort, mother of the first Tudor king, is the first English translator of the text known by name; the text would also play a prominent role in the court of her grandson, Henry VIII. The lives of medieval saints and medieval prophetic texts remained largely (but not exclusively) the domain of Catholic readers after the Reformation, but the amphibious, seemingly immortal *Imitatio Christi* continued to be read, printed, and retranslated with exceptional frequency on either side of the confessional divide.

The text's extensive use of biblical quotations is often claimed to have been one of the keys to its enduring success, yet it still retained (for translators of many centuries) its roots in the fifteenth-century devotional culture fostered by the *devotio moderna* in the Low Countries.[12] Its Biblicism is treated as the main factor in its unmatched transconfessional popularity, but one would be hard-pressed to find many works of fifteenth-century piety *without* a roughly similar degree of quotation and stylistic influence from the Bible. Indeed, the text seems to have functioned in a liminal role: just biblical enough for its authority to persevere across denominational boundaries (and to justify the portions of the text in which Christ speaks extensively in the first person), but also definitively nonbiblical in its narrative structure and overall emphases, and thus more amenable to substantial emendation in translation. Even the Epistle of James, for instance, was never eliminated from the biblical canon (*pace* Martin Luther), but the entire fourth book of the four-book *Imitatio*, focusing on Eucharistic theology, was regularly omitted in Protestant translations of Kempis's text (or replaced with any of a number of other devotional texts).[13]

Many of the devotional motifs explored thus far in this book, which collectively help to define English popular spiritual literature of the late fourteenth and fifteenth centuries, can also be found (albeit in a reimagined form) in the *Imitation of Christ*, the medieval book that can claim the very first truly global audience in European literature.[14] An unparalleled success of devotional writing—in sheer numbers, the *Golden Legend* is its only real rival—it was only completed by 1427 (a holograph manuscript also survives from 1441),[15] and yet at least 848 manuscripts survive.[16] More than 745 editions are known to have been printed before

1650 (including 106 incunables), in at least fifteen European and Asian languages. Maximilian von Habsburg's recent catalogue, extending to 1650, lists 71 Dutch, 50 English, 112 French, 68 German, 110 Italian, 255 Latin, 56 Spanish, and 23 "miscellaneous" vernacular editions (Chinese, Croatian, Czech, Greek, Hungarian, Japanese, and Polish); a Welsh translation appeared in 1684.[17] After 1563, the *Imitation of Christ* could be found in two main Latin versions, and diverse English translations of this pair of texts were tailored to appeal to an ever-changing array of Protestant, Anglican, or Catholic audiences (and later, Puritan and Methodist readers). It was used by Franciscan and Jesuit missionaries around the world, with a translation into Japanese appearing by 1596; extracts from it were published in Tamil translation in 1832.[18] Its popularity has not diminished with time, and it seems to succeed in every possible literary sphere, including across the New World: it was translated into Nahuatl (Aztec) in 1570 and first printed in English in the Americas in Philadelphia in 1749.[19]

These networks of transmission and translation, astounding as they already are, of necessity cannot take into account the loss rate in early print: for incunable editions, this has been estimated at between 10 and 25 percent. One recent statistical analysis has proposed a 30 to 33 percent loss rate, if one includes in this overall rate an estimated 60 percent mean loss rate for broadside issues (the loss rate for folios, for instance, the authors only estimate to be 14 to 16 percent).[20] The survival of sixteenth-century editions, even if not as well studied or exhaustively catalogued, may not be drastically different. Franklin Williams, for instance, has found that roughly 15 percent of the printed books in divinity and science (i.e., nonephemera) recorded as having been seen or owned by the printer Andrew Maunsell in 1595 can no longer be traced in any surviving copies; Andrew Pettegree's study of twenty years of late sixteenth-century French books sold at the Frankfurt book fair found that about 10 percent cannot be traced to a single extant copy.[21] More comprehensive recent studies have suggested even greater loss rates, particularly for smaller, vernacular books.[22] In the case of a text reprinted as many times in the vernacular as the *Imitation of Christ*—and used primarily by devotional readers, not typically acquired by libraries or collected by connoisseurs in its early centuries—the chances of a stray edition simply falling through the cracks are, one would imagine, even higher still.

The Latin title varies across regions, too, making comprehensive manuscript or print counts similarly challenging (as does the long-running authorship dispute). Most Latin manuscripts of English provenance refer to it as the *Musica Ecclesiastica*, while "sixteenth-century Spanish readers of Kempis's *Imitatio* would have referred to this work as *Contemptus mundi.*"[23] In English translation, it appears most commonly as *The Imitation of Christ*, but is also given the titles *The Following of Christ* and *The Christian's Pattern* (or, in some of the few Middle English manuscripts, its insular Latin name, *Musica Ecclesiastica*). The general popularity of the text in Anglican, Protestant, and Catholic devotion continued unabated in more recent centuries: John Wesley translated the *Imitation* in 1735, leading to its widespread use among Methodists in the centuries to follow. In Victorian England, perhaps most famously, the book features prominently in George Eliot's *The Mill on the Floss* (1860): Maggie Tulliver's encounter with the text transforms her life.[24] Under a wide range of titles, and in a remarkable range of contexts and translations, it was, and remains, quite simply, an astonishingly successful book.

As Nandra Perry has written, the *Imitation of Christ* drew some of its effectiveness from the attempt to solve a linguistic paradox inherent in its very title, and echoed in the texts we have studied in previous chapters: can "human words imitate, perhaps even participate in, the miracle of signification made present in the living Word?"[25] The distinction between *imitating* Christ and *following* Christ, too, becomes a theoretical tension around which prefaces of the *Imitatio* regularly circle. These schools of devotional literature must always grapple with the intersecting challenges presented by linguistic representation writ large, the ethical goal of imitation of the God-man, and the thorny realm of biblical translation. Each contemplative author aims to create a text that can hope to contribute to a faithful reader's emotional experience of a truth that is, ultimately, biblical; the composition of each translation of the *Imitatio* addresses these literary and ethical issues anew (often quite directly in a translator's preface). What does it mean to attempt to imitate Christ in the fifteenth century, and what does it mean to write a contemplative guide instructing readers in the imitation of Christ? How were these ideals of imitation, and the modes of representation involved, in turn transformed during the confessional upheavals of the sixteenth and seventeenth centuries?

The history of texts promoting the imitation of Christ is, of course, almost as long as Christianity itself—beginning already in Saint Stephen's proto-martyrdom in Acts and subsequent late antique depictions of martyrdom (imitating the death of Christ) as a saintly ideal. The path to Calvary, in these instances, is the explicit model to be followed. But this quickly changed.[26] Imitation meant something quite different in Suso and Rolle, for whom causal exemplarity meant that their authorship and their textual presence as characters in their work provided a stimulus to the performance of devotion in the life of the reader (an imitation, however tempered, of the author-character and *their* imitation of Christ).[27]

In the culture of the Modern Devout, imitation of Christ was not defined by martyrdom, persecution, asceticism, or isolation, but rather a more generalized, interior sense of suffering coupled with intense humility and regular prayer. The literature most closely associated with the movement emphasizes contemplative interiority, vernacular paraliturgical prayer and song, and spiritual note-taking (in John van Engen's terms, a process of "examining the self, making progress, and experiencing peace"); Henry Suso was also, it bears mentioning, among their most frequently read authors.[28] Kempis's text, then, connects these common, shared interests with Christic imitation. The rhetorical style of the *Imitation of Christ* has also drawn significant commentary, particularly its likely origins in the spiritual note-taking practiced by members of the Modern Devout. David Harrap summarizes the output of this process neatly: "Kempis's audience placed greater value on sententious phrases than cohesive texts."[29] This textual culture, both individual and communal, centered on *rapiaria* ("personal collections of inspirational passages in which devout readers filled a quire with moving writings—dicta, memorable excerpts, or any other engaging paragraph")[30] and extended beyond textual devotion alone, however.

The interaction between musical and contemplative culture, for instance, was especially widespread among the Modern Devout. Their song collections, Ulrike Hascher-Burger has demonstrated, can in many instances best be interpreted as a musical analogue to the notebooks of the Modern Devout. She writes that "viewing the songbooks as *rapiaria* explains the striking mixture of disparate text types that is peculiar to some of them: inserted between songs are prayers, edifying legends, proverbs, and passages from the Bible . . . the result is a series of thematic blocks which served as the basis for individual meditative exercises."[31] The book known as *Zwolle VI*, for instance, a manuscript primarily of devotional Latin hymns, also contains both a sermon by Guerric d'Igny and a long excerpt from the *Imitatio Christi*.[32] Considering the extensive rhetorical ornamentation of the *Imitatio* alongside the interaction between song-texts and miscellanies, perhaps the rhythmic sententiousness of the *Imitatio* and its related texts can best be compared to the prose-poem of later literary movements.

The text's translation (or adaptation) from Latin to Latin in 1563 by Swiss reformer Sebastian Castellio gave it a unique status in post-Reformation Europe: a work of late medieval Netherlandish devotion treasured by Catholic readers, but a work of wisdom literature purged of medieval grammatical constructions, monastic terminology, and Catholic Eucharistic theology for evangelical readers and translators (Protestant translations in many languages, following Castellio's lead, simply omitted the fourth book, on the Eucharist). The history of the *Imitation of Christ* in England has an especially paradoxical relationship to its fifteenth-century genesis, however: its translators pay careful attention to disputes over its medieval authorship (it was regularly attributed to Jean Gerson for centuries) and its textual history (by examining and commenting in detail on Castellio's revisions of Kempis).[33] By doing so, they aim to establish each new translation as a uniquely authoritative, confessionally sanctioned, definitive English version of an unparalleled pan-European best seller, a process motivated by a complex network of theological, political, and commercial concerns.

THE *IMITATIO* IN FIFTEENTH-CENTURY ENGLAND

The manuscript context of the *Imitation of Christ* is relatively subdued in England, particularly in comparison to the success the text would have in the era of print. What is likely the first manuscript in England of the Latin text is found in Oxford, Magdalen College MS lat. 93.[34] Roger Lovatt notes that "the first English translation, which was undertaken during the middle decades of the fifteenth century, has survived in only four manuscripts . . . the English reputation of the *Imitatio* was essentially created by the successive editions which appeared from 1502 onwards."[35]

In stark contrast to the text's later treatment, none of the four surviving Middle English manuscripts has prefatory material; internal and scribal evidence links them strongly to Sheen, with one manuscript being copied at the request of Elizabeth Gibbs, the abbess of Syon.[36]

The four Middle English manuscripts present, however, a text that stylistically provides a close analogue to the Latin *Imitatio*: not only the content, but the form of Kempis's text was a part of its appeal to English readers from this first instance of its translation. Brendan Biggs concludes, for instance, that "in its vocabulary it is innovative without being slavishly Latinate; its syntax follows the Latin clause by clause but makes adaptations of individual constructions to English idiom where appropriate; and it reproduces many of the rhetorical figures present in the original."[37] From its first arrival in England, the most influential literary production of the *devotio moderna* was appreciated by readers and translators alike for both its content and style; the English translation helps to demonstrate the particular appeal of the rhetorical style of the Latin original to a new vernacular audience.

The treatment of sacred reading, for instance, demonstrates some of its effectiveness in guiding the contemplative efforts of its readers: "We owe as gladly to rede symple and devoute bokes as highe bokes and profounde sentences. Lete not þe auctorite of hym þat wryteþ, wheþer he be of grete lettur [o]r lytel, chaunge þi conceyte, but lette þe love of pure trouþe drawe þe to þe love of God. . . . Menne passeþ, but þe trowþe of our Lorde abydeþ euerlastingly. . . . Oure curiouste oftetymes in redinge of scriptures [deceyveþ vs], in þat we serche curiouse sentence where hit is to be passed over symply and not curiously enquered. If þou wolte drawe profite in redinge, rede mekely, simply, and truly, not desiringe to haue a name of kunnynge."[38] The text encourages appreciation of some of its own features: the personal authority of a particular author is to be ignored in favor of the eternal authority of God, while stylistic or rhetorical subtleties can distract readers whose souls need more simple or straightforward language. The fifteenth-century English translation is also notable for the number of emotional terms first attested to in the vernacular within: *anxietie, abjectely, imperturbable, subjective,* and *vilyfie,* among others.[39] It is the emphasis on this interior, emotional imitation of Christ that sets the text apart from earlier meditations on either the Passion or the life of Christ.

ATKYNSON AND BEAUFORT: PRINTING THE *IMITATIO* DURING THE REIGN OF HENRY VII

Lady Margaret Beaufort (1443–1509), mother of Henry VII, has attracted substantial critical attention for her position at the intersection of pious learning, the nascent printing industry, and political power (as the mother of the first Tudor king).[40] Her work as an author and translator began with a translation of book 4 of the *Imitation of Christ*; it was published by Richard Pynson in 1504, preceded by a translation of the first three books of the text by William Atkynson. Her interest in fifteenth-century Netherlandish devotion does not end with the *Imitation*, however. She also translated (again via a French intermediary) the Dutch Carthusian Jacobus de Gruitrode's *Mirror of Gold for the Sinful Soul*; it was first published in 1506 and reprinted three times after her death.[41] The Atkynson–Beaufort translation of the *Imitatio Christi* was reprinted four times between 1504 and 1519, the beginning of a quite complicated and truly expansive English tradition of printed translations of the text.

Brenda Hosington, describing Lady Margaret Beaufort's translations as "mirrors of practical piety," points out that one of the most significant omissions of Lady Margaret's translation of the *Mirror of Gold for the Sinful Soul* is the source-text's lengthy discussion of the human fetus's feeding on menstrual blood during pregnancy.[42] The grotesque depiction of an almost cannibalistic fetus also emphasizes, in the source-text, the magical and poisonous qualities of menstrual blood—mere contact with it, for example, can kill plants or prevent trees from bearing fruit. Some of the emphasis on the painful hideousness of pregnancy is included (perhaps especially apt given the very young age at which Lady Margaret gave birth to the future Henry VII); some of the rather baroque details the Dutch Carthusian associates with menstrual blood itself are omitted. Her translation of book 4 of the *Imitatio*, however, is especially noteworthy for a range of rhetorical effects—among them the repeated addition of first-person plural pronouns—which serve to create "a mood of greater intimacy and immediacy"[43] in the encouragement of a heightened affective response to the Eucharist.

Both the *Mirror of Gold* and the *Imitation of Christ* translations have been described by Stephanie Morley as instances of "compensatory power" in which Lady Margaret is able to "ventriloquize" male-authored texts in order to harness their preexisting authority during the first decade of the sixteenth century.[44] Rather than translation being pious busywork or the elaborate vanity project of a devout laywoman as she prepares her soul for death, these acts of translation instead give her the possibility to wield an authorial presence that fuses royal authority with the sophisticated devotional and textual authority of both the Modern Devout and Dutch Carthusians. The translation itself has recently been examined for its rich vocabulary and rhetorical elegance in rendering the French source-text into English prose; similarly, Lady Margaret's understanding of the Eucharistic theology and devotional psychology involved in the treatise demonstrates the "ease with which she makes sense through sounds, colouring and reshaping words to affect other people."[45]

RICHARD WHITFORD, THE WRETCH OF SYON, AND QUEEN KATHERINE PARR: THE *IMITATIO* FROM 1530 TO 1560

Richard Whitford (d. 1543?), the prolific author and self-styled "Wretch of Syon"—brother at the Bridgettine house of Syon Abbey until its dissolution—was long thought to have been the translator of a version of the *Imitatio* first published in 1531.[46] His authorship of the translation is uncertain, however, and may have been mistakenly attributed to him on the basis of a 1556 edition that names him as the translator of the *Golden Epistle* (printed there alongside the *Imitatio*).[47] Whether the 1531 *Imitatio* is Whitford's work or that of an unknown and anonymous author, this third translation of the *Imitatio* before the English break with Rome begins an extensive English tradition of substantial prefaces describing the choices made by the translation, justifying its position as a new vernacular *Imitatio*. In this instance, the translator's preface acknowledges the already existing translation of "famous clerke" William Atkynson and the "ryght noble & excellent princess Margaret." He points out, however, that Lady Margaret translated from a French translation of the Latin, and that the text of "the sayde noble pryncesse" regrettably "could not folowe the latyn so nyghe, ne so dyrectly, as if it had been translated out of Latyn."[48] The desire to hew closely and accurately to the Latin source-text—even as that very source-text will itself bifurcate early in the 1560s—will indeed be a recurring theme in future prefaces to the *Imitatio*.

Rather than put himself in the position of directly criticizing his monarch's grandmother in establishing his own text as superior in its faithfulness to the Latin, the translator equivocates. He does not list specific complaints about Lady Margaret's translation, claiming that his is translated directly out of Latin, "yet nevertheless it kepeth the substaunce & the effect of the first translacion out of french, though somtyme it vary in wordes, as to the reders wyll appere."[49] We might say the substance is the same, though the accidents vary considerably. In aiming to have his translation render the original more faithfully (the search for a purity of origins rather akin to that still found in many studies of transmission and translation today), he is able to claim to discard only minor aspects of Lady Margaret's literary accomplishment, just twenty years after her death. There is already the assumption, too, that some readers will be familiar enough with the Atkynson–Beaufort text to recognize and appreciate this gesture to fidelity. Maximilian von Habsburg points out, however, that the translation restores passages omitted by Atkynson: criticism of pilgrimage, miracles, monastic garb, and the external performance of devotion.[50] Florian Kubsch finds some persuasive evidence of an "enhanced Biblicism" in this pseudo-Whitfordian translation, but the claim that the *Imitatio* functioned in both this translation and the Atkynson–Beaufort translation primarily as a "proxy English Bible" is not altogether convincing given the radical differences, on nearly every level imaginable, between the Bible and the *Imitatio*.[51]

The popularity of the text, however, continued unabated, and the translation lived on in complicated ways, even in the dangerous decades just after the Henrician Reformation. On the one hand, it was reprinted by John Cawood during the reign of Queen Mary in 1556, and again in 1566 with a brief new preface (claiming that the *Imitatio* is one of a few dependable books of devotion which the Holy Ghost provided during a time of general ecclesiastical error), during the early years of Elizabeth's reign. The printer was again John Cawood, who managed to remain as joint royal printer, with Richard Jugge, until Cawood's death in 1572.[52] Soon, however, both pre-Reformation translations would be seen as in need of replacement: by 1575 the "Whitford" translation could only be printed by a secret English press. In 1585 it was firmly a recusant text, printed by a press in Rouen for predominantly Catholic readers.[53]

It survived in another form during and beyond the reign of Henry VIII, however. Just as translating a portion of the first printed *Imitatio* may

have been a source of proxy authority for Lady Margaret in the first decade of the sixteenth century, another royal woman turned to the *Imitatio*,
in this case the 1531 translation, in crafting a work of vernacular piety.
The body of Katherine Parr's *Prayers or Meditations* (first printed June
1545), as C. F. Hoffman first addressed, is (save its opening and concluding prayers) an abridgment of book 3, chapters 15–50, of the 1531 *Imitatio*.[54] Appearing in ten editions by 1559 (and reprinted as late as 1640),
Parr's text dramatically changes the *Imitatio*: not only compressing and
eliding passages, but recasting Kempis's dialogue between the soul and
Jesus as "a continuous prose meditation emphasising the inclusiveness
and universalism of the human yearning for spiritual redemption."[55] Janel
Mueller has examined the literary techniques employed in detail, concluding: "From the densely scriptural weave of the original *Imitatio* she
consistently selects lyric and affective verses couched in the first person
(or restyles them in this form). The result is to center her abridgment of
Whitford's version in a degendered, generically human speaker."[56]

Parr's *Prayers or Meditations* (and her earlier translation of John
Fisher) balanced ambiguously between conservative and evangelical religion.[57] In a detailed study of the rhetorical effects of Parr's text,
David Harrap writes that "the non-determinacy of the *Prayers* ultimately
demonstrates the extent to which the text was incomplete until actual-
ised by performance," concluding that Parr is participating in a mode of
authorship in which "rather than creating a radical new symbolic structure, evangelicals were able to assign new meanings to the compunctious
emotional scripts of *Imitatio*."[58] This "transformative intertextual appropriation" of Kempis via Whitford (or Pseudo-Whitford) was clearly cele-
brated in the Henrician court: it was even translated into Latin, Italian,
and French by the twelve-year-old future Queen Elizabeth at the end of
1545 as a New Year's present to the king and queen.[59]

EDWARD HAKE, THOMAS ROGERS, AND
SEBASTIAN CASTELLIO: A PROTESTANT *IMITATIO*
AND CONFESSIONAL TEXTUAL CRITICISM

The first two definitively post-Reformation English translations of Thomas
a Kempis's *Imitatio Christi*—those of Edward Hake (1568) and Thomas
Rogers (1580)—both depend not only on the original Latin text of Thomas à

Kempis, but also on the revised, classicized and Protestantized *De Imitatione Christi* (first published in 1563) of Sebastian Castellio (1515–63).[60] The English authors evince a deep-rooted anxiety about the status of their translation project—they must, on some level, be hostile to a Catholic past that includes their very source-text, yet they abandon neither classical learning nor patristic authority in creating their translations. And although Castellio, Hake, and Rogers all join with Kempis in establishing Christ as the ideal imitative model, the three post-Reformation writers nevertheless find themselves, almost inevitably, developing a weighty mediating hierarchy as both translators and authors. They create intricate texts that must balance themselves carefully between scripture, Kempis, and the demands of the Protestant reader.[61]

These and subsequent translations all include detailed prefaces by the translators, demonstrating a consistent, peculiar form of what I term "confessional textual criticism" brought to bear on the text (which might be seen as a particularly textual and post-Reformation subset of devotional cosmopolitanism). Each new English translator, rather than dismissing the text's medieval roots and relying wholly on Castellio's new Latin version, instead emphasized his careful study of the differences between the Latin texts of Castellio *and* Thomas à Kempis, correcting previous translators—and Castellio himself—for the sake of accuracy (or the perception of accuracy) in their translations. Demonstrating a profoundly uneasy tension between respect for the fifteenth-century text and its author, on the one hand, and, on the other, a need to interrogate and correct passages that conflicted with their preexisting understanding of a "proper" imitation of Christ for a Protestant audience, these new generations of sixteenth-century translators evince a more ambivalent, nuanced understanding of fifteenth-century Catholicism and its most universally popular text than is conventionally thought.

Castellio's belief in reason as an eternal and preexisting aspect of humanity might have helped him see the transhistorical value of Kempis's text; that is, despite its fifteenth-century roots, the text's combination of Biblicism and interior piety may have struck him as valuable evidence of human reason helping to produce pre-Reformation, postbiblical Christian truth.[62] Castellio's complicated work of translation not only draws on the Latin of Kempis, however, but also on an anonymous 1551 translation of Kempis into German, printed in Zurich (Castellio was also interested in possible contributions to the English Reformation beyond the *Imitatio*—in 1551 he dedicated his translation of the Bible into classical Latin to King Edward VI).[63] In the preface, Castellio "invokes the censoring (he calls it 'castration') of a classical author for a precedent."[64] The censorship of the *Imitatio*, however, is both theological and linguistic; it was perhaps a textual castration too radical for many of his later translators because English Protestant vernacularizations of the Castellio text would repeatedly compare his work to the original fifteenth-century text in establishing new versions of the *Imitatio* for sixteenth- and seventeenth-century reformed readerships.[65]

Hake's title page immediately emphasizes these sources: it was "at the first written by Thomas Kempise a Dutchman, amended and polished by Sebastianus Castalio, an Italian, and Englished by E. H."[66] The preface of Hake's translation, dedicating it to the Duke of Norfolk, aims to justify the new translation. By way of explanation, he claims that "no difficult questions at all are pursued (I meane in matters of religion), yet ghostly instructions and right Godly lessons at large are dilated: knowledge of letters and literall sense, therein so much is nothing supported, as amendement of life & manners advanced."[67] Highlighting its lack of interest in doctrinal questions—perhaps especially appropriate in this decade following the Elizabethan Settlement—Hake hastens to emphasize its straightforward use in the pragmatic advancement of moral virtue; rather than stoking controversy, this preface attempts to sell the book's benefits to readers of any potential sectarian commitment. The dedication to Norfolk is then followed by an address to the reader:

> Thou hast here (gentle Reader) the pathway to perfit lyfe, vnder the tytle of *The Imitation of Christ*, whose footesteps if thou follow, thou canst neuer go astray, for he is the *way,* the *truth,* and the *life.* Learne here wyth Christ to contemne the worlde, learne his modestie, his meekenesse and humilitie. In doctrine, learne his synceritie, simplicitie & veritie. Learne his loue & vncomparable charity. And to conclude, learne to beare thine owne Crosse after Christ manfully. This shalt thou soone learne to doe, if thou canst once become humble in thine owne eyes.[68]

Humility is the most essential virtue in this address, and although doctrine makes an appearance here, it is stripped of any real denominational content, summarized instead as "sincerity, simplicity, and verity."

Within fifteen years, however, Thomas Rogers (d. 1616) would criticize Hake's text as insufficiently de-Catholicized; in 1580 he published a translation of Castellio–Kempis that would prove far more popular over the following decades. Seth Lerer has written that the errata sheets in early print demonstrate a new cultural understanding of—and structural procedure for dealing with—error. The mechanical reproduction of texts changed the way in which errors are seen, recognized, categorized, and emended (and the way in which academic selves were imagined as eradicators of error). It is in the preface to Rogers, however, that we see the birth of confessional textual criticism in the English translations of Kempis. One finds in this a process similar to Lerer's examples of the errata sheets in which he sees "the need to narrativize the story of . . . errors—to offer up a personal history of detection and correction," which in turn "makes the true subject of the early humanist book not so much its content but the complex relationships between textual and political fealty that write the history of its own production."[69] In writing of Tyndale's 1526 New Testament, for instance, the errata slips detail a wide range of errors; here the errata sheets are "the place where the past is publicly brought into line with the present, where errors of all kinds could be confessed and corrected. To explore the early history of these sheets is to explore the loci of authority and action that make academic life both a performance and a defense."[70] In the case of the *Imitation of Christ*, the dedicatory epistles and translators' prefaces offer a site for a quite similar variety of error-seeking in the construction of a sixteenth-century vernacular text that situates itself between its two sources, one Catholic and one Reformed.

Most straightforward of Rogers's changes when compared to Hake are the excisions of some potentially unacceptable terms and the inclusion of hundreds of marginal notes indicating scriptural quotations or parallels. In the chapter on solitariness and silence, for instance, Hake writes of a "cell or closet" in which one prays and avoids temptation. Rogers, uncomfortable with the monastic resonance of "cell," writes, "For commonlie thou shalt finde that in thy closet, which thou wouldest leese abrode. The more thou vsest thy closet, the more thou wilt like it: the lesse thou comest thereinto, the more thou wilt loath it."[71] David Crane points out that Hake's sentence "I say, there is no man lyuing voyde of all calamitie and traueyle: no not the King, no not the Pope himselfe" becomes in Rogers the moderately more anti-Catholic "man is not without miserie and troble, no not a King, nor the proud Pope himselfe."[72] Rogers also omits terms that potentially might resonate as Catholic but that are found in Hake: *vocation, congregation,* and *intercession* (but not *Superior, confession, Obedience,* and *Rule,* as Crane claims—these are found in both, and *Purgatory* is found in neither).[73]

Rogers's preface grants us a particularly clear perspective on the process of the confessional textual criticism he engages in: a complicated process of denuding a fifteenth-century text of its Catholic particularities, even in the process of attempting to rectify the perceived failure of an earlier coreligionist's attempt. David Harrap describes this process of emendation as a part of a project of "a Protestant 'myth of eternal return'" in which translators aimed for "the recovery of a valid text from a papist original [which] was conceptually enabled by the trans-historical working of the Spirit in both author and interpreter."[74] The *Imitatio,* then, was a text Castellio, Hake, and Rogers all sought to "liberate" from its status as a fifteenth-century text, representing it to their readers as part of a hidden proto-Protestant textual heritage beyond scripture (even as Hake and Rogers disagreed on the level of fidelity one should have toward the original text). This conception of the (potential) purity of some pre-Reformation texts, however, does not wholly account for the concern with the possibility or necessity of imitation the translators espouse, nor the careful way in which they explicitly negotiate between their own recovery of the text and the ways in which previous translators (from Castellio on) had done so.

Rogers's version begins with a translator's preface, for instance, which issues this opening salvo: "Who entereth into a due consideration of mans nature, shal easilie perceave that most stranglie it is addicted unto Imitation; and, though in truth, we should live by lawes not by examples, that examples doe more move than doe lawes."[75] Servants, soldiers, and subjects are cited as the best instances of this; he takes this to indicate that those who are imitated must be especially careful in their actions, citing Cicero's maxim on judicial malfeasance and the book of Wisdom's claim that "the mighty will be mightily punished." These claims to a universal human trait of "strange addiction" to imitation, coupled with marginal notes referring to Jerome, an apocryphal book of the Old Testament, and the pre-Christian Cicero, set a pattern that will continue in the preface: a methodological eclecticism that looks well beyond Protestant Biblicism for its authorities. Not in itself exceptional, there is also an undertone of discomfort in this preface, tempered by a grudging respect of the rhetorical and ethical efficacy of the *Imitatio*. A partial resolution is found in the references to the two key sources of pre-Christian wisdom: the Old Testament and the classical heritage. By emphasizing the need for upstanding textual exemplars in both cases, Rogers tacitly acknowledges that this approach to authorities applies to the Catholic past, but he can invoke this and still avoid direct reference to the conditions of his source-text's fifteenth-century composition.

We are then told that the following of a bad exemplar does not excuse sinfulness in the imitator, and that care must be chosen in our choice of model for imitation:

> The precept therefore which is giuen to an imitator of Orators, I could wish were folowed of a Christian Imitator. In oratorie imitation two sortes of examples there be: one alwaies, and most necessarie to be folowed, the other but sometime and in somethings. The example <u>alwaies</u> necessarilie to be folowed of an Orator is among the Graecians Demosthenes, Cicero among the Latins: they who are but <u>sometime</u>, and in <u>some things</u> to be followed, are Poëts and Historiographers.[76]

These examples are particularly notable in their reach to the classical past as an age of possible virtue as yet untainted by Catholicism. Indeed, in his 1589 *Historical Dialogue touching Antichrist and Poperie*, Rogers spends a good deal of time, Habsburg writes, "ridiculing the notion that any resemblance existed between Christ and Saint Francis"—the single saint mentioned by name in the *Imitatio*.[77] The universality of imitation as a mode of ethical behavior is here given an emphatically classical (and even universal) heritage *before* it is given a Christian one.

In next turning to the Bible, however, the models of imitation proposed become still more muddled—some biblical models, indeed, are worthy to be followed in some instances but not in others. We are told that Abraham's faith, Joseph's chastity, Tobias's mercy to the poor, and David's zeal are all worthwhile exemplars for the particular virtues associated with them. On the other hand, David's adultery, Moses's and Aaron's incredulity, Peter's denial of Christ, and the undefined "ambition" of the apostles are all included in the Bible as negative examples. These instances of vice were put in the Bible with four chief goals in mind: first, to show us that all sin, even "the elect" (thinking otherwise, Rogers remarks, has been a sadly overprevalent notion); second, to inspire us to greater care in our own lives (frailer as they are than those of great biblical patriarchs); third, to teach us not to despair in our sinfulness; and fourth, to show examples of God's mercy (and thus to inspire us to similar acts of mercy).[78] In some few instances, however, Rogers then indicates that biblical example is not to be followed in *any* circumstance: the circumcision of male children, blood sacrifice, and marrying the widow of one's brother are all now uniformly an "offence to God." And other deeds are classified as "singular"—that is to say, we may not imitate them today "without the special and extraordinarie motion of the holie Spirit."[79] The only two examples given of this category are Abraham's readiness to kill Isaac and the plundering of the Egyptians' silver and gold by the Jews as they fled captivity.

With this, Rogers then returns to the third of three epigraphs from the frontispiece: Paul's complicated, mediated command from 1 Corinthians ("Folowe me, as I folowe Christ"). Rogers here paraphrases it in a concise encapsulation of its troublesome ambiguity: based on the preceding biblical examples, particularly the final pair, he writes, "it is apparent that good men are not in al things to be imitated. But as S. Paule would be so folowed, as he folowed Christ, so should they be."[80] Paul is the model to be followed, and the model for how we should follow other good men, who should be followed insofar as they followed Christ. This is scriptural support of a sort, to be certain, but one far more convoluted than the epigraph that precedes it on the frontispiece: Mark 8:34, "Whosoeuer wil folowe me, let him forsake himselfe, and take vp his crosse, and folowe me." He does go on to explain that following Christ is proper because both Christ and his apostles "have commanded us to do so," but the rhetorical effect is a jarring series of transitions from classical rhetoric, to biblical examples both positive and negative, to Paul's admonition to follow him in the following of Christ. Rogers develops a framework that will persist throughout his translation: a hierarchical model of imitation melding both classical and Christian that aims to provide an unmediated connection between Christ and the contemporary Christian, yet cannot but gradate that connection, recognizing its mediatedness through multiple, overlapping layers of text, tradition, and language.

The possibility of our imitation of Christ is thoroughly qualified, analyzed, and dissected. For he immediately follows the mention of the command of Christ and his apostles to follow him with this skeptical gesture: "But here mistake me not, I beseech you. For albeit I saie our Sauior Christ is alwaies; yet do I not saie in al things: and though necessarilie to be folowed; yet not as he was God."[81] Christ as God fasted forty days, commanded the waves to cease, walked on water, and fed 5,000 men (besides women and children), and so on. These are all, Rogers writes, "unimitable (as I maie saie) of mortal man." In fact, he continues, those who try to imitate Christ in his divinity "offend greatlie, whether they do it of superstition, as Papists; or of meere zeale, as did the God of Norweigh."[82] Not only is imitating Christ impossible in many instances, but even when it is, some aspects of imitating Christ are forbidden (the Catholics, in presuming to replicate the Last Supper in the Mass; the God of Norway apparently was a charismatic figure who fasted for forty days). He continues, "we are not commanded to make a new world, to create things visible or inuisible; no nor in the world to do miracles, and to raise the dead, said Augustine, and so do I."[83] Just after the text's first mention of the errors of papists comes the first reference within Rogers's preface to an authority figure both nonbilical and nonclassical. Augustine here serves to buttress Rogers's already potent qualification of the forms of the imitation of Christ to be aimed for, even as it brings up the specter of the centuries of Catholic past being abrogated in the attempt to follow Christ and Christ alone. He concludes: "He that loueth and hateth what Christ as a God, doth loue and detest, imitates Christ as much as man maie imitate God, he that doth that which Christ did as a man, doth folowe Christ as a Christian should."[84] One imitates Christ's divine nature simply in adopting his judgments (but Rogers leaves open the vexing question of what precisely Christ-as-God loves and hates); inspiring and guiding the imitation of Christ's humanity is the chief goal of the text to follow.

With the models for Christian imitation thus delineated and qualified, Rogers turns again to the nature of imitation itself. Why exactly should one imitate Christ? Rogers writes:

Partlie for that he is our God. Therefore is it our partes to imitate
him, whome we worship and serue. Partlie, because we are by nature giuen to imitation. Wisedome would therefore we should imitate the best. And partlie because we are Englishmen, who of al other
people are most famous, and infamous too for imitation. A shame
were it therefore for vs to imitate so painefulie as manie do in eloquence Cicero; in philosophie Aristotle; in lawe Iustinian; in Physick
Galen for worldlie wisedome; yea to imitate, as most do, the French
in vanitie, the Dutch in Luxurie, in brauerie the Spanish, the Papists
in idolatrie, in impietie and al impuritie of life the Atheists, and not
to folowe our Sauior Christ in heauenlie wisedome, and in al godlines of manners.[85]

A return to the opening, with its claim that imitation is universally found,
inherent in human nature, is now expanded and redefined: imitation of
classical figures, first described in the opening paragraph as an analogue
for Christian imitation, is now dismissively linked in parallel formation
with comically negative national and religious stereotypes. Demosthenes
has now fallen away, as have the poets and historiographers of the earlier passage.

There then follows a second prefatory epistle in which Rogers discusses his choices as translator, beginning by mentioning the justification
for Castellio's own Latin-to-Latin translation of the *Imitatio*. Neither Castellio's Latin nor this new English translation are produced for novelty's
sake, but rather they stand in a great tradition of the textual criticism of
classical works—and even the Bible itself. Humanist scholarship, he
maintains, has provided humanity with "sundrie and diuers interpretations
of the workes of *Aristotle*, and *Plato* for philosophie; of *Demosthenes*
and *Isocrates*, for Oratorie; of *Galen* and *Hippocrates*, for Physick; for
Diuinitie of the sacred Bible." He goes on to explain his improvements
upon the text proper: because previous translations were not sufficiently
rigorous in their use of scripture, he has included both relevant scriptural
quotations and citations to chapter and verse. This, of course, raises the
question at the heart of a great deal of devotional literature, but especially
those works praised for their biblicism in an era of widespread scriptural
translation—why not simply read the Bible instead? This is not, indeed,
directly addressed, but the overall method is to create an *Imitatio* that

replicates as much of the Bible as possible even as it presents a text compiled in the fifteenth century. Rogers explains that his method has been to use scripture whenever possible to replace the source-text, eliminating whatever novel phrases he can in favor of scriptural ones; he claims that it is a commendation to do so, equivalent to how the most devout of Ciceronians treat phrases of Cicero's. A methodology, that is, forged in imitation of the most zealous of neoclassical rhetoricians.

He then details Hake's mistakes, citing first Castellio's Latin and then Hake's translation thereof. The first example is a mention of the sign of the cross being in heaven, which, Rogers reports, "for somuch as I see neither the Scripture, nor any <u>good</u> writer doth confirme the same, I haue left out altogether"—an abrupt dismissal of his immediate predecessor in translation, but even more so of Castellio and his project.[86] The second is also a mention of the cross: "Naie thou shalt not feare the enimitie of the Diuel neither, if thou be armed with faith, and marked with the crosse of Iesus." Rogers comments, "What needes these words, *And marked with the crosse of Iesus?* I haue therefore not mentioned them." The third difference Rogers points to is a mention of merit. Hake's text reads: "*Neither is our merit, and the comming forward in our dutie consisting in plentie of pleasures and comfortes, &c.*" Rogers writes, "I haue thus Englished, *Neither doth our comming forward consist in the stoare of pleasures, and comfort, &c.* leauing out the worde <u>merit</u>. Because both the scripture is cleene against our meriting, and the Autor too in manie places condemnes the same," offering a note for the curious, or skeptical reader: "[Note: As most principalie in the third boke chap. 26, cha. 52, pag. 227, chap. 58.]."[87] The precision this offers may preempt criticism of his changes, but it also draws the reader's attention immediately and directly to these very alterations and their locations.

The final change removes a reference to the location of the justified before the Passion, doing away with the harrowing of hell and limbo at once. If the justified were not in heaven, Rogers comments, "Where then were they? In hel? I thinke none wil saie it. In Abrahams bosome, as some, in *Lymbo patrum*, as other Papists do saie? but that wil not easilie be proued. Wherefore as that which otherwise might offend the godlie, I haue cleane omitted, & left out that sentence."[88]

Deletion of the offending sentence avoids the debate, on some level. Of course, he has instead (in this preface, at least) highlighted them, both pointing out the four greatest failings of Castellio's translation even as he grants them a privileged position in the preface of his book, a contradiction highlighted by his subsequent mention immediately hereafter that he has "added some godlie sentences, which haue bene omitted both by *Castellio*, and such as folowed him." He cursorily gives the reader their chapter and location in the book, without any explanation or emphasis on the importance of their reinclusion, perhaps out of a desire to minimize further mention of the text's history *before* Castellio's revision.

And yet for all this, Rogers is largely sympathetic to the Catholic past and its texts: in justifying his notes, he heads off criticism by comparing them to those of Erasmus, and claims that there "were other bookes, that I could name, excellent for manie good points, yet for some things superstitious, purged and corrected, sure I am, both God would greatlie like thereof, and manie man would reade them, who now reject them; and much profit would be reaped, whereas now there is either litle or no profit at al taken."[89] Just a slight dose of improvement and emendation is necessary to bring these old, neglected texts into profitable circulation. The opinions of the imagined Protestant reader are influenced not by the origin of the devotional text nor by its potential doctrinal implications, but rather a few unfortunate (and easily altered) words or phrases.

Despite the significant attention given to classical models in this preface, the significance of the Catholic heritage is not altogether effaced, even as he recreates aspects of the hierarchical relationship between man and God that many Protestants had believed themselves to have fought against. Since Paul, that is, the idea of imitating Christ is something that can only ever be done with several intermediaries: Paul, patristic authority, textual interpretation, translatorial intervention, marginal annotation, and so forth.[90] Indeed, most of Rogers's hostility is directed toward contemporary Catholics, rather than the Catholic past writ large—he amply cites sources both patristic and medieval. The very title page of Rogers's translation acknowledges its Catholic and Latin heritage: "Of the imitation of Christ, three, both for wisdome, and godlines, most excellent bookes; made 170 yeeres since by one Thomas of Kempis, and for the worthines therof oft since translated out of Latine into sundrie languages by diuers godlie and learned men: now newlie corrected, translated, and with most ample texts, and sentences of holie Scripture." The three books, however, would—in recognition of the original four-book structure of the

Kempis text—become four. In 1592 his translation added a translation of Kempis's *Soliloquium animae* as a fourth book, transforming "Kempis into a would-be Protestant" and endorsing the text's "doctrinal purity, authorizing Kempis as suitable reading for Protestants."[91] Despite the multiple prefaces detailing his method of revising, refining, and purifying the text for the late sixteenth-century reader, the four-book structure of the original—and the implicit authority of Kempis himself in providing pious reading material for Protestant readers—would be restored.

BEYOND ROGERS: EARLY MODERN IMITATIONS

The late sixteenth-century success of Rogers's text did not dissuade future authors from translating the *Imitatio*, however. Moreover, it encouraged other non-Catholic writers to appropriate Catholic texts, purging and rewriting them in imitation of the process employed by Castellio and Rogers. Accounting for the entirety of the translated theology of the late sixteenth and early seventeenth centuries, of course, would be considerable. Jaime Goodrich, in exploring the gendering of translation in the period, also notes that "Protestant translators working with Catholic texts claimed authorial agency even more openly by taking advantage of the gatekeeping aspect of translation"—that is, they carefully sculpted early modern, medieval, and patristic sources into agreement with Protestant doctrine as they translated them into English.[92]

Only four years after Rogers's first *Imitatio*, indeed, the moderate Puritan rector Edmund Bunny (1540–1619), former fellow of Merton College, recognized the significance of the model of the textual emendation employed in the Rogers/Castellio/Kempis *Imitation of Christ*. Reading *The Book of Christian Exercise* (1582) by the English Jesuit Robert Persons (1546–1610), Bunny found its impressive rhetoric and finely tuned prose style too difficult to resist. He rewrote the Jesuit work (which had been imagined, in part, as a polemical overture to wavering Christians in England), taking out or altering whatever he found inappropriately Catholic or insufficiently biblical, thus both creating and plagiarizing a tremendously popular spiritual guide for domestic, nonrecusant consumption. Bunny's text went through thirty editions from 1584 to 1630, and six editions of an abridged version.[93] In the preface, Bunny describes his process of de-Catholicizing as a devout imitation of the precise form of emendation both Castellio and Rogers performed on Kempis:

> For whereas it may be the perswasion of some, that no such worke as is at the first so corrupt in it selfe, should be brought foorth to light by any of us, though never so warily we purged it before. . . . In which kinde of labour, as *Castalion* first, then also Maister *Rogers* have done very well, in that little booke of *Kempicius*, that is called *The Imitation of Christ*, leaving out the corruption of it, and taking onely that which was sounde.[94]

The purging and refining of texts both medieval *and* contemporary—Augustinian and Jesuit—is treated as equivalent in the approach described here. In this "almost unique opportunity to study the meeting point of Roman Catholic and English Protestant in the reign of Elizabeth"[95] we find the emendation of *Kempis* cited as the methodological inspiration for the successful attempt to redirect a work of Jesuit piety to insular, Puritan ends.

As Brad Gregory notes, although Bunny "deletes points of controversial doctrine, biblical exegesis, and specific Catholic practices, he retains fundamental practical admonitions about the sort of attitude Christians ought to have and the type of life they ought to lead."[96] Bunny approves of the program of providing precise Christian truths initiated in Persons's text. Yet Bunny elaborates: Persons "desireth al, though they dissent from him in religion: yet laieng aside hatred, malice, and wrathful contention, to join togither in amendment of life, and in praieng one for another. Which we might have hearde in his own words, but that he interlaceth other things withal, that I dare not in conscience and dutie to God commend unto thee."[97] This near approval of a lengthy Jesuit treatise demonstrates some of the malleability possible between factions at a time when the bulk of confessional polemic, Catholic and Protestant alike, tended toward some of the most hyperbolic demonization imaginable. Bunny then discusses the sources drawn on in the text: scholastic authors writing persuasively on the reformation and improvement of life are all the more important as examples insofar as they lived in the "corrupter time of the church."[98] As Victor Houliston argues, however, imagining Bunny as a thoughtful ecumenist was the last thing on Persons's mind when news came of Bunny's version of his text.[99] Persons quickly published a vitriolic complaint of Bunny's theft of his text, to which Bunny responded with *A briefe Answer unto those idle and frivolous quarrels of R. P. against the late edition of the Resolution* (1589).[100] The dispute continued to be discussed in the prefaces to editions of the text as late as 1619, the year of Bunny's death, and nine years after Persons died.

This was not the only work of Persons's, nor the only Jesuit text, to be used for Protestant ends: Nancy Bradley Warren mentions the use of Persons's *Conference* by Oliver Cromwell's publicist, Henry Walker, writing of the utter incongruence of the Jesuit text on "the divine legitimacy of a Catholic monarch being turned to Republican ends."[101] And the prefatory material to a 1633 English edition of *A Paradise of Prayers* (a translation of Louis of Granada) includes a dedication to the sheriff of London, Hugh Perry, claiming that the translation has taken off the "Spanish habit" of these meditations and prayers, and replaced them with "English attire"—and that the resulting text is not "a popish relique, but as a precious Iewell of inestimable price and valew."[102] Alison Shell notes that Louis of Granada's "highly affective approach to prayer made him one of the most popular devotional writers in Tudor and Stuart England," published (and plagiarized) by Catholic and mainstream presses alike.[103]

Bunny found Kempis's treatment in the latter half of the sixteenth century a methodological inspiration for his own authorial program of turning Jesuit texts to Protestant ends, but Lady Grace Mildmay (1552–1620) instead saw in Kempis's devotional method and authorial style a rich model for personal, private imitation.[104] She is best known today for the autobiographical section of her manuscript, and her intellectual and devotional life was deeply shaped by Kempis; her most prized books, given to her by her mother, were the Bible, Foxe's *Acts and Monuments*, Wolfgang Musculus's *Common Places*, and the *Imitatio Christi*.[105] Lady Grace praised the *Imitatio* "for containing a 'true and lively description & difference betwixt the flesh and the spirit' and offering a 'direction of lyfe and good conversation.'"[106] She adapted the book, drawing on its style of compilation and commonplacing, allowing her to speak in a scriptural voice. Female poets in the period often "figure God as husband, their poems as offspring, and their godly 'motions' as the movements of the child in the womb, but Mildmay characterizes her meditations instead as love tokens. God is a spiritualized lover who bestows meditations as favors or pledges that are tokens of his presence."[107] This private work of devotional writing, imitating both style and content of the *Imitatio*, is further testament to the ongoing appeal of Kempis's text across seventeenth-century English culture.

Despite the continued success of Rogers's edition among Protestant readers, new translations of the *Imitatio* appeared throughout the seventeenth century, including two metrical versions, inspired by a 1651 French verse translation, in the second half of the century.[108] The Whitford translation was reprinted for recusants for much of the sixteenth century, but it was replaced in 1613 by Anthony Hoskins, S.J. (Saint-Omer, 1613), with a translation dedicated to Elizabeth Vaux.[109] This translation was reprinted a number of times between 1636 and 1687 by Protestant and Catholic plagiarizing "translators" printing in Paris, Oxford, Cambridge, London, Rouen, and Antwerp.[110] The 1640s and 1650s also saw a remarkable expansion in a variety of medieval Continental mystical material translated for the first time into early modern English.[111] Perhaps most remarkably, 1653 saw the posthumous publication of a number of John Everard's (ca. 1582–1640/41) sermons as *Some Gospel-Treasures Opened*, a particularly surprising publication given Everard's arrests throughout the 1630s, and finally his conviction for heresy in 1639.[112] Just three years earlier, his translation of Nicholas of Cusa and one section of Hermes Trismegistus had been posthumously published.[113] *Some Gospel-Treasures Opened*, however, also contains passages translated from John Tauler, and mentions on its title page that it includes an English translation of Pseudo-Dionysius's *Mystical Theology*; the dedicatory epistle commends the work to Oliver Cromwell. T. A. Birrell notes that the translation "was popular in Quaker and Pietistic circles (Penn called Everard 'the great spiritual separatist')",[114] demonstrating the long afterlife of both late antique and medieval mystical texts in certain circles.

In 1735, however, Thomas à Kempis found yet another confessional audience. The third publication of John Wesley (1703–91) was an abridged translation of the *Imitation of Christ*. He had encountered it in his youth in George Stanhope's (1660–1728) version of 1698 and found the translation's style wanting; later he recommended his translation (in 1746) as one among eight titles for daily reading for devout students.[115] The ongoing concern with fidelity to Kempis's source-text led to the very title page declaring that the translation had been "Compared with the

Original, and corrected throughout." Wesley claims in the preface that his detailed study led to a translation that "differed from his source in four particulars: it was in distinct sentences (like the Latin), closer to the original, plainer, and clearer."[116] He then made a Latin abridgment that was printed in Bristol in 1748; another edition of his English translation was first published in 1741, with seven more editions by 1800.[117] Wesley's interest in Kempis continued after this: in 1742 he translated the Eucharistic book 4 of the *Imitatio*, excised from so many Protestant translations of Kempis, as *A Companion for the Altar*.[118]

The post-Reformation English fate of the *Imitation of Christ* would be hard to imagine replicated for any other text. The reception and editing of Chaucer in the period is particularly revealing in understanding how early modern scholars understood the medieval past, but no other medieval text received the level of attention—both in retranslating and reprinting—from so many prominent (and anonymous) English figures as the *Imitatio*.[119] Approval or condemnation of Catherine of Siena largely split along confessional lines, and Henry Suso's work simply gradually grew less and less popular, but the *Imitatio* was able to attract English readers and publishers of every stripe, in every century since its composition. Following the bifurcation of the source-text as a result of Sebastian Castellio's revision of the text according to Protestant doctrine and Neo-Latin grammatical ideals, English authors continually sought to reconcile the two. Through their detailed prefaces, we can see a little-studied corner of the birth of textual criticism: a discourse born not out of a desire to recover the pure origins of biblical or classical texts, but rather one intimately concerned with the ability of both Kempis and Castellio to instruct new generations of readers in the proper imitation of Christ.

Authorship, Canon, and Popularity

While literary study has tended to conceptualize the development of national literatures in terms of the aesthetic accomplishment of individual authors, along with some form of philosophical or theoretical sophistication (however these happen to be defined at the time the critic is writing), shifting the focus to the *popular* literature of an international European readership yields a very different picture of the cultural, literary, and religious landscape of the late Middle Ages. Quite simply, people wanted their souls, and the souls of their loved ones, to be saved; the books we have discussed in the preceding chapters offered a rich variety of methods for achieving this foremost goal. The questions to be asked of this body of work, and the scholarly lenses used to interpret it, must change markedly: this book might best be considered as part of a subdiscipline such as the "social history of religious literature" in order best to appreciate its approach to medieval and early modern best sellers across linguistic boundaries; the change to the set of analytic tools and interpretive questions required by such a subfield is considerable. This field might dwell in the intersections of book history, translation studies, philology, the history of devotion, and literary history more broadly construed. Studies of the social history of pious texts (or of devotional theology and mobility, as I have framed it in this work) in particular need to be cognizant of corresponding trends in the study of visual and aural culture.

My book has aimed to move beyond "the long-upheld point of view of monomedial determinism, which regards the printed book as the driving force behind cultural revolutions,"[1] alongside a host of other misconceptions often inherent in the all-too-unrelentingly Whiggish or presentist study of the period. Instead, I focus on the histories of texts that succeeded in both manuscript and print, both in England and beyond its borders. With the growth of vernacular literature in fifteenth- and sixteenth-century England, among an audience both clerical and lay, what do the numbers tell us about the success of various texts? In even broader terms, if we rethink the history of English and European literature from the perspective of the popularity of works—the more a work is copied or printed, the larger a place it gains in our history—what changes, fundamentally, to our understanding of "literature" writ large? Considering these texts anew, what can we consequently learn about the role of scholarly canon-making in the reception of English literature in the years since the birth of English literary study in the nineteenth century? I have written with the long-held conviction that clerics are people too, and literature produced by ecclesiastical figures has every right to be considered an integral part of popular literature. Centuries of Lutheran historiography have tainted our view of clerical and monastic texts, and a general distaste for religious didacticism has further alienated these texts from contemporary critical appreciation. "Popular" literature, however, can be produced and consumed by a wide range of people in any period, including members of various elite communities (in Latin or in the vernacular); in an era when book ownership was relatively rare, and the present-day survival of books often dependent in part on their costliness, the question of just what might *not* be considered, in some sense or another, "elite" literature becomes rather moot. I have aimed in this book not to produce a revisionist love letter to the medieval Church, but rather (I hope) to contribute to a growing recognition of the ways in which the study of literature and popularity can also include didactic vernacular works, and to reconsider the English reception of three key Continental devotional corpora that have rarely been included in discussions of popular English literature.

From three different half centuries and three different regions in continental Europe, Suso, Catherine of Siena, and Thomas à Kempis demonstrate three considerably different paths toward the transmission of piety and the process of translating devotional theology in trans-Reformation England. Yet far more connects them than divides them, united as they are in their popularity, whether in manuscript or in early print—and united, too, by their relative exclusion in so many venues of contemporary canonicity. What, then, do canonicity and popularity mean for the study of the fifteenth and sixteenth centuries? How can texts such as these be reincorporated into contemporary literary studies? Translation studies and interest in female authorship have brought some of the texts in this book to the attention of wider scholarly communities in recent decades (particularly Catherine of Siena), but broader studies of the interaction between devotion, translation, and literature are still rare. By looking at devotional culture and devotional mobility in England and the Continent from this perspective, and by examining the history of the books that were most widely read across Western Europe, I hope to have demonstrated what we might consider a new canon of "popular" literature that deserves a central position in our understanding of literary history. From this perspective, England is neither marginal nor insular, but was a thriving part of a textual culture that incorporated Continental mysticism into a broader discourse concerning the role of reading in shaping ethical behavior, the status and authority of revelatory visions, and, ultimately, the salvation of souls.

In all these cases, the status of the "author" is not a one-dimensional march from mind to page, from medieval manuscript to contemporary monograph. Neither pages, nor minds, nor languages are that straightforward—in any time period. And, as is entirely unsurprising for any medieval text, the layers of compiling, translating, copying, reporting, and editing all variously contribute to the intermingled, hybrid spiritual text as it was experienced then, and as it is read today—all these interconnected facets of what Sarah Poor calls "cloaking the body in text."[2] Just as medievalists have, for the better part of a half century, been able to recognize the forces at work in limiting medieval literature by employing postromantic ideals of authorship, so too do the barriers between source-text and translation, life and *Life*, Latin and vernacular, medieval and "Renaissance," seem increasingly restrictive to me. There is far, far more to be gained by looking across languages, genres, types of textual production, and the boundaries of periodization than there is to be lost.

By studying the trans-Reformation history of the translation of the texts in this study, and recalibrating our understanding of how translation functions as a positive form of intellectual production, we encounter an otherwise missing link between the visionaries and prophets of high and late medieval Europe and, for instance, the seventeenth-century prophetic figures of Quakerism, Methodist spirituality in the eighteenth, and New World visionaries from the late sixteenth century onward.[3] Similarly, the extraordinary diversity of gender imagery in representations of Jesus in the texts studied here evince an understanding of divine gender that is far closer to contemporary ideals of genderfluidity and performativity than one might otherwise have expected. In reconsidering canonicity, popularity, and mobility in the fifteenth and sixteenth centuries, we might also see a turn away from the affective and the vernacular in the study of devotion. While these have undoubtedly proved rifts laden with ore in recent decades, yet they too often reinforce existing canons and notions of popularity, excluding lesser-known texts and noninsular literary traditions to our detriment. By instead focusing on aurality, gender, and translation across regions and across time periods, I hope this book can reframe discussion of what Rolle, Suso, Catherine, and Kempis meant to readers in England and across Europe for centuries—and what they might mean to us today.

NOTES

INTRODUCTION

1. Moira Fitzgibbons has confronted this issue quite directly in the classroom with regard to the most popular Middle English poem, *The Prick of Conscience*, and has argued that the poem can be understood today in relation to practical and vocational writing. That hundreds of Middle English readers wanted something akin to a poetic handbook for salvation is certainly to be expected. See Fitzgibbons, "Critical Pleasure, Visceral Literacy, and *The Prik of Conscience*," *Pedagogy* 13, no. 2 (2013): 245–66.

2. The study of medieval romance seems most eager to claim the mantle of popularity. See, for instance, Nicola McDonald, ed., *Pulp Fictions of Medieval England: Essays in Popular Romance* (Manchester: Manchester University Press, 2004), in which romance is "'popular' in its capacity to attract a large and heterogeneous medieval audience, as well as in its ability to provide that audience with enormous enjoyment . . . judged low-class, on account of its non-aristocratic audience, its reliance on stereotypes, formulae and conventional plot structures, and its particular brand of unadulterated good fun" (2). The opening paragraph of this "polemical introduction," however, is careful to exclude any consideration of religious literature as potentially popular, emphasizing that romance is "medieval England's most popular secular genre" and "the 'principal secular literature of entertainment'" (1), citing Stephen Knight, "The Social Function of the Middle English Romances," in *Medieval Literature: Criticism, Ideology, and History*, ed. David Aers (New York: St. Martin's Press, 1986), 99.

3. Some of the most important exceptions can be found in Maximilian van Habsburg, *Catholic and Protestant Translations of the "Imitatio Christi," 1425–1650: From Late Medieval Classic to Early Modern Bestseller* (Aldershot: Ashgate, 2011), and the work of Géraldine Veysseyre's OPVS project, the results of which are forthcoming in Veysseyre, ed., *Ad aedificationem multorum: The Circulation and Adaptation of the Most Widely Disseminated Vernacular Works of Late Medieval Europe/Circulation et adaptation des œuvres vernaculaires les plus diffusées en Europe (13e–15e s.)*. For an important recent exception in American literary-cultural

213

studies, see Jess McHugh, *Americanon: An Unexpected U.S. History in Thirteen Bestselling Books* (New York: Dutton, 2021).

4. On intellectual life in Syon, see especially Vincent Gillespie's edition of the registrum for the library of the Syon brethren, published along with A. I. Doyle's work on what survives of catalogues of Carthusian libraries; Vincent Gillespie and A. I. Doyle, *Syon Abbey, with the Libraries of the Carthusians* (London: The British Library, 2001).

5. Some religious and literary historians have already embraced this type of trans-Reformation scholarship; see, especially, Virginia Blanton, *Signs of Devotion: The Cult of St. Æthelthryth in Medieval England, 695–1615* (University Park: Pennsylvania State University Press, 2007), and Laura Ackerman Smoller, *The Saint & the Chopped-up Baby: The Cult of Vincent Ferrer in Medieval & Early Modern Europe* (Ithaca, NY: Cornell University Press, 2014), for two important examples.

6. Berndt Hamm's formulation of devotional theology is especially useful in its desire to offer a framework able to incorporate spiritual movements across the divide of the Reformation: the development and expansion of devotional theology between the fourteenth and seventeenth century is, he argues repeatedly, more significant to the history of religion than its respective Catholic, Protestant, or "humanist" instantiations. His term is *Frömmigkeitstheologie*: "pietistic theology" or "the theology of piety" sounding rather awkward in English, I have chosen "devotional theology" as an equivalent. The term "devotion" appears in English first circa 1225 in the *Ancrene Riwle*, and the main category the *OED* gives for "piety" (in this sense first appearing ca. 1500) is "senses relating to devotion" (*OED* s.vv. "piety," "devotion"). See Berndt Hamm, "Was ist Frömmigkeitstheologie? Überlegungen zum 14. bis 16. Jahrhundert," in *Praxis Pietatis: Beiträge zu Theologie und Frömmigkeit in der frühen Neuzeit*, ed. Hans-Jörg Nieden and Marcel Nieden (Stuttgart: Kohlhammer, 1999), 9–45. See also the collection of essays in Berndt Hamm, *The Reformation of Faith in the Context of Late-Medieval Theology and Piety: Essays by Berndt Hamm*, ed. Robert Bast (Leiden: Brill, 2004), and Hamm, "*Normative Zentrierung*—eine gemeinsame Vision von Malern und Literaten in Zeitalter der Renaissance," in *Künstler und Literat: Schrift- und Buchkultur in der europäischen Renaissance* (Wiesbaden: Harrassowitz, 2006), 46–74.

7. "Die Wahl der Adressaten und Adressatinnen" (Hamm, "Was ist Frömmigkeitstheologie?," 13; my translation).

8. "Die Wahl der Themen" (ibid., 14; my translation).

9. "erbaulichen 'Kleinliteratur'" (ibid., 15; my translation).

10. The intersection between literature and theology is perhaps best seen in the work of Barbara Newman, especially her development of the concept of "imaginative theology" in Newman, *God and the Goddesses: Vision, Poetry, and Belief in the Middle Ages* (Philadelphia: University of Pennsylvania Press, 2003), and her study of "medieval crossover."

11. "Die damit unmittelbar verbundene Wahl des theologischen 'modus loquendi'" . . . "Sie wurden transformiert in eine lebens- und frömmigkeitsnahe,
(mehr oder weniger) einfache und anschauliche, oft eher affektive als kognitiv-
intellektuelle Theologie der Kanzel und des Beichtstuhls, der Bürgerstube und der
Klosterzelle, der beruflichen Alltagswelt und des Sterbelagers" (Hamm, "Was ist
Frömmigkeitstheologie?," 16–17; my translation).

12. Horst Laubner, Wolfgang Urban, and Walter Simon, eds., *Paltz. Werke 3
(Opuscula)* (Berlin: De Gruyter, 1989), 155–284.

13. "Wie unterschiedlich die Umstellung der Theologie auf einer erbaulichen
Stil selbst beim gleichen Autor ausfallen konnte: Sie konnte, sozusagen auf halb-
akademischen Ebene, sehr scholastiknah bleiben, indem sie sich z.b. weiterhin des
Quästionenstils bediente, aber ihn zugleich durch die überführung der diskursiven
'Sic-et-non'-Methode in einen affirmativen 'Sic'-stil vereinfachte" (Hamm, "Was ist
Frömmigkeitstheologie?," 17; my translation).

14. Michel de Certeau, *The Mystic Fable*, vol. 1, *The Sixteenth and Seventeenth
Centuries*, trans. Michael B. Smith (Chicago: University of Chicago Press, 1992), 76.
See also Denys Turner's similar argument in Turner, *The Darkness of God: Negativity in Christian Mysticism* (Cambridge: Cambridge University Press, 1995), in particular the chapters "Denys the Carthusian and the Problem of Experience" (chap. 9,
211–25) and "From Mystical Theology to Mysticism" (chap. 11, 252–73).

15. Anselm, *The "Prayers and Meditations" of Saint Anselm with the "Proslogion,"* trans. Sister Benedicta Ward, S.L.G. (New York: Penguin, 1973), 90. "In qui-
bus quamvis quaedam sint quae ad vestram personam non pertinent, omnes tamen
volui mittere, ut, si cui placuerint, de hoc exemplari eas possit accipere"; Anselmus
Cantuariensis, *Orationes siue meditationes*, Brepols Library of Latin Texts, 3:3.

16. "Your Highness has told me that you have not got the Prayers and Meditations which I myself have copied and I thought you had got. I send them to you
by my son, Alexander" (ibid.). On the history of both the *Prayers and Meditations*
and related works of devotion written by men for (often distant) women readers, see
Sarah McNamer, "The Genealogy of a Genre," in *Affective Meditation and the Invention of Medieval Compassion* (Philadelphia: University of Pennsylvania Press,
2010), 58–85.

17. Ward, trans., *"Prayers and Meditations,"* 95. "Heu mihi, qui videre non
potui dominum angelorum humiliatum ad conversationem hominum, ut homines
exaltaret ad conversationem angelorum! . . . Cur, o anima mea, te praesentem non
transfixit gladius doloris acutissimi?"; *Orationes siue meditationes*, Brepols Library
of Latin Texts (online), 3:7. The same motif is found in Suso, *Horologium Sapientiae*
I.15: "O Deus meus, utinam fuisset tunc famulus tuus praesens, dum haec agebantur,
ut pietas et compassio, quae eis defuit, per me suppleta fuisset" (K 500, 13–15) (O my
God, if only your servant had been present when these things were being done, that
the pity and compassion that they lacked might have been mine to supply) (C 209).

Citations from Suso's Latin work throughout will be from Pius Künzle, ed., *Horologium Sapientiae* (Freiburg, Switzerland: Universitätsverlag, 1977), with citations to page and line numbers preceded by "K"; translations from Edmund Colledge, trans., *Wisdom's Watch on the Hours* (Washington, DC: Catholic University of America Press, 1994), when used, will be cited by "C" followed by page numbers.

18. Certeau, *Mystic Fable*, 81 (italics original).

19. On the specifically *auditory* nature of the resolution of this encounter, see Rainer Warning, "Seeing and Hearing in Ancient and Medieval Epiphany," in *Rethinking the Medieval Senses: Heritage, Fascinations, Frames*, ed. Stephen G. Nichols, Andreas Kablitz, and Alison Calhoun (Baltimore: Johns Hopkins University Press, 2008), 102–16.

20. Ward, trans., *"Prayers and Meditations,"* 101. "ut dignus sim corpori tuo, 'quod est ecclesia,' incorporari, et sim membrum tuum et tu caput meum, et maneam in te et tu in me" (*Orationes siue meditationes*, 3:10). The speaker of the Prayer to Christ addresses Jesus, expressing his remorse that he was not able to enjoy "the glorious contemplation of your face," and berates his soul for not being "there to be pierced by a sword of bitter sorrow" nor "drunk with bitter tears when they gave him bitter gall to drink." The speaker then wishes that he might have, with Joseph, wrapped Christ "in spiced grave-clothes" and, with the Magdalene, "heard from the angel's mouth" that Jesus is risen. He begs the Lord for recompense "for not having kissed the place of the wounds where the nails pierced" (Ward, trans., *"Prayers and Meditations,"* 95–97).

21. Katherine Zieman, "The Perils of *Canor*: Mystical Authority, Alliteration, and Extragrammatical Meaning in Rolle, the *Cloud*-Author, and Hilton," *Yearbook of Langland Studies* 22 (2008): 149.

22. Carmel Davis, in her exploration of the use of space and spatial terminology in Rolle's work, draws further attention to the inherent mobility of his devotional system; see Davis, *Mysticism and Space: Space and Spatiality in the Works of Richard Rolle, the "Cloud of Unknowing" Author, and Julian of Norwich* (Washington, DC: Catholic University of America Press, 2008).

23. O-T 26.4–6. Citations from Richard Rolle's Middle English texts will often be cited from *Richard Rolle: Prose and Verse*, edited by S. J. Ogilvie-Thomson, Early English Text Society original series 293 (1988); citations from this edition will be by page and line number (when appropriate) prefaced by "O-T." I provide translations of complicated passages of Middle English in many instances, followed by a parenthetical citation of the original text, as in this quotation. Christopher Roman argues that stability of place is the central prerequisite for Rolle's experience of the divine, but he also notes that in the *Incendium amoris* Rolle tends to describe two distinct levels of rapture: a lower one that is sedentary and numbing, and a superior one in which "his entire being is lifted to God"; Roman, "Opening the Inner Doors: Richard Rolle and the Space of the Soul," *Mystics Quarterly* 32, no. 3-4 (2006): 35.

24. Nicholas Watson writes of one likely source for Rolle, Hugh of St. Victor's *De Laude Caritatis*, as describing love itself as a *via* (*via hominis ad Deum, et via Dei ad homines*); *PL* 176:974, quoted by Watson, *Richard Rolle and the Invention of Authority* (Cambridge: Cambridge University Press, 1991), 20.

25. Davis, *Mysticism and Space*, 148.

26. In the fifteenth century, for instance, Charles d'Orléans "translated himself into English" following his capture at Agincourt in 1415. "His example witnesses to the fluidity of geographical and cultural boundaries, and the mobility of the translator, in the late Middle Ages"; Edward Wheatley, "The Developing Corpus of Literary Translation," in *The Oxford History of Literary Translation in English*, vol. 1, *To 1550*, ed. Roger Ellis (Oxford: Oxford University Press, 2008), 181.

27. Greenblatt writes, "Mobility was facilitated through a wholesale reinterpretation of history, a change in its valence, so that Moses could be understood (and represented) at once as a significant person in the history of Israel and as a type or prefiguration of Christ," a process of historical interpretation which bears a curious "blend of homage and aggression"; Stephen Greenblatt, "Cultural Mobility: An Introduction," in *Cultural Mobility: A Manifesto* (Cambridge: Cambridge University Press, 2010), 13.

28. "Die grenzüberschreitende, ausweitende Tendenz der Frömmigkeitstheologen": "Sie nehmen ganz Neues—in der akademischen Theologie nicht Enthaltenes—in die Theologie hinein, bestimmte Erfahrungen von Seelsorge und frommer Lebenspraxis in Ordenskonventen, ordensnahen Lebensformen oder weltlichen Bereichen. Theologie wird also nicht nur transponiert und transformiert, sondern gewinnt als Frömmigkeitstheologie religiöse Inhalte und Vertrautheit mit konkreten Lebensbedingungen hinzu, damit aber auch eine neue Art von Intensität und Einfühlsamkeit" (Hamm, "Was ist Frömmigkeitstheologie?," 35; my translation).

29. Indeed, Nicholas Watson writes that the "the emphasis of these prologues [examined in his study] on language drawn from the physical, ethical, and social realms offers evidence, not of the vagueness, but rather of the stability of the role translation sustains at the centre of the place of knowledge and exchange that is medieval vernacular culture, as an essential mediator between, on the one hand, the riches of learning, the past, and elsewhere, and, on the other, the 'lewed,' the now, and here" (Watson, "Theories of Translation," in Ellis, ed., *Oxford History of Literary Translation in English*, 1:75–76).

30. Discussing here the *Mirror of Perfection* (*Spieghel der Volcomenheit*) of the Franciscan Hendrik Herp, d. 1477 (Certeau, *Mystic Fable*, 1:118).

31. Ibid.

32. On this phenomenon, see Alexander Murray, "Should the Middle Ages Be Abolished?," *Essays in Medieval Studies* 21 (2004): 1–22.

33. Certeau, *Mystic Fable*, 1:299 (emphasis original).

CHAPTER 1

1. The section of the *Horologium* quoted is Künzle, I.1 (383.1–4), here in Edmund Colledge's translation: Colledge, trans., *Wisdom's Watch upon the Hours* (Washington, DC: Catholic University of America Press, 1994), 75. "Videamus eciam quid deuotissimus ille discipulus in horologio sapiencie de hac materia dicat: Contigit inquit frequenter quod cor suum pre amoris vehemencia sensibiliter feruere inciperet, & motu ac pulsu vehementissimo amoris vim proderet, & per alta suspira ardorem ignite caritatis aperiret" (195.147–52); quotation from Michael Sargent, "Contemporary Criticism of Richard Rolle," in *Kartäusermystik und -mystiker*, ed. James Hogg and Robert Rackowitz (Salzburg: Institut für Anglistik und Amerikanistik, 1981), 195. Sargeant's transcription is from the unique surviving copy, Uppsala Universitetsbiblioteket MS C.621. Citations from Suso's German works in this book will be from Karl Bihlmeyer, ed., *Heinrich Seuse: Deutsche Schriften* (Stuttgart: Druck und Verlag von W. Kohlhammer, 1907), with citations to page numbers preceded by "B." Translations from the Middle High German are my own.

2. This, in turn, plays a significant role in our understanding of the patterns of textual transmission and translation between these two regions in the later Middle Ages. The study of Suso is also central to an understanding of the development of late medieval Netherlandish spirituality, taken up in greater detail in chapter 4 herein. Lists of suggested reading materials in communities of the New Devout, for instance, often contained only *one* text written after the thirteenth century: Suso's *Horologium Sapientiae*; see John van Engen, *Sisters and Brothers of the Common Life: The Devotio Moderna and the World of the Later Middle Ages* (Philadelphia: University of Pennsylvania Press, 2008), 276–78.

3. Rather than constantly resort to phrases precise but prolix, such as "the textual figure called 'the Servant' in Henry Suso's semi-autobiographical *Vita*" or "the hermit-character depicted in the text most commonly ascribed to Richard Rolle," it will be assumed that "Suso" and "Rolle" as they appear in their texts are never precise references to historically verifiable authors (witnesses to which are extremely scarce and mostly conjectural) speaking in a first-person that can only ever be yoked to the author himself, but that there will always be a considerable degree of textual construction in our understanding of the characters to whom these names refer. Debates surrounding the historicity of these pseudo-autobiographical texts and their authors are at times useful and interesting (as exercises in *historical* research), but my interests center on their literary existence: as characters in popular devotional *literature*.

4. Eckhart's trial was not completed because of his untimely death in 1327 or 1328, but Pope John XXII's vehement condemnation of his work in 1329 (*In agro dominico*) certainly resonated with Suso, whose first known work, the *Büchlein der Wahrheit*, sought to defend Eckhart posthumously from the pope's charges (though he appears to have written it around 1329, that he included it decades later in the

Exemplar demonstrates his unyielding devotion to defending Eckhart's orthodoxy). See "Documents Relating to Eckhart's Condemnation," in *Meister Eckhart: The Essential Sermons, Commentaries, Treatises, and Defense*, trans. Edmund Colledge, O.S.A., and Bernard McGinn (Mahwah, NJ: Paulist Press 1981), 71–81. See also Bernard McGinn, *The Presence of God: A History of Western Christian Mysticism*, vol. 4, *The Harvest of Mysticism in Medieval Germany* (New York: Crossroad, 2005), 197–200. For a complete look at the heresy trial, see Winfried Trusen, *Der Prozeß gegen Meister Eckhart: Vorgeschichte, Verlauf und Folgen* (Paderborn: Ferdinand Schöningh, 1988).

5. See his recent work on biblical commentary and the widespread "appeal of the academic," in Andrew Kraebel, *Biblical Translation and Commentary in Later Medieval England* (Cambridge: Cambridge University Press, 2020).

6. In a quite different genre, John of Rupescissa's popular fourteenth-century prophetic text, *Vade mecum in tribulatione*, also received a very wide audience across Europe: the attempt to foresee the future could also prove astonishingly popular in pan-European writing. An edition of the text in *seven* different medieval vernaculars (French, Catalan, Castilian, Italian, German, Czech, and English) has recently been published: *Vade mecum in tribulatione*, ed. Robert Lerner and Pavlína Rychterová (Milan: Vita e Pensiero, 2019).

7. This has been noted in many places; the thesis is developed with most comprehensive detail in Jules-Augustin Bizet, *Suso et le Minnesang, ou, la morale de l'amour courtois* (Paris: Aubier, Éditions Montaigne, 1947).

8. Laurence De Looze, *Pseudo-autobiography in the Fourteenth Century: Juan Ruiz, Guillaume de Machaut, Jean Froissart, and Geoffrey Chaucer* (Gainesville: University Press of Florida, 1997). De Looze goes on to explain that the key difference between contemporary approaches to pseudo-autobiography and medieval modes of reading is that readers and scholars today seem more inclined to resolve the tension between fact and fiction, rather than revel in its indeterminacy.

9. Ibid., 2.

10. Ibid., 27.

11. Ibid., 2.

12. A. C. Spearing, *Medieval Autographies: The "I" of the Text* (Notre Dame, IN: University of Notre Dame Press, 2012), 257. For a broad overview of these categories at work in late antique and medieval texts, also bridging sacred and secular, see John V. Fleming, "Medieval European Autobiography," in *The Cambridge Companion to Autobiography*, ed. Maria DiBattista and Emily O. Wittman (Cambridge: Cambridge University Press, 2014), 35–48.

13. Again, Spearing's work on autography highlights this: the pleasure of reading these texts, he writes, "would depend on a willingness to tolerate ambiguities and inconsistencies, contradictions and loose ends, as opposed to an insistence on obtaining resolution by attributing these features to the errors and inadequacies of supposed 'speakers' or 'narrators'" (Spearing, *Medieval Autographies*, 257).

14. See, most recently, Antje Willing, *Heinrich Seuses "Büchlein der ewigen Weisheit": Vorstudien zu einer kritischen Neuausgabe* (Berlin: Erich Schmidt Verlag, 2019).

15. On some iconographic observations of Suso's French reception, see Steven Rozenski, "Henry Suso's *Horologium Sapientiae* in Fifteenth-Century France: Images of Reading and Writing in Brussels Royal Library MS IV 111," *Word & Image* 26, no. 4 (2010): 364–80. See also the facsimile of the images of this manuscript with an interpretive introduction by Peter Rolfe Monks, *The Brussels Horloge de Sapience: Iconography and Text of Brussels, Bibliothèque Royale, MS. IV 111, with an Edition of the Déclaration des Hystoires and a Translation by K. V. Sinclair* (Leiden: Brill, 1990). Further information on the French reception of Suso is scarce, and a critical edition of the second book of the French translation remains a desideratum.

16. The authoritative count of Dutch manuscripts may indeed increase as research into Suso's Dutch reception continues; Stephanus Axters extends his manuscript count to include Geert Grote's Dutch translation of the Latin *Cursus de Aeterna Sapientia*, of which he reports 354 MSS, and 22 MSS recorded but now lost, and the vernacular *Hundert Betrachtungen* in 135 MSS; see *Bibliotheca dominicana neerlandica manuscripta, 1224–1500* (Louvain: Publications universitaires de Louvain, 1970), 213–42, 310–17, and 186–99. But see José van Aelst, *Vruchten van de Passie: De laatmiddeleeuwse passieliteratuur verkend aan de hand van Suso's* Honderd artikelen (Hilversum: Verloren, 2011), and Aelst, *Passie voor het lijden: De "Hundert Betrachtungen und Begehrungen" van Henricus Suso en de oudste drie bewerkingen uit de Nederlanden* (Leuven: Peeters, 2005), for an updated analysis of the reception of the *Hundert Betrachtungen*. For an edition of Geert Grote's text based on Antwerp, Museum Plantin-Moretus MS 14.12, fol. 38r–52v, see Anton Weiler, *Getijden van de Eeuwige Wijsheid* (Amsterdam: Uitgeverij Van Gennep, 2008); a reprint of Baarn: Ambo, 1984.

17. See Giovanna della Croce, *Enrico Suso: La sua vita, la sua fortuna in Italia* (Milan: Editrice Àncora, 1971).

18. These will be discussed in detail in chapter 2. It is a complicated linguistic tradition to summarize briefly, given its subsequent usage by various authors. Initially we can account for eight complete MSS of the *Seven Points*, nine MSS containing fragments of the *Seven Points* or other independent translations of parts of the *Horologium*, and Caxton's 1491 print, *The Book of Diverse Ghostly Matters*, with six extant copies (from Dirk Schultze's edition of the *SP*, lxxvii–civ). The earliest record of the translation of Suso in England is almost certainly *Chastising of God's Children*, written near London between 1395 and 1405; see chapter 2 for more details. In addition, Hope Emily Allen points out early printed editions claiming to include works by Rolle that in fact contain the third section of the *Horologium*, the *Cursus de Aeterna Sapientia*: viz., the *Hore beate Marie*, Sarum Use, printed by Wynkyn de Worde, July 31, 1503 (RSTC 15899), and a 1531 Paris printing of the Sarum Hours (RSTC 15973); this text then appears in the vernacular Sarum Books of Hours. There

is another English translation of Suso, not yet discussed in any scholarship on Suso in England, by Richard Braithwaite (ca. 1588–1673), in his compilation, *A Spiritual Spicerie: Containing Sundrie sweet Tractates of Devotion and Piety*, printed in London in 1638 (RSTC 3586). A translation of Suso's *Centum meditationes* in English verse, copied around 1525 by a Carthusian in Hull, is uniquely found in Bodleian Library MS E Museo 160 (see, again, chapter 2).

19. My gratitude to Stephen Mitchell for this information, taken from *H. Susos Gudeliga snilles väckare (Horologium aeternae sapientae)*, ed. Richard Bergström (Stockholm: P. A. Norstedt & sönner, 1868–70), which differs slightly from the account of Suso's Scandinavian reception given in the introduction to Künzle's edition of the *Horologium*.

20. The basis for this information comes from Pius Künzle's 1977 edition of the *Horologium*, 250–76; research on the French, Scandinavian, and English medieval reception all have had further developments since its publication. On Suso's frequent appearance in print up until the seventeenth century, see Dieter Breuer, "Zur Druckgeschichte und Rezeption der Schriften Heinrich Seuses," in *Frömmigkeit in der frühen Neuzeit: Studien zur religiösen Literatur des 17. Jahrhunderts in Deutschland*, ed. Dieter Breuer (Amsterdam: Rodopi, 1984), 29–49. It is also worth noting that more medieval Susonian material, in both the vernaculars and Latin, is still being discovered and identified.

21. *Gesamtkatalog der Wiegendrucke*, http://www.gesamtkatalogderwiegen drucke.de.

22. See Aelst, *Passie voor het lijden*, which examines only the first two of the seven Middle Dutch adaptations of Suso's *One Hundred Meditations*. Her meticulous second monograph, Aelst, *Vruchten van de Passie*, completes the groundwork of the reception of this text. See also the foundational work of J. Deschamps, "De Middelnederlandse vertalingen en bewerkingen van de *Hundert Betrachtungen und Begehrungen* van Henricus Suso," *Ons geestelijk erf* 63 (1989): 309–69.

23. See Richard Pfaff, *New Liturgical Feasts in Later Medieval England* (Oxford: Clarendon Press, 1970), 62–83, and Denis Renevey, "Name Above Names: The Devotion to the Name of Jesus from Richard Rolle to Walter Hilton's *Scale of Perfection*," in *The Medieval Mystical Tradition: England, Ireland and Wales*, ed. Marion Glasscoe (Cambridge: D. S. Brewer, 1999), 103–21, and chapter 2 herein.

24. For a comprehensive description of these manuscripts, see *Emendatio Vitae*, ed. Rüdiger Spahl, 25–86. Allen, *Writings Ascribed*, has recently been revised and updated by the late A. I. Doyle, with revisions by Ralph Hanna, significantly expanding our understanding of Rolle's Latin manuscript context, with numerous Continental manuscripts added since Hope Allen's time. See Doyle and Hanna, eds., *Hope Allen's Writings Ascribed to Richard Rolle: A Corrected List of Copies* (Turnhout: Brepols, 2019).

25. Ralph Hanna, *The English Manuscripts of Richard Rolle: A Descriptive Catalogue* (Exeter: University of Exeter Press, 2010). He includes manuscripts of

the *Speculum spiritualium*: the bulk of the text is in Latin, but the final chapter of book 2 consists of extracts from Rolle's *Form of Living* in English. For an edition and discussion of this chapter, see E. A. Jones, "A Chapter from Richard Rolle in Two Fifteenth-Century Compilations," *Leeds Studies in English* 27 (1997): 139–62.

26. See A. I. Doyle, "Carthusian Participation in the Movement of Works of Richard Rolle between England and Other Parts of Europe in the 14th and 15th Centuries," in *Kartäusermystik und und -mystiker*, ed. James Hogg, Analecta Carthusiana 55 (Salzburg: Institut für Anglistik und Amerikanistik, 1981), 2:109–20. For Rolle's reception in Bohemia, see Michael van Dussen, *From England to Bohemia: Heresy and Communication in the Later Middle Ages* (Cambridge: Cambridge University Press, 2012), and Michael Van Dussen, "Richard Rolle's Latin Psalter in Central European Manuscripts," *Medium Ævum* 87, no. 1 (2018): 41–71. See also Ralph Hanna, "The Transmission of Richard Rolle's Latin Works," *The Library* 14 (2013): 313–33.

27. Denis Renevey, "Richard Rolle," in *Approaching Medieval English Anchoritic and Mystical Texts*, ed. Dee Dyas, Valerie Edden, and Roger Ellis (Cambridge: D. S. Brewer, 2005), 64.

28. Using Hanna's manuscript numbering, Walter Hilton appears in Rolle MSS 12, 15, 17, 36, 48, 51, 61, 63, 68, 85, 94, 111, 114, and 118; the *Meditationes vitae Christi* in 3, 4, 35, 68, and 71; William Flete in 26, 49, and 118; and Bridget of Sweden in 4 and 114.

29. For a detailed study of this manuscript, see Marleen Cré, *Vernacular Mysticism in the Charterhouse: A Study of London, British Library, MS Additional 37790* (Turnhout: Brepols, 2006).

30. Manuscript information is taken from Hanna, *English Manuscripts of Richard Rolle*.

31. For preliminary information on this manuscript, see Elizabeth Psakis Armstrong, "Heinrich Suso's *Horologium sapientiae*: A Recently Discovered Excerpt," *Manuscripta* 12 (1968): 101–3.

32. See Jill C. Havens, "A Narrative of Faith: Middle English Devotional Anthologies and Religious Practice," *Journal of the Early Book Society* 7 (2004): 67–84.

33. Wolfgang Riehle, *The Middle English Mystics*, trans. Bernard Standring (London: Routledge and Kegan Paul, 1981), 32.

34. McGinn, *Presence of God*, 4:225. It should be noted that this synaesthetic approach to mystical experience, combining many sensory impressions—among them sweetness, song, and warmth—will remain central to my discussion in chapter 2, which stresses the synaesthetic aspect of Rolle's and Suso's mysticism beyond the reduction we assign today to Rolle as being solely an exponent of a tripartite ascending program of *fervor-dulcor-canor*.

35. Jeffrey Hamburger, *The Visual and the Visionary: Art and Spirituality in Late Medieval Germany* (New York: Zone Books, 1998), 229–31. See also Tamás Karáth, "*Altum sapere*: The Risks of Authority and the Responsibility of Knowledge in Late Medieval English Extramural Literary Texts" (PhD diss., Eötvös Loránd

University, 2008), for a comparative discussion of Rolle's and Suso's approaches to authority and learning.

36. See, for instance, David Wallace, ed., *Europe: A Literary History, 1348–1418*, 2 vols. (Oxford: Oxford University Press, 2016), and Jonathan Hsy, *Trading Tongues: Merchants, Multilingualism, and Medieval Literature* (Columbus: Ohio State University Press, 2013).

37. Ross Fuller describes the spirituality associated with the *devotio moderna* in similar terms. Writing of *The Ymage of Love* (RSTC 21471.5), he describes the text's link "to the religious life of the continent, revealing elements of a common late medieval nonscholastic spirituality which entered significantly into the movements of Christian humanism, Counter-Reformation Catholicism and even Protestantism. Here, all roads lead through the experimental asceticism of the New Devotion to the truths of an earlier age. The New Devotion was a bridge"; Fuller, *The Brotherhood of the Common Life and Its Influence* (Albany: State University of New York Press, 1995), 74.

38. Steven Rozenski, "Exemplarity and Authority in Henry Suso and Richard Rolle," in *The Medieval Mystical Tradition: Papers Read at Charney Manor, July 2011*, ed. E. A. Jones (Rochester, NY: Boydell & Brewer, 2013), 93–108. On the exemplar cause, see Leonard J. Bowman, "The Cosmic Exemplarism of Bonaventure," *Journal of Religion* 55, no. 2 (1975): 181–98. A similar understanding of the exemplarism of the divine ideas can be found in Thomas Aquinas; see Gregory Doolan, *Aquinas on the Divine Ideas as Exemplar Causes* (Washington, DC: Catholic University of America Press, 2008). I was initially made aware of the role this played in Suso's conception of authorship by Peter Ulrich, *Imitatio et configuratio: Die philosophia spiritualis Heinrich Seuses als Theologie der Nachfolge des Christus passus* (Regensburg: Verlag Friedrich Pustet, 1995).

39. As Jörg Seelhorst writes, "Christus ist das Exemplar, dem es nachzufolgen gilt; der Diener leistet diese Nachfolge in vorbildlicher Weise, wodurch sein Leben selbst zum Exemplar, zur *glichnús*, für den Leser wird"; Seelhorst, *Autoreferentialität und Transformation: Zur Funktion mystischen Sprechens bei Mechthild von Magdeburg, Meister Eckhart, und Heinrich Seuse* (Tübingen: A. Francke Verlag, 2003), 275.

40. On the key role emotional responses play in this process, see Vincent Gillespie, "Mystic's Foot: Rolle and Affectivity," in *The Medieval Mystical Tradition in England: Papers Read at Dartington Hall, July 1982*, ed. Marion Glasscoe (Exeter: University of Exeter Press, 1982), 199–230.

41. Jessica Barr, "Modelling Holiness: Self-Fashioning and Sanctity in Late Medieval English Mystical Literature," in *Sanctity as Literature in Late Medieval Britain*, ed. Eva von Contzen and Anke Bernau (Manchester: Manchester University Press, 2015), 84.

42. For two important studies of the role of exemplarity in the history of Christianity, see Peter Brown, "The Saint as Exemplar in Late Antiquity,"

Representations 2 (1983): 1–25, and Caroline Walker Bynum, *Docere verbo et exemplo: An Aspect of Twelfth-Century Spirituality* (Missoula, MT: Scholars Press, 1979). On the relationship between Suso's Passion meditation and other dominant discourses of the imitation of Christ, see Nigel Palmer, "Antiseusiana: *Vita Christi* and Passion Meditation before the *Devotio Moderna*," in *Inwardness, Individualization, and Religious Agency in the Late Medieval Low Countries: Studies in the "Devotio Moderna" and Its Contexts,* ed. Rijcklof Hofman, Charles Caspers, Peter Nissen, Mathilde van Dijk, and Johan Oosterman (Turnhout: Brepols, 2020), 87–120.

43. For a detailed study of scriptural references to the imitation of Christ and their application in early Christianity, see Candida R. Moss, *The Other Christs: Imitating Jesus in Ancient Christian Ideologies of Martyrdom* (Oxford: Oxford University Press, 2010), 3–44.

44. Ibid., 4.

45. Gábor Klaniczay writes of the development of this form of living, describing it as a paradox of later medieval Christianity: "On the one hand, a greater awareness of the self and individuality, and on the other, a great capacity to conform to historical models of life," particularly insofar as both the Dominicans and the Franciscans offered charismatic founder-saints (that is, new and contemporary figures to imitate) who yet strove to reproduce the assumed purity of early Christianity; see Klaniczay, "Legends as Life Strategies of Aspirant Saints in the Later Middle Ages," *Journal of Folklore Research* 26, no. 2 (1989): 152.

46. Claire McIlroy writes of the ways in which Rolle relies "on affective language to construct a separate discourse in each work that appeals to each reader as an individual soul, and so potentially invites a wider audience"; McIlroy, *The English Prose Treatises of Richard Rolle* (Rochester: D. S. Brewer, 2004), 22.

47. Nicholas Watson, *Richard Rolle and the Invention of Authority* (Cambridge: Cambridge University Press, 1991), 228.

48. McIlroy, however, argues against this identification, showing that the incipit "to moniali de ʒedyngham"—which for a long time led critics to assume that this did in fact originate as an epistle written for a specific religious—is not contained in all MSS (McIlroy, *English Prose Treatises of Richard Rolle*, 62). Some MSS claim it was "wrot to an ankress" or assume that it is, like some of the other tracts, originally written for Margaret of Kirkby, and group it accordingly. Additionally, many fifteenth-century MSS include the rubric *Ego Dormio* at the beginning of the text, indicating that many scribes treated it more as a free-standing tract than as a copy of an actual letter (ibid., 64).

49. On the importance of imitative devotion, see Richard Kieckhefer, "Major Currents in Late Medieval Devotion," in *Christian Spirituality: High Middle Ages and Reformation*, ed. Jill Raitt (New York: Crossroads, 1987), 2:75–108, esp. 100–102 ("General Trends in Devotionalism").

50. Watson, *Richard Rolle and the Invention of Authority*, 195–221.

51. Indeed, it is tempting, if misleading, to see the *Horologium Sapientiae* as largely a vehicle for subsequent retranslation into vernacular languages across Europe, if not intentionally so. However, the order in which the *Horologium* and the *LBEW* were composed is a matter of some debate, and establishing the priority of one against the other cannot yet be conclusively argued. Claire Champollion follows J. A. Bizet, *Henri Suso et le déclin de la scolastique* (Paris: Aubier, 1946), in arguing that "Suso must have made use of earlier fragments and notes for both [the *Horologium* and the *Little Book of Eternal Wisdom*]" (für beide müsse Seuse frühere Fragmente und Aufzeichnungen benutzt haben), but she admits that some parts of the text must originally have been composed in German (including, of course, the *Hundert Betrachtungen*, as Suso himself claims); see Claire Champollion, "Zum intellektuellen Wortschatz Heinrich Seuses OP," in *Heinrich Seuse: Studien zum 600. Todestag, 1366–1966*, ed. Ephrem Filthaut (Köln: Albertus Magnus Verlag, 1966), 78.

52. See, especially, Jeremy Catto, "Written English: The Making of the Language 1370–1400," *Past & Present* 179 (May 2003): 24–59. He argues for a lack of common literary or even linguistic culture among early Middle English texts, and the central role of Latin and Anglo-Norman literacy for the three centuries following the Norman Conquest. The most prominent texts in nearly every genre are indeed based on Anglo-Norman or Latin models, with those providing entertainment and pleasure tending toward the former and those geared toward instruction the latter. In comparing French, German, and English "literary consciousness," for instance, *The Cambridge History of Literary Criticism* concludes, in strong terms with which I agree, that "in the British Isles, a developed literary consciousness does not, with some notable exceptions, make itself felt in Middle English writing until the latter half of the fourteenth century, this being concurrent with the rise of national consciousness and the firm establishment of English as a literary vernacular"; see Kevin Brownlee, Tony Hunt, Ian Johnson, Nigel F. Palmer, and James Simpson, "Vernacular Literary Consciousness c. 1100–c. 1500: French, German and English Evidence," in *The Cambridge History of Literary Criticism*, vol. 2, *The Middle Ages*, ed. Alastair Minnis and Ian Johnson (Cambridge: Cambridge University Press, 2009), 423. The complex and contested status of the vernacular is addressed in Nicholas Watson, "Censorship and Cultural Change in Late-Medieval England: Vernacular Theology, the Oxford Translation Debate, and Arundel's Constitutions of 1409," *Speculum* 70, no. 4 (1995): 822–64.

53. If Suso's status as a Dominican minimizes his worries about the vernacular vis-à-vis Rolle, however, he nevertheless takes upon himself a still greater challenge: reestablishing Eckhart's authority in the wake of John XXII's condemnation of Eckhart in *In agro Dominico* (1329). Indeed, it seems likely that the defense of Eckhart in the *Büchlein der Wahrheit* (*Little Book of Truth*) was Suso's first work.

54. For Misyn's translations, see *The Fire of Love and The Mending of Life or The Rule of Living*, ed. Ralph Harvey, EETS o.s. 106 (Oxford: Oxford University

Press, 1896). Citations from the Misyn translation will be by page number from this edition preceded by "M."

55. The literature on the role of Latin and the vernacular in Eckhart's work is considerable. See, especially, Erik Panzig, "Lateinische und deutsche Terminologie in der Theologie Meister Eckharts," *Meister-Eckhart-Jahrbuch* 1 (2007): 157–66, and Susanne Köbele, *Bilder der unbegriffenen Wahrheit: Zur Struktur mystischer Rede im Spannungsfeld von Latein und Volkssprache* (Tübingen: A. Francke Verlag, 1993).

56. Erich Auerbach, *Literary Language and Its Public in Late Latin Antiquity and in the Middle* Ages, trans. Ralph Manheim (Princeton, NJ: Princeton University Press, 1965), 330.

57. Bernard McGinn, *The Mystical Thought of Meister Eckhart: The Man from Whom God Hid Nothing* (New York: Herder and Herder, 2001), 34 (emphasis original). See also Frank Tobin, *Meister Eckhart: Thought and Language* (Philadelphia: University of Pennsylvania Press, 1986); Benno Schmoldt, *Die deutsche Begriffssprache Meister Eckharts: Studien zur philosophischen terminologie des Mittelhochdeutschen* (Heidelberg: Quelle & Meyer, 1954), and Alois Haas, "Meister Eckhart und die Sprache: Sprachgeschichtliche und sprachtheologische Aspekte seines Werkes," and "Meister Eckhart und die deutsche Sprache," both in Alois Haas, *Geistliches Mittelalter* (Freiburg, Switzerland: Universitätsverlag Freiburg Schweiz, 1984), 193–214 and 215–37.

58. "nâch der wîse, als der geist enpfenclich is"; *Meister Eckhart: Werke I*, ed. Niklaus Largier (with the text of Josef Quint) (Frankfurt a.M.: Deutscher Klassiker Verlag, 2008), Sermon 1, 20. Translations are mine.

59. On this, see especially Kurt Flasch, *Meister Eckhart: Philosopher of Christianity* (New Haven, CT: Yale University Press, 2015), 57–74.

60. "Daz selbe, daz mîn munt got sprichet und offenbâret, daz selbe tuot des steines wesen, und verstât man mê an dem werke dan an den worten" (*Meister Eckhart: Werke I*, Sermon 53, 568, lines 5–8).

61. "Do er in der klage stûnt, do kamen sine inren sinne in ein ungewonlich ufgezogenheit" (B 196).

62. "Und dar umb so screib er die betrahtunge an und tet daz ze tútsche, wan sú im och also von gotte waren worden" (B 197).

63. "geschah nit mit einem liplichen kosenne noh mit bildricher entwúrt, es geschah allein mit betrachtunge in dem lieht der heiligen schrift, der entwúrt bi núti getriegen mag, also daz die entwúrt genomen sint eintweder von der Ewigen Wisheit munde, die si selber sprach an dem evangelio, oder aber von dien höhsten lerern; und begrifent eintweder dú selben wort oder den selben sin oder aber sogtan warheit, dú nah dem sinne der heiligen scrift geriht ist, usser der mund dú Ewig Wisheit hat geredet" (B 197).

64. In the case of the *Vitaspatrum*, a favorite patristic text for Suso, however, the vernacular is, in fact, quite possible. Ulla Williams, ed., *Die Alemannischen*

Vitaspatrum (Tübingen: Max Niemeyer Verlag, 1996), mentions that vernacular reception of the *Vitaspatrum* began at the end of the thirteenth century with a 41,000-line verse translation and that the prose Alemannic version she edits was likely composed in the first half of the fourteenth century (7–18).

65. For a detailed study of the use of Bernardine spirituality in the works of the Rhineland Dominicans, see Georg Steer, "Bernhard von Clairvaux als theologische Autorität für Meister Eckhart, Johannes Tauler, und Heinrich Seuse," in *Bernhard von Clairvaux: Rezeption und Wirkung im Mittelalter und in der Neuzeit*, ed. Kaspar Elm (Wiesbaden: Harrassowitz, 1994), 235–59.

66. "Und die lere git er also vúr vragwise, dar umb daz si dest begirlicher sie, nút daz er der si, den es an gehöret, oder daz es von im selber hab gesprochen. Er meint dar inne ein gemein lere geben, da beidú, er und ellú menschen, mugen an finden ein ieklicher daz, daz in an gehöret" (B 197). The reliance on parabolic speech when describing matters transcendent can be traced directly from Mark 4. The Vulgate reads: "et talibus multis parabolis loquebatur eis verbum prout poterant audire. Sine parabola autem non loquebatur eis" (Mark 4:33–34).

67. "Notandum quoque, quod locutio ista quantum ad interrogationem discipuli et responsionem sapientiae vel econverso solum posita est ad ferventiorem modum tradendi. Nec est aliter accipiendum, quasi discipulus fuerit ille talis, de quo sapientia in persona propria solum intenderit, vel qui sapientiam solus prae ceteris tantum amaverit, vel cui sapientia tot et tanta fecerit, sed reversa pro quolibet in genere dictum habeatur. Siquidem per modum doctoris nunc loquitur in persona hominis perfecti, deinde in persona imperfecti. . . . Et sic diversimode stilum vertit secundum quod tunc materiae congruit. Nunc etiam Dei Filium ut devotae animae sponsum inducit; postea eundem tamquam aeternam sapientiam viro iusto desponsatam introducit" (K 366.6–19) (It should also be noted that I have used the device of questions and answers between the Disciple and Wisdom only to convey matters more vividly. It is not to be understood that there ever will be a disciple as this, or that Wisdom will be concerned with him to everyone else's exclusion, or that only he, more than all others, will love Her so much, or that She will do so many great things for him, but take him to represent everyone who is like him. So, as teachers do, sometimes he speaks as if he were a perfect man, and then as one who is imperfect. . . . And so the style changes from time to time, to suit what is then the subject. Sometimes the Son of God is presented as the spouse of the devout soul; then later the same Son is introduced as Eternal Wisdom, wedded to the just man) (C 54–55).

68. "Die sinne, die hie stant, sint einvaltig; so sint dú wort noh einveltiger, wan sú gant uzzer einer einvaltigen sele und gehörent zú einvaltigen menschen" (B 198).

69. "Als unglich ist, der ein süzes seitenspil selber horti süzklich erklingen gegen dem, daz man da von allein hört sprechen, als ungelich sint dú wort, dú in der lutren gnade werdent enpfangen und usser einem lebenden herzen dur einen lebenden munt us fliezent gegen den selben worten, so sú an daz töt bermit koment, und sunderliche in tútscher zungen; wan so erkaltent sú neiswe und verblichent als die

abgebrochnen rosen, wan dú lustlich wise, dú ob allen dingen menschlich herz rüret, dú erlöschet denne, und in der túrri der túrren herzen werdent sú denn enphangen. Es enwart nie kein seiten so süze: der in richtet uf ein túrres schit, er erstumbet. Ein minnerichen zungen ein unminneriches herze enkan als wenig verstan, als ein tútscher einen walhen" (B 199). An earlier generation of critics saw this as evidence of Suso's distaste for the German language; I find considerably more convincing interpretations that see this passage as demonstrating Suso's devotion to the vernacular, and simply his dislike of seeing it written down, outside of the realm of aural immediacy. The overall importance of aurality to Suso, as demonstrated in Steven Rozenski, "The Visual, the Textual, and the Auditory in Henry Suso's Vita or Life of the Servant," *Mystics Quarterly* 34, no. 1-2 (2008), also lends this understanding of the passage further credence.

70. "do sú in ir leblichi, in ir wúnklicher schonheit waren" (B 200).

71. "mag eigenlich kumme iemer dis überlesen, sin herz müze inneklich bewegt werden" (B 200).

72. Maria Bindschedler works against the peculiar assumptions of an earlier generation of scholars who saw German as a hindrance. See Bindschedler, "Seuses Auffassung von der deutschen Sprache," in *Heinrich Seuse: Studien zum 600. Todestag*, 71–75. See also Alois Haas, "Sprache und mystische Erfahrung nach Tauler und Seuse," in Haas, *Geistliches Mittelalter*, 239–47.

73. For an overview of earlier work on the relationship between the *Horologium* and the *LBEW*, see Künzle's edition, 28–54.

74. "Ins besondere finden wir kaum eine Entsprechung für ratio, intellectus, mens. Nicht, daß die Wörter fehlten; sie sind da, sie werden aber kaum gebraucht"; Claire Champollion, "Zum intellektuellen Wortschatz Heinrich Seuses OP," 85.

75. "mag man merken an sinem büchlin der wisheit in tútsch und in latin" (B 11).

76. C 54. "Obsecro autem devotos lectores, ut sermo imperitus et incultus, etiam si barbarum aliquid fortassis sonare videatur, non displiceat. Non multum etenim curo vitia incurrere artium sermocinalium, dummodo vitia animorum eo commodius possem fervida locutione corrigere et emendare" (K 365.6–10).

77. C 54. "Verum, quoniam eaedem materiae dudum a multis subtiliter et luculenter declaratae sunt et paene ex frequenti usu iamiam plerisque in fastidium vertuntur, ideo non fuit opus ad singula quaeque auctoritates adducere; nam ex hoc consonantia motiva huius voluminis utique intercepta fuisset" (K 366.1–5).

78. Watson, *Richard Rolle and the Invention of Authority*, 223.

79. Ibid.

80. As one prologue has it, "copyed has this Sauter ben of yuel men of lollardry: / And afturward hit has bene sene ympyd in with eresy" (Bramley 2.49–50). See the three recent volumes of Anne Hudson, ed., *Two Revisions of Rolle's English Psalter Commentary and the Related Canticles*, EETS o.s. 340, 341, and 343 (Oxford: Oxford University Press, 2012–2014).

81. Bramley 1.17–20.

82. Bramley 1.25–29.

83. Bramley 2.41–46.

84. Bramley 3.

85. Bramley 4–5.

86. See Hanna, *English Manuscripts of Richard Rolle*. Hanna rules out the unwieldy nature of including descriptions of manuscripts containing short excerpts of Rolle's English works, as it would "open the way to describing a large percentage of late medieval religious miscellanies" (xxiv), but the *Speculum spiritualium* is his one exception, as the final chapter of book 2 is "entirely Rolle in English, three excerpts from 'The Form' . . . [and is] clearly designed to communicate the English text" (xxv). On the two collections containing Rolle, see Doyle, "Carthusian Participation in the Movement of Works of Richard Rolle." For an edition and discussion of this chapter, see E. A. Jones, "A Chapter from Richard Rolle in Two Fifteenth-Century Compilations," *Leeds Studies in English* 27 (1997): 139–62.

87. Wolfgang Riehle briefly gestures toward this commonality in Riehle, *The Middle English Mystics*, trans. Bernard Standring (London: Routledge and Kegan Paul, 1981) (even though claims to Rolle's originality are more central to his argument): "The closest links between England and the continent have, however, turned out to be in the area of female mysticism. . . . Richard Rolle, too, shows a clear affinity of spirit with female mysticism, and in this he has a remarkable counterpart on the continent in the person of Henry Suso who also has close contacts with mystically inclined women" (163). See also Anne Astell, "Feminine Figurae in the Writings of Richard Rolle: A Register of Growth," *Mystics Quarterly* 15, no. 3 (1989): 117–24.

88. Watson, *Richard Rolle and the Invention of Authority*, 224. On this topic, see most extensively Olli Lampinen, "Just Friends? Richard Rolle and the Possibility of Christian Friendship between Men and Women" (MA thesis, University of Helsinki, 2014).

89. On the overall sense of queerness in Rolle's eremetic form of living, represented both in this famous scene and the well-known encounter in the *Officium* when Rolle's sister gives him her tunics as makeshift vestments, see Christopher Roman, *Queering Richard Rolle* (New York: Palgrave, 2018), 1–19. On *The Doctrine of the Hert*, a text that minimizes the famous discussion of the breasts of the beloved in the Song of Songs, see Annie Sutherland, "'Comfortable Wordis': The Role of the Bible in *The Doctrine of the Hert*," in *A Companion to the Doctrine of the Hert*, ed. Denis Renevey and Christiania Whitehead (Liverpool: Liverpool University Press, 2010), 109–30.

90. Sermon 9, "On the Breasts of the Bride and the Bridegroom," and 10, "The Breasts and Their Perfumes," most especially. See the Cistercian Fathers Series 4 (Collegeville, MN: Liturgical Press, 2008), 53–68; the first volume of four providing a modern English translation of the sermons.

91. "En conditor orbis corpora caelestia ornavit sideribus, corpora elementa-ria animantibus ac volatilibus, nemora foliis virentibus, prata floribus ridentibus; sed super haec omnia, virgo beata, corpus tuum sanctissimis decoravit uberibus" (K 508.8–11).

92. Colledge writes in his note on the passage that Suso "follows Bonaven-ture, *Soliloquy*, chap. 1, as do Eckbert of Schönau, *Meditations*, chap. 2, and Pseudo-Anselm, *Meditation XIII*, 'Of Christ.' But none of the three makes this comparison with Mary" (C 219n12).

93. "*In vino* namque *est luxuria* et delectatio terrena, in his autem phialis au-reis concupiscentiae noxiae plenissima exstinctio, et caelestis quaedam et supernatu-ralis delectatio. Novis, qui gustavit, quam citissime et perfectissime omnis voluptas carnalis evanuit, cum de lacte gratiarum tuarum gustatum fuit. Ad fraglantiam quippe unguentorum supernorum virulenti serpentes territi fugabantur, et sustinere non poterant praesentiam tantae puritatis" (K 509.3–10).

94. Both the *Stimulus amoris* and a sermon by Umiltá of Faenza describe a mixed drink of the blood of Christ and the sweet milk of the Virgin, a related, if dis-tinct, conceit. See Atsushi Iguchi, "A Study of Vernacular Devotional Translation in Late-Medieval England" (PhD diss., University of Cambridge, 2008), 224–26.

95. "et cum ipsum iam habere velut sponsum carissimum gauderem, subito divinitatis eius recordatione stupefactus, ut iudicem meum deprecabar. Et cum in-terdum lac peterem, repulit, et quasi *ablactando super matre sua* acetosam exhibuit austeritatem" (K 510.10–13).

96. "Ecce quaerenti mihi tuam divinitatem, ostendis humanitatem; quaerenti dulcedinem, profers amaritudinem; petenti mamillas sugere, das robusta certamina decertare" (K 388.15–17).

97. Eternal Wisdom expresses this similarly in the *LBEW*: "Ich bin es, din brůder, lůg, ich bin es, din gemahel!" (B 213).

98. "O paternorum viscerum pietas inaudita. O fraternae fidelitatis dilectio stupenda" (K 401.9–10). Colledge's translation silently omits *viscerum*. In the *LBEW* a similar conflation of fatherhood and brotherhood is voiced by the servant: "Owe vater miner, owe brůder miner" (B 214).

99. On the creative ways in which Wycliffite translators dealt with the Song of Songs, see Helen Cooper, "Translation and Adaptation," in *A Concise Companion to Middle English Literature*, ed. Marilyn Corrie (Chichester: Wiley-Blackwell, 2009), 171–73.

100. Quotations from Rolle's commentary on the Song of Songs will be taken from the edition by Sister Elizabeth Marian Murray, S.C., "Richard Rolle's Com-ment on the Canticles" (PhD diss., Fordham University, 1958), and cited by page number preceded by "Murray." Translations are my own. "Et, allegorice loquendo, ad quemlibet sanctum potest dici illud quod mulier dixit in evangelio ad Christum. *Beatus venter, qui te portavit, et ubera que suxisti.* Quemadmodum namque ante-quam in mundum nascimur corporaliter in matris utero portamur, ut priusquam

ambulare vel currere aliquem cibum forte sumere possumus necessarie est ut lac ab uberibus matris capiamus; ita, spiritualiter, ante baptismum vel ante penitenciam, in utero Christi, id est, in paciencia sua" (Murray 29–30).

101. Denis Renevey, *Language, Self and Love: Hermeneutics in the Writings of Richard Rolle and the Commentaries on the Song of Songs* (Cardiff: University of Wales Press, 2001), 84. He goes on to point out the similar patterns at play in the *Oleum effusum.*

102. *Richard Rolle: Uncollected Prose and Verse*, ed. Ralph Hanna (EETS o.s. 329), 114.

103. David Tinsley, *The Scourge and the Cross: Ascetic Mentalities of the Later Middle Ages* (Leuven: Peeters, 2010), however, makes the argument that Stagel is intended to represent a follower of a spiritual path *superior* to Suso's.

104. "Das Engagement der fiktionalen Elsbeth für die Entstehung des *Exemplars* ist zunächst ein erzählerisches Mittel, um die Vorbildlichkeit des Dieners aufzubauen . . . Frauen fungieren in der *Vita* als Resonanz-Figuren: Ihre Aufmerksamkeit, Lernwilligkeit, Bereitschaft zum rückhaltlosen Vertrauen sind Ausdruck der Anerkennung und werfen ein sehr helles Licht auf den charismatischen Diener"; Hildegard Elisabeth Keller, *Die Stunde des Hundes: Auf dem mystischen Weg zu Gott* (Schlieren, Switzerland: NZZ Fretz, 2007), 33.

105. See also Werner Williams-Krapp, "Henry Suso's *Vita* between Mystagogy and Hagiography," in *Seeing and Knowing: Women and Learning in Medieval Europe 1200–1500*, ed. Anneke B. Mulder-Bakker (Turnhout: Brepols, 2004): "The feminization of the role and the reduction of the Servant's *Vita activa* to a bare minimum are further aspects of the narrative that are designed to optimize the possibilities of the female readership's identification with the Servant" (41).

106. Jeffrey Hamburger, *The Visual and the Visionary: Art and Spirituality in Late Medieval Germany* (New York: Zone Books, 1998), 249.

107. Walter Blank, "Heinrich Seuses 'Vita': Literarische Gestaltung und pastorale Funktion seines Schrifttums," *Zeitschrift für deutsches Altertum und Literatur* 122 (1993), for instance, argues for the uniqueness of Elsbeth's own spiritual path. Tinsley, *The Scourge and the Cross*, however, remains the strongest proponent for a postfeminist interpretation of Stagel's role in the *Vita*, which manages to avoid the "temptation to blame." In Barbara Newman's words, the common historiographical injustice "regards the women in question as complicit in their own victimization and sees every missed opportunity to rebel as an implicit betrayal" (Barbara Newman, "On the Ethics of Feminist Historiography," *Exemplaria* 2, no. 2 [1990]: 704).

108. Watson, *Richard Rolle and the Invention of Authority*, 225.

109. But, *because* of their gender, Suso and Rolle have been left out of the relatively recently established canon of female spirituality, despite the significance of these two authors for the history of gender in the later Middle Ages.

110. Riehle, *Middle English Mystics*, 36.

111. Richard Kieckhefer, *Unquiet Souls: Fourteenth-Century Saints and Their Religious Milieu* (Chicago: University of Chicago Press, 1984), 172.

112. On Bernard of Clairvaux and bridal mysticism, see, most especially, Line Engh, *Gendered Identities in Bernard of Clairvaux's Sermons on the Song of Songs: Performing the Bride* (Turnhout: Brepols, 2014).

113. Citations from the *Contra amatores mundi* and its translation will be by page number of the edition of Paul F. Theiner, *The "Contra Amatores Mundi" of Richard Rolle of Hampole* (Berkeley: University of California Press, 1968), and preceded by "*CAM*." Note that the Latin text and Theiner's English translation are printed sequentially, not facing-page. The text cited above is *CAM* 157; the Latin text is: "hec est dilecta mea sapienca increata, vere amabilis et in amore gratissima" (*CAM* 3.75–80). Wisdom is also discussed as a lover earlier in the text: "this wisdom of God comes as one beloved; she embraces and kisses the one she loves just as a sister would. . . . She so gives herself as a lover to the hearts of holy men that they have no desire for any other love" (*CAM* 148), "Ut amica venit dei sapienca; ut soror amplecitur, deosculans quem diligit. . . . Prebet se amantem in cordibus sanctorum, ut iam non eis libeat aliam cupere" (*CAM* 1.41–42, 51–53).

114. "Nunc etiam Dei Filium ut devotae animae sponsum inducit; postea eundem tamquam aeternam sapientiam viro iusto deponsatam introducit" (K 366.17–19).

115. For a wide range of perspectives on nonnormative gender identities and representations of sexual difference in the Middle Ages, see Karl Whittington, "Medieval Intersex in Theory, Practice, and Representation," *postmedieval* 9 (2018): 231–47. Jessica Boon has recently written with great nuance and beauty on similar dynamics in the works of Juana de la Cruz, in which "Juana's life and sermons . . . propose a new mystical language of bigender, genderqueer, trans, and intersex, culminating in a gender performance continuum that transgresses and transmutes all boundaries between heaven and earth"; see Boon, "At the Limits of (Trans)Gender: Jesus, Mary, and the Angels in the Visionary Sermons of Juana de la Cruz (1481–1534)," *Journal of Medieval and Early Modern Studies* 48, no. 2 (2018): 284. See also Anne J. Cruz, "Transgendering the Mystical Voice: Angela de Foligno, San Juan, Santa Teresa, Luisa de Carvajal," in *Echoes and Inscriptions: Comparative Approaches to Early Modern Spanish Literatures*, ed. Barbara Simerka and Christopher Weimer (Lewisburg, PA: Bucknell University Press, 2000), 127–41.

116. Hamburger, *The Visual and the Visionary*, 249.

117. Elizabeth A. Clark, "The Celibate Bridegroom and His Virginal Brides: Metaphor and the Marriage of Jesus in Early Christian Ascetic Exegesis," *Church History* 77, no. 1 (2008): 18. For a contemporary author who seems to overlook the potential of patristic and medieval writers to enrich this discourse, see, for instance, Justin Sabia-Tanis, *Trans-Gender: Theology, Ministry, and Communities of Faith*, 2nd ed. (Eugene, OR: Wipf & Stock, 2018). His chapter 3, for instance, "Gender Variance and the Scriptures" (55–84), discusses Genesis, Deuteronomy, Isaiah,

Matthew, Acts, and Galatians in exploring scriptural understanding of variance. The books most important to Suso's conception of a nonbinary Jesus, Proverbs and Wisdom, are not discussed (for the latter, perhaps in part because of the noncanonicity of Wisdom for many non-Catholics). See also Austen Hartke, *Transforming: The Bible & the Lives of Transgender Christians* (Louisville: Westminster John Knox Press, 2018), and Gabrielle Bychowski, "Trans Literature: Transgender Histories and Genres of Embodiment, Medieval and Post-Medieval" (PhD diss., George Washington University, 2017). For an intriguing study of the life of a medieval saint (whose cult has gained a renewed contemporary following) and the saint's relationship to recent trans discourse, see especially Lewis Wallace, "Bearded Woman, Female Christ: Gendered Transformations in the Legends and Cult of Saint Wilgefortis," *Journal of Feminist Studies in Religion* 30, no. 1 (2014): 43–63.

118. Sophie Sexon, "Gender-Querying Christ's Wounds: A Non-Binary Interpretation of Christ's Body in Late Medieval Imagery," in *Trans and Genderqueer Subjects in Medieval Hagiography*, ed. Alicia Spencer-Hall and Blake Gutt (Amsterdam: Amsterdam University Press, 2021), 137.

119. See Leah DeVun, "The Jesus Hermaphrodite: Science and Sex Difference in Premodern Europe," *Journal of the History of Ideas* 69, no. 2 (2008): 193–218, with fascinating examples from early fifteenth-century manuscript images.

120. The idea of earthly love as a withering flower is also found in one of Rolle's lyrics: "Bot fleschly lufe sal fare as dose þe flowre in May / And lastand be na mare þan ane houre of a day" (EETS o.s. 329, 27).

121. "tanta est generationis meae profunditas, ut cunctorum mortalium ingenia excedat" (K 421.10–11). The adjective here, too, is feminine.

122. On Wycliffite versions of the Song of Songs and their attention to the genders of the characters portrayed in its (mystical) marriage, see Helen Cooper, "Translation and Adaptation," in *A Concise Companion to Middle English Literature*, ed. Marilyn Corrie (Chichester: Wiley-Blackwell, 2009), 166–87.

123. "sic igitur dilectus in dilecto semper eram manens, ac dilectus ex dilecto [Cant. 5:9] semper manans, in dilecto ab aeterno ludens eram" (K 422.10–12).

124. "Porro quid sim in essentia, quantum ad plenam comprehensionem, ab huius perscrutatione iubet ratio quiescere, cum natura ordinata non tendat ad impossibilia" (K 422.13–15).

125. Newman, *God and the Goddesses*, 210. On discussions of God's potential for polygamy in early Christian texts, see Clark, "The Celibate Bridegroom and His Virginal Brides."

126. "Owe herr, weri mir nu ein kúnegin gemehelt, dez gasti sich min sele; owe, nu bist du mins herzen keisrin und aller gnaden geberin" (B 15). David Tinsley draws attention to still another moment of gender oscillation in the *Vita*: when the courtship of the Servant and Eternal Wisdom begins, "she shifts genders, assuming the mantle of patriarchal wisdom and calling to Suso with the voice of Solomon" and

then becomes "the queen, the lady, the *domina*, the ultimate object of the knight's desire, who rules heaven, earth, and the chasms of calamity below" (Tinsley, *The Scourge and the Cross*, 127–28).

127. Newman, *God and the Goddesses*, 206.

128. Werner Williams-Krapp writes that "Suso appears to feminize the role [of the Servant in the *Vita*] in order to achieve a maximum of possible identification with the figure of the exemplary Servant within his predominantly female audience" (Williams-Krapp, "Henry Suso's *Vita* between Mystagogy and Hagiography," 41).

129. On the performative aspects of masculine norms in Suso, and their connections to his great predecessor in spiritual autobiography, see Jennifer Ash, "Holy Virility: Masquerading Masculinity in the Autobiographical Texts of Augustine of Hippo and Henry Suso" (PhD diss., Northwestern University, 2000). For a wide-ranging examination of the performance of femininity and masculinity in devotional texts (as a preface to a discussion of these themes in a particular Middle English treatise), see Michelle Sauer, "Cross-Dressing Souls: Same-Sex Desire and the Mystic Tradition in *A Talkyng of the Loue of God*," in *Intersections of Sexuality and the Divine in Medieval Culture: The Word Made Flesh*, ed. Susannah Chewning (Aldershot: Ashgate, 2005), 157–82.

130. Italics here in the critical edition and my translation indicate quotations from scripture. "*Viriliter agite* (1 Cor 16:13) etc. So ein ersamer ritter einen knapen dez ersten in den ring füret, so spricht er wakerlich zů ime: 'eia, werder held, tů hut als ein frumer man' . . . *Viriliter* etc., daz sprichet: gebarend kůnlich un manlich ir alle, die got getrúwent!" (B 370.22–31).

131. *CAM* 158. "Viriliter hostium expugnavit iacula, devicit regna, castra destruxit . . . vestem strangulatam sibi fecit: Hec mulier non est mollis in moribus femineis, nec se prebuit verbis iuvenum pestiferis; sed . . . ut vir stetit in viribus" (*CAM* 75–76).

132. J. Christian Straubhaar-Jones, "The Rivalry of the Secular and the Spiritual in the Masculine Personae of Henry Suso's *The Life of the Servant*," in *Rivalrous Masculinities: New Directions in Medieval Gender Studies*, ed. Ann Marie Rasmussen (Notre Dame, IN: University of Notre Dame Press, 2019), 45.

133. The most important studies are Newman, *God and the Goddesses*, and Caroline Walker Bynum, *Jesus as Mother: Studies in the Spirituality of the High Middle Ages* (Berkeley: University of California Press, 1982).

134. Caroline Walker Bynum, *Fragmentation and Redemption: Essays on Gender and the Human Body in Medieval Religion* (New York: Zone Books, 2012), 161.

135. The literature on this miscellany is considerable, but see especially Jessica Brantley, *Reading in the Wilderness: Private Devotion and Public Performance in Late Medieval England* (Chicago: University of Chicago Press, 2007).

136. Establishing events of self-naming in the absence of autograph manuscripts is, of course, fraught with difficulties. Incipits, explicits, and colophons are all employed in various places to identify Suso or Rolle as authors of both authentic

and spurious works, but this is likely the result of scribal intervention with paratextual material. Within the body of the texts itself such references are exceedingly scarce: for instance, Suso's *Vita* begins with an incipit "here begins the books called the Suso," but this is more likely to be a scribal addition, when the text that follows refers to the Suso-character only as "the Servant of Eternal Wisdom." Similarly, the *Horologium* describes the Suso-character as being given the name *Amandus* to signify his loving relationship with Eternal Wisdom.

137. Suso and Rolle both take their devotion to the monogram to rhetorical extremes, but the monogram was employed by the late third century to imbue an aura of reverence to the name of Christ, analogous to the sacral setting apart of the Hebrew tetragrammaton (yet it is uncertain if there was any direct crossover in the earliest stages of Christian writing). Hildegard Keller, "Kolophon im Herzen: Von beschrifteten Mönchen an den Rändern der Paläographie," *Das Mittelalter* 7 (2002): 157–82, argues that the monogram can also stand for *Jesus hominum salvator*, and the *HS* portion of it also standing for *Heinrich Seuse* (with the *I* perhaps standing in for *Ich?*), but however tempting this interpretation might seem, it is unlikely to be correct, as the vast majority of the monograms in Suso manuscripts read *IHC*, not *IHS* (and even though it happens to be the reading for the manuscript she uses, Einsiedeln, there is no evidence to suggest this fifteenth-century manuscript represents an earlier tradition in relation to the fourteenth-century Strasbourg MS 2929.

138. On the numerous ways in which text becomes iconic in medieval manuscripts and art, see Jeffrey Hamburger, *Script as Image* (Leuven: Peeters, 2014), and Hamburger, "The Iconicity of Script," *Word & Image* 27, no. 3 (2011): 249–61. On the cult of the Holy Name in England, see Rob Lutton, "The Name of Jesus, Nicholas Love's *Mirror*, and Christocentric Devotion in Late Medieval England," in *The Pseudo-Bonaventuran Lives of Christ: Exploring the Middle English Tradition*, ed. Ian Johnson and Allan F. Westphall (Turnhout: Brepols, 2013), 19–53; Lutton, "'Love this Name that is IHC': Vernacular Prayers, Hymns and Lyrics to the Holy Name of Jesus in Pre-Reformation England," in *Vernacularity in England and Wales, c. 1300–1550*, ed. Elizabeth Salter and Helen Wicker (Turnhout: Brepols, 2011), 119–45, and Denis Renevey, "Name above Names: The Devotion to the Name of Jesus from Richard Rolle to Walter Hilton's *Scale of Perfection I*," in *The Medieval Mystical Tradition: England, Ireland and Wales*, ed. Marion Glasscoe (Cambridge: D. S. Brewer, 1999), 103–21.

139. For a broader look at Arthurian influences in Suso, see Deborah Rose-Lefmann, "Lady Love, King, Minstrel: Courtly Depictions of Jesus or God in Late-Medieval Vernacular Mystical Literature," in *Arthurian Literature and Christianity: Notes from the Twentieth Century*, ed. Peter Meister (New York: Garland, 1999), 138–58.

140. Quoted from Renevey's transcription of British Library Additional MS 6686, fol. 319 ("Name above Names," 116).

141. "machete do dez selben namen glich unzallichen vil namen und schůf, daz der diener die namen alle uf sin herz bloss leit und sú mit einem götlichen segen sinen geischlichen kinden hin und her sante" (B 155.1–4). Keller points out that in Suso's text the heart "is a medium used for the transfer of the miraculous. In it the semantics of the means, the intermediary, and the mediation all build upon each other" (Das Herz ist also ein für wundersamen Transfer eingesetztes Medium. In ihm potenziert sich die Semantik der Mitte, des Mittlers, der Vermittlung) (Keller, "Kolophon im Herzen," 159).

142. On the intimacy and sexualization of this scene, see J. Christian Straubhaar-Jones, "Understanding the Visuality of a Medieval Visionary: Fourteenth-Century Dominican Henry Suso's Interwoven Concepts of Divine Image, Gendered Identity, and Epistemology" (PhD diss., University of North Carolina, Chapel Hill, and Duke University, 2015), 120–23.

143. C 321, "quia plerumque facta plus movent quam verba" (K 596.5).

144. Text taken from Brussels, Royal Library of Belgium MS 10981, fol. 235v.

145. "Guldinen bůchstaben allenthalb dar inne geschriben: Jesus, Jesus, Jesus" (B 393). It is important to note that this aspect of the legend of Saint Ignatius's martyrdom was of fairly recent coinage in Suso's day, first appearing in the thirteenth century. See Marie-Anne Polo de Beaulieu, "La légende du cœur inscrit dans la littérature religieuse," in *Education, prédication, et cultures au Moyen Âge: Essais sur Jean Gobi le Jeune (†1350)* (Lyon: Presses Universitaires de Lyon, 1999), 185–96.

146. Citations from the edition of Rolle's main vernacular works will be taken from S. J. Ogilvie-Thomson, ed., *Richard Rolle: Prose and Verse*, EETS o.s. 293 (1988), and preceded with "O-T." O-T 18.615–20. See also the language of wounding in *Ego Dormio*: "In loue þou wound my thoght, and lift my hert to þe" (O-T 31.203).

147. "Hoc nomen Ihesu, fideliter in mente retentum, vicia eradicat, virtutes plantat, caritatem inserit, saporem celestium infundit, discordiam vastat, pacem reformat, quietem internam exhibit, carnalium desideriorum molestam prorsus delet, omnia terrena vertit in fastidio, amantem spiritali replet gaudio" (Murray 43).

148. "O Ihesu pie, infunde in visceribus nostris hoc oleum; scribe in cordibus nostris nomen tuum" (Murray 39). Praise of the name reaches a fever pitch in this passage: "Et hoc est nomen tuum et hoc est opus tuum! Nomen delectabile, opus salubre!" (Murray 39).

149. "Et sic nomen ymaginis et similitudinis tue in cordibus nostris imprimatur" (Murray 41).

150. On the use of the Holy Name in marginalia and other decorative forms, see Denis Renevey, "The Name Poured Out: Margins, Illuminations and Miniatures as Evidence for the Practice of Devotions to the Name of Jesus in Late Medieval England," in *The Mystical Tradition and the Carthusians*, ed. James Hogg (Salzburg: Institut für Anglistik und Amerikanistik, 1996), 9:127–47.

151. Hanna, ed., EETS o.s. 329, p. 111, lines 317–18 and 320–27.

152. Michael S. Batts, ed., *Bruder Hansens Marienlieder* (Tübingen: Max Nie-meyer Verlag, 1963). "Ick wold voel gern in graven / End prenten in miin herne / Ave die drie buecstaven" (lines 1231–23).

153. Bramley 244.

154. O-T 18.611–15.

155. Quotations from the *Incendium amoris* will be taken from Margaret Dean-esly, ed., *The Incendium Amoris of Richard Rolle of Hampole* (Manchester: Uni-versity Press, 1915); cited by page number, they will be preceded by "D." "O bone Ihesu ligasti cor meum in cogitacione nominis tui, et illud iam non canere non ualeo" (D 278) / "O gude Ihesu, my hart þou has bun in þoght of þi name, & now I can not bot synge it" (M 103).

156. Gillespie, "Mystic's Foot," 215.

157. Certeau, *Mystic Fable*, 145.

158. Norman MacKenzie, ed., *The Poetical Works of Gerard Manley Hopkins* (Oxford: Oxford University Press, 1990), 112.

159. Most recently, see Andrew Albin, "Canorous Soundstuff: Hearing the Offi-cium of Richard Rolle at Hampole," *Speculum* 91, no. 4 (2016): 1026–39, and Andrew Albin, *Richard Rolle's Melody of Love* (Toronto: University of Toronto Press, 2018). The only detailed explorations of this topic in Suso to date have been Rozenski, "The Visual, the Textual, and the Auditory," 35–72, and Rozenski, "Music, Mysticism, and the Task of Popularization: The Case of Meister Eckhart and Henry Suso," in *Musik der mittelalterlichen Metropole: Räume, Identitäten und Kontexte der Musik in Köln und Mainz, ca. 900–1400*, ed. Fabian Kolb (Kassel: Merseberg Verlag, 2016), 477–90.

160. Watson, *Richard Rolle and the Invention of Authority*, 139. This system, though undeniably present in Rolle, is even more abundantly commented on in the studies of contemporary scholars, trained as we are to reduce the textual complexity of the past to frameworks and schemata that demand a logical consistency and or-derly pattern of thought (a desire or expectation not necessarily shared by medieval authors or readers).

161. See John Bugbee, "Sight and Sound in *St Erkenwald*: On Theodicy and the Senses," *Medium Ævum* 77, no. 2 (2008): 202–22, for an adversarial article on the relationship between vision and audition in a different fourteenth-century English text. He acknowledges the traditional superiority of vision but argues that "hearing is, boldly put, a more humble sense than seeing. One could even argue phenomeno-logically that it is essentially so: *looking* carries with it some sense of intentional pry-ing into what is distant, since one can control, for example, the direction and duration of one's gaze, and fix it on any object this side of the horizon. The listener, by con-trast, is more dependent on the sounds that happen to make it to her ear" (211–12). See also the study by Elizabeth Sears, "The Iconography of Auditory Perception in the Early Middle Ages: On Psalm Illustration and Psalm Exegesis," in *The Second Sense: Studies in Hearing and Musical Judgment from Antiquity to the Seventeenth*

Century, ed. Charles Burnett, Michael Fend, and Penelope Gouk (London: Warburg Institute, 1991), 19–42.

162. The best historical overview of this intersection of mystical rapture and musical experience can be found in Wolfgang Fuhrmann, *Herz und Stimme: Innerlichkeit, Affect, und Gesang im Mittelalter* (Kassel: Bärenreiter, 2004), 286–317, namely "Unaussprechlichkeit (2): Der mystische Jubilus."

163. Zieman, "The Perils of *Canor*: Mystical Authority, Alliteration, and Extragrammatical Meaning in Rolle, the *Cloud*-Author, and Hilton," *Yearbook of Langland Studies* 22 (2008): 137.

164. See also Racha Kirakosian, "Musical Heaven and Heavenly Music: At the Crossroads of Liturgical Music and Mystical Texts," *Viator* 48, no. 1 (2017): 121–44.

165. McIlroy, *English Prose Treatises of Richard Rolle*, 67.

166. Riehle, *Middle English Mystics*, writes of the importance of music in many of Rolle's Latin works: "This music emanates from God because God himself is music. Rolle indeed addresses him as the medieval musical instrument 'cithara': 'O amor meus! O mel meum! O cithara mea!' . . . We constantly observe in Rolle how the images of music, together with those of fire, are linked with other sense experiences, and this helps to give his mystical language the greatest possible compactness" (120).

167. Watson, *Richard Rolle and the Invention of Authority*, 229.

168. "Und do im in der betrahtunge die sinne neiswi entsunken, do duht in in einer gesiht, er wurdi gefüret uf ein schön, grünen heide, und gie ein stolzer himelscher jungling bi ime und fürte in an siner hand. Also erhůb der selb jungling in dez brůder sele ein lied, und daz erschal als frölich, daz es im alle sin sinne verflogte von überkraft des süssen gedönes" (B 139) (And while he was in this contemplation his senses somehow dissolved. He seemed to be taken in a vision to a beautiful green heath; and a glorious heavenly young man walked by him and led him with his hand. Then this same young man began to sing a song in the friar's soul, and it sounded so joyfully that all his senses flew away because of the overwhelming power of the sweet sounds).

169. "und duhte in, daz sin herz als reht vol wurdi inbrünstiger minne und jamers na gote, daz daz herz ward varnd und wütende in dem libe, als ob es von übriger not zerbrechen wölte, und můste die rehten hand legen uf daz herz im selber ze hilfe, und sinů ogen wurden als vol, daz die trehen über ab runnen. Do daz lied us kom, do ward im ein bild für geworfen, in dem man in leren wolte daz selb lied, daz er sin nit vergessen möhte" (B 139–40).

170. "der anvang dez liedes . . . geschriben mit schönen, wolgeflorierten bůchstaben, und waz du scrift als togen, daz si nit menlich gelesen konde" (B 140).

171. On the crossover between Marian hymns and secular love lyrics, see David Rothenberg, *The Flower of Paradise: Marian Devotion and Secular Song in Medieval and Renaissance Music* (Oxford: Oxford University Press, 2011).

172. "mundi quippe amatores scire possunt uerba uel carmina nostrarum cancionum, non autem cantica nostrorum carminum; quia uerba legunt, sed notam et tonum ac suauitatem odarum addiscere non possunt" (D 278) (Warldly lufars sothely wordis or ditis of owr songe may knaw, for þe wordis þai rede, bot not & toyne & swetnes of songe þai may not lere) (M 103).

173. "Siquidem si clamorem illum canorem ab extrinsecis auribus omnino absconditum arbitrer (quod et uere esse audeo annunciare), utinam et illius modulaminis inueniam auctorem hominem, qui esti non dictis, tamen scriptis mihi gloriam meam decantaret, et pneumataque nexus in nomine nobilissimo coram amato meo edere non erubui, canendo ac pneumatizando depromeret" (D 244) (fforsoth if I demyd þat cry or songe fro bodily eris is all-way hyd, & þat I dar wele say, wold god of þat melody a man I myȝt fynde Autor, þe qwhilk þof not in worde ȝitt in writtynge my ioy he sulde synge, & notis of lufe þe qwhilk in þe worþiest name before my lufe I schamyd nott to say, syngand and Ioyand he suld shew owt) (M 77).

174. R. Jacob McDonie, "Performing Friendship in Richard Rolle's *Incendium Amoris*," *New Medieval Literatures* 17 (2017): 81–114.

175. "Sed utinam uel sodalem in itinere ostendisses, ut illius exhortacione langor letificaretur . . . Interim autem exultans in ympnis tuis degerem dulciter cum socio quem dedisses" (D 245) (Bot wald god þou had owdyr schewd me a fela in þe way, þat with his stirynge heuynes myȝt ha bene gladynd. . . . Emonge certan Ioyand in ympnis of louyng sweytly I suld ha restyd with my fela þat þou had gyfyn me) (M 78).

176. Watson interprets this, for instance, as being "his desire to find (or justify having found) a woman to play, as it were, Clare to his Francis" (Watson, *Richard Rolle and the Invention of Authority*, 224).

177. McDonie, "Performing Friendship in Richard Rolle's *Incendium Amoris*," 100.

178. "Et hec est musica spiritualis, que incognita monet omnibus qui seculi negociis licitis uel illicitis occupantur; nec aliquis qui eam nouit nisi qui soli Deo uacare studuit" (D 257) (Þis is gostely musyk, þat is vnknawen till all þat with wardly bisyness lefull or vnlefull ar occupyde. No man þer is þat þis has knawen bot he þat has stodyyd to god onely to take hede) (M 87).

179. "Et tota oracio nostra cum affectu et effectu erit; ut iam non uerba in oracione transcurramus, sed omnes eciam pene sillabas, cum clamore valido et desiderio incenso, Deo nostro offeremus"; Nicholas Watson, ed., *Emendatio Vitae*; *Orationes Ad Honorem Nominis Ihesu* (Toronto: Pontifical Institute of Mediaeval Studies, 1995), 50 (chap. 7, lines 31–34). "And all our prayer with desire and effect sal be, so þat we ouer-rynne not þe wordis, but nerehand all sillabyls with grete cry & desire we sal offyr to owr lorde" (M 118).

180. See Robert Boenig, "St. Augustine's *jubilus* and Richard Rolle's *canor*," in *Vox Mystica: Essays on Medieval Mysticism*, ed. Anne Clark Bartlett (Cambridge: D. S. Bewer, 1995), 75–86. Wybren Scheepsma notes a passage in Limburg Sermon

45 in which the experience of either music or heat leads to a glossolalic outburst: see Wybren Scheepsma, *The Limburg Sermons: Preaching in the Medieval Low Countries at the Turn of the Fourteenth Century*, trans. David F. Johnson (Leiden: Brill, 2008), 352.

181. "quia dum in oracione ineffabilis dulcor oranti infunditur, ipsa oracio in iubilum commutatur" (Watson, ed., *Emendatio Vitae*, 51).

182. Zieman, "Perils of *Canor*," 145. Francesco Ciabattoni's study of Dante's *Commedia* offers a persuasive account of a similar use of celestial music in the *Paradiso*, which he summarizes thus: "Music is employed to accompany the more mystical and mysterious steps of the pilgrim's ascent. Indeed the exact meaning of the songs' words becomes incomprehensible to the pilgrim, who is more and more left with a sweet lingering feeling of the extraordinary spiritual experience, but is incapable of recollecting it rationally or transcribing it. Such impenetrable songs carry out the mystical component of Dante's own *itinerarium mentis in Deum*. Music becomes the tightrope by means of which the poet attempts to bridge the gap between the physical plane of his mortal limitedness and the metaphysical plane of his vision's subject. Like a rain pervading the entire universe, Grace is delivered through music"; Francesco Ciabattoni, *Dante's Journey to Polyphony* (Toronto: University of Toronto Press, 2010), 155.

183. Albin, "Canorous Soundstuff," 1035.

184. Vincent Gillespie, "Postcards from the Edge: Interpreting the Ineffable in the Middle English Mystics," in *Interpretation, Medieval and Modern*, ed. Piero Boitani and Anna Torti (Cambridge: D. S. Brewer, 1993), 156.

185. As Watson writes, Rolle's "new, daring readiness to talk about *canor* actually is (is a form of, is equivalent to) *canor* . . . [The *Melos Amoris*] both is and is about *canor*" (Watson, *Richard Rolle and the Invention of Authority*, 178).

186. Wolfgang Riehle writes, for instance, that Rolle's use of music is not "a conscious synaesthetic effect in the romantic sense" but rather "the *ineffable* character of his experience makes him reach for several sense concepts at the same time, in order to put across the intensity of his experience in the most effective way" (Riehle, *Middle English Mystics*, 120).

187. *CAM* 174. "Sed alii sunt qui aliter dicunt; videlicet, quod viderunt clare celestia. Asserant qui hoc noverunt; ego id non expertus sum, nec puto experiri dum in carne sum. Paulus vero, qui raptus fuit usque ad tercium celum, non dixit quod vidit deum facie ad faciem, aut cives celestes, sed quod audivit archana dei. . . . Et cum causam temptacionis sue exponeret, scripsit, *ne magnitudo revelacionum*—non dixit visionum—*extollat me; datus est michi stimulis carnis (2 Cor. 12:7)*. Unde audeo dicere quod nullis sanctorum conceditur in hac vita perfecta visio eternorum, nisi ex aliqua spirituali causa, ut aliquid convertatur" (*CAM* 90).

188. A somewhat contrary position can be found in the *Ego Dormio*, but instead of the depth of argumentation found in the *CAM*, it expresses a simple expression of

longing for the vision of Christ: "Þou art þat I haue soght; thy face when may I se?" (O-T 31.206).

189. See William Pollard, "Richard Rolle and the 'Eye of the Heart,'" in *Mysticism and Spirituality in Medieval England*, ed. William Pollard and Robert Boenig (Cambridge: D. S. Brewer, 1997), 85–105.

190. C 167. "Confessores radiant igneo fulgore, virginesque emicant *niveo candore*; tota denique caelestis frequentia quomodo divina affluit dulcedine, repletur iucunditate. Haec caelestia agmina, simul iuncta, cum ineffabili ducentes choros laetitia, coram throno sua depromunt modulamina" (K 464.12–16).

191. C 218. "Gaudent pueri ad sonitum organi, et ad laetos rumores corda exhilarantur universa; sic ad tuam quoque suavissimam memoriam totus aestuo divini amoris incendio, te laudare cupiens" (K 507.4–6).

192. C 276. "Deinde devota anima me audire faciat vocem suam cantando mihi *de canticis Sion* (Ps. 136:3), cuius melodia ex triplici proportione composita suavissimum reddit sonum, videlicet ex perfecta oblivione terrenorum, fervido affectu aeternorum et laudis quadam inchoatione spirituum beatorum" (K 558.1–5) (Aftirwarde a devoute sowle schalle make me to hire his voyce, singinge to me wiþ þe songes of Syoon, whereof þe melodye made of þre manere proporciones ȝeldith alþer swettest sowne, þat is to seye, of perfyte forȝetynge of erþelye þinges and feruent affeccione of euerlastinge þinges and a manere bygynnynge of lovynge of þe blessed sperites) (*SP* VI.316–22). Cf. in the *LBEW*, "Si sol mir singen des gesanges von Syon, daz ist ein inbrünstiges minnen mit einem grundlosen lobenne" (B 297). In French the *ex triplici proportione composita* becomes a simple "chant de trois," indicating that what could be quite precise musical terminology in the Latin text was not fully understood by the translator in this instance (text taken from Brussels, Royal Library of Belgium MS 10981, fol. 193v).

193. Translation mine. "Felix, qui haec gustu interno percipere meruit, qui haec per veram experientiam magis quam per verba vel scripta cognovit" (K 558.5–6) (Welle is him þat maye perceyue and fele þese þinges wiþ inwarde taste & þat may knowe hem by soþfast experience [more] þan by wordes or writinggis) (*SP* VI.322–24).

194. Translation mine. "Quid fecit ille tuus symphonides, homo secundum cor tuum, qui *nudatus velut unus de scurris*, cum organis armigatis, *totis viribus saltavit* (2 Samuel 6:20, 14), coram arca?" (K 561.3–5) (Waz tet din knecht David, der vor der arke, da allein lipliches himelbrot und liplichúding inne warent, so vrölich mit allen sinen kreften sprang!) (B 298).

195. Translation mine. "Quia si cuncta corporis mei membra innumerositate arenam maris excedentia essent organa dulcisona, et omnes potentiae meae essent voces iubilosae, his omnibus te laudare cuperem totis viribus meis, conditor orbis" (K 561.11–15). For a roughly parallel passage in which singing the *Sursum corda* grants Suso a vision of every creature and plant giving praise to God—although he

yet qualifies this as a *seitenspil*, a song on stringed instruments—see Rozenski, "The Visual, the Textual, and the Auditory," 48–49.

196. Citations from Rolle's *English Psalter* will be taken from *The Psalter or Psalms of David and Certain Canticles*, ed. H. R. Bramley (Oxford: Clarendon, 1884); references to this edition will be given by the page and line number prefaced by "Bramley."

197. Translation mine. "O *surge, surge* nunc, anima mea, et *loquere canticum* (Judges 5:12). Canticum utique laudis *in voce exultationis* (Ps. 41:5). Cymbala concrepent, corda coniubilent, tellus omnis resultet in laudem creatoris. O amantissima sapientia, bonitas aeterna, te precor, ut omni mane diluculo, cum ad te surrexero et oculos aperuero, simul quoque cor meum in laude tua aperiatur, et quondam lucifero splendore ac flammeo ardore laudis tuae facula immensa ex eo simul exsurgat, in se continens tui amoris intensissimum gradum cordi humano unquam desursum concessum. Similitudinem quoque ardoris in se gerens spiritus illius, qui inter supremi ordinis caelestia agmina in te et de te ardentia maxime tuo calet in amore. Ad exemplar nihilominus illius supersubstantialis et superessentialis ac ineffabilis caritatis, in qua tu, o Pater caelestis, ferventissime diligis tuum unigenitum in Spiritu Sancto" (K 583.20–22).

198. Translation mine. "Et peto, ut haec laus tam suaviter ac blande resonet in corde tuo paterno, sicut sonare consuevit suo modo omnium citharoedorum ac musicalium instrumentorum suavis modulatio in corde iucundo, statu iuventutis florido. Et in hac laudis facula simul ascendat tuae laudis tam odorifera *fumi virgula* tam gratiosa, ac si esset composita *ex* omnibus *aromatibus myrrhae et thuris et universi pulveris pigmentarii* (Cant. 3:6): Tam speciosa, sicut cum vernali tempore flores herbarum pullulant in campis, pulchris coloribus, et arbores stant frondibus ornatis, gratis odoribus" (K 583–84.22–25, 1–5).

199. Translation mine. "Sitque laudis huius facula tam amorosa ac deliciosa, ut in eam oculi tui delectabiliter ferantur, totaque caelestis aula resultet. Et haec iugiter sine intermissione fervidissimo aestu et rapidissimo calore tui amoris sursum exsurgat ex corde per devotam meditationem, ex labiis per fervidam locutionem et ex omnibus operibus meis per sanctam ac caelestem conversationem; et haec laudis facula sua virtute omnes inimicos repellat, gratiam augeat, finem beatum obtineat et gloriam aeternae beatitudinis acquirat, ut finis huius laudis temporalis sit initium aeternae laudis patriae caelestis. Amen" (K 584.6–14).

200. "Minneklicher herr, min zartú Ewigú Wisheit, ich beger, swenne minú ögen dez morgens erst uf gant, daz och min herz uf gange, und von ime uf breche ein ufflammendú vúrinú minnevackel dins lobes mit der lieplichesten minne des minnendesten herzen, daz in zit ist, nach der bitzigosten minne des höhsten geistes von Seraphin in ewikeit, und der grundlosen minne, also du, himelscher vatter, din gemintes kint minnest in der usblikenden minne úwer beider geistes, und daz lob als süzklich erklinge in dinem vätterlichen herzen, als in zit in siner achte kein süz gedöne aller minneklichen seitenspil in keinem vrien gemüt ie gedonde, und in der

minnevackel uf tringe ein als süzer smak des lobes, als es usgenomenlich von allen edlen krütern und wurzen und allen apotekan aller tugenden in ir höhstennn luterkeit zesamen púlverlich geröchet weri, und sin anblik als schone in gnaden geblümet wart, daz es dinen götlichen ögen und allem himelschen here werde ein lustliches ansehen; und beger, daz dú minnevackel ze allen ziten inbrúnstklich uf schlahe in allem minem gebette, uz dem munde, in dem gesange, an gedenken, worten und werken, daz si alle mine viende verjage, alle mine gebresten verswende, gnade erbitte und ein heiliges ende erwerbe, daz ein ende dises zitlichen lobes si ein anvang des iemer werenden ewigen lobes. Amen" (B 313–14).

201. Rozenski, "The Visual, the Textual, and the Auditory," 52–54.

202. On the relationship in intellectual history between birdsong, music, and poetry more generally (though neither Suso nor Rolle are specifically discussed), see Elizabeth Eva Leach, *Sung Birds: Music, Nature, and Poetry in the Later Middle Ages* (Ithaca, NY: Cornell University Press 2007), and Michael J. Warren, *Birds in Medieval English Poetry: Metaphors, Realities, Transformations* (Rochester, NY: Boydell & Brewer, 2018).

203. Translation mine. "nimirum videmus, quod plerumque inter dulcissimas nemoris aviculas et cincinnantes philomenas corvi quoque crocitantes assunt, in hoc eodem modico, quod acceperunt, creatori suo subservientes" (K 579.19–22).

204. "Minneklicher herre, nu lobent dich doch die fröschen in den graben, und mugent su nit singen, so gewzent su aber" (B 305).

205. Translation mine. "ego quoque peccator cum sim, cantum ad manus habeo peccatorum, et prout possum Deum meum per ipsum laudo et glorifico in aeternum" (K 579.23–25).

206. Translation mine. "Hoc suave canticum anima mea usque in saeculum inter spirituale genus avium cum laeto dulci canit carmine" (K 580.2–3).

207. Tellingly, the translator of the *Seven Points* apparently did not know quite what to make of the "spiritual race of birds," and omitted it from his otherwise faithful translation of K 579.3–580.5 (*SP* VII.124–49).

208. "luf copuls God and manne" (*Richard Rolle: Uncollected Prose and Verse with related Northern Texts*, ed. Ralph Hanna, EETS o.s. 329, 26).

209. "In principio enim conuersionis mee, et propositi singularis, cogitaui me uelle assimilari auicule, que pre amore languet amati sui, sed languendo eciam letatur adueniente sibi quod amat et letando canit, canendo eciam languet, sed in dulcedine et ardore. Fertur enim philomena tota nocte cantui et melo indulgere, ut ei placeat, cui copulatur" (D 277) (In the begynnynge truly of my conuersion & syngulere purpoys I þoght I wald be lyke þe lityll byrde þat for lufe of þe lemman longis, bot in longynge it is gladynd qwhen he cumys þat it lufis, Also it longis, bot in swetnes & heet. It is sayd þe nyghtgale to songe & melody all nyght is gyfyn, þat sche may pleis hym to qwhome sche is Ioynyd) (M 102).

This theme also appears near the end of the *Melos amoris*: "Perfruens Factore sic funditus affectus fio ut philomena que concinens continue usque ad mortem in melos diligit dulcissime quia hec demum moritur melum amando et mesticia amati deducta deficit, ut dicitur, pre dileccione" (Richard Rolle, *Le chant d'amour*, ed. E. J. F. Arnould, 2 vol. [Paris: Les Éditions du Cerf, 1971], 1:178). A similar metaphor is used for Mechthild of Hackeborn: "one of her sisters records in the *Liber specialis gratiae*, Mechthild was known as 'God's nightingale' (Philomenae suae)"; Bruce Holsinger, *Music, Body, and Desire in Medieval Culture: Hildegard of Bingen to Chaucer* (Stanford, CA: Stanford University Press, 2001), 241.

210. "Quanto magis cum suauitate maxima canerem Christo meo Ihesu, qui est sponsus anime mee per totam uitam presentem que nox est respectu future claritatis, ut langueam, et languendo deficiam pre amore. Sed deficiendo conualescam et nutriar in ardore, iubilemque ac iubilando canam delicias amoris cum amenitate, et tanquam ex fistula perflet canora ac feruens deuocio, et emittat odas altissimo interius incensas" (D 277) (How mykill more with grettyst swetnes to criste, me Ihesu, I suld synge, þat is spouse of my saule, be all þis present lyfe þat is nyght in regarde of clerenes to cum, to longe, longyngly in lufe dee, deyngly I sal wax stronge & in heet I sal be norischyd, & ioy I sal & Ioyand likynges of lufe synge with myrth, & as wer of a pype hote deuocion sal gif songe & aungelis melody my sa[u]l to þe hyest sal 3elde with-inforth dressyd) (M 102–3).

211. "With this he came into a custom, when he heard songs of praise being sung or sweet stringed instruments sounding, or speaking and singing about secular love, he was suddenly transported into his heart and mind with a detached in-looking on his loveliest love, from which all love flows" (Hie mite kom er in ein gewonheit, wenn er loblieder horte singen oder süzzú seitenspil erklingen oder von zitlichem lieb hort sagen ald singen, so wart im sin herz und mût geswintlich in gefürt mit einem abgescheiden inblik in sin lieplichostes lieb, von dem alles liep flússet) (B 15).

212. Zieman, "The Perils of *Canor*," 141–42. She cites the Latin: "si non ualeat sustinere clamorem psallencium nisi canor eius interior ad cogitatum redigatur."

213. From the *Table des Équivalences*, in Rolle, *Le chant d'amour*, 2:323–25.

214. "O height of ineffable devotion, how most sweetly and superbly do these instruments resound in a sorrowful ear" (*SP* III.71–72). Citations from the *Seven Points* will be to chapter (also called "points") and line number from Schultze's edition preceded by "*SP*." The *LBEW* contains equivalent passages in German that also reveal aspects of Suso's nomenclature for the experience of heavenly music: "Ach süzer, minneklicher herre, wel ein süzes harphen dis ist einem lidenden menschen! Herr, wöltist du mir also minneklich psalterjen in minem lidenne, so wölt ich gern liden, so were mir baz mit lidenne denn ane liden" (B 250).

215. "In fact, when you play the psaltery so sweetly, the spirit weighed down by sadness is lightened and your heavenly song drives out, at least for a time, sadness from the spirit and the mind, that suffering might be borne more lightly" (my translation).

216. Translation mine. "Audire vis citharam spiritualis musicae pulchre resonantem. Sursum erigere, et pretiosum fructum temporalium adversitatum diligenter

attende. Sicut enim in cithara cordae proportionaliter protensae sonum reddunt suavem, sic electus quisque, dum adversitate premitur, quasi vi quadam extra se tenditur, et ad reddendam dulcem ac caelestem melodiam plenius facilitator" (K 488.9–14). Künzle's footnote to this passage notes a similar metaphor used in Gregory the Great, *Moralia in Job* 20.41 (*PL* 76:185C).

217. For an overview, see Holsinger, *Music, Body, and Desire in Medieval Culture*, 191–258: "The Musical Body in Pain: Passion, Percussion, and Melody in Thirteenth-Century Religious Practice."

CHAPTER 2

1. Ian Johnson, "Translational Topographies of Language and Imagination in Nicholas Love's *Mirror* and *A Mirror to Devout People*," in *The Medieval Translator*, ed. Alessandra Petrina (Turnhout: Brepols, 2013), 15:246.

2. Elizabeth Westlake, "Learn to Live and Learn to Die: Heinrich Suso's *Scire Mori* in Fifteenth Century England" (PhD diss., University of Birmingham, 1993), examined Suso's contribution to the *ars moriendi* tradition, largely agreeing with Lovatt's argument about the dullness of the texts she studied. She also provided editions of two unpublished translations of Suso's *Ars moriendi*: one found in Lichfield, Cathedral Library MS 16, the other found in Glasgow University Library MS Hunter 496 and Oxford, Bodleian Library MS Bodley 789.

3. Roger Lovatt, "Henry Suso and the Medieval Mystical Tradition in England," in *The Medieval Mystical Tradition in England: Papers Read at Dartington Hall, July 1982*, ed. Marion Glasscoe (Exeter: University of Exeter Press, 1982), 57. See also Lovatt, "The Influence of the Religious Literature of Germany and the Low Countries on English Spirituality c. 1350–1475" (PhD diss., University of Oxford, 1975).

4. Rebecca Selman produced a comprehensive study of most of Suso's medieval appearances in medieval England, focusing on their increased dialogic element and their contribution to vernacular sapiential literature; see Selman, "Voices and Wisdom: A Study of Henry Suso's *Horologium Sapientiae* in Some Late Medieval English Religious Texts" (PhD diss., University of Exeter, 1998).

5. For instance, Sarah James, "A Previously Unnoticed Extract of Suso's *Horologium Sapientiae* in English," *Notes & Queries* 59, no. 1 (2012), 28–30, and James, "Rereading Henry Suso and Eucharistic Theology in Fifteenth-Century England," *Review of English Studies* 63, no. 262 (2012): 732–42.

6. Previously, it had only been printed by Horstmann in the journal *Anglia* in the late nineteenth century, and this was only a transcription of one witness, Bodleian MS Douce 114. Dirk Schultze, ed., *"The Seven Points of True Love and Everlasting Wisdom*: A Middle English Translation of Henry Suso's *Horologium Sapientiae*, edited from Aberystwyth, National Library of Wales, Brogyntyn II.5" (PhD diss., Ernst-Moritz-Arndt-Universität Greifswald, 2005). Citations of the

Seven Points will be from this edition, cited using Schultze's Point and line numbers preceded by *"SP."*

7. Steven Rozenski, "'Your Ensaumple and Your Mirour': Hoccleve's Amplification of the Imagery and Intimacy of Henry Suso's *Ars Moriendi*," *Parergon* 25, no. 2 (2008): 1–16. Most recently, discussions of Hoccleve's translation strategies have appeared in Shannon Gayk, *Image, Text, and Religious Reform in Fifteenth-Century England* (Cambridge: Cambridge University Press, 2010); Karen Smyth, *Imaginings of Time in Lydgate and Hoccleve's Verse* (Aldershot: Ashgate, 2011); David Watt, *The Making of Thomas Hoccleve's Series* (Liverpool: University of Liverpool Press, 2013); and Amy Appleford, *Learning to Die in London, 1380–1540* (Philadelphia: University of Pennsylvania Press, 2015).

8. For a more detailed study of Blacman and his intellectual life, see Roger Lovatt, "The Library of John Blacman and Contemporary Carthusian Spirituality," *Journal of Ecclesiastical History* 43, no. 2 (1992): 195–230.

9. Barry Windeatt, "1412–1534: Texts," in *The Cambridge Companion to Medieval English Mysticism*, ed. Samuel Fanous and Vincent Gillespie (Cambridge: Cambridge University Press, 2011), 197.

10. Vincent Gillespie, "Anonymous Devotional Writings," in *A Companion to Middle English Prose*, ed. A. S. G. Edwards (Cambridge: D. S. Brewer, 2004), 143.

11. The present-day Konzilgebäude (once a fourteenth-century warehouse), home to the conclave that elected Martin V, is now a museum dedicated to the council, and the Dominican monastery is a luxury hotel (with a bar named after Suso). For the significance of the Council of Constance in the changing shape of the English Church and English devotional literature, see especially Vincent Gillespie, "Chichele's Church: Vernacular Theology in England after Thomas Arundel," in *After Arundel: Religious Writing in Fifteenth-Century England*, ed. Kantik Ghosh and Vincent Gillespie (Turnhout: Brepols, 2011), 3–42.

12. Kathryn Kerby-Fulton, *Books under Suspicion: Censorship and Tolerance of Revelatory Writing in Late Medieval England* (Notre Dame, IN: University of Notre Dame Press, 2006), 74–75. For a broader discussion of insular awareness and repression of Joachimism, see the entire chapter in ibid., "'Through the Hiding of Books': The Codicological Evidence for Joachite Franciscanism and Censorship in England before and after Wyclif," 71–108.

13. Selman, "Voices and Wisdom," 268–81, drawing on A. I. Doyle, "A Survey of the Origins and Circulation of Theological Writings in English in the 14th, 15th, and Early 16th Centuries, with Special Consideration of the Role of the Clergy Therein" (D Phil diss., University of Cambridge, 1953), Wiltrud Wichgraf, "Susos *Horologium Sapientiae* in England nach Handschriften des 15. Jahrhunderts," *Anglia: Zeitschrift für Englische Philologie* 53, no. 1-2 (1929): 123–33, and 53, no. 3 (1929): 345–73, and Roger Lovatt, "The Influence of the Religious Literature of Germany and the Low Countries on English Spirituality, c. 1350–1475" (PhD diss., University of Oxford, 1965). Unfortunately Künzle does not use any of these in his

edition of the *Horologium* (he considers variants from eleven Continental MSS), making an evaluation of which, if any, of the extant MSS were used by the English translators reliant on manuscript study. The Latin translations of the *One Hundred Meditations* all seem to come from the Low Countries: on this tradition, see Van Aelst, *Vruchten van de Passie* and *Passie voor het lijden*, and also my discussion below of the one English translation that survives from this tradition in Oxford, Bodleian Library MS E Museo 160.

14. Gilbert Ouy, *La librairie des frères captifs: Les manuscrits de Charles d'Orléans et Jean d'Angoulême* (Turnhout: Brepols, 2007). For an edition of book 1 of the French translation of the *Horologium*, see Marie-France Piaggesi-Ajdnik, ed., "L'Orloge de Sapience: Edition critique avec introduction, notes et glossaire, d'après le manuscrit no. 926 de la Bibliothèque Nationale de Paris" (PhD diss., Université de Nancy II, 1984).

15. Schultze, ed., *"The Seven Points of True Love and Everlasting Wisdom,"* lxiii. The grant to Witham is found in 50 Edward III, Public Record Office 143/389/7.

16. It draws on Suso's *Horologium* briefly, but the *Chastising* is best known for translating a significant portion of Jan van Ruusbroec's *The Spiritual Espousals* into English, via Geert Grote's Latin translation of the Dutch source-text. See G. B. de Soer, "The Relationship of the Latin Versions of Ruysbroek's 'Die Geestelike Brulocht' to 'The Chastising of God's Children,'" *Mediaeval Studies* 21 (1959): 129–46, Michael Sargent, "Ruusbroec in England: *The Chastising of God's Children* and Related Works," in *Historia et spiritualitas cartusiensis: Colloquiii Quarti Internationalis acta, Gandavi, Antverpiae, Brugis, 16–19 Sept. 1982* (Destelbergen: De Grauwe, 1982), 303–12, and Steven Rozenski, *"The Chastising of God's Children* from Manuscript to Print," *Études Anglaises* 66, no. 3 (2013): 369–78.

17. An ownership inscription of the unique manuscript of *The Cleansing of Man's Soul* that refers to the *Chastising* by name dates the MS to 1401 and establishes Fenton's ownership; the year, however, has been added by a second, undatable hand; see Annie Sutherland, *"The Chastising of God's Children*: A Neglected Text," in *Text and Controversy from Wyclif to Bale: Essays in Honour of Anne Hudson*, ed. Helen Barr and Ann M. Hutchison (Turnhout: Brepols, 2005), 356–57. On Bodleian Library MS Douce 322 and British Library MS Harley 1706 and their connection to Dartford and Barking, respectively, see Paul Lee, *Nunneries, Learning and Spirituality in Late Medieval English Society: The Dominican Priory of Dartford* (Woodbridge: Boydell & Brewer, 2000), 135–65.

18. On Caxton, Wynkyn de Worde, and Pynson as translators and as printers of translated literature, see Julia Boffey, "Banking on Translation: English Printers and Continental Texts," in *The Medieval Translator*, vol. 15, *In Principio Fuit Interpres*, ed. Alessandra Petrina (Turnhout: Brepols, 2013), 317–29.

19. *The Chastising of God's Children and the Treatise of Perfection of the Sons of God*, ed. Joyce Bazire and Eric Colledge (Oxford: Basil Blackwell, 1957), 25.

See also Michael Sargent, "Ruusbroec in England: *The Chastising of God's Children and Related Works*," in *Historia et spiritualitas cartusiensis: Colloquiii Quarti Internationalis acta, Gandavi, Antverpiae, Brugis, 16–19 Sept. 1982* (Destelbergen: De Grauwe, 1982).

20. Susan H. Cavanaugh, "A Study of Books Privately Owned in England, 1300–1450" (PhD diss., University of Pennsylvania, 1980), 54–55.

21. On this passage, see also Brantley, *Reading in the Wilderness*, 259–68.

22. Transcription provided by Dirk Schultze.

23. From Sargent's introduction to Love's *The Mirror of the Blessed Life of Jesus Christ: A Full Critical Edition*, edited by Michael Sargent (Exeter: Exeter University Press, 2005), 1. All citations are taken from this edition and presented by page and line number. See also the recent study by David Falls, *Nicholas Love's Mirror and Late Medieval Devotio-Literary Culture* (London: Routledge, 2016).

24. On the genesis of the *Meditationes Vitae Christi*, see most recently Sarah McNamer, ed., *"Meditations on the Life of Christ": The Short Italian Text* (Notre Dame, IN: University of Notre Dame Press, 2018).

25. "Imagination thus conceived constitutes a restriction for Love, a means to distance the meditant from imagined scenes, where it had provided the meditant of the [*Meditationes Vitae Christi*] with a means to engage in precisely those scenes"; Michelle Karnes, *Imagination, Meditation, and Cognition in the Middle Ages* (Chicago: University of Chicago Press, 2011), 221.

26. Nicholas Love, *Mirror of the Blessed Life of Jesus Christ*, will be cited as *Mirror*. Anonymous, *Mirror to Devout People/Speculum devotorum*, will be cited as *Spec.*

27. This is established with some certainty in Elizabeth Zeeman, "Two Middle English Versions of a Prayer to the Sacrament," *Archiv für das Studium der neueren Sprachen und Literaturen* 194 (1957): 113–21.

28. For a nuanced and perceptive discussion of Nicholas Love's translation practices, alongside a briefer mention of the strategies employed in the *Speculum devotorum*, see Ian Johnson, "Translational Topographies of Language and Imagination in Nicholas Love's *Mirror* and *A Mirror to Devout People*," in *The Medieval Translator*, vol. 15, *In Principio Fuit Interpres*, ed. Alessandra Petrina (Turnhout: Brepols, 2013).

29. This affective intensity is seen especially vividly in Juliette Vuille's study of Middle English treatments of the *Noli me tangere* episode after the Resurrection: Love, "while accepting the fact that Christ uttered the objectionable words, cannot believe that the Magdalene was not allowed to touch him later on during their encounter. He goes on to reduce the episode's import by presenting it as utterly metaphorical, and by turning this apparent rejection into a token of Christ's affection for the Magdalene" (see Juliette Vuille, "'Towche me not': Uneasiness in the Translation of the *noli me tangere* Episode in the Late Medieval English Period," in Petrina, ed., *Medieval Translator*, 15:220).

30. Katie Bugyis, "Through the Looking Glass: Reflections of Christ's 'Trewe Louers' in Nicholas Love's *Mirror of the Blessed Life of Jesus Christ,*" in *Devotional Culture in Late Medieval England and Europe*, ed. Stephen Kelly and Ryan Perry (Turnhout: Brepols, 2014), 485.

31. *Spec* 6. Citations are from Paul Patterson, ed., *A Mirror to Devout People (Speculum devotorum)*, EETS o.s. 346, by page number preceded by "*Spec.*"

32. Paul Patterson notes that Nicholas of Lyra may have been chosen for the perception that he was particularly well versed in historical Jewish customs and other local details of the ancient Near East; see Patterson, "*Myrror to Devout People (Speculum Devotorum)*: An Edition with Commentary" (PhD diss., University of Notre Dame, 2006), 41–42.

33. On the emphasis of Wycliffe and his followers on the historical/literal meaning of scripture, see Kantik Ghosh, *The Wycliffite Heresy: Authority and the Interpretation of Texts* (Cambridge: Cambridge University Press, 2002), 1–21.

34. "eintweder von der Ewigen Wisheit munde, die si selber sprach an dem evangelio, oder aber von dien höhsten lerern" (B 197).

35. See Rebecca Selman, "Spirituality and Sex Change: *Horologium Sapientiae* and *Speculum Devotorum,*" in *Writing Religious Women: Female Spiritual and Textual Practices in Late Medieval England*, ed. Denis Renevey and Christiania Whitehead (Cardiff: University of Wales Press, 2000), for an account of the text's Marian focus and the method in which the translator transformed a Passion meditation to appeal specifically to a female readership.

36. On the translator's handling of his sources and his project of translation, particularly in comparison to Nicholas Love, see Ian Johnson, *The Middle English Life of Christ: Academic Discourse, Translation, and Vernacular Theology* (Turnhout: Brepols, 2013), 147–75.

37. Vincent Gillespie, "The Haunted Text: Reflections in the *Mirour to Deuote Peple,*" in *Medieval Texts and Contexts*, ed. Denis Renevey and Graham Caie (New York: Routledge, 2008), 139. Michael Sargent, "Versions of the Life of Christ: Nicholas Love's *Mirror* and Related Works," *Poetica* 42 (1995): 39–70, does claim that the "author of the *Speculum* thus seems to have had the *Meditationes Vitae Christi* and *The Mirror of the Blessed Life of Jesus Christ* constantly in mind in shaping his own work. The *Speculum* follows the *Meditationes* and the *Mirror* in some ways, complements them in others; but seems never to ignore them" (65).

38. A translation of K 549.7–10: "Certissime et veraciter et absque omni dubitatione in hoc sacramento contineor, Deus et homo cum corpore et anima, carne et sanguine, sicut cum prodii ex utero matris et in cruce pependi ac sedeo ad dexteram Patris." For comparison, the *Seven Points* rendering of this passage reads: "In moste certeynte and soþfastelye and wiþoute any doute I am conteynede in þis Sacrament, god and man wiþ body and sowle, flesche and blode, as I wente oute of my modere wombe and henge on þe Crosse & sitte on þe fadere Righte hande" (*SP* VI.43–47).

39. See also Selman, "Spirituality and Sex Change," 63–79, for a perspective on the gender dynamics possibly at work in the translation. On the approved women, see Paul Patterson, "Preaching with the Hands: Carthusian Book Production and the *Speculum Devotorum*," in *Medieval Latin and Middle English Literature: Essays in Honour of Jill Mann*, ed. Christopher Cannon and Maura Nolan (Cambridge: D. S. Brewer, 2011), 134–51.

40. *Chastising* 98 and note. Citations from the *Chastising* are given by page number from *The Chastising of God's Children and the Treatise of Perfection of the Sons of God*, ed. Joyce Bazire and Eric Colledge (Oxford: Basil Blackwell, 1957), and preceded with "*Chastising*."

41. *Chastising* 99, from *Horologium* 1.8.

42. *Chastising* 186, from *Horologium* 2.5.

43. *Chastising* 204, from *Horologium* 2.5.

44. Hanna describes the Suso text itself, retrospectively in the manner of a blind taste test: "The first booklet of the MS, which contains the biblical texts, ends (ff. 85–93) with an unpublished tract 'how [in] þe sacrament of þe auter crist is [to] be resceyued worþili and deuotly'; this text addresses what is always taken as the defining heretical tenet of the movement and is neither overtly Lollard nor overtly orthodox but accommodating of any view"; see Ralph Hanna, "English Biblical Texts before Lollardy and Their Fate," in *Lollards and Their Influence in Late Medieval England*, ed. Fiona Somerset, Jill Havens, and Derrick Pitard (Woodbridge: Boydell Press, 2003), 149.

45. It has been edited by Dirk Schultze, "Henry Suso's *Treatise on the Sacrament* in Cambridge, St John's College G.25: An Edition," *Anglia* 132, no. 3 (2014): 439–72.

46. James, "Rereading Henry Suso and Eucharistic Theology," 737.

47. Westlake, "Learn to Live and Learn to Die," 85. She also edits both texts in appendices to the dissertation.

48. Ibid., 121.

49. On Winter, see, especially, Vincent Gillespie, "Syon and the New Learning," in *The Religious Orders in Pre-Reformation England*, ed. James G. Clark (Woodbridge: Boydell & Brewer, 2002), 75–95, and George Keiser, "Patronage and Piety in Fifteenth Century England: Margaret, Duchess of Clarence, Simon Wynter and Beinecke MS 317," *Yale University Library Gazette* 60–61 (1985): 32–46.

50. Pseudo-Jerome, *Epistolae de magnificentiis et miraculis beati Hieronymi*; *PL* 22:281–326.

51. Claire Waters, ed., *Virgins and Scholars: A Fifteenth-Century Compilation of the Lives of John the Baptist, John the Evangelist, Jerome, and Katherine of Alexandria* (Turnhout: Brepols, 2008), 180. Translating K 527, 10–18: "Scientia utilissima et cunctis artibus praeferenda est haec scientia, scire videlicet mori. Scire quidem se esse mortalem, omnibus commune est, cum *nemo sit, qui semper vivat vel*

qui huius rei fiduciam habeat. Sed paucissimos invenies, qui scire mori sciant; quia hoc donum Dei permaximum est. Scire namque mori est paratum habere cor et animam omnni tempore ad superna, ut quandocumque mors venerit, paratum eum inveniat, ut absque omni retractione eam recipiat, quasi qui socii sui dilecti adventum desideratum exspectat." In the *Seven Points* this passage reads, "Soþely, a man forto kunne dye is forto haue his herte and his sowle *in* alle tymes vpwarde to þo þinges þat beþ abouen, þat is to seye, þat what time deth comyth hit [fynde him] redye, so þa*t* he receyue hit gladlye wiþoute any wiþdrawynge, right as he þat abideþ þe desyred comynge of his dere louyd felawe" (*SP* V.14–8).

52. The troublesome final page of Bodleian MS Douce 114 (assigned the siglum <**D**> by Schultze), which we will see again in chapter 3, bears a heavily erased colophon beginning with an *S* that, even under ultraviolet light, remains indecipherable. The argument has been made that the term *scriptus* is unlikely to have been used to describe a scribe's work, thus making it in some way stem from the translator himself. Combined with the reference to "this place of grace" in the preface and the Nicholas Love connection, this lends support to Mountgrace Charterhouse as the place of composition. Others have argued that the "Dere worshipfull lady" translator's preface makes Carthusian authorship unlikely. The question remains open, particularly insofar as Künzle's edition does not include any of the English-provenance MSS.

53. See Schultze, ed., "*Seven Points*," 247–53, for a complete concordance, including page numbers keyed to Künzle and Horstmann.

54. Michael Sargent, "Versions of the Life of Christ: Nicholas Love's *Mirror* and Related Works," *Poetica* 42 (1995): 47.

55. Jolliffe J.2(c)/J.3(b), *Index of Printed Middle English Prose* (*IPMEP*), 142.

56. Hartung, *A Manual of the Writings in Middle English, 1050–1500*, vol. 8, XXIII.3.81.

57. *IPMEP* 281, 197.

58. There are two copies recorded in Cambridge University Library, and one each in Durham Cathedral Library, the British Library (Grenehalgh's copy), the John Rylands Library, and the Pierpont Morgan Library.

59. Schultze, ed., "*Seven Points*," lxxvii–cii, with slight emendations regarding the Caxton incunable (Schultze omits *The Twelve Profits of Tribulation*).

60. Rebecca Selman's insightful dissertation, which has unfortunately remained unpublished, focuses on the role of voices and wisdom in the text: particularly the changing audience, the use of Augustine, and the emphasis on sapiential literature in the adaptations.

61. A. C. Spearing, "Language and Its Limits: *The Cloud of Unknowing* and *Pearl*," in *Approaching Medieval English Anchoritic and Mystical Texts*, ed. Dee Dyas, Valerie Edden, and Roger Ellis (Cambridge: D. S. Brewer, 2005), 75 (emphasis original).

62. For a detailed look at the significance of this passage to the overall strategy of the *Seven Points* (particularly its use of Augustine), see Rebecca Selman, "Hearing Voices? Reading *Horologium Sapientiae* and *The Seven Poyntes of Trewe Wisdom*," in *The Medieval Translator*, Proceedings of the International Conference of Göttingen (22–25 July 1996), ed. Roger Ellis, René Tixier, and Bernd Weitemeier (Turnhout: Brepols, 1998), 6:254–69.

63. Indeed, despite significant evidence that there *was* a limited English awareness of and reaction against Free Spiritism. In vernacular literature, this is most marked in *Chastising of God's Children* (see Kerby-Fulton, *Books under Suspicion*, particularly, "*The Chastising of God's Children* and the Context for Porete's *Mirror* in England: Evidence of Insular Awareness of the Free Spirit Heresy in Carthusian Circles and Beyond," 260–71). For the interesting case of the insular reception of Marguerite Porete, see Robert Lerner, "New Light on the *Mirror of Simple Souls*," *Speculum* 85 (2010): 91–116.

64. On some consistent aspects of the copying of paratextual features of the *Seven Points*, see Dirk Schultze, "Wisdom in the Margins: Text and Paratext in *The Seven Points of True Love and Everlasting Wisdom*," *Études anglaises* 66, no. 3 (2013): 341–56.

65. K 366.17–19. Barbara Newman made this suggestion to me in private correspondence. MS P (New York, Columbia University MS Plimpton 256) omits a line, which might make the gendering more complicated still, slipping from one gender to another within the same clause, but it is more likely a case of eye skip. "[I]n þese wordis of þe boke of wisdam" is omitted in Caxton's text, perhaps indicating an awareness of the apocryphal nature of the book of Wisdom or a greater concern regarding some forms of biblical translation when explicitly labeled as such. See also Karáth, "*Altum sapere*," 70–76, on the translator's transformation of the gender dynamics in the *Seven Points*.

66. Newman, *God and the Goddesses*, 209. But in some instances the gendered language used in both is identical.

67. Not to mention the luscious iconography of a female Sapientia in Brussels Royal Library MS IV 111, which Newman goes on to discuss: one of the miniatures, depicting the marriage of the Servant and Eternal Wisdom "may well be unique as a representation of the male Christian joined in marriage to his feminine God" (Newman, *God and the Goddesses*, 220). She also notes the unique *Déclaration des Hystoires*, a contemporary description of the iconography of the miniatures, which does not hesitate to explain the main figure in the frontispiece as "Sapientia in the image and likeness of a woman [en forme et figure de femme] representing Jesus"; Peter Rolfe Monks, *The Brussels Horloge de Sapience: Iconography and Text of Brussels, Bibliothèque Royale, MS. IV 111, With an Edition of the Déclaration des Hystoires and a Translation by K.V. Sinclair* (Leiden: E. J. Brill, 1990), 134.

68. Schultze, ed., *Seven Points*, Translator's Prologue (hereafter TP), lines 2–3.

69. See Karáth, "*Altum sapere*," 75–76.

70. Indeed, elsewhere too the translator omits from his source-text: "When he has been so devoutly received, I shall lead him to his own place, that is my heart's couch, the spiritual marriage bed" (C 141).

71. Certeau, *Mystic Fable*, 1:114

72. B 342.

73. *Pseudo-Dionysius: The Complete Works*, trans. Colm Luibheid (Mahwah, NJ: Paulist Press 1987), 101.

74. On Hoccleve's use of first-person allegory in a broader French context, see Stephanie A. V. G. Kamath, *Authorship and First-Person Allegory in Late Medieval France and England* (Rochester, NY: Boydell & Brewer, 2012).

75. Citations are from Roger Ellis, ed., *"My Compleinte" and Other Poems* (Exeter: University of Exeter Press, 2001).

76. Sebastian Langdell, *Thomas Hoccleve: Religious Reform, Transnational Poetics, and the Invention of Chaucer* (Liverpool: Liverpool University Press, 2018), 4 (emphasis original). See also Amy Appleford, "The Sea Ground and the London Street: The Ascetic Self in Julian of Norwich and Thomas Hoccleve," *Chaucer Review* 51, no. 1 (2016): 49–67.

77. David Watt, *The Making of Thomas Hoccleve's "Series"* (Liverpool University Press, 2013), 11.

78. For a more detailed analysis, see Steven Rozenski, "'Your Ensaumple and Your Mirour': Hoccleve's Amplification of the Imagery and Intimacy of Henry Suso's *Ars Moriendi*," *Parergon* 25, no. 2 (2008): 1–16. This section is in part adapted from that article. See also Ashby Kinch's helpful corrective to my essay in Kinch, *Imago Mortis: Mediating Images of Death in Late Medieval Culture* (Leiden: Brill, 2013), 35–68. On Hoccleve and translation more broadly, see Jerome Mitchell, *Thomas Hoccleve: A Study in Early Fifteenth-Century English Poetic* (Urbana: University of Illinois Press, 1968), esp. 34–43, on Hoccleve's translations of Christine de Pisan and the *Gesta Romanorum*. And see Nicholas Perkins, *Hoccleve's Regiment of Princes: Counsel and Constraint* (Cambridge: D. S. Brewer, 2001), 85–121, on his translations of the three major sources of the *Regiment* (the *Secretum secretorum*, Giles of Rome's *De regimine principum*, and *De ludo scaccorum*).

79. Appleford, *Learning to Die*, 136.

80. Kurtz, "The Relation of Occleve's *Lerne to Dye* to Its Source," *PMLA* 40 (1925): 275 and 270. See also Westlake, "Learn to Live and Learn to Die."

81. On the complicated sense of self Hoccleve manufactures in his poetry, see especially Lee Patterson, "'What Is Me?': Self and Society in the Poetry of Thomas Hoccleve," *Studies in the Age of Chaucer* 23 (2001): 437–70.

82. Spearing, *Medieval Autographies*, 174.

83. Caroline Walker Bynum, *Christian Materiality: An Essay on Religion in Late Medieval Europe* (Cambridge: Zone Press, 2011), 30.

84. Ibid., 35.

85. Ibid.

86. For the most detailed study of its sources, see Walter Kay Smart, "Some English and Latin Sources and Parallels for the Morality of Wisdom" (PhD diss., University of Chicago, 1912).

87. See especially Milton Gatch, "Mysticism and Satire in the Morality of *Wisdom*," *Philological Quarterly* 53, no. 3 (1974): 342–62, and Richard Beadle, "The Scribal Problem in the Macro Manuscript," *English Language Notes* 21 (1984): 1–13, and Donald Baker's introduction to the EETS edition of the play (o.s. 262, 1982).

88. The text will be cited by line number from EETS o.s. 262, 114–52. Stage directions are not given line numbers; this *s.d.* appears on page 114.

89. This is a fairly direct adaptation of the *SP*: "Firste, if þou wilt wite þe propirte and resoun of my name þow schalt vndirstande þat y am cleped of hem þat levin in erþe "euerlastynge wisdam", þe whiche name is moste conuenient and beste acordynge to myne nobleye. For þough it so be þat euery persone of þe holye trenite taken by hit selfe is wisdam, and alle þe persones togedere one euerlastynge wisdam, neuerþeles for als myche as wisdam is applied propirly to the sone and also hit falliþ to him be resoun of his generacioun specially, þerfore þe beloued sone of þe fader is takin and vndirstande in þat manere significacioun of wisdam custummabely [now] as god & now as man, now as he þat is þe spouse of his chirche, & now as sche þat is þe spowse & wyfe of euery chosen sowle" (*SP* I.4–16). This passage is, in turn, translating two portions of the *Horologium*: "Imprimis ergo rationem et interpretationem nominis mei scire si vis, Sapientiam aeternam me appellari a terrigenis cognosce, quod utique meae congruit peroptime nobilitati" (K 420.12–14), and "Verum licet quaelibet persona per se accepta sit sapientia, et omnes personae simul una aeterna sapientia, tamen quia sapientia attribuitur Filio, et quia ratione suae generationis sibi convenit, ideo dilectum Patris Filium sub eodem significato consuetudinaliter accepit nunc quidem ut Deum, deinde ut hominem" (K 381.13–17).

90. On the ambiguities of gender and the role of cross-dressing in the mystery plays (and more general instances), see Meg Twycross, "'Transvestism' in the Mystery Plays," *Medieval English Theatre* 5 (1983): 123–80.

91. Karáth, "*Altum sapere*," 81.

92. Karáth argues that the play masculinizes both Wisdom *and* Anima: "although Anima appears as a queen on stage, and is dressed in a queen's ritual robes for coronation ceremonies," her performance of gender is far more complicated and subtle ("*Altum sapere*," 81).

93. Adapting from the *SP*: "*Hanc amaui et exquisiui a iuuentute mea, & quesiui eam sponsam michi assumere, & amator factus sum forme illius.*—Sche, þis y haue louyd and I haue vttirly sowȝte fro my ȝowþe, and y haue desyred forto haue hir to my spowse, & I am made a lover of hir forme & schappe. And also in [þe] selfe boke þus: *Super salutem & omnem pulcritudinem dilexi sapien*ciam, *& proposui pro luce habere illam. Venerunt michi omnia bona pariter cum illa.*— Abouen heele and alle bewte I haue loued wisdam, and y haue purposed for to haue hir as for my liht. And alle godes haue comyn to me wiþ hire" (I.18–28).

94. Adapting from the *Seven Points*: "*Sapiencia speciosior est sole* [the remainder of the passages from Wisdom are quoted in full]' . . . Þat is to seye: 'Wisdam is feyrere þanne þe sonne; and in comparisoun of hir to lihte sche is foundin passinge aboue alle þe disposicioun of sterres.' 'Sche is forsoþe þe briȝtenesse of euerlastynge liȝte and þe mirrour wiþoute wemme of goddis maieste and þe ymage of his goodnesse.' Also þus: '*Melior est sapiencia cunctis opibus preciosissimis* [the remainder of the passages from Proverbs are quoted in full]' . . . 'Wisdam ys bettir þanne alle manere of moste precious godes, & alle þat may be desirede may not be in comparisoun lyke to hir.' 'Þe lengþe of ȝeres is in her rihte side, & in hir lifte syde rychessis and ioye'" (I.29–44).

95. The author's dependence on the *Seven Points* can be easily seen in this passage, insofar as he retains the text's loose rendering of *longitudo dierum* as "length of *years*" (rather than *days*). Although this play was written many decades after Arundel, it is still rather striking to see vernacular biblical verse staged so dramatically, even if it came via the intermediary of the *Seven Points*—the initial line of Latin definitely tagging it as elevated language, even if not definitively identifying what follows as translated scripture.

96. Eleanor Johnson, *Staging Contemplation: Participatory Theology in Middle English Prose, Verse, and Drama* (Chicago: University of Chicago Press, 2018), 139.

97. The general sense of the superlatives is spoken by the Disciple in the *SP*: "O lord god, how manye gode þingis here I spoken of þis souereynlye fayre and worþy spouse! . . . Why assayest not wheþer þou myghtist wedde hire and haue hir in to þi spowse!" (I.78–82).

98. Compare this to the *SP*'s exposition of the same: "First, þou schalt besilye examyne þi selfe, what þou art in þe absence of my grace, and anone þou schalt fynde þat þou seechiste. . . . Now þanne, yf þou dist euer proue þe godenesse and þe lykynge of my presence, or ellis þe bareynnesse & myslykinge of myne absence, bringe forth into knowynge and telle hit opunlye, so þat þou mayhte knowe þe flowres amonge þe wedis" (I.244–54).

99. Bynum, *Christian Materiality*, 282–83.

100. Laviece Cox Ward, "Historiography in an Early Sixteenth-Century English Manuscript, *e Museo 160*," *Medieval Perspectives* 3, no. 1 for 1988 (1990): 288. Ward's other studies of the manuscript are Ward, "The *E Museo* 160 Manuscript: Writing and Reading as Remedy," in *The Mystical Tradition and the Carthusians*, ed. James Hogg (Salzburg: Institut für Anglistik und Amerikanistik, 1995), 4:68–87; Ward, "Historiography on the Eve of the Reformation," in *The Work of Dissimilitude: Essays from the Sixth Citadel Conference on Medieval and Renaissance Literature*, ed. David G. Allen and Robert A. White (Newark: University of Delaware Press, 1992), 81–90; and Ward, "A Study of MS e Museo 160, a Middle English Devotional History" (PhD diss., University of Colorado-Boulder, 1978). My deep gratitude to Ward for her extraordinary generosity in sharing her research materials with me. For the most detailed manuscript description, see D. C. Baker and

J. L. Murphy, "The Bodleian MS *E Mus.* 160 *Burial* and *Resurrection* and the Digby Plays," *Review of English Studies*, n.s., 19, no. 75 (1968): 290–93. This printed universal history was closely associated with its technical innovations throughout its roughly half century of considerable pan-European popularity. What must have been a close collaboration between Rolewinck and his printer resulted in an intricately designed book incorporating dozens of woodcuts, hundreds of roundels (with type sometimes set in concentric rings), and several intersecting timelines. Indeed, the text's overwhelmingly elaborate mise-en-page is considered to be the first use of a timeline to represent the progression of historical events.

101. "The two page continuation of the chronicle, on fol 108v and fol 114r, is devoted largely to events in England, or concerning Englishmen, which makes it rather different in content to that which preceded it. It opens with the death of the emperor Maximilian, and describes the visit of Henry VIII and Katherine of Aragon to the Field of the Cloth of Gold, with its jousting and games. Then the author describes the terrible floods and storms in England that year, and how many people were killed"; C. B. Rowntree, *A Carthusian World View: Bodleian MS e Museo 160*, Spiritualität Heute und Gestern 9 (Salzburg: Institut für Anglistik und Amerikanistik, 1990), 44.

102. Ibid., 17. She also notes that "on some of the blank picture frames in the early folios, drawings seem to have been inserted at a later date, mostly depicting Tudor gentlemen in elaborate costumes. They appear to have been drawn by a child" (29).

103. My sincere thanks to José van Aelst for access to her typescript of the Jordaens translation, allowing me to more speedily compare Jordaens to the text of MS E Museo 160.

104. Transcriptions of the Passion meditation are mine; standard scribal abbreviations are expanded silently.

105. This work is not considered in Richard Rex's monograph on Fisher's theology—indeed, the Susonian material clearly dear to Fisher is not even included in Rex's appendix allegedly listing "all the separate works John Fisher owned, cited, mentioned or (in a very few cases) clearly alluded to"; Rex, *The Theology of John Fisher* (Cambridge: Cambridge University Press, 1991), 192. Some medieval visionary authors are mentioned, however: Bridget of Sweden, Elizabeth of Schöngau [*sic*], Hildegard von Bingen [*Scivias*], "Mechtild" [*sic*, presumably "of Hackeborn"?], and Rupert of Deutz.

106. Selman, "Voices and Wisdom," 260.

107. See also Thomas Lawler, "Fruitful Business: Medieval and Renaissance Elements in the Devotional Method of St. John Fisher," *Medievalia et humanistica* 4 (1973): 145–59.

108. Cecilia A. Hatt, ed., *English Works of John Fisher, Bishop of Rochester: Sermons and Other Writings, 1520–1535* (Oxford: Oxford University Press, 2002), 368. Further citations will be by page number from this edition preceded by "*Spiritual Consolation.*"

109. The book still survives, in Yale's Beinecke Library. For a study of More's annotations in some parts of the book, including a short English prayer he wrote in the margins, see Eamon Duffy, *Marking the Hours: English People & Their Prayers, 1240–1570* (New Haven, CT: Yale University Press, 2006), 107–18. On the general implications of this text on the literature of the later Middle Ages, see Paul Saenger, "Books of Hours and the Reading Habits of the Later Middle Ages," in *The Culture of Print: Power and the Uses of Print in Early Modern Europe*, ed. Roger Chartier (New York: Polity Press, 1989), 141–73.

110. Ellis, ed., *The Oxford History of Literary Translation in English*, 264.

111. See Edgar Hoskins, *Horæ Beatæ Mariæ Virginis, or, Sarum and York Primers: with kindred books and Primers of the reformed Roman use, together with an introduction* (London: Longmans, Green, and Co., 1901), 122–23, for a complete list of the contents of the book, https://books.google.com/books?id=jVArAAAAYAAJ. On the confusing terminology sometimes applied to English vernacular Books of Hours (particularly the term "primer") and the complicated array of texts included in them, see Kathleen E. Kennedy, "Reintroducing the English Books of Hours, or 'English Primers,'" *Speculum* 89, no. 3 (2014): 693–723.

112. On the development of an office for the Feast of the Name of Jesus in England (without any recognition that the text comes from Suso), see R. W. Pfaff, *New Liturgical Feasts in Later Medieval England* (Oxford: Clarendon, 1970), 62–83. On the *Cursus* in some early Sarum Use printed Hours and two earlier manuscripts (Bodleian MS Dugdale 47 [second quarter of the fifteenth century], fol. 116 ff., and Oxford, Trinity College MS 13, fol. 98 ff.), see ibid., 68–69. Nigel Thorp, *The Glory of the Page: Medieval and Renaissance Illuminated Manuscripts from Glasgow University Library* (Oxford: Oxford University Press, 1987), 90, also mentions the inclusion of the Susonian "Hours" (identified as such by his listing them as identical to those of the Dugdale MS, with the comment that they are a relatively rare inclusion in English Hours) in Glasgow University Library MS Hunter 268 (*olim* U.5.8); this is dated to the early fifteenth century in the catalogue of Hunterian MSS. There are, it seems certain, more to be found; it also seems quite possible that the independent *Iesus Mattens* are taken either directly from an English-language Hours or newly translated in 1575 from an earlier insular Latin Book of Hours.

113. This print may also attribute the vespers to Rolle—I have not yet been able to view an original, and the Early English Books Online digital image for the beginning of Vespers appears to have some (rubricated?) text at the header, but it is either badly faded or poorly reproduced.

114. See Denis Renevey, "Anglo-Norman and Middle English Translations and Adaptations of the Hymn *Dulcis Iesu Memoria*," in *The Medieval Translator*, vol. 5, *The Theory and Practice of Translation in the Middle Ages*, ed. Roger Ellis and René Tixier (Turnhout: Brepols, 1996), 264–83, for a brief mention of this Book of Hours.

115. On the widespread theological interests of the sixteenth-century Cologne Carthusians and their activity translating the Rhineland mystics into Latin, see,

especially, Carlos Eire, "Early Modern Catholic Piety in Translation," in *Cultural Translation in Early Modern Europe*, ed. Peter Burke and R. Po-chia Hsia (Cambridge: Cambridge University Press, 2007), 83–100.

116. Compiled by Augustine Baker after Gertrude More's death, this collection was published in Paris in 1657. The table of recommended works is found on pp. 35–36. On the spirituality of the English Benedictines in Belgium and France during the period, see Laurence Lux-Sterritt, *English Benedictine Nuns in Exile in the Seventeenth Century: Living Spirituality* (Manchester: Manchester University Press, 2017).

117. James Gaffney, *Augustine Baker's Inner Light: A Study in Recusant Spirituality* (Scranton, PA: University of Scranton Press, 1989), 54. Baker's own translations from both Suso and Tauler may be found in York, Ampleforth Abbey MS 127; on this manuscript, see John Clark, ed., *Augustine Baker, O.S.B.: Collections I–III and The Twelve Mortifications of Harphius*, Analecta Cartusiana 119/21 (Salzburg: Institut für Anglistik und Amerikanistik, 2004). On Augustine Baker's complicated and controversial position among the Benedictines (and the role Cressy played in promoting his posthumous reputation), see Liam P. Temple, "The Mysticism of Augustine Baker, OSB: A Reconsideration," *Reformation & Renaissance Review* 19, no. 3 (2017): 213–30.

118. As James Simpson has argued, the very concept of a sharp line between periods falls prey to the "logic of the revolutionary moment"; see James Simpson, "Diachronic History and the Shortcomings of Medieval Studies," in *Reading the Medieval in Early Modern England*, ed. Gordon McMullan and David Matthews (Cambridge: Cambridge University Press, 2007), 27.

119. The main work on Brathwaite remains Matthew Wilson Black, "Richard Brathwait: An Account of His Life and Works" (PhD diss., University of Pennsylvania, 1928). Black writes that the burlesque "may be defined as that literary *genre* which has for its purpose to render ridiculous that which is dignified and serious, by the method of distorted or exaggerated imitation" (101). Widener Library's copy of this dissertation bears a poignant marginal note: the dissertation begins, "Richard Brathwait is a minor writer of the seventeenth century who has been strangely neglected by literary historians." A reader has underlined *strangely* and rather archly put a question mark in the margins. More recently, see John Bowes, *Richard Brathwait: The First Lakeland Poet* (Ings, Cumbria: Hugill, 2007), a biographical study by a figure who was intrigued about the poet upon learning that his sixteenth-century home had once been occupied by the Brathwaite family. Jennifer Summit, *Lost Property: The Woman Writer and English Literary History, 1380–1589* (Chicago: University of Chicago Press, 2000), begins the introduction with a brief discussion of Brathwaite's consideration of the ways in which women are missing in the English literary tradition in his 1641 *A Ladies Love-Lecture*.

120. See Jeffrey Masten, *Textual Intercourse: Collaboration, Authorship, and Sexualities in Renaissance Drama* (Cambridge: Cambridge University Press, 1999), 28–37.

121. On this, with an introduction to his life and works and an edition of "Chaucer's Ghost Incensed," see Caroline F. E. Spurgeon, ed., *Richard Brathwait's Comments, in 1665, upon Chaucer's Tales of the Miller and the Wife of Bath* (London: Chaucer Society, 1901).

122. Thomas Prendergast, "Revenant Chaucer: Early Modern Celebrity," in *Chaucer and Fame: Reputation and Reception*, ed. Isabel Davis and Catherine Nall (Rochester, NY: Boydell & Brewer, 2015), 185–201, and Louise Bishop, "Father Chaucer and the Vivification of Print," *Journal of English and Germanic Philology* 106, no. 3 (2007): 336–63.

123. See chapter 4 for a discussion of his *Mirror of Gold* and its translation by Lady Margaret Beaufort.

124. On *A Spiritual Spicerie* and its perspective on the role of knowledge in contemplation, see Paul Cefalu, *The Johannine Renaissance in Early Modern English Literature and Theology* (Oxford: Oxford University Press, 2017), 29–30.

125. Debora Shuger, "Literature and the Church," in *The Cambridge History of Early Modern English Literature*, ed. David Loewenstein and Janel Mueller (Cambridge: Cambridge University Press, 2002), 541.

126. See especially the three insightful articles by T. A. Birrell, "English Catholic Mystics in Non-Catholic Circles—I, II, and III," *Downside Review* 94 (1976): 60–81, 99–117, and 213–31.

127. On Thomas à Kempis's limited use of Suso, however, and the considerable differences between them, see Pierre Debongnie, "Henri Suso et l'Imitation de Jesus-Christ," *Revue d'ascétique et de mystique* 21 (1940): 242–68.

CHAPTER 3

1. For a general study of the significance of Christian sainthood, see Peter Brown, *The Cult of the Saints: Its Rise and Function in Latin Christianity*, 2nd ed. (Chicago: University of Chicago Press, 2014), and Robert Bartlett, *Why Can the Dead Do Such Great Things? Saints and Worshippers from the Martyrs to the Reformation* (Princeton, NJ: Princeton University Press, 2013). For the later Middle Ages, see especially André Vauchez, *Sainthood in the Later Middle Ages*, trans. Jean Birrell (Cambridge: Cambridge University Press, 1989), and Richard Kieckhefer, *Unquiet Souls: Fourteenth-Century Saints and Their Religious Milieu* (Chicago: University of Chicago Press, 1984). For a more specific background to the use of narratives of virginity in constructing sanctity in England, see Karen Winstead, *Virgin Martyrs: Legends of Sainthood in Late Medieval England* (Ithaca, NY: Cornell University Press, 1997).

2. Boston, also, is ultimately derived from "Saint Botolph's stone," perhaps after a boulder from which he preached, a stone cross to mark a site of preaching or conversion, or a stone church erected in his name. On the geography of the British

Isles and its changes, see Alexandra Walsham, *The Reformation of the Landscape: Religion, Identity, and Memory in Early Modern Britain and Ireland* (Oxford: Oxford University Press, 2011).

3. See, for instance, Daniel A. Dombrowski, *Contemporary Athletics and Ancient Greek Ideals* (Chicago: University of Chicago Press, 2009), and the range of essays in Peter Jan Margry, ed., *Shrines and Pilgrimage in the Modern World: New Itineraries into the Sacred* (Amsterdam: Amsterdam University Press, 2008).

4. Comparing contemporary heroes and superheroes to medieval saints, indeed, is a reversal of an earlier skeptical tradition. As Robert Bartlett notes, the notion that Christian saints simply correspond to ancient heroes of various stripes was deployed by David Hume in the *Natural History of Religion*, and by a considerable number of anticlerical polemicists: see Bartlett, *How Can the Dead Do Such Great Things?*, 611–12. The recent attempt to create what seemed a thoughtful and satirical comic, *Second Coming*, with Jesus as a peaceful contrast to the often violent morals of both superheroes and some contemporary Christians, however, seems to have been a bridge too far, leading hundreds of thousands to sign petitions encouraging its cancellation: see, for instance, Carol Kuruvilla, "DC Relinquishes Rights to Comic Book Series about Jesus after Conservative Backlash," *Huffington Post*, February 18, 2019, https://www.huffingtonpost.co.uk/entry/second-coming-jesus-comic-book -series_n_5c6ad4c0e4b01757c36e497b.

5. Simon Yarrow, *Saints: A Very Short Introduction* (Oxford: Oxford University Press, 2018), 1.

6. Adam Barkman, *Imitating the Saints: Christian Philosophy and Superhero Mythology* (Hamden, CT: Winged Lion Press, 2013); Greg Garrett, *Holy Superheroes! Exploring the Sacred in Comics, Graphic Novels, and Film*, 2nd ed. (Louisville, KY: Westminster John Knox Press, 2008).

7. Neither Rolle nor Suso became saints, but (like Margery Kempe) the character they performed in their texts is clearly meant to be associated with a wide array of contemporary expectations of sanctity. In Rolle's case, this led to a somewhat substantial local cult (and the production of the *Officium* in liturgical support of a potential canonization); Suso's veneration, too, seems to have persisted in southern Germany, especially around Lake Constance, into the nineteenth century (leading to his beatification in 1831). Little about Suso's personal identity was maintained across the many strands of his English reception (outside of his status as a Dominican), and, of course, his autohagiographical *Life* never reached medieval or early modern England.

8. As Jennifer Summit writes, for instance, "even as unimpeachable a Protestant classic as Foxe's own *Acts and Monuments* shares some iconography with the detested *Legenda aurea*, the immensely influential work of pre-Reformation hagiography that appeared in eight editions before 1527"; Jennifer Summit, *Lost Property: The Woman Writer and English Literary History, 1380–1589* (Chicago: University of Chicago Press, 2000), 113. On the role the *Acts and Monuments* played in the identity of English Christians, see Alice Dailey, *The English Martyr from Reformation*

to Revolution (Notre Dame, IN: University of Notre Dame Press, 2012); Susannah Brietz Monta, *Martyrdom and Literature in Early Modern England* (Cambridge: Cambridge University Press, 2005); and John N. King, *Foxe's "Book of Martyrs" and Early Modern Print Culture* (Cambridge: Cambridge University Press, 2006). This hagiographic project as an attempt to replace the medieval cult of saints was addressed directly in English Jesuit Robert Persons's (1545–1610) three-volume *A Treatise of Three Conversions of England from Paganisme to Christian Religion* (RSTC 19416), published in 1604. He produces extensive facing-page calendars to compare Foxe's martyrs with Catholic saints, even highlighting the presence of "000" virgin martyrs in Foxe's calendar of saints, something in the manner of a virgin martyr odometer (he also stresses the overall greater number of all types of saints in the Catholic calendar). This emphasis on precisely "000" virgin martyrs in Foxe apparently resonated with international audiences: it is even reproduced exactly in a 1750 Italian translation of Persons.

9. The most thorough study to date of Catherine of Siena's late medieval and early modern reception in England (and in English communities outside of England) is Jennifer N. Brown, *Fruit of the Orchard: Reading Catherine of Siena in Late Medieval and Early Modern England* (Toronto: University of Toronto Press, 2019). See also Brown, "The Many Misattributions of Catherine of Siena: Beyond *The Orchard* in England," *Journal of Medieval Religious Cultures* 41, no. 1 (2015): 67–84, and Dirk Schultze, "Translating St Catherine of Siena in Fifteenth-Century England," in *Catherine of Siena: The Creation of a Cult*, ed. Jeffrey Hamburger and Gabriela Signori (Turnhout: Brepols, 2013), 185–214, and Schultze, "Spiritual Teaching by Catherine of Siena in BL Harley 2409: An Edition," *Anglia* 136, no. 2 (2018): 296–325. Given the wide range of hagiographic verse about women in the fifteenth century (see Catherine Sanok, "Saints' Lives and the Literary after Arundel," in *After Arundel: Religious Writing in Fifteenth-Century England*, ed. Vincent Gillespie and Kantik Ghosh [Turnhout: Brepols, 2011], 469–86), it is perhaps something of a surprise that nothing of Catherine of Siena's life found its way into verse.

10. Brown, *Fruit of the Orchard*, 9 and 20.

11. The foundation is studied in greatest detail in Jane Chance, "St. Catherine of Siena in Late Medieval Britain: Feminizing Literary Reception through Gender and Class," *Annali d'Italianistica* 13 (1995): 163–203.

12. Although the EETS edition and most scholars use the Middle English spelling, *Orcherd*, I believe making the text less distantly medieval may be a better strategy overall in connecting contemporary readers to the Middle English reception of Catherine. For general overviews of Catherine's place in Syon's readerly communities, see Rebecca Krug, *Reading Families: Women's Literate Practice in Late Medieval England* (Ithaca, NY: Cornell University Press, 2002), "Reading at Syon Abbey," 153–206; and Phyllis Hodgson, "*The Orcherd of Syon* and the English Mystical Tradition," *Proceedings of the British Academy* 50 (1964): 229–49. On Syon Abbey, see, most recently, E. A. Jones, *England's Last Medieval Monastery: Syon*

Abbey 1415–2015 (Leominster: Gracewing, 2015), and Susan Powell, *The Birgittines of Syon Abbey: Preaching and Print* (Turnhout: Brepols, 2017), esp. "Syon Abbey in the Reign of Henry VIII and Beyond," 214–69.

13. The four Middle English translations of his *Remedies against Temptations* have recently been edited in Jessica Lamothe, ed., "An Edition of the Latin and Four Middle English Versions of William Flete's *De remediis contra temptaciones* (*Remedies against Temptations*)" (PhD diss., University of York, 2017). See also Benedict Hackett, *William Flete, O.S.A., and Catherine of Siena: Masters of Fourteenth Century Spirituality* (Villanova, PA: Augustinian Press, 1992). On the role of English clerics in Italy, and ecclesiastical and cultural exchange between the two regions more generally, see Robert Brentano, *Two Churches: England and Italy in the Thirteenth Century* (Berkeley: University of California Press, 1968).

14. *Dominican Penitent Women*, ed. and trans. Maiju Lehmijoki-Garner (Mahwah, NJ: Paulist Press, 2005), 97. On the related devotional and visual cultures in which Margery Kempe and Catherine of Siena operated, see David Wallace, "Mystics and Followers in Siena and East Anglia: A Study in Taxonomy, Class and Cultural Mediation," in *The Medieval Mystical Tradition in England: Papers Read at Dartington Hall, July 1984*, ed. Marion Glasscoe (Cambridge: D. S . Brewer, 1984), 169–91; Robert Brentano, "Catherine of Siena, Margery Kempe, and a *caterva virginum*," in *Bishops, Saints, and Historians: Studies in the Ecclesiastical History of Britain and Italy*, ed. William North (Aldershot: Ashgate, 2008), 45–55; and, most recently, Carol F. Heffernan, "The Middle English *Orcherd of Syon* in Late Medieval England: A Reconsideration," *Magistra* 22, no. 1 (2016): 3–24.

15. Fenn 326. Citations of the 1609 translation (RSTC 4830) will be by page number of the EEBO digitization preceded by "Fenn"; citations of the ca. 1493 Wynkyn de Worde translation (RSTC 24766, reprinted 1500 RSTC 24766.3) will be by page number of the Horstmann edition (*Archiv für das Studium der neueren Sprachen und Literaturen* 76 [1886]: 33–112, 265–314, and 353–91) preceded by "WdW." When needed, the Latin text will be taken from Silvia Nocentini, ed., *Legenda maior* (Florence: Galluzzo, 2013); English translations of the Latin from George Lamb, trans., *The Life of St. Catherine of Siena* (Rockford, IL: Tan Books, 2003).

16. Brown, *Fruit of the Orchard*, also traces the iconographic record in England in admirable detail.

17. On the complicated case of Marguerite Porete in England, see, especially, Nicholas Watson, "Melting into God the English Way: Deification in the Middle English Version of Marguerite Porete's *Mirouer des simples âmes anienties*," in *Prophets Abroad: The Reception of Continental Holy Women in Late-Medieval England*, ed. Rosalynn Voaden (Cambridge: D. S. Brewer, 1996), 19–50; Robert Lerner, "New Light on *The Mirror of Simple Souls*," *Speculum* 85, no. 1 (2010): 91–116; and Marleen Cré, "Further Thoughts on M.N.'s Middle English Translation of Marguerite's *Mirouer des simples âmes anienties*," in *A Companion to Marguerite Porete and The*

Mirror of Simple Souls, ed. Wendy Terry and Robert Stauffer (Leiden: Brill, 2017), 240–63.

18. Sara Poor, *Mechthild of Magdeburg and Her Book: Gender and the Making of Textual Authority* (Philadelphia: University of Pennsylvania Press, 2004), 85.

19. For the German translation of Raymond of Capua's *Vita* and a thorough introduction on its role in vernacular Dominican spirituality, particularly Dominican reform, see Thomas Brakmann, ed., *Ein Geistlicher Rosengarten: Die Vita der heiligen Katharina von Siena zwischen Ordensreform und Laienfrömmigkeit im 15. Jahrhundert. Untersuchungen und Edition* (Berlin: Peter Lang, 2011). The *Vita*'s Middle French translation has been edited recently; see Piotr Tylus, ed., *La "Legenda maior" de Raymond de Capoue en français ancien* (Turnhout: Brepols, 2015).

20. On recusant women religious and their descriptions of exile more broadly considered, see Claire Walker, "The Experience of Exile in Early Modern English Convents," *Parergon* 34, no. 2 (2017): 159–77.

21. See Ruth Dean, "Manuscripts of St Elizabeth of Schönau in England," *Modern Language Review* 32, no. 1 (1937): 62–71. The copy of the English *Liber viarum Dei* (RSTC 7605.5) reproduced in EEBO is from the former Ushaw College Library, Durham; little is currently known about the volume's place of printing or its date. For a unique interpolation mentioning "the holy woman hyldegardis" in a Middle English translation of David of Augsburg in Cambridge University Library MS Dd.2.33, see Iguchi, "Study in Vernacular Devotional Translation in Late-Medieval England," 192–93.

22. The most complete study of the reception of female Continental religious authors in England remains the collection of essays in Voaden, ed., *Prophets Abroad*. An excellent survey of the topic can also be found in Alexandra Barratt, "Continental Women Mystics and English Readers," in *The Cambridge Companion to Medieval Women's Writing*, ed. Carolyn Dinshaw and David Wallace (Cambridge: Cambridge University Press, 2003), 240–55; her brief discussion of the late Middle English translation of Marie of Oisterwijk in British Library MS Harley 494 (p. 244) is one of the few references to the translation of this Flemish beguine's work into English and the evidence it provides of possible connections between Syon Abbey and the rich intellectual community of the Cologne Carthusians. On this, see also Mary Erler, *Reading and Writing during the Dissolution: Monks, Friars, and Nuns, 1530–1558* (Cambridge: Cambridge University Press, 2013), 124. On the Cologne Charterhouse as the focal point of a "mystical Renaissance," see Bernard McGinn, *The Varieties of Vernacular Mysticism, 1350–1550*, vol. 5 of *The Presence of God: A History of Western Christian Mysticism* (New York: Herder & Herder, 2014), 141–43.

23. For a translation of this rule, and an explanation of the varieties of lay female involvement in Dominican spiritual circles before the formalization of a rule (and associated terminology) for the *mantellate*, see Lehmijoki-Garner, ed. and trans., *Dominican Penitent Women*. For a reevaluation of the category of *mantellate* and

Catherine's role in their community, see F. Thomas Luongo, "Cloistering Catherine: Religious Identity in Raymond of Capua's *Legenda Maior* of Catherine of Siena," *Studies in Medieval and Renaissance History* 3 (2006): 25–69, and forthcoming work by Mary Doyno, along with Doyno, *The Lay Saint: Charity and Charismatic Authority in Medieval Italy, 1150–1350* (Ithaca, NY: Cornell University Press, 2019).

24. Grazia Mangano Ragazzi, *Obeying the Truth: Discretion in the Spiritual Writings of Saint Catherine of Siena* (Oxford: Oxford University Press, 2014), 12–13. See also Karen Scott, "St. Catherine of Siena, 'Apostola,'" *Church History* 61, no. 1 (1992): 34–46.

25. Emma Shackle, "The Effect of Twinship on the Mysticism of Catherine of Siena (1347–1380): A Vergotean Analysis," *Archiv für Religionspsychologie/Archive for the Psychology of Religion* 25 (2003): 129–41.

26. McGinn, *Varieties of Vernacular Mysticism,* 197.

27. On the many strands of development of her local cult over the past 550 years, see Gerald Parsons, *The Cult of Saint Catherine of Siena: A Study in Civil Religion* (Aldershot: Ashgate, 2008). For an overview of the history of the study of Catherine, see F. Thomas Luongo, "The Historical Reception of Catherine of Siena," in *A Companion to Catherine of Siena,* ed. Carolyn Muessig, George Ferzoco, and Beverly Mayne Kienzle (Leiden: Brill, 2012), 23–45. For the spread of the cult of another critical Dominican saint, canonized shortly before Catherine, see Laura Smoller, *The Saint and the Chopped-Up Baby: The Cult of Saint Vincent Ferrer in Medieval and Early Modern Europe* (Ithaca, NY: Cornell University Press, 2014).

28. Sigrid Undset, *Catherine of Siena,* trans. Kate Austin-Lund (New York: Sheed and Ward, 1954). It was originally published posthumously in Norwegian in 1951; see also Natalie Van Deusen, "'Doubleday affaren': The Story of Sigrid Undset's *Catarina av Siena,*" *Scandinavian Studies* 87, no. 3 (2015): 383–400. The descriptive bibliography of Catherinian studies from 1901 to 2010 is now in six volumes (totaling 1,600 pages); the reader will, I hope, forgive me for the extremely selective overview above.

29. On Sister Nancy Murray, O.P., see for instance Mark Zimmermann, "Nun and Sister of Original 'Ghostbusters' Star Says Acting Is Preaching," *Crux,* July 16, 2016, https://web.archive.org/web/20160717160925/https://cruxnow.com/church-in-the-usa/2016/07/16/nun-sister-original-ghostbuster-sees-acting-preaching/.

30. McGinn, *Varieties of Vernacular Mysticism,* 244–45.

31. Ragazzi, *Obeying the Truth,* 69. McGinn, too, has written that her notion of self-knowledge is inseparable from her development of a system of discernment that embraces both a proper understanding of God's love and the proper way in which to behave in light of that understanding: "For Catherine, discernment is more than judging visions and finding the proper balance in acting—the intimate connection of discernment with self-knowledge, humility, and love demonstrates that it is essentially the process of realizing God's love for us and knowing how to put the message into practice" (McGinn, *Varieties of Vernacular Mysticism,* 236).

32. McGinn, *Varieties of Vernacular Mysticism*, 208. See also Heather Webb, "Catherine of Siena's Heart," *Speculum* 80, no. 3 (2005): 802–17.

33. André Vauchez, *Catherine of Siena: A Life of Passion and Purpose*, trans. Michael F. Cusato (Mahwah, NJ: Paulist Press, 2018), 27–28 and 106–7. In a later tradition, an interpolated version of Raymond's *Legenda* even describes her face transforming before his eyes into a likeness of Jesus.

34. Warren, *The Embodied Word: Female Spiritualities, Contested Orthodoxies, and Religious Cultures, 1350–1700* (Notre Dame, IN: University of Notre Dame Press, 2010), 42.

35. See, for instance, Karen Scott, "'*Io Caterina*': Ecclesiastical Politics and Oral Culture in the Letters of Catherine of Siena," in *Dear Sister: Medieval Women and the Epistolary Genre*, ed. Karen Cherewatuk and Ulrike Wiethaus (Philadelphia: University of Pennsylvania Press, 1993), 87–121, and Scott, "Not Only with Words, but with Deeds: The Role of Speech in Catherine of Siena's Understanding of Her Mission" (PhD diss., University of California, Berkeley, 1989).

36. Cited in Jane Tylus, "Mystical Literacy: Writing and Religious Women in Late Medieval Italy," in Muessig, Ferzoco, and Kienzle, eds., *A Companion to Catherine of Siena*, 156–57.

37. Cited in ibid., 157.

38. Luongo, "The Historical Reception of Catherine of Siena."

39. This, in turn, led some historians to argue that her ability to write was fabricated from whole cloth by Caffarini (asserting an emendation on his part to the aforementioned letter to Raymond in order to heighten its miraculousness).

40. Lehmijoki-Garner, ed. and trans., *Dominican Penitent Women*, 183.

41. Catherine Mooney, "Wondrous Words: Catherine of Siena's Miraculous Reading and Writing According to the Early Sources," in *Catherine of Siena: Creation of a Cult*, ed. Jeffrey Hamburger and Gabriela Signori (Turnhout: Brepols, 2013), 273.

42. Mooney, for instance, concludes that Catherine's use of the motifs of Christ-as-Book and Blood-as-Ink (not original to Catherine) must, in the end, supersede historical notions of literacy; see Mooney, "Wondrous Words," 287. Christ's blood as ink dates back to at least the fourth century and Prudentius, however, as does the saintly person as book, applied to martyrs.

43. Jane Tylus, "Writing versus Voice: Tommaso Caffarini and the Production of a Literate Catherine," in Hamburger and Signori, eds., *Catherine of Siena*, 302.

44. George Ferzoco, "The *Processo Castellano* and the Canonization of Catherine of Siena," in Muessig, Ferzoco, and Kienzle, eds., *A Companion to Catherine of Siena*, 201. He notes the lack of a contemporary shelf mark that results from this rather unique shelving arrangement.

45. Jane Tylus, *Reclaiming Catherine of Siena: Literacy, Literature, and the Signs of Others* (Chicago: University of Chicago Press, 2009), 275–77. See also Ruth Mortimer, "St. Catherine of Siena and the Printed Book," *Papers of the Bibliographic Society of America* 86 (1992): 11–22.

46. See, especially, Kathryn Kerby-Fulton, *Books under Suspicion: Censorship and Tolerance of Revelatory Writing in Late Medieval England* (Notre Dame, IN: University of Notre Dame Press, 2006), and the introduction to Jennifer N. Brown, *Three Women of Liege: A Critical Edition of and Commentary on the Middle English Lives of Elizabeth of Spalbeek, Christina Mirabilis, and Marie d'Oignies* (Turnhout: Brepols, 2008).

47. See, for instance, Paul Patterson, "Preaching with the Hands: Carthusian Book Production and the *Speculum Devotorum*," in *Medieval Latin and Middle English Literature: Essays in Honor of Jill Mann*, ed. Christopher Cannon and Maura Nolan (Rochester, NY: Boydell & Brewer, 2011), and Ian Johnson, *The Middle English Life of Christ: Academic Discourse, Translation, and Vernacular Theology* (Turnhout: Brepols, 2013), 147–75.

48. Felicity Riddy, "'Women Talking of the Things of God': A Late Medieval Sub-culture," in *Women & Literature in Britain, 1150–1500*, ed. Carol M. Meale (Cambridge: Cambridge University Press, 1993), 110.

49. Denise Despres, "Ecstatic Reading and Missionary Mysticism: *The Orcherd of Syon*," in Voaden, ed., *Prophets Abroad*, 150. See chapter 4 for more on Lady Margaret's devotional reading interests and activity as a translator and patron.

50. On the wide range of Protestant polemic that treats the Catholic Church (or other forms of "deviant" religion) as a disgraced woman, and the ways in which gendered spaces were associated with recusants, see Frances Dolan, *Whores of Babylon: Catholicism, Gender, and Seventeenth-Century Print Culture* (Notre Dame, IN: University of Notre Dame Press, 1999).

51. On the relationship of the first printers in England to mystical literature more generally, see George R. Keiser, "The Mystics and the Early English Printers: The Economics of Devotionalism," in *The Medieval Mystical Tradition in England: Papers Read at Dartington Hall, July 1987*, ed. Marion Glasscoe (London: D. S. Brewer, 1988), 9–26.

52. On this text, extant in one manuscript in addition to the two de Worde printings, see Sarah McNamer, ed., *The Two Middle English Translations of the Revelations of St. Elizabeth of Hungary* (Heidelberg: Universitätsverlag C. Winter, 1996). On the Töss Sisterbook and Stagel's authorship, see Gertrud Jaron Lewis, *By Women, for Women, about Women: The Sister-Books of Fourteenth-Century Germany* (Toronto: Pontifical Institute of Mediaeval Studies, 1995).

53. RSTC 4815. On this motif, see Brown, *Fruit of the Orchard*, 136–39, and Jennifer N. Brown, "From the Charterhouse to the Printing House: Catherine of Siena in Medieval England," in *Middle English Religious Writing in Practice: Texts, Readers, and Transformations*, ed. Nicole Rice (Turnhout: Brepols, 2013), 17–45.

54. Catherine Grisé, "Holy Women in Print: Continental Female Mystics and the English Mystical Tradition," in *The Medieval Mystical Tradition in England: Symposium VII—Papers Read at Charney Manor, July 2004*, ed. E. A. Jones (Cambridge: D. S. Brewer, 2004), 84–85. On *The Mirror of Our Lady*, especially its

relationship to Bridgettine reading culture more broadly, see, most recently, Michael Sargent, "The Anxiety of Authority, the Fear of Translation: The Prologues to *The Myroure of Oure Ladye*," in *Booldly bot meekly: Essays on the Theory and Practice of Translation in the Middle Ages in Honour of Roger Ellis*, ed. Catherine Batt and René Tixier (Turnhout: Brepols, 2018), 231–44. On the *Fifteen Oes*, see also Summit, *Lost Property*, 111–26, and Rebecca Krug, "*The Fifteen Oes*," in *Cultures of Piety: Medieval English Devotional Literature in Translation*, ed. Anne Clark Bartlett and Thomas Bestul (Ithaca, NY: Cornell University Press, 1999), 107–17.

55. On this text, see Brown, *Fruit of the Orchard*, 164–70. On the extract from Margery Kempe's *Book* that also appears in the Pepwell miscellany, see Allyson Foster, "*A Shorte Treatyse of Contemplacyon: The Book of Margery Kempe* in Its Early Print Contexts," in *A Companion to the Book of Margery Kempe*, ed. John Arnold and Katherine Lewis (Cambridge: D. S. Brewer, 2004), 95–112.

56. Jennifer N. Brown, "The Many Misattributions of Catherine of Siena: Beyond *The Orchard* in England," *Journal of Medieval Religious Cultures* 41, no. 1 (2015): 67–84, and Schultze, "Spiritual Teachings by Catherine of Siena in BL Harley 2409."

57. For the *Documento* (in two versions, one with emendations by Maconi), see R. Fawtier, "Catheriniana," *Mélanges d'archéologie et d'histoire* 34 (1914): 86–93.

58. The three passages following "Cleanness of Soul" have been given these titles by Brown, "Many Misattributions," 68. The text is edited in Schultze, "Spiritual Teachings by Catherine of Siena in BL Harley 2409," 296–325.

59. ST 1–4. Citations are from Schultze, "Spiritual Teachings by Catherine of Siena in BL Harley 2409," preceded by "ST" and followed by Schultze's line number.

60. Brown, *Fruit of the Orchard*, 177. The first edition of Whitford's text also features an apology for Syon's support of Elizabeth Barton just months previously: see Alexandra da Costa, *Reforming Printing: Syon Abbey's Defence of Orthodoxy, 1525–1534* (Oxford: Oxford University Press, 2012), 116–18, and Appleford, *Learning to Die in London, 1380–1540* (Philadelphia: University of Pennsylvania Press, 2014), 189–96.

61. Brown, "From the Charterhouse to the Printing House," 18.

62. Brown, *Fruit of the Orchard*, 119–20, posits three Latin translations circulating after Catherine's death, of which the Middle English translation is made from the Latin of Cristofano di Gano Guidini (a copy of which survives in Edinburgh, Edinburgh University Library MS 87, and in Siena, Biblioteca comunale, Cod. T.II.4). Cristofano's translation, however, may well have been made in collaboration with Maconi, leaving us only two Latin versions; a second (by either Raymond of Capua or Stefano Maconi) was more successful: it was printed in Brescia in 1496 and Cologne in 1553. The Wynkyn de Worde print of the *Orchard* includes a translation of the preface of the Brescia edition. See Johannes Jørgensen, *Catherine of Siena*, trans. Ingeborg Lund (Eugene, OR: Wipf & Stock, 2012), 405; Hodgson, "*The Orcherd of*

Syon and the English Mystical Tradition," 230; and Lisa Tagliaferri, "Lyrical Mysticism: The Writing and Reception of Catherine of Siena" (PhD diss., City University of New York, 2017), 155–56. Citations of the Italian text of the *Dialogue* are taken from the critical edition of Giuliana Cavallini (Siena: Edizioni Cantagalli, 1995) and are cited by page number prefaced with "ID," followed by Suzanne Noffke's translation (Paulist Press, 1980) (page numbers of Noffke's translation will be provided preceded by "Noffke"). Quotations from the Middle English are taken from the critical edition of Phyllis Hodgson and Gabriel Liegey, EETS o.s. 258 (1966), and are cited by page number preceded by "*Orchard*." Citations of the probable Latin source-text are my transcription (with scribal abbreviations silently expanded) taken when needed from Edinburgh, Edinburgh University Library MS 87, and cited by folio preceded by MS 87. With my limited time in Edinburgh, I have not been able to compare the Middle English in every instance to the Latin, but that remains a desideratum.

63. See, especially, the detailed textual study of the manuscripts, their provenance, and the Wynkyn de Worde print in Sister Mary Denise, "'The Orchard of Syon': An Introduction," *Traditio* 14 (1958): 269–93. On Julian of Norwich and Catherine of Siena, see Reneé Neu Watkins, "Two Women Visionaries and Death: Catherine of Siena and Julian of Norwich," *Numen* 30, no. 2 (1983): 174–98.

64. *Orchard* 351.

65. On Dante and Catherine of Siena, see, especially, Cornelia Wild, *Göttliche Stimme, irdische Schrift: Dante, Petrarca und Caterina da Siena* (Berlin: Walter de Gruyter, 2017), and Sister Mary Denise, "'The Orchard of Syon': An Introduction," 269–93. See also the classic study by Edmund G. Gardner, *Saint Catherine of Siena: A Study in the Religion, Literature and History of the Fourteenth Century in Italy* (London: J. M. Dent, 1907). On Christine de Pisan in England, see Jane Chance, "Gender Subversion and Linguistic Castration in Fifteenth-Century English Translations of Christine de Pizan," in *Violence against Women in Medieval Texts*, ed. Anna Roberts (Gainesville: University Press of Florida, 1998), 161–94, and Elizabeth Dearnley, *Translators and Their Prologues in Medieval England* (Cambridge: D. S. Brewer, 2016), 174–77.

66. Despres, "Ecstatic Reading and Missionary Mysticism," 141.

67. On imaginative theology, see, especially, Newman, *God and the Goddesses.* On interpreting the *Dialogue* as literature, see McGinn, *Varieties of Vernacular Mysticism*, 216–18; Hodgson, "*The Orcherd of Syon* and the English Mystical Tradition"; and F. Thomas Luongo, *The Saintly Politics of Catherine of Siena* (Ithaca, NY: Cornell University Press, 2006), 10–16. See also the poet Geoffrey Hill's book of contemporary verse in some ways linked to the text; Hill, *The Orchards of Syon* (Washington, DC: Counterpoint, 2002).

68. Schultze, "Spiritual Teachings by Catherine of Siena in BL Harley 2409," 301.

69. Stephen Kelly and Salvador Ryan, "Devotional Cosmopolitanism in Fifteenth-Century England," in Gillespie and Ghosh, eds., *After Arundel*, 365.

70. Alexandra da Costa, for instance, points out the challenge both Bridget of Sweden and Catherine of Siena pose, as practitioners of a mixed life with considerable engagement in the affairs of the world, to a cloistered Bridgettine audience (da Costa, *Reforming Printing*, 143–63). For the role of mystical literature at Syon more broadly, see Vincent Gillespie, "Dial M for Mystic: Mystical Texts in the Library of Syon Abbey and the Spirituality of the Syon Brethren," in *The Medieval Mystical Tradition in England: England, Ireland, and Wales. Papers Read at Charney Manor, July 1999*, ed. Marion Glasscoe (Cambridge: D. S. Brewer, 1999), 241–68, and the catalogue of the brothers' library: Vincent Gillespie and Ian Doyle, eds., *Syon Abbey, with the Libraries of the Carthusians*. On the connection between Syon and the *Orchard*, see Catherine Grisé, "'In the Blessid Vyneȝerd of oure Holy Saueour': Female Religious Readers and Textual Reception in the *Myroure of Oure Ladye* and the *Orcherd of Syon*," in Glasscoe, ed., *The Medieval Mystical Tradition in England* (1999), 193–211, and on their libraries, Catherine Grisé, "Proliferation and Purification: The Use of Books for Nuns," in Gillespie and Ghosh, eds., *After Arundel*, 503–19.

71. Noffke 43.

72. *Orchard* 42.

73. *Orchard* 149.

74. *Orchard* 188. "E però intendono più la scrittura litteralmente che con intendimento; unde ne gustano solo la lettera rivollendo molti libri, e non gustano il mirollo della scrittura perché s'ànno tolto il lume con che è dichiarata e formata la scrittura" (ID 225) (They read Scripture literally rather than with understanding. They taste only its letter in their chasing after a multiplicity of books, never tasting the marrow of Scripture because they have let go of the light by which Scripture was formed and proclaimed) (Noffke 157).

75. *Orchard* 206. "Quanto pericolo, oltre al danno spirituale della privazione de la grazia che à fatta nell'anima, n'esce in danno temporale! Che per le parole avete veduto e udito venire mutazioni di stati, disfacimento delle città e molti altri mali e omicidii perché la parola entrò nel mezzo del cuore a colui a cui fu detta: intrò dove non sarebbe passato il coltello" (ID 251) (What a danger do such wicked words pose! They not only rob souls of grace, but bring temporal harm as well. You have seen and heard how words have caused revolutions, the ruin of cities, murders, and many other evils, when words entered the heart of the one to whom they were said more deeply than a sword could have entered) (Noffke 173).

76. Fenn 109.

77. *Orchard* 93.

78. *Orchard* 323. On the relationship between the practice of music and its spiritual meanings, see Klaus Pietschmann, "Religion and the Senses in Fifteenth-Century Europe," trans. James Steichen, in *The Cambridge History of Fifteenth-Century Music*, ed. Anna Maria Busse Burger and Jesse Rodin (Cambridge: Cambridge University Press, 2015), 40–52. For a detailed study of the motif in Mechthild of Hackeborn, see Anne Marie Caron, R.S.M., "Mechthild of Hackeborn, Prophet of Divine

Praise: To Sing God's Praise, to Live God's Song," *Cistercian Studies Quarterly* 36 (2001): 145–61.

79. *Orchard* 360. "L'affetto de l'anima fa alora uno giubilo e uno suono, temperate e acordate le corde con prudenzia e lume, acordandole tutte a uno suono, cioè a gloria e loda del nome mio" (ID 489–90) (The soul's movements, then, make a jubilant sound, its chords tempered and harmonized with prudence and light, all of them melting into one sound, the glorification and praise of my name) (Noffke 310).

80. *Orchard* 360, Noffke 310, MS 87 ff. 249v–250r.

81. *Orchard* 361.

82. *Orchard* 167. "Prima parla a me con la lingua che sta nella bocca del santo desiderio suo, ciò è la lingua della santa e continua orazione. Questa lingua parla attuale e mentale: mentale offerendo a me dolci e amorosi desideri in salute dell'anime, e attuale parla annunziando la dottrina della mia Verità, amonendo consigliando e confessando senza alcuno timore di propria pena che il mondo le volesse dare, ma arditamente confessa inanzi ad ogni creatura in diversi modi, e a ciascuno secondo lo stato suo" (ID 196–97) (First she speaks to me with the tongue of holy and constant prayer that is in the mouth of her holy desire. This tongue has an external and an interior language. Interiorly, the soul offers me tender loving desires for the salvation of souls. Externally, she proclaims the teaching of my Truth, admonishing, advising, testifying, without any fear for the pain the world may please to inflict on her. And she adapts her enthusiastic testimony to the situation of each person she confronts) (Noffke 140).

83. *Orchard* 167.

84. *Orchard* 167.

85. "Sum mensa, et illis est filius meus cibus, et spiritus sanctus eis servit, qui a me, patre, filioque procedit" (MS 87, fol. 103v). There is a related culinary metaphor in Mechthild of Hackeborn in which the visionary speaker claims she is not worthy to wash the Lord's dishes, and Jesus explains that the kitchen is his heart, the cook is the Holy Spirit, and the dishes are, he says, "the hearts of all my saints and chosen ones, which are constantly flooded with wondrous sweetness from the overflow of my divine heart"; Mechthild of Hackeborn, trans. Barbara Newman, *The Book of Special Grace* (Mahwah, NJ: Paulist Press, 2017), 127–28.

86. This use of Jeremiah to express mystical ineffability is also found, for example, in *A Ladder of Eight Rungs*, a Dutch Franciscan text of the fifteenth century: the rung to be contemplated on Wednesday, the fourth rung, is the "rung of amazement," when one exclaims these same words along with the prophet. See Rik van Nieuwenhove, Robert Faesen, S.J., and Helen Rolfson, eds., *Late Medieval Mysticism of the Low Countries* (Mahwah, NJ: Paulist Press, 2008), 108.

87. See, especially, Niels Christian Hvidt, *Christian Prophecy: The Post-Biblical Tradition* (Oxford: Oxford University Press, 2007). My thanks to Regina Schwartz for discussing this aspect of prophecy with me.

88. On short and single-syllable prayers, see Alastair Bennet, *"Brevis oratio penetrat celum*: Proverbs, Prayers, and Lay Understanding in Late Medieval England," *New Medieval Literatures* 14 (2012): 127–63; A. C. Spearing, "Language and Its Limits: *The Cloud of Unknowing* and *Pearl*," in *Approaching Medieval English Anchoritic and Mystical Texts*, ed. Dee Dyas, Valerie Edden, and Roger Ellis (Woodbridge: D. S. Brewer, 2005), 75–86; and Jordan Kirk, "The Hideous Noise of Prayer: The Cloud of Unknowing on the Syllable-Word," *Exemplaria* 28, no. 2 (2016): 97–117.

89. "E che dirò? Farò come troglio, dirò 'A, a'; perché non so che mi dire altro, però che la lingua finita non può esprimere l'affetto de l'anima che infinitamente desidera te" (ID 519) (And what shall I say? I will stutter, "A-a," because there is nothing else I know how to say. Finite language cannot express the emotion of the soul who longs for you infinitely) (Noffke 325).

90. On medical and philosophical theories surrounding speech impairment, see Irina Metzler, *Disability in Medieval Europe: Thinking about Physical Impairment during the High Middle Ages, c. 1100–1400* (London: Routledge, 2006), 65–125.

91. Catherine Grisé, "Translating Tears in *The Orcherd of Syon*," in *Booldly bot meekly: Essays on the Theory and Practice of Translation in the Middle Ages in Honour of Roger Ellis*, ed. Catherine Batt and René Tixier (Turnhout: Brepols, 2018), 267.

92. On Catherine's use of this motif, and its use by those around her to describe her revelatory experiences, see Cornelia Wild, *Göttliche Stimme, irdische Schrift: Dante, Petrarca und Caterina da Siena* (Berlin: Walter de Gruyter, 2017), 124–26 ("Extase").

93. *Orchard* 18.

94. See especially Suzanne Noffke, O.P., "The Physical in the Mystical Writings of Catherine of Siena," *Annali d'italianistica* 13 (1995): 109–29.

95. H. Howes, "In Search of Clearer Water: An Exploration of Water Imagery in Late Medieval Devotional Prose Addressed to Women" (PhD diss., Queen Mary University of London, 2016), 35.

96. *Orchard* 127.

97. Howes, "In Search of Clearer Water," 125.

98. Noffke 365–66.

99. Jane Chance, "St. Catherine of Siena in Late Medieval Britain: Feminizing Literary Reception through Gender and Class," *Annali d'Italianistica* 13 (1995): 163–203. The Italian text, but not the Middle English, also claims that Christ's "divinity is kneaded into the clay of your humanity like one bread" (Noffke 65). London, British Library MS Harley 3432 marginally glosses "anefeeld" as "an instrument which smythis han wheron þei forge what werk þei wil haue" (*Orchard* 69).

100. *Orchard* 58. Hodgson, "*The Orcherd of Syon* and the English Mystical Tradition." On Julian of Norwich and Catherine of Siena, see also Elisabeth Dutton,

Julian of Norwich: The Influence of Late-Medieval Devotional Compilations (Woodbridge: D. S. Brewer, 2008), 34–35.

101. *Orchard* 68. "Of my having joined myself with your humanity, which I formed from the earth's clay" (Noffke 64) (l'unione che Io ò fatta ne l'uomo, il quale Io formai del limo della terra" (ID 69).

102. Noffke 38.

103. Regina Schwartz, *Loving Justice, Living Shakespeare* (Oxford: Oxford University Press, 2016), 120.

104. On Francis and his marriage to Lady Poverty, see, for instance, Michael Robson, *The Franciscans in the Middle Ages* (Woodbridge: Boydell & Brewer, 2006), esp. 37–47, and Kenneth Baxter Wolf, *The Poverty of Riches: Saint Francis of Assisi Reconsidered* (Oxford: Oxford University Press, 2003), 30–39.

105. *Orchard* 370. Catherine's Italian, however, notes rather that it is the Son of the Virgin who has no place to rest his head, not the Son of Man (ID 511).

106. See Newman, *God and the Goddesses*, 209–20.

107. *Orchard* 371. Noffke comments in her translation that "the metaphors become crossed here" (321n80). "Tutte le virtù, tutte le grazie e piaceri e diletti che l'anima sa desiderare, e più che non sa desiderare, truova l'anima che piglia per sposa la reina della povertà" (ID 512).

108. ID 512/Noffke 321.

109. Noffke 336. "Raguarda Benedetto con quanto ordine ordinò la navicella sua" (ID 537–38).

110. *Orchard* 388. "by a singular grace, the wounds of my Truth appeared in his body to show in the vessel of his body what was in his soul's affection. Thus did he make a path for the others" (Noffke 337).

111. *Orchard* 388–89, even specifying individual and collective ownership of property as warranting the curse of both Dominic and God (cf. Noffke 337).

112. Noffke 339. "Larga, tutta gioconda e tutta odorifera: uno giardino dilettissimo in sé" (ID 542). The *MED*, s.v. *viridarie*, points out that the translation likely stems from a misidentification of *viridarium* for *viridarius*.

113. *Orchard* 391. "Like a true knight without any slavish fear he went forth onto the battlefield" (Noffke 340).

114. "I could tell you about many others who, though they never suffered actual martyrdom, did so in spirit, as did Dominic/E così molti te ne potrei contare I quali, perché non avessero il martirio attualmente, l'avevano mentalmente, sì come ebbe Domenico" (Noffke 340/ID 543).

115. *Orchard* 391. The Middle English largely preserves the spirit of this chapter, but it does here omit that final comparison of the two in the Italian: "Truly Dominic and Francis were two pillars of holy Church: Francis with the poverty that was his hallmark and Dominic with learning/Veramente Domenico e Francesco sono stati due colonne nella santa Chiesa: Francesco con la povertà che principalmente gli fu propria come detto è, e Domenico con la scienzia" (Noffke 340/ID 543).

116. Christopher Roman, "*The Dialogue* of Catherine of Siena: A Charity Born of Solitude," *Magistra* 21, no. 1 (2015): 131.

117. *Orchard* 138. On Julian's theology of deification, see Louise Nelstrop, *On Deification and Sacred Eloquence: Richard Rolle and Julian of Norwich* (Abingdon: Routledge, 2020), 126–74. After twenty years of contemplating the parable first revealed to her, she comes to understand how the servant's falling into the ditch is simultaneously both the fall and the Incarnation, and the servant both Christ and all of humanity: "In the servant is comprehended the seconde person of the trinite, and in the servant is comprehended Adam: that is to sey, all men"; see *The Writings of Julian of Norwich: A Vision Showed to a Devout Woman and A Revelation of Love*, ed. Nicholas Watson and Jacqueline Jenkins (University Park: Pennsylvania State University Press, 2006), 283.

118. On the preexistence of the soul in God as understood by Julian of Norwich and other Middle English writers, see Denise Baker, "Julian of Norwich and the Varieties of Middle English Mystical Discourse," in *A Companion to Julian of Norwich*, ed. Liz Herbert McAvoy (Woodbridge: D. S. Brewer, 2008), 53–63.

119. See Hugh Feiss, O.S.B., ed., *On Love: A Selection of Works of Hugh, Adam, Achard, Richard, and Godfrey of St. Victor* (Turnhout: Brepols, 2011), especially, in that volume, Andrew Kraebel's translation of Richard of Saint Victor's *Four Degrees of Violent Love*, 263–300.

120. Warren, *The Embodied Word*, 45.

121. *Orchard* 66. "Keep in mind that each of you has your own vineyard. But every one is joined to your neighbors' vineyards without any dividing lines. They are so joined together, in fact, that you cannot do good or evil for yourself without doing the same for your neighbors. All of you together make up one common vineyard, the whole Christian assembly, and you are all united in the vineyard of the mystic body of the holy Church" (Noffke 62).

122. *Orchard* 420. "Clothe, clothe me with yourself, eternal Truth, so that I may run the course of this mortal life in true obedience and in the light of most holy faith. With that light I sense my soul once again becoming drunk! Thanks be to God! Amen" (Noffke 366). On the language of spiritual drunkenness in other Middle English devotional texts, especially the *Ladder of Four Rungs*, see Gina Brandolino, "God's Gluttons: Middle English Devotional Texts, Interiority, and Indulgence," *Studies in Philology* 110, no. 3 (2013): 403–31.

123. *Orchard* 176. "aufero eis ludum dilectionis eundi et redeundi. Qui vocatur 'dilectionis ludus' quia ex amore discedo et ex amore redeo: non proprie ego, quam ego sum dominus vobis immobilis . . . sed sensus quem in animam caritas mea dat, ille est qui vadit et redit" (MS 87, fol. 105r)/"lo' tolgo il giuoco dell'amore d'andare e tornare, il quale si chiama 'giuoco d'amore' perché per amore parto e per amore torno; non propriamente Io, ché Io so' lo Dio vostro immobile che non mi muovo, ma il sentimento che dà la mia carità nell'anima è quello che va e torna" (ID 209)/"I relieve them of this lover's game of going and coming back. I call it a 'lover's

game' because I go away for love and I come back for love—no, not really I, for I am your unchanging and unchangeable God; what goes and comes back is the feeling my charity creates in the soul" (Noffke 147). On the development of this motif from James of Milan's *Stimulus Amoris* onward, see Riehle, *Middle English Mystics*, 40–42.

124. *Orchard* 50. "God let himself be forced by her tears and chained by her holy desire"/"Dio . . . lassandosi costrignere alle lagrime e lassandosi legare alla fune del santo desiderio suo" (Noffke 50/ID 45); God goes on to tell the Soul, "your weeping has power over me and the pain in your desire binds me like a chain"/"la lagrima mi costrigne . . . e mi legano i penosi desideri vostri" (Noffke 50/ID 45).

125. *Orchard* 375–76, noted in Riehle, *Middle English Mystics*, 45.

126. On Syon in the age of print, see J. T. Rhodes, "Syon Abbey and Its Religious Publications in the Sixteenth Century," *Journal of Ecclesiastical History* 44, no. 1 (1993): 11–25.

127. On the possibility of the role played in the production of the manuscript by the nearby Augustinian priory of Thurgarton, famous as the home of Walter Hilton, see Jennifer Brown, *Three Women of Liège*, 12.

128. For an edition of these three lives, see Brown, *Three Women of Liège*. On Christina the Astonishing, see, especially, the introduction to Barbara Newman, trans., *Thomas of Cantimpré, The Collected Saints' Lives: Abbot John of Cantimpré, Christina the Astonishing, Margaret of Ypres, and Lutgard of Aywières* (Turnhout: Brepols, 2008). See also Rachel J. D. Smith, *Excessive Saints: Gender, Narrative, and Theological Invention in Thomas of Cantimpré's Mystical Hagiographies* (New York: Columbia University Press, 2018).

129. Sarah Macmillan, "Mortifying the Mind: Asceticism, Mysticism, and Oxford, Bodleian Library, MS Douce 114," in *The Medieval Mystical Tradition: Papers Read at Charney Manor, July 2011*, ed. E. A. Jones (Rochester: Boydell & Brewer, 2013), 109–24, and Macmillan, "Asceticism in Late-medieval Religious Writing: Oxford, Bodleian Library, MS Douce 114" (PhD diss., University of Birmingham, 2010).

130. Brian Vander Veen, "The *Vitae* of Bodleian Library MS Douce 114" (PhD diss., University of Nottingham, 2007), 191.

131. Jennifer N. Brown, "Gender, Confession, and Authority: Oxford, Bodleian Library, MS Douce 114 in the Fifteenth Century," in Ghosh and Gillespie, eds., *After Arundel*, 416.

132. Vincent Gillespie, "1412–1534: Culture and History," in *The Cambridge Companion to Medieval English Mysticism*, ed. Samuel Fanous and Vincent Gillespie (Cambridge: Cambridge University Press, 2011), 181.

133. Brown, "From the Charterhouse to the Printing House"; see also Brown, *Fruit of the Orchard*, 42–44, and Jennifer N. Brown, "Gender, Confession, and Authority: Oxford, Bodleian Library, MS Douce 114 in the Fifteenth Century," in Gillespie and Ghosh, eds., *After Arundel*.

134. Fols. 86r–87v. "Saint James the Apostle says that whoever does not sin with his tongue is a perfect man. Therefore the turner of this English, who is only simple in understanding as the truth here proves, lowly and meekly, beseeches all men and women who may by chance read or hear this English, that they be not too questioning or curious about the many clauses and changes in style, or the way the English is sometimes southern, sometimes northern. Because the reason why does not need to be told. And he especially [beseeches] educated men and clerks, if they deign to see this book, that they be favorable and harmless readers or hearers of this English, and forgive him all the errors that he made in compiling (attributing his uneducated state to simple ignorance and obedience, rather than to pride or presumption). For all men should know that he who wrote this English, out of Latin, knowing his own simpleness and unknowing, dared not have presumed to undertake such a labor unless his master had commanded him (he whom the translator might not contradict)." Transcriptions are mine, made in consultation with Carl Horstmann's 1885 edition in *Anglia*, with scribal abbreviations silently expanded and punctuation added.

135. Dirk Schultze, review of Claire Waters, ed., *Virgins and Scholars: A Fifteenth-Century Compilation of the Lives of John the Baptist, John the Evangelist, Jerome, and Katherine of Alexandria* and Jennifer Brown, ed., *Three Women of Liége: A Critical Edition of and Commentary on the Middle English Lives of Elizabeth of Spalbeek, Christina Mirabilis, and Marie d'Oignies, Anglia* 127, no. 2 (2009), 341–47.

136. Fol. 83r. "At times in Rome, she took only the sacrament of the altar. Nevertheless, the manner of whipping she kept for a long time, as I saw for many years, is this: meat, wine, sweets, and eggs she loathed greatly. But women that were with her commonly gave to her green herbs, when they might get any, or else a mess of roots with oil. Of an eel she only ate the head and the tail, but she ate no cheese at all (unless it were very old and rotten), and similarly grapes and other things. Nevertheless, she didn't eat these, but chewed them with her teeth. Sometimes with bread, sometimes without bread, sucking the juice, and spitting out every morsel of the grease, supping often on clear water by itself. And she stayed at the table as long as other women were eating there. Afterwards she rose, and said 'now we go for the justice of this wreched sinner.' And with a stalk of fennel or a different thing she stuck into her stomach, and brought out violently by the same way the juice and the water that she had ingested. And some times she suffered such great violence in doing this that fresh blood came out of her mouth."

137. "She ended the last day in my presence. When I bore her with my own hands to the tomb, that is to the church of the Friars Preachers to be buried, ye, rather to be kept in a coffin of cypress and a respectful tomb. Truly, while she labored towards her death, she commanded some men what they should do after her death. Afterward, turning her face to me, she said—stretching forth her finger—'Truly, I bid thee, on God's behalf and in the virtue of obedience, by any means necessary go to the Carthusian order. He hath called and chosen thee!' Then she, seeing us beside her weeping, said 'full dear children, you should not weep in any way, but rather joy

in our Lord and make a merry day! For I am delivered out of this prison, going this day to the most special spouse of my soul'" (ff. 78r–v).

138. Virginia Blanton, *Signs of Devotion: The Cult of St. Æthelthryth in Medieval England, 695–1615* (University Park: Pennsylvania State University Press, 2007), 1–2.

139. On the mains strands of transmission of the text, see Silvia Nocentini, "The *Legenda maior* of Catherine of Siena," in Muessig, Ferzoco, and Kienzle, eds., *A Companion to Catherine of Siena*, 339–57. On the early Italian translations of the Latin, see Silvia Nocentini, "'Pro solatio illicteratorum': The Earliest Italian Translations of the *Legenda maior*," in Hamburger and Signori, eds., *Catherine of Siena*, 169–83, and, in the same volume, Alison Frazier, "Humanist Lives of Catherine of Siena: Latin Prose Narratives on the Italian Peninsula (1461–1505)," in Hamburger and Signori, eds., *Catherine of Siena*, 109–34.

140. On the *Life* as proto-novel, see Ann W. Astell, "Heroic Virtue in Blessed Raymond of Capua's *Life of Catherine of Siena*," *Journal of Medieval and Early Modern Studies* 42, no. 1 (2012): 35–57.

141. John W. Coakley, *Women, Men, and Spiritual Power: Female Saints and Their Male Collaborators* (New York: Columbia University Press, 2006), "Managing Holiness: Raymond of Capua and Catherine of Siena," 170.

142. Karen Scott, "Mystical Death, Bodily Death: Catherine of Siena and Raymond of Capua on the Mystic's Encounter with God," in *Gendered Voices: Medieval Saints and Their Interpreters*, ed. Catherine Mooney (Philadelphia: University of Pennsylvania Press, 1999), 136.

143. Ruth Mortimer, "St. Catherine of Siena and the Printed Book," *Papers of the Bibliographic Society of America* 86 (1992): 11–22, 12.

144. As Nancy Bradley Warren has demonstrated, the idea of "Englishness" extends "beyond England's shores" throughout this period; see Warren, *The Embodied Word*, 8.

145. *Oxford Dictionary of National Biography* (online), s.v. John Fenn.

146. A comprehensive study or edition of this text is lacking. But on Lancellotto more generally, see, most recently, Giorgio Caravale, *Beyond the Inquisition: Ambrogio Catarino Politi and the Origins of the Counter-Reformation* (Notre Dame, IN: University of Notre Dame Press, 2017); the *Life* of Catherine is discussed briefly on 14–15.

147. Following in the footsteps of Warren, *The Embodied Word*, exploring the cultural valences of female monasticism and their textual communities, this builds on recent studies of the enduring forms in which cloistered medieval female spirituality was remembered and reconstructed, both in England and on the Continent. For Bridget of Sweden, see, for example, E. A. Jones and Alexandra Walsham, eds., *Syon Abbey and Its Books: Reading, Writing and Religion, c. 1400–1700* (Woodbridge: Boydell Press, 2010), and Susan Powell, *The Birgittines of Syon Abbey: Preaching and Print* (Turnhout: Brepols, 2017).

148. Blanton, *Signs of Devotion*, 289.

149. On the spaces of Siena and their relationship to Catherine's spiritual development, see Karen Scott, "Urban Spaces, Women's Networks, and the Lay Apostolate in the Siena of Catherine Benincasa," in *Creative Women in Medieval and Early Modern Italy: A Religious and Artistic Renaissance*, ed. E. Ann Matter and John Coakley (Philadelphia: University of Pennsylvania Press, 1994), 105–19.

150. WdW 40.

151. Fenn 14.

152. WdW 40–41.

153. Fenn 14–15.

154. On the wider context of bridal mysticism in the period, see Elizabeth Clarke, *Politics, Religion, and the Song of Songs in Seventeenth-Century England* (New York: Palgrave Macmillan, 2011), and Randall Pederson's chapter on Francis Rous, Puritan author of *The Mystical Marriage* (1635, translated into Latin 1655), in Pederson, *Unity in Diversity: English Puritans and the Puritan Reformation, 1603–1689* (Leiden: Brill 2014), 153–209.

155. Fenn 39.

156. Fenn 40–41.

157. Fenn 41.

158. Caroline Walker Bynum, *Holy Feast and Holy Fast: The Religious Significance of Food to Medieval Women* (Berkeley: University of California Press, 1987), 246. See also Andrew Jacobs, *Christ Circumcised: A Study in Early Christian History and Difference* (Philadelphia: University of Pennsylvania Press, 2012).

159. Fenn 104.

160. The term appears in a discussion of Herbert and Crashaw that turns to an analysis of Catherine's marriage to Jesus; see Richard Rambuss, "Pleasure and Devotion: The Body of Jesus and Seventeenth-Century Religious Lyric," in *Queering the Renaissance*, ed. Jonathan Goldberg (Durham, NC: Duke University Press, 1994), 263. Richard Crashaw's father, William, it has been noted, owned one of the currently extant manuscripts of the *Orchard of Syon*.

161. See, especially, Claudia Rattazzi Papka, "The Written Woman Writes: Caterina da Siena between History and Hagiography, Body and Text," *Annali d'italianistica* 13 (1995): 131–49.

162. Fenn 111. In Wynkyn de Worde, her face also transforms: Raymond, saying Mass, turns to make the general absolution, and "he sawe hyr face lyke the face of an angell, sendyng out bemys of bryghtnesse, in soo moche that he meruaylled and sayd in hymself to oure lord thus: 'Thys is not Katheryns face, but certeyne, lorde, this is thy dere spouse'" (WdW 354–55).

163. James White, "Hungering for Maleness: Catherine of Siena and the Medieval Public Sphere," *Religious Studies and Theology* 33, no. 2 (2014): 168.

164. Fenn 165.

165. WdW 104.

166. Fenn 166.

167. On these representations of the side-wound, see Amy Hollywood, "That Glorious Slit: Irigary and the Medieval Devotion to Christ's Side Wound," in *Acute Melancholia and Other Essays* (New York: Columbia University Press, 2016). On the birth of Ecclesia and its femininity, see Lora Walsh, "Ecclesia Reconsidered: Two Premodern Encounters with the Feminine Church," *Journal of Feminist Studies in Religion* 33, no. 2 (2017): 73–91.

168. On the use of the heart-exchange theme more broadly, and its relationship to contemporary stories about heart transplant surgery, see Barbara Newman, "Exchanging Hearts: A Medievalist Looks at Transplant Surgery," in *Rethinking the Medieval Legacy for Contemporary Theology*, ed. Anselm Min (Notre Dame, IN: University of Notre Dame Press, 2014), 17–42.

169. Fenn 183.

170. Fenn 184.

171. Fenn 187–88. See also Shackle, "The Effect of Twinship on the Mysticism of Catherine of Siena (1347–1380): A Vergotean Analysis," *Archiv für Religionspsychologie/Archive for the Psychology of Religion* 25 (2003): 129–41.

172. Fenn 211–12.

173. Fenn 212.

174. Jenna Lay, *Beyond the Cloister: Catholic Englishwomen and Early Modern Literary Culture* (Philadelphia: University of Pennsylvania Press, 2016), 10.

175. Nancy Bradley Warren, "Owning the Middle Ages: History, Trauma, and English Identity," in *Renaissance Retrospections: Tudor Views of the Middle Ages*, ed. Sarah A. Kelen (Kalamazoo, MI: Medieval Institute Publications, 2013), 191. See also E. A. Jones, *England's Last Medieval Monastery Syon Abbey, 1415–2015* (Leominster: Gracewing, 2015), 85–87.

176. Warren, "Owning the Middle Ages," 187.

177. Warren, *The Embodied Word*, 213–20.

178. Diane Watt, "The Prophet at Home: Elizabeth Barton and the Influence of Bridget of Sweden and Catherine of Siena," in Voaden, ed., *Prophets Abroad*, 161–76. See also Watt, "Of the Seed of Abraham: Elizabeth Barton, the 'Holy Maid of Kent,'" in *Secretaries of God: Women Prophets in Late Medieval and Early Modern England* (Cambridge: D. S. Brewer, 1997), 51–80.

179. Brown, *Fruit of the Orchard*, 198.

180. *The Blessings on Mount Gerizzim, and the Curses on Mount Ebal, Or, The happie estate of Protestants compared with the miserable estate of papists under the Popes tyrannie* (RSTC 23466), 122.

181. Ibid., 116.

182. *A true relation of Englands happinesse, under the raigne of Queene Elizabeth, and the miserable estate of papists, under the Popes tyrany* (RSTC 23467), [London], 1629, 104.

183. RSTC 983, 525–26. For a modern English translation of the *Audi Filia*, see Joan Gormley, trans., *Audi Filia—Listen, O Daughter* (Mahwah, NJ: Paulist Press, 2006). See also Girolamo Piatti, S.J., *The Happiness of a Religious State*, trans. Henry More, S.J. (1586–1661) (Rouen, 1632) (RSTC 20001), 87–88.

184. *The life of Gregorie Lopes, that great servant of God, natiue of Madrid* (Paris, 1638) (RSTC 16828), 277–78.

185. This text was first destroyed when the secret press was discovered in England in 1602, but it was printed in both English and French in 1609. Then, however, in 1646 the Puritan preacher Giles Randall published his own translation of the third part of the *Rule of Perfection*, renaming it *A Bright Starre*. Birrell notes that Randall also translated into English Nicholas of Cusa's *The Vision of God* and Sebastian Castellio's Latin translation of the *Theologia Germanica*, a key text in Martin Luther's understanding of medieval mysticism. See Birrell, "English Catholic Mystics in Non-Catholic Circles: Part 1," *Downside Review* 94 (1976): 64–65. The *Rule of Perfection* also had a reception history in most European languages: Birrell mentions it "was translated into Latin, French, Flemish, Italian and Spanish"; see Birrell, "English Counterreformation Book Culture," *Recusant History* 22 (1994): 115.

186. *The Rule of Perfection* (1609), 104.

187. On Hawkwood, see, especially, William Caferro, *John Hawkwood: An English Mercenary in Fourteenth-Century Italy* (Baltimore: Johns Hopkins University Press, 2006).

CHAPTER 4

1. On the status of the Low Countries as both a region in the later Middle Ages (extending as far up the Rhine as Cologne) and as a historiographical conceit in religious studies, see John Van Engen, "New Devotion in the Low Countries," *Ons geestelijk erf* 77 (2005): 235–63. On the relationship between the Dutch *Elckerlijc* and *Everyman*, see Clifford Davidson, Martin W. Walsh, and Ton J. Broos, eds., *Everyman and Its Dutch Original, "Elckerlijc"* (Kalamazoo, MI: Medieval Institute Publications, 2007). On Caxton's printing career in Bruges, Ghent, and Cologne, see N. F. Blake, *Caxton: England's First Printer* (London: Osprey, 1976), 20–32. On Caxton's command of Dutch, see Blake, *William Caxton and English Literary Culture* (London: Hambledon Press, 1991), 231–58, and Wytze Hellinga and Lotte Hellinga, "Between Two Languages: Caxton's Translation of Reynaert de Vos," in *Studies in Seventeenth-Century English Literature, History and Bibliography*, ed. G. A. M. Janssens and F. G. A. M. Aarts (Amsterdam: Rodopi, 1984), 119–32.

2. Jonathan Hsy, *Trading Tongues: Merchants, Multilingualism, and Medieval Literature.* (Columbus: Ohio State University Press, 2013), 1–26. See also Andrew Fleck, "'Ick verstaw you niet': Performing Foreign Tongues on the Early

Modern English Stage," *Medieval & Renaissance Drama in England* 20 (2007): 204–21.

3. On the relationship between the Modern Devout and the wool trade, see John van Engen, *Sisters and Brothers of the Common Life: The Devotio Moderna and the World of the Later Middle Ages* (Philadelphia: University of Philadelphia Press, 2008), "Labor: Living from the Work of Their Own Hands," 188–93.

4. David Wallace, "In Flaundres," *Studies in the Age of Chaucer* 19 (1997): 63–91, explores the significance of Flanders across Chaucer's lifetime and throughout his poetry, for instance. On the relationship between the two regions more generally, see, especially, the essays in Caroline Barron and Nigel Saul, eds., *England and the Low Countries in the Late Middle Ages* (New York: St. Martin's Press, 1995), and Steven Gunn and Antheun Janse, eds., *The Court as a Stage: England and the Low Countries in the Later Middle Ages* (Woodbridge: Boydell Press, 2006).

5. A. S. G. Edwards, "Continental Influences on London Printing and Reading in the Fifteenth and Early Sixteenth Centuries," in *London and Europe in the Later Middle Ages*, ed. Julia Boffey and Pamela King (London: Queen Mary and Westfield College, University of London, 1995), 230. See also Elizabeth Armstrong, "English Purchases of Printed Books from the Continent, 1465–1526," *English Historical Review* 94 (1979): 268–90, and Lotte Hellinga, "Importation of Books Printed on the Continent into England and Scotland before c. 1520," in *Printing the Written Word: The Social History of Books, circa 1450–1520*, ed. Sandra Hindman (Ithaca, NY: Cornell University Press, 1991), 205–24. On the errors Continental printers sometimes introduced into English texts as a result of their unfamiliarity with the language, see Curt Bühler, "At Thy Golg First eut of the hous vlysse the saynge thus," *Studies in the Renaissance* 6 (1959): 223–35.

6. See, for instance, Liesbeth Corens, "Catholic Nuns and English Identities: English Protestant Travellers on the English Convents in the Low Countries, 1660–1730," *Recusant History* 30, no. 3 (2011): 441–59.

7. See G. B. de Soer, "The Relationship of the Latin Versions of Ruysbroek's 'Die Geestelike Brulocht' to 'The Chastising of God's Children,'" *Mediaeval Studies* 21 (1959): 129–46. On Ruusbroec's Latin reception more generally, see Kees Schepers, "Ruusbroec in Latin: Impulses and Impediments," in *A Companion to John of Ruusbroec*, ed. John Arblaster and Rob Faesen (Leiden: Brill, 2014), 237–85.

8. London, British Library MS Additional 37790. *The Treatise of Perfection of the Sons of God* has been edited alongside *The Chastising of God's Children* by Colledge and Bazire (229–58); see also Marleen Cré's detailed study of the Amherst manuscript, *Vernacular Mysticism in the Charterhouse: A Study of London, British Library, MS Additional 37790* (Turnhout: Brepols, 2006), and Natalie Dear, "Representations of Continental Mysticism in British Library MS. Additional 37790: Mystical Union's Relationship with Courtly Love" (PhD diss., University of Calgary, 2005). On Ruusbroec and his broader literary connections in the Low Countries and

beyond, see Geert Warnar, *Ruusbroec: Literature and Mysticism in the Fourteenth Century*, trans. Diane Webb (Leiden: Brill, 2007).

9. Klaus Pietschmann and Steven Rozenski, "Singing the Self: The Autobiography of the Fifteenth-Century German Singer and Composer Johannes von Soest," *Early Music History* 29 (2010): 127–28.

10. On this text, see Steven Rozenski, "Ave Ave Ave [Ave]: The Multilingual Poetics of Exuberance in Bruder Hans," *New Medieval Literatures* 20 (2020): 107–42. For an edition of this idiosyncratic poem, see Michael S. Batts, *Bruder Hansens Marienlieder* (Tübingen: Max Niemeyer Verlag, 1963). For the most substantial discussion of his use of English, see H. M. Flasdieck, "Mittelenglische Verse vom deutschen Niederrhein," in *Studies for William A. Read: A Miscellany Presented by Some of His Colleagues and Friends*, ed. Nathaniel M. Caffee and Thomas A. Kirby (Baton Rouge: Louisiana State University Press, 1940), 35–66. See also David Wallace's discussion of a Deschamps poem set in Calais in Wallace, *Premodern Places: Calais to Surinam, Chaucer to Aphra Behn* (Malden, MA: Wiley Blackwell, 2004), 54–56, for one of the only other rare uses of English as a poetic language by a Continental author in the Middle Ages.

11. On English wisdom literature, see especially Christopher Cannon, "Proverbs and the Wisdom of Literature: *The Proverbs of Alfred* and Chaucer's *Tale of Melibee*," *Textual Practice* 24, no. 3 (2010): 407–34.

12. On the status of post-Reformation English Bibles and Bible commentary, see Andrew Taylor, "The Bible," Donald Mackenzie, "The Psalms," and Taylor, "Biblical Commentary," in *The Oxford History of Literary Translation in English*, vol. 2, *1550–1660*, ed. Gordon Braden, Robert Cummings, and Stuart Gillespie (Oxford: Oxford University Press, 2010), 121–40, 141–54, and 155–63.

13. On the complicated Lutheran and Evangelical relationship to the "Epistle of Straw," see, most recently, Jason D. Lane, *Luther's Epistle of Straw: The Voice of St. James in Reformation Preaching* (Berlin: De Gruyter, 2018).

14. As a Latin incunable with 72 printings (not taking into account incunable printings of translations, that is), it ranks only twenty-eighth in Michael Milway's list of Latin incunable best sellers, below liturgical books such as the top-ranking Breviary (449 printings), Hours (404), Missal (359), and Psalter (239); educational texts such as the *Donatus* (284) and *Distichs* of Cato (217); devotional works such as the *Golden Legend* (150) and the *Ars moriendi* (80); and classical works such as Terence's comedies (103), Virgil's *Aeneid* (96), and Boethius's *Consolation of Philosophy* (75 printings). The Bible itself is the eighth most popular incunable, with 178 printings. See Michael Milway, "Forgotten Best-Sellers from the Dawn of the Reformation," in *Continuity and Change: The Harvest of Late Medieval and Reformation History*, ed. Robert J. Bast and Andrew C. Gow (Leiden: Brill, 2000), 113–42. On the various successes of vernacular English texts in manuscript, see Michael Sargent, "What Do the Numbers Mean? Observations on Some Patterns of Middle

English Manuscript Transmission," in *Design and Distribution of Late Medieval Manuscripts in England*, ed. Margaret Connolly and Linne Mooney (York: York Medieval Press, 2008), 205–44.

15. The autograph manuscript has been examined most thoroughly by L. M. J. Delaissé, *Le manuscrit autographe de Thomas à Kempis et "L'imitation de Jésus Christ": Examen archéologique et édition diplomatique du Bruxellensis 5855–61* (Paris, 1956).

16. On the manuscript transmission, see, especially, S. G. Axters, O.P., *De Imitatione Christi: Een handschrifteninventaris bij het vijfhonderdste verjaren van Thomas Hemerken van Kempen* (Kempen: Thomas-Druckerei, 1971), and Uwe Neddermeyer, "*Radix Studii et Speculum Vitae*: Verbreitung und Rezeption der 'Imitatio Christi' in Handschriften und Drucken bis zur Reformation," in *Studien zum 15. Jahrhundert: Festschrift für Erich Meuthen*, ed. Johannes Helmrath and Heribert Müller (Munich: R. Oldenbourg Verlag, 1994), 457–81.

17. Maximilian von Habsburg, *Catholic and Protestant Translations of the Imitatio Christi, 1425–1650: From Late Medieval Classic to Early Modern Bestseller* (Burlington, VT: Ashgate, 2011), 255–307. See also the exhibition catalogue: Martine Delaveau and Yann Sordet, eds., *Un succès de librairie européen: l'Imitatio Christi, 1470–1850* (Paris: Éditions des Cendres, 2012). My thanks to Yann Sordet for thoughtfully providing me with a copy of this excellent work.

18. John Murdoch, *Classified Catalogue of Tamil Printed Books* (Madras: Christian Vernacular Education Society, 1865), 117.

19. It appeared in Philadelphia as *The Christian Pattern: Or the Imitation of Christ, Being an Abridgement of the Works of Thomas à Kempis by a Female Hand* (Germantown, PA: Christopher Sauer, 1749). For a study of the multiple extant translations of the text into Nahuatl (in manuscript, and thus not mentioned in Habsburg's survey) and its use in the Franciscan mission in colonial Mexico, see David Tavárez, "Nahua Intellectuals, Franciscan Scholars, and the *Devotio Moderna* in Colonial Mexico," *The Americas* 70, no. 2 (2013): 203–35.

20. Green and McIntyre estimate "around 42,500 total editions printed in the fifteenth century, compared to the 29,000-odd editions known to the ISTC today"; see Jonathan Green and Frank McIntyre, "Lost Incunable Editions: Closing in on an Estimate," in *Lost Books: Reconstructing the Print World of Pre-Industrial Europe*, ed. Flavia Bruni and Andrew Pettegree (Leiden: Brill, 2016), 60.

21. Franklin B. Williams Jr., "Lost Books of Tudor England," *The Library* 33, no. 1 (1978): 1–14; Andrew Pettegree, "French Books at the Frankfurt Fair," in *The French Book and the European Book World*, ed. Andrew Pettegree (Leiden: Brill, 2007), 129–76.

22. See Alexandra Hill, *Lost Books and Printing in London, 1557–1640: An Analysis of the Stationers' Company Register* (Leiden: Brill, 2018), and the above-mentioned work by Green and McIntyre, "Lost Incunable Editions," and also their earlier essay, J. Green, F. McIntyre, and P. Needham, "The Shape of Incunable

Survival and Statistical Estimation of Lost Editions," *Papers of the Bibliographical Society of America* 105, no. 2 (2011): 141–75.

23. Tavárez, "Nahua Intellectuals," 211. On the *Musica Ecclesiastica* manuscripts, see Roger Lovatt, "*The Imitation of Christ* in Late Medieval England," *Transactions of the Royal Historical Society* 18 (1968): 97–121. To this can be added at least two other manuscripts identified by Benjamin Gallucci-Wright of the University of Notre Dame—my thanks to him for providing me with the fruits of some of his recent doctoral research.

24. On the role of ascetic ideals, including those addressed in the *Imitation of Christ*, in the novel, see Paul Yeoh, "*Saint's Everlasting Rest*: The Martyrdom of Maggie Tulliver," *Studies in the Novel* 41, no. 1 (2009): 1–21.

25. Nandra Perry, *Imitatio Christi: The Poetics of Piety in Early Modern England* (Notre Dame, IN: University of Notre Dame Press, 2014), 21.

26. Candida Moss writes: "Rhetorically, the narrative reenactment of Jesus traditions clothed Christ in ecclesiastical attire. The martyrs served to demonstrate the Christly response to persecution, communal conflicts, perceived heresies, and oppression"; Candida R. Moss, *The Other Christs: Imitating Jesus in Ancient Christian Ideologies of Martyrdom* (Oxford: Oxford University Press, 2010), 6.

27. Rozenski, "Authority and Exemplarity in Richard Rolle and Henry Suso," in *The Medieval Mystical Tradition: Papers Read at Charney Manor, July 2011*, ed. E. A. Jones (Rochester: Boydell & Brewer, 2013), 93–108. The concept is also addressed in Peter Ulrich, *Imitatio et configuratio: Die philosophia spiritualis Heinrich Seuses als Theologie der Nachfolge des Christus passus*, chap. 1.

28. Van Engen, *Sisters and Brothers of the Common Life*, 294–304. Van Engen also mentions the reading list of Geert Grote, founder of the Modern Devout, and its sole contemporary author, Henry Suso (16). See also John Van Engen, ed. and trans., *Devotio Moderna: Basic Writings* (Mahwah, NJ: Paulist Press, 1988), and Thom Mertens, "Collatio und Codex im Bereich der Devotio Moderna," in *Der Codex in Gebrauch*, ed. Christel Meier (Munich: Fink, 1996), 163–82.

29. David Alexander Harrap, "The Phenomena of Prayer: The Reception of the *Imitatio Christi* in England (1438–c. 1600)" (PhD diss., Queen Mary University of London, 2016), 26.

30. Sara Ritchey, "Wessel Gansfort, John Mombaer, and Medieval Technologies of the Self: Affective Meditation in a Fifteenth-Century Emotional Community," *Fifteenth-Century Studies* 38 (2013): 156. See also Nikolaus Staubach, "*Diversa raptim undique collecta*: Das Rapiarium im geistlichen Reformprogramm der Devotio moderna," in *Literarische Formen des Mittelalters: Florilegien, Kompilationen, Kollektionen*, ed. Kaspar Elm (Wiesbaden: Harrassowitz, 2000), 115–47.

31. Ulrike Hascher-Burger, "Religious Song and Devotional Culture in Northern Germany," in *A Companion to Mysticism and Devotion in Northern Germany in the Late Middle Ages*, ed. Elizabeth Andersen, Henrike Lähnemann, and Anne Simon (Leiden: Brill, 2014), 268.

32. For a detailed study of this book, a hybrid of incunables and a manuscript still in its original binding (the manuscript was bound with two incunables: *De spiritualibus ascensionibus* by fourteenth-century Dutch theologian Gerhard Zerbolt van Zutphen and *De exterioris et interioris hominis compositione* by the thirteenth-century German Franciscan David of Augsburg), see Ulrike Hascher-Burger, *Singen für die Seligkeit: Studien zu einer Liedersammlung der Devotio moderna: Zwolle, Historisch Centrum Overijssel, coll. Emmanuelshuizen, cat. VI. Mit Edition und Faksimile* (Leiden: Brill, 2007).

33. For an overview of the authorship arguments, see Nikolaus Staubach, "Eine unendliche Geschichte? Der Streit um die Autorschaft der 'Imitatio Christi,'" in *Aus dem Winkel in die Welt: Die Bücher des Thomas von Kempen und ihre Schicksale,* ed. Ulrike Bodemann and Nikolaus Staubach (Frankfurt a.M.: Peter Lang, 2006), 9–35.

34. For a detailed study of this manuscript, see Ralph Hanna, "Producing Magdalene College MS lat. 93," *Yearbook of English Studies* 33 (2003): 142–55.

35. Lovatt, "*The Imitation of Christ* in Late Medieval England," *Transactions of the Royal Historical Society* 18 (1968): 100.

36. "The earliest surviving Latin manuscript copied in England was written by John Dygon, a recluse at Sheen, in 1438, and two of the four surviving manuscripts were written by Sheen scribes, Dublin, Trinity College MS 678, by Stephen Dodesham; and Glasgow, University Library MS Hunterian T.6.18, by Wilham Darker, the latter for Elizabeth Gibbs, Abbess of Syon"; Brendan Biggs, "The Style of the First English Translation of the *Imitatio Christi,*" in *The Medieval Translator* 5 (1996): 188.

37. Biggs, "The Style of the First English Translation of the *Imitatio Christi,*" 202.

38. *The Imitation of Christ: The First English Translation of the "Imitatio Christi,"* ed. Brendan Biggs, EETS o.s. 309 (1997), 9.

39. Ibid., lxxx.

40. For a general overview of her life and works (with an emphasis on political, dynastic, and institutional history), see Malcolm Underwood and Michael K. Jones, *The King's Mother: Lady Margaret Beaufort, Countess of Richmond and Derby* (Cambridge: Cambridge University Press, 1992). On her religious and cultural life, see Susan Powell, "Lady Margaret Beaufort: Books, Printers, and Syon Abbey," in *The Birgittines of Syon Abbey: Preaching and Print* (Turnhout: Brepols, 2017), 152–213. See also Anne Clark Bartlett, "Translation, Self-Representation, and Statecraft: Lady Margaret Beaufort and Caxton's *Blanchardyn and Eglantine* (1489)," *Essays in Medieval Studies* 22 (2005): 53–66.

41. RSTC 6894.5. The Latin *Mirror of Gold* is sometimes misattributed to Denys the Carthusian. See Elizabeth Nugent, ed., *The Thought and Culture of the English Renaissance: An Anthology of Tudor Prose, 1481–1555* (Cambridge: Cambridge University Press, 1956), 384–86.

42. Brenda Hosington, "Lady Margaret Beaufort's Translations as Mirrors of Practical Piety," in *English Women, Religion, and Textual Production, 1500–1625*, ed. Micheline White (Burlington, VT: Ashgate, 2011), 185–204.

43. Ibid., 198.

44. Stephanie Morley, "Translating Lady Margaret Beaufort: A Case for Translation as Compensatory Power," in *The Medieval Translator*, ed. Denis Renevey and Christiania Whitehead (Turnhout: Brepols, 2009), 12:251–61. Morley is also preparing an edition of Lady Margaret's translations for the Middle English Texts Series (METS).

45. Patricia Demers, "'God may open more than man maye vnderstande': Lady Margaret Beaufort's Translation of the '*De Imitatione Christi*,'" *Renaissance and Reformation/Renaissance et Réforme* 35, no. 4 (2012): 55.

46. RSTC 23961. On the relationship between Whitford and Syon's larger publication project, see Alexandra da Costa, *Reforming Printing: Syon Abbey's Defence of Orthodoxy, 1525–1534* (Oxford: Oxford University Press, 2012).

47. James P. Carley and Ann M. Hutchison, "William Peto, O.F.M.Obs., and the 1556 Edition of *The folowinge of Chryste*: Background and Context," *Journal of the Early Book Society* 17 (2014): 98.

48. RSTC 23961, *The Following of Christ*, sig. a1v–a2r.

49. RSTC 23961, *The Following of Christ*, sig. a1v–a2r.

50. Habsburg, *Catholic and Protestant Translations of the Imitatio Christi*, 91–92. He assumes the attribution to Whitford is correct, and thus interprets these changes as signaling a greater capacity to criticize monasticism, stemming from Whitford's almost unimpeachable position as a Syon brother.

51. Kubsch, *Crossing Boundaries in Early Modern England: Translations of Thomas à Kempis's "De imitatione Christi"* (1500–1700) (Zürich: Lit Verlag, 2018), 60–61.

52. Carley and Hutchison, "William Peto, O.F.M.Obs., and the 1556 Edition of *The folowinge of Chryste*," 100–101. On the political transformations of the Marian period, see Christopher Haigh, *English Reformations: Religion, Politics, and Society under the Tudors* (Oxford: Oxford University Press, 1993), 203–34.

53. The Cawood prints are RSTC 23966 and 23967.5. On the varieties of post-Marian English Catholicism, insular and Continental, see Andrew Muldoon, "Recusants, Church-Papists, and 'Comfortable' Missionaries: Assessing the Post-Reformation English Catholic Community," *Catholic Historical Review* 86, no. 2 (2000): 242–57.

54. C. Fenno Hoffman, "Catherine Parr as a Woman of Letters," *Huntington Library Quarterly* 23, no. 4 (1960): 355–56. Janel Mueller has edited the *Prayers or Meditations* (including a holograph fragment) in Katherine Parr, *Complete Works and Correspondence*, ed. Janel Mueller (Chicago: University of Chicago Press, 2011). On Parr's earlier authorship, see also Micheline White, "The Psalms, War, and Royal Iconography: Katherine Parr's *Psalms or Prayers* (1544) and Henry VIII as

David," *Renaissance Studies* 29, no. 4 (2015): 554–75. On Parr's encouragement of literary activity in her stepchildren, the two future queens Mary and Elizabeth, see Sheryl Kujawa-Holbrook, "Katherine Parr and Reformed Religion," *Anglican and Episcopal History* 72, no. 1 (2003): 55–78.

55. Andrew Hiscock, "'A supernal liuely fayth': Katherine Parr and the Authoring of Devotion," *Women's Writing* 9, no. 2 (2002): 185. He also notes, "Parr's principal focus here upon strategies of compilation, abridgement and textual reconfiguration is a timely reminder to dispense with anachronistic thinking which foregrounds 'original' creativity as the defining characteristic of authorship—this was intellectual baggage with which the Renaissance reader would not have been burdened" (ibid.). An incomplete autograph manuscript of the text on vellum also survives in Kendal, Cumbria.

56. Janel Mueller, "Devotion as Difference: Intertextuality in Queen Katherine Parr's 'Prayers or Meditations' (1545)," *Huntington Library Quarterly* 53, no. 3 (1990): 177.

57. On Parr and Fisher, see Janel Mueller, "Complications of Intertextuality: John Fisher, Katherine Parr, and 'The Book of the Crucifix,'" in *Texts and Cultural Change in Early Modern England*, ed. Cedric Brown and Arthur Marotti (New York: Palgrave Macmillan, 1997), 15–36.

58. Harrap, "The Phenomena of Prayer," 181 and 195.

59. See Janel Mueller and Joshua Scodel, eds., *Elizabeth I: Translations, 1544–1589* (Chicago: University of Chicago Press, 2009), 129–200; the Parr text is referred to as a "transformative intertextual appropriation" at 130. On the Latin translations, and Elizabeth's other translations into Latin, see Brenda Hosington, "The Young Princess Elizabeth, Neo-Latin, and the Power of the Written Word," in *Elizabeth I in Writing: Language, Power and Representation in Early Modern England*, ed. Donatella Montini and Iolanda Plescia (New York: Palgrave Macmillan, 2018), 11–36, and Roger Ellis, "The Juvenile Translations of Elizabeth Tudor," *Translation and Literature* 18, no. 2 (2009): 157–80.

60. Castellio is perhaps best known today for his quarrels with John Calvin and his defense of religious freedom. See, for instance, Sebastian Castellio, *Concerning Heretics* (New York: Columbia University Press, 1935), and Stefan Zweig, *The Right to Heresy: Castellio against Calvin*, trans. Eden Paul and Cedar Paul (New York: Viking Press, 1936).

61. For a comparative study demonstrating that conservative/Anglican English authors and readers were more likely than evangelicals/Puritans to prefer Christ as an exemplar for personal imitation, see Elizabeth K. Hudson, "English Protestants and the *imitatio Christi*, 1580–1620," *Sixteenth-Century Journal* 19, no. 4 (1988): 541–58. On the status of various strands of English Catholicism during the reign of Elizabeth, see Alexandra Walsham, *Church Papists: Catholicism, Conformity and Confessional Polemic in Early Modern England* (London: Royal Historical Society, 1993); and Christopher Highly, *Catholics Writing the Nation in Early Modern Britain and Ireland* (Oxford: Oxford University Press, 2008).

62. Hans R. Guggisberg, *Sebastian Castellio, 1515–1563: Humanist and Defender of Religious Toleration in a Confessional Age*, trans. Bruce Gordon (Aldershot: Ashgate, 2003).

63. Kubsch, *Crossing Boundaries*, 74 and 68–69. Kubsch also notes that comparing his Bible translation with his translation of Kempis allows us to see Castellio's differing treatment of sacred scripture and devotional literature.

64. Ibid., 75.

65. I am grateful to Rand Johnson, of Western Michigan University, for sharing some of his unpublished research into Castellio with me.

66. RSTC 23969, sig. a1r.

67. RSTC 23969, sig. a2v–a3r.

68. RSTC 23969.5c (1568), sig. a4r.

69. Seth Lerer, *Error and the Academic Self: The Scholarly Imagination, Medieval to Modern* (New York: Columbia University Press, 2003), 18.

70. Ibid., 17.

71. Citations are taken from the EEBO reproduction of RSTC 23973. All underlining and emphases in quotations are from the original text.

72. David Crane, "English Translations of the *Imitatio Christi* in the Sixteenth and Seventeenth Centuries," *Recusant History* 13 (1975): 84.

73. Ibid., 79–100.

74. Harrap, "The Phenomena of Prayer," 201.

75. Rogers 1580, sig. a3r.

76. Rogers 1580, sig. a3v.

77. Habsburg, *Protestant and Catholic Translations of the "Imitatio Christi,"* 173.

78. Rogers 1580, sigs. a4r–a5r.

79. Rogers 1580, sig. a5v.

80. Rogers 1580, sig. a5v.

81. Rogers 1580, sig. a5v.

82. Rogers 1580, sigs. a6r–a6v.

83. Rogers 1580, sig. a6v.

84. Rogers 1580, sig. a6v.

85. Rogers 1580, sigs. a7r–v.

86. Emphasis original. Rogers 1580, sig. a9v.

87. Emphasis original. Rogers 1580, sig. a9v.

88. Rogers 1580, sig. a10r.

89. Rogers 1580, sig. a10v.

90. Similarly, scripture itself was mediated by technologies of interpretation; Protestant attempts to liberate the biblical text from medieval commentary tended themselves to introduce new forms of mediation in their very attempt to repudiate earlier commentary. See the conclusion to Andrew Kraebel, *Biblical Commentary and Translation in Later Medieval England: Experiments in Interpretation* (Cambridge: Cambridge University Press, 2020), and, more generally, James Simpson,

Burning to Read: English Fundamentalism and Its Reformation Opponents (Cambridge, MA: Harvard University Press, 2007).

91. Jaime Goodrich, *Faithful Translators: Authorship, Gender, and Religion in Early Modern England* (Evanston, IL: Northwestern University Press, 2014), 21.

92. Ibid., 20.

93. On Persons, see, especially, Victor Houliston, *Catholic Resistance in Elizabethan England: Robert Persons's Jesuit Polemic, 1580–1610* (Aldershot: Ashgate, 2007). See also his critical edition of *The Book of Resolution*, ed. Victor Houliston (Leiden: Brill, 1998). On the popularity of Persons's text among recusants, see Thomas H. Clancy, S.J., "Spiritual Publications of English Jesuits, 1615–1640," *Recusant History* 19 (1989): 426–46.

94. RSTC 19358. *A Book of Christian Exercise*, sig. a3r.

95. Robert McNulty, "The Protestant Version of Robert Parsons' 'The First Booke of the Christian Exercise,'" *Huntington Library Quarterly* 22, no. 4 (1959): 276.

96. Brad Gregory, "The 'True and Zealouse Seruice of God': Robert Parsons, Edmund Bunny, and *The First Booke of the Christian Exercise*," *Journal of Ecclesiastical History* 45, no. 2 (1994): 253.

97. RSTC 19358. *A Book of Christian Exercise*, sig. a3r.

98. For a comprehensive study of Bunny's changes to Persons, see McNulty, "The Protestant Version of Robert Parsons' 'The First Booke of the Christian Exercise.'"

99. Victor Houliston, "Why Robert Persons Would Not Be Pacified: Edmund Bunny's Theft of *The Book of Resolution*," in *The Reckoned Expense: Edmund Campion and the Early English Jesuits*, ed. Thomas McCoog, S.J. (Woodbridge: Boydell Press, 1996), 159–77.

100. Tina Skouen, *The Value of Time in Early Modern English Literature* (New York: Routledge, 2018), x.

101. Nancy Bradley Warren, "Owning the Middle Ages: History, Trauma, and English Identity," in *Renaissance Retrospections: Tudor Views of the Middle Ages*, ed. Sarah A. Kelen (Kalamazoo, MI: Medieval Institute Publications, 2013), 193.

102. Citation from the fourth edition, RSTC 16917, sig. A3r. It goes on to say that the work "was now out of Print and almost raked up and buried in the dust of ingratefull Oblivion: I therefore conceyved it to be a resolution and enterprise, as worthy of my cost and labour, as that is of a Christian afresh to revive it, and so once more, to make it salute both the Presse and the world" (sig. A4v).

103. Alison Shell, "Spiritual and Devotional Prose," in *The Oxford History of Literary Translation in English*, vol. 2, *1550–1660*, ed. Gordon Braden, Robert Cummings, and Stuart Gillespie (Oxford: Oxford University Press, 2010), 426.

104. On Grace's family's background and the varieties of Protestantism of others in her sphere, see Nancy Bradley Warren, "Tudor Religious Cultures in Practice: The

Piety and Politics of Grace Mildmay and Her Circle," *Literature Compass* 3, no. 5 (2006): 1011–43.

105. Ibid.

106. Retha Warnicke, "Lady Mildmay's Journal: A Study in Autobiography and Meditation in Reformation England," *Sixteenth Century Journal* 20, no. 1 (1989): 62.

107. Kate Narveson, "Authority, Scripture, and Typography in Lady Grace Mildmay's Manuscript Meditations," in *English Women, Religion, and Textual Production, 1500–1625*, ed. Micheline White (London: Taylor & Francis, 2011), 182.

108. See Kubsch, *Crossing Boundaries in Early Modern England*, "'Verse may render it yet more pleasant': The Metrical Versions by Anonymous (1694) and Luke Milbourne (1696)," 150–97.

109. RSTC 23987. On the literary and devotional culture of the English Benedictines, see, especially, Heather Wolfe, "Reading Bells and Loose Papers: Reading and Writing Practices of the English Benedictine Nuns of Cambrai and Paris," in *Early Modern Women's Manuscript Writing: Selected Papers from the Trinity/Trent Colloquium*, ed. Victoria Burke and Jonathan Gibson (Aldershot: Ashgate, 2004), 135–56; Marion Norman, "Dame Gertrude More and the English Mystical Tradition," *Recusant History* 13 (1976): 196–211; and James Gaffney, *Augustine Baker's Inner Light: A Study in Recusant English Spirituality* (Scranton, PA: University of Scranton Press, 1989).

110. Kubsch, *Crossing Boundaries in Early Modern England*, 3.

111. Randall Pederson writes, for instance, that "little overall attention has been given to mysticism within English Puritanism"; Pederson, *Unity in Diversity: English Puritans and the Puritan Reformation, 1603–1689* (Leiden: Brill, 2014), 72–73). Studies of alchemy and the occult have been more numerous: see, for instance, Walter Woodward, *Prospero's America: John Winthrop, Jr., Alchemy, and the Creation of New England Culture, 1606–1676* (Chapel Hill: University of North Carolina Press, 2011). Pederson notes one of the main recent exceptions is Tom Schwanda, *Soul Recreation: The Contemplative-Mystical Piety of Puritanism* (Eugene, OR: Pickwick, 2012), which focuses primarily on the thought of Isaac Ambrose (1604–64). See also Bernard McGinn's recent general overview, McGinn, "Mysticism in the English Reformation," in *Mysticism in the Reformation: 1500–1650, Part 1*, vol. 6 of *The Presence of God: A History of Western Christian Mysticism* (New York: Herder & Herder, 2016), 211–98, especially McGinn's discussion of Richard Sibbes (1577–1635) and his commentary on the Song of Songs, *Bowels Opened* (1639), and Francis Rous (ca. 1580–1659) and his treatise, *The Mystical Marriage* (1638), in the section "Puritan Mysticism," 262–74.

112. On Everard's life and works, with a detailed account of his heresy trial, see Paul Robert Hunt, "John Everard: A Study of His Life, Thought, and Preaching" (PhD diss., University of California, Los Angeles, 1977).

113. On these, see T. Wilson Hayes, "John Everard and Nicholas of Cusa's *Idiota*," *Notes & Queries* 28, no. 1 (1981): 47–49, and Hayes, "Nicholas of Cusa and

Popular Literacy in Seventeenth-Century England," *Studies in Philology* 84, no. 1 (1987): 80–94.

114. Birrell, "English Catholic Mystics in Non-Catholic Circles, Part 1," 66. The book was reprinted in 1757 in Philadelphia, without the medieval texts. Regina Schwartz has written of the varying ways in which mystical discourse entered poetry during this period in Schwartz, *Sacramental Poetics at the Dawn of Secularism: When God Left the World* (Palo Alto, CA: Stanford University Press, 2008).

115. On his frustration with Stanhope's translation of Kempis, see Albert C. Outler, *John Wesley* (Oxford: Oxford University Press, 1980), 61; on his reading recommendations, see 162.

116. Isabel Rivers, *Vanity Fair and the Celestial City: Dissenting, Methodist, and Evangelical Literary Culture in England, 1720–1800* (Oxford: Oxford University Press, 2018), 169.

117. Richard Green, *Works of John and Charles Wesley—a Bibliography* (London: C. H. Kelly, 1896), items 3, 26, and 114.

118. Rivers, *Vanity Fair and the Celestial City*, 169.

119. On Chaucer, see, most recently, Nancy Bradley Warren, *Chaucer and Religious Controversies in the Medieval and Early Modern Eras* (Notre Dame, IN: University of Notre Dame Press, 2019), and Megan Cook, *The Poet and the Antiquaries: Chaucerian Scholarship and the Rise of Literary History, 1532–1635* (Philadelphia: University of Pennsylvania Press, 2019).

CONCLUSION

1. Willem Heijting, "The Media in Reformation Historiography," in *Between Lay Piety and Academic Theology: Studies Presented to Christoph Burger on the Occasion of His 65th Birthday*, ed. Ulrike Hascher-Burger, August den Hollander, and Wim Janse (Leiden: Brill, 2010), 416.

2. Sara Poor, *Mechthild of Magdeburg and Her Book: Gender and the Making of Textual Authority* (Philadelphia: University of Pennsylvania Press, 2004), 57–78.

3. On Quaker women, see, especially, Phyllis Mack, *Visionary Women: Ecstatic Prophecy in Seventeenth Century England* (Berkeley: University of California Press, 1992). On Methodist spirituality and mysticism, see Isabel Rivers, *Vanity Fair and the Celestial City: Dissenting, Methodist, and Evangelical Literary Culture in England, 1720–1800* (Oxford: Oxford University Press, 2018).

BIBLIOGRAPHY

MANUSCRIPTS

Brussels, Royal Library of Belgium MS 10981
Brussels, Royal Library of Belgium MS IV.111
Cambridge, Cambridge University Library MS Ff.v.45
Edinburgh, Edinburgh University Library MS 87r
Einsiedeln, Stiftsbibliothek MS 710 (322)
Lichfield, Lichfield Cathedral Library MS 16
London, British Library MS Additional 6686
London, British Library MS Additional 37049
London, British Library MS Add 37790 (Amherst)
London, British Library MS Cotton Faustina B.VI (Pt. II)
Oxford, Bodleian Library MS Douce 114
Oxford, Bodleian Library MS Douce 322
Oxford, Bodleian Library MS E Museo 160
Oxford, Bodleian Library MS Laud Misc. 528
Oxford, University College MS 14
Strasbourg, National-University Library MS German 2929

PRIMARY TEXTS

Anselm of Canterbury. *Orationes siue meditationes*. Library of Latin Texts. Brepols: Online Database.
———. *The Prayers and Meditations of Saint Anselm with the Proslogion*. Translated by Sister Benedicta Ward, S.L.G. New York: Penguin, 1973.
Bernard of Clairvaux. *The Works of Bernard of Clairvaux*. Vol. 2, *Song of Songs I*. Translated by Kilian Walsh, O.C.S.O. Collegeville, MN: Liturgical Press, 2008.
Biblia Sacra Vulgata. Stuttgart: Deutsche Bibelgesellschaft, 1994.
Bonaventure. *Itinerarium Mentis in Deum. Opera Omnia S. Bonaventurae*. Vol. 5. Edited by the Fathers of the Collegium S. Bonaventurae. Ad Claras Aquas [Quaracchi]: Ex typographia Colegii S. S. Bonaventurae, 1891.

Brathwaite, Richard. *Richard Brathwait's Comments, in 1665, upon Chaucer's Tales of the Miller and the Wife of Bath*. Edited by Caroline F. E. Spurgeon. London: Chaucer Society, 1901.

———. *A Spiritual Spicerie: Containing Sundrie sweet Tractates of Devotion and Piety*. London, 1638.

Bridget of Sweden. *The Liber Celestis of St Bridget of Sweden: The Middle English Version in British Library MS Claudius B i, together with a life of the saint from the same manuscript*. Edited by Roger Ellis. EETS o.s. 291 (1987).

Bruder Hans. *Marienlieder*. Edited by Michael S. Batts. Tübingen: Max Niemeyer Verlag, 1963.

Catherine of Siena. *Il Dialogo*. Edited by Giuliana Cavallini. Siena: Edizioni Cantagalli, 1995.

———. *The Dialogue*. Translated by Suzanne Noffke, O.P. Mahwah, NJ: Paulist Press, 1980.

———. *The Orchard of Syon*. Edited by Phyllis Hodgson and Gabriel M. Liegey. EETS o.s. 258 (1966).

The Chastising of God's Children and the Treatise of Perfection of the Sons of God. Edited by Joyce Bazire and Eric Colledge. Oxford: Basil Blackwell, 1957.

Davidson, Clifford, Martin W. Walsh, and Ton J. Broos, eds. *Everyman and Its Dutch Original, "Elckerlijc."* Kalamazoo, MI: Medieval Institute Publications, 2007.

Eccles, Mark, ed. *The Macro Plays: The Castle of Perseverance, Wisdom, Mankind*. EETS o.s. 262 (1969).

Elizabeth I. *Elizabeth I: Translations, 1544–1589*. Edited by Janel Mueller and Joshua Scodel. Chicago: University of Chicago Press, 2009.

Fisher, John. *English Works of John Fisher, Bishop of Rochester: Sermons and Other Writings, 1520–1535*. Edited by Cecilia A. Hatt. Oxford: Oxford University Press, 2002.

Flete, William. "An Edition of the Latin and Four Middle English Versions of William Flete's *De remediis contra temptaciones* (*Remedies against Temptations*)." Edited by Jessica Lamothe. PhD diss., University of York, 2017.

Heinrich von Meissen (Frauenlob). *Frauenlob's Song of Songs: A Medieval German Poet and His Masterpiece*. Translated by Barbara Newman (with the critical edition of Karl Stackmann). University Park: Pennsylvania State University Press, 2006.

Hoccleve, Thomas. *"My Compleinte" and Other Poems*. Edited by Roger Ellis. Exeter: University of Exeter Press, 2001.

Hopkins, Gerard Manley. *The Poetical Works of Gerard Manley Hopkins*. Edited by Norman MacKenzie. Oxford: Oxford University Press, 1990.

Horstmann, Carl, ed. *Prosalegenden: Die Legenden des MS. Douce 114. Anglia* 8 (1885): 102–96.

Julian of Norwich. *The Writings of Julian of Norwich: A Vision Showed to a Devout Woman and A Revelation of Love*. Edited by Nicholas Watson and Jacqueline Jenkins. University Park: Pennsylvania State University Press, 2006.

Love, Nicholas. *The Mirror of the Blessed Life of Jesus Christ: A Full Critical Edition*. Edited by Michael Sargent. Exeter: Exeter University Press, 2005.

Mechthild of Hackeborn. *The Book of Special Grace*. Translated by Barbara Newman. Mahwah, NJ: Paulist Press, 2017.

Meister Eckhart. *Die deutschen und lateinischen Werke*. Edited by Joseph Quint et al. Stuttgart: Kohlhammer, 1958–.

————. *Meister Eckhart: The Essential Sermons, Commentaries, Treatises, and Defense*. Edited and translated by Edmund Colledge, O.S.A., and Bernard McGinn. Mahwah, NJ: Paulist Press, 1981.

————. *Meister Eckhart: Teacher and Preacher*. Edited and translated by Bernard McGinn. Mahwah, NJ: Paulist Press, 1986.

————. *Meister Eckhart: Werke I*. Edited by Niklaus Largier, with the text of Josef Quint. Frankfurt a.M.: Deutscher Klassiker Verlag, 2008.

"*Myrror to Devout People* (*Speculum Devotorum*): An Edition with Commentary." Edited by Paul Patterson. PhD diss., University of Notre Dame, 2006.

Paltz, Johannes von. *Paltz. Werke 3 (Opuscula)*. Edited by Horst Laubner, Wolfgang Urban, and Walter Simon. Berlin: De Gruyter, 1989.

Parr, Katherine. *Complete Works and Correspondence*. Edited by Janel Mueller. Chicago: University of Chicago Press, 2011.

Pseudo-Dionysius. *Pseudo-Dionysius: The Complete Works*. Translated by Colm Luibheid. Mahwah, NJ: Paulist Press 1987.

Raymond of Capua. *Die Legenda Maior (Vita Catharinae Senensis) des Raimund von Capua*, ed. by Jörg Jungmayr (Berlin: Weidler, 2004).

————. *Ein Geistlicher Rosengarten: Die Vita der heiligen Katharina von Siena zwischen Ordensreform und Laienfrömmigkeit im 15. Jahrhundert. Untersuchungen und Edition*. Edited by Thomas Brakmann. Berlin: Peter Lang, 2011.

————. *La "Legenda maior" de Raymond de Capoue en français ancien*. Edited by Piotr Tylus. Turnhout: Brepols, 2015.

————. *Legenda maior*, ed. by Silvia Nocentini (Florence: Galluzzo, 2013).

Rolle, Richard. *The Contra Amatores Mundi of Richard Rolle of Hampole*. Edited and translated by Paul F. Theiner. Berkeley: University of California Press, 1968.

————. *De emendatione vitae: eine kritische Ausgabe des lateinischen Textes von Richard Rolle. Mit einer Übersetzung ins Deutsche und Untersuchungen zu den lateinischen und englischen Handschriften*. Edited and translated by Rüdiger Spahl. Göttingen: V&R Unipress, 2009.

————. *Emendatio Vitae; Orationes Ad Honorem Nominis Ihesu*. Edited by Nicholas Watson. Toronto: Pontifical Institute of Mediaeval Studies, 1995.

————. *The Fire of Love and The Mending of Life or The Rule of Living*. Translated by Richard Misyn; edited by Ralph Harvey. EETS o.s. 106 (1896).

————. *The Incendium Amoris of Richard Rolle of Hampole*. Edited by Margaret Deanesly Manchester: Manchester University Press, 1915.

————. *Le chant d'amour*. Edited by E. J. F. Arnould. 2 vol. Paris: Les Éditions du Cerf, 1971.

————. *The Officium and Miracula of Richard Rolle of Hampole*. Edited by Reginald Maxwell Woolley. London: Society for Promoting Christian Knowledge, 1919.

————. *The Psalter or Psalms of David and Certain Canticles*. Edited by H. R. Bramley Oxford: Clarendon, 1884.

————. *Richard Rolle: Prose and Verse*. Edited by S. J. Ogilvie-Thomson. EETS o.s. 293 (1988).

————. *Richard Rolle: Uncollected Prose and Verse with related Northern Texts*. Edited by Ralph Hanna. EETS o.s. 329 (2007).

————. *Richard Rolle's Song of Love*. Translated by Andrew Albin. Toronto: University of Toronto Press, 2018.

————. *Tractatus Super Apocalypsim: Texte Critique avec Traduction et Commentaire*. Edited by Nicole Marzac. Paris: Librairie Philosophique J. Vrin, 1968.

————. *Writings Ascribed to Richard Rolle, Hermit of Hampole*. Edited by Hope Emily Allen. New York: D. C. Heath and Company, 1927.

————. *Yorkshire Writers: Richard Rolle of Hampole, an English Father of the Church, and His Followers*. Edited by C. Horstman. London: Swan Sonnenschein & Co., 1895.

Sargent, Michael, ed. "Contemporary Criticism of Richard Rolle." In *Kartäusermystik und -mystiker*, edited by James Hogg and Robert Rackowitz, 160–205. Salzburg: Institut für Anglistik und Amerikanistik, 1981.

Seneca. *Epistles*. Vol. 1. Edited and translated by Richard M. Gummere. Cambridge, MA: Harvard University Press, 1917.

Seymour, M. C. "Mandeville and Marco Polo: A Stanzaic Fragment." *AUMLA: Journal of the Australasian Universities Language and Literature Association* 21 (1964): 39–52.

Speculum Devotorum. Edited by Paul Patterson. EETS o.s. 346 (2016).

Suso, Henry. *Getijden van de Eeuwige Wijsheid*. Translated by Geert Grote; edited by Anton Weiler. Amsterdam: Uitgeverij Van Gennep, 2008.

————. *Heinrich Seuse. Deutsche Schriften*. Edited by Karl Bihlmeyer. Stuttgart: Druck und Verlag von W. Kohlhammer, 1907.

————. *Henry Suso: The Exemplar, with Two German Sermons*. Translated by Frank Tobin. Mahwah, NJ: Paulist Press, 1989.

————. *Horologium Sapientiae*. Edited by Pius Künzle. Freiburg, Switzerland: Universitätsverlag, 1977.

————. *H. Susos Gudeliga snilles väckare (Horologium aeternae sapientae)*. Edited by Rich Bergström. Stockholm: P. A. Norstedt & sönner, 1868–70.

————. "*L'Orloge de Sapience*: Edition critique avec introduction, notes et glossaire, d'après le manuscrit no. 926 de la Bibliothèque Nationale de Paris." Edited by Marie-France Piaggesi-Ajdnik. PhD diss., Université de Nancy II, 1984.

———. "The Seven Points of True Love and Everlasting Wisdom: A Middle English translation of Henry Suso's *Horologium Sapientiae*, Edited from Aberystwyth, National Library of Wales, Brogyntyn II.5." Edited by Dirk Schultze. PhD diss., Ernst-Moritz-Arndt-Universität Greifswald, 2005.

———. *Wisdom's Watch upon the Hours.* Translated by Edmund Colledge. Washington, DC: Catholic University of America Press, 1994.

Thomas of Cantimpré. *Thomas of Cantimpré, The Collected Saints' Lives: Abbot John of Cantimpré, Christina the Astonishing, Margaret of Ypres, and Lutgard of Aywières.* Translated by Barbara Newman. Turnhout: Brepols, 2008.

Van Nieuwenhove, Rik, Robert Faesen, S.J., and Helen Rolfson, eds. *Late Medieval Mysticism of the Low Countries.* Mahwah, NJ: Paulist Press, 2008.

Waters, Claire, ed. *Virgins and Scholars: A Fifteenth-Century Compilation of the Lives of John the Baptist, John the Evangelist, Jerome, and Katherine of Alexandria.* Turnhout: Brepols, 2008.

SECONDARY SOURCES

Aelst, J. J. van. *Passie voor het lijden: De "Hundert Betrachtungen und Begehrungen" van Henricus Suso en de oudste drie bewerkingen uit de Nederlanden.* Leuven: Peeters, 2005.

———. *Vruchten van de Passie: De laatmiddeleeuwse passieliteratuur verkend aan de hand van Suso's "Honderd artikelen."* Hilversum: Verloren, 2011.

Albin, Andrew. "Auralities: Sound Cultures and the Experience of Hearing in Late Medieval England." PhD diss., Brandeis University, 2010.

———. "Canorous Soundstuff: Hearing the *Officium* of Richard Rolle at Hampole." *Speculum* 91, no. 4 (2016): 1026–39.

Alford, John A. "The Scriptural Self." In *The Bible in the Middle Ages: Its Influence on Literature and Art*, edited by Bernard S. Levy, 1–22. Binghamton, NY: Medieval & Renaissance Texts & Studies, 1992.

Appleford, Amy. *Learning to Die in London, 1380–1540.* Philadelphia: University of Pennsylvania Press, 2014.

———. "The Sea Ground and the London Street: The Ascetic Self in Julian of Norwich and Thomas Hoccleve." *Chaucer Review* 51, no. 1 (2016): 49–67.

Armstrong, Elizabeth. "English Purchases of Printed Books from the Continent, 1465–1526." *English Historical Review* 94 (1979): 268–90.

———. "Heinrich Suso's *Horologium sapientiae*: A Recently Discovered Excerpt." *Manuscripta* 12 (1968): 101–3.

Ash, Jennifer. "Holy Virility: Masquerading Masculinity in the Autobiographical Texts of Augustine of Hippo and Henry Suso." PhD diss., Northwestern University, 2000.

Astell, Anne W. "Feminine Figurae in the Writings of Richard Rolle: A Register of Growth." *Mystics Quarterly* 15, no. 3 (1989): 117–24.

————. "Heroic Virtue in Blessed Raymond of Capua's *Life of Catherine of Siena.*" *Journal of Medieval and Early Modern Studies* 42, no. 1 (2012): 35–57.

Auerbach, Erich. *Literary Language and Its Public in Late Latin Antiquity and in the Middle Ages.* Translated by Ralph Manheim. Princeton, NJ: Princeton University Press, 1965.

Axters, Stephanus. *Bibliotheca dominicana neerlandica manuscripta 1224–1500.* Leuven: Publications universitaires de Louvain, 1970.

————. *De Imitatione Christi: Een handschrifteninventaris bij het vijfhonderdste verjaren van Thomas Hemerken van Kempen.* Kempen: Thomas-Druckerei, 1971.

Baker, D. C., and J. L. Murphy. "The Bodleian MS *E Mus.* 160 *Burial* and *Resurrection* and the Digby Plays." *Review of English Studies*, n.s., 19, no. 75 (1968): 290–93.

Baker, Denise. "Julian of Norwich and the Varieties of Middle English Mystical Discourse." In *A Companion to Julian of Norwich*, edited by Liz Herbert McAvoy, 53–63. Woodbridge: D. S. Brewer, 2008.

Barkman, Adam. *Imitating the Saints: Christian Philosophy and Superhero Mythology.* Hamden, CT: Winged Lion Press, 2013.

Barr, Jessica. "Modelling Holiness: Self-Fashioning and Sanctity in Late Medieval English Mystical Literature." In *Sanctity as Literature in Late Medieval Britain*, edited by Eva von Contzen and Anke Bernau, 80–95. Manchester: Manchester University Press, 2015.

Barratt, Alexandra. "Continental Women Mystics and English Readers." In *The Cambridge Companion to Medieval Women's Writing*, edited by Carolyn Dinshaw and David Wallace, 240–55. Cambridge: Cambridge University Press, 2003.

Barron, Caroline, and Nigel Saul, eds. *England and the Low Countries in the Late Middle Ages.* New York: St. Martin's Press, 1995.

Bartlett, Anne Clark. "Translation, Self-Representation, and Statecraft: Lady Margaret Beaufort and Caxton's *Blanchardyn and Eglantine* (1489)." *Essays in Medieval Studies* 22 (2005): 53–66.

Bartlett, Robert. *How Can the Dead Do Such Great Things? Saints and Worshippers from the Martyrs to the Reformation.* Princeton, NJ: Princeton University Press, 2013.

Beadle, Richard. "Monk Thomas Hyngham's Hand in the Macro Manuscript." In *New Science out of Old Books: Studies in Manuscripts and Early Printed Books in Honour of A. I. Doyle*, edited by Richard Beadle and A. J. Piper, 315–37. Aldershot: Scolar Press, 1995.

————. "The Scribal Problem in the Macro Manuscript." *English Language Notes* 21 (1984): 1–13.

Bennet, Alastair. "*Brevis oratio penetrat celum*: Proverbs, Prayers, and Lay Understanding in Late Medieval England." *New Medieval Literatures* 14 (2012): 127–63.

Biggs, Brendan. "The Style of the First English Translation of the *Imitatio Christi.*" *The Medieval Translator* 5 (1996): 187–211.

Bindschedler, Maria. "Seuses Auffassung von der deutschen Sprache." In *Heinrich Seuse: Studien zum 600. Todestag, 1366–1966*, edited by Ephrem Filthaut, O.P., 71–75. Köln: Albertus Magnus Verlag, 1966.

Birrell, J. A. "English Catholic Mystics in Non-Catholic Circles." *Downside Review* 94 (1976): 60–81, 99–117, 213–31.

———. "English Counterreformation Book Culture." *Recusant History* 22 (1994): 113–22.

Bishop, Louise. "Father Chaucer and the Vivification of Print." *Journal of English and Germanic Philology* 106, no. 3 (2007): 336–63.

Bizet, J.-A. *Henri Suso et le déclin de la scolastique*. Paris: Aubier, Éditions Montaigne, 1946.

———. *Suso et le Minnesang, ou, la morale de l'amour courtois*. Paris: Aubier, Éditions Montaigne, 1947.

Black, Matthew Wilson. "Richard Brathwait: An Account of His Life and Works." PhD diss., University of Pennsylvania, 1928.

Blake, N. F. *Caxton: England's First Printer*. London: Osprey, 1976.

———. *William Caxton and English Literary Culture*. London: Hambledon Press, 1991.

Blank, Walter. "Heinrich Seuses 'Vita': Literarische Gestaltung und pastorale Funktion seines Schrifttums." *Zeitschrift für deutsches Altertum und Literatur* 122 (1993): 285–311.

Blanton, Virginia. *Signs of Devotion: The Cult of St. Æthelthryth in Medieval England, 695–1615*. University Park: Pennsylvania State University Press, 2007.

Boenig, Robert. "St. Augustine's *jubilus* and Richard Rolle's *canor*." In *Vox Mystica: Essays on Medieval Mysticism*, edited by Anne Clark Bartlett, 75–86. Cambridge: D. S. Brewer, 1995.

Boffey, Julia. "Banking on Translation: English Printers and Continental Texts." In *The Medieval Translator*, vol. 15, *In Principio Fuit Interpres*, edited by Alessandra Petrina, 317–29. Turnhout: Brepols, 2013.

Bolduc, Michelle. "The Poetics of Authorship and Vernacular Religious Devotion." In *The Varieties of Devotion in the Middle Ages*, edited by Susan Karant-Nunn, 125–43. Turnhout: Brepols, 2003.

Boon, Jessica. "At the Limits of (Trans)Gender: Jesus, Mary, and the Angels in the Visionary Sermons of Juana de la Cruz (1481–1534)." *Journal of Medieval and Early Modern Studies* 48, no. 2 (2018): 261–300.

Bowes, John. *Richard Brathwait: The First Lakeland Poet*. Ings: Hugill, 2007.

Bowman, Leonard J. "The Cosmic Exemplarism of Bonaventure." *Journal of Religion* 55, no. 2 (1975): 181–98.

Braden, Gordon, Robert Cummings, and Stuart Gillespie, eds. *The Oxford History of Literary Translation in English*. Vol. 2, *1550–1660*. Oxford: Oxford University Press, 2010.

Brandolino, Gina. "God's Gluttons: Middle English Devotional Texts, Interiority, and Indulgence." *Studies in Philology* 110, no. 3 (2013): 403–31.

Brantley, Jessica. *Reading in the Wilderness: Private Devotion and Public Performance in Late Medieval England.* Chicago: University of Chicago Press, 2007.

Brentano, Robert. "Catherine of Siena, Margery Kempe, and a *caterva virginum*." In *Bishops, Saints, and Historians: Studies in the Ecclesiastical History of Britain and Italy*, edited by William North, 45–55. Aldershot: Ashgate, 2008.

———. *Two Churches: England and Italy in the Thirteenth Century.* Berkeley: University of California Press, 1968.

Breuer, Dieter. "Zur Druckgeschichte und Rezeption der Schriften Heinrich Seuses." In *Frömmigkeit in der frühen Neuzeit: Studien zur religiösen Literatur des 17. Jahrhunderts in Deutschland*, edited by Dieter Breuer, 29–49. Amsterdam: Rodopi, 1984.

Brown, Jennifer N. "From the Charterhouse to the Printing House: Catherine of Siena in Medieval England." In *Middle English Religious Writing in Practice: Texts, Readers, and Transformations*, edited by Nicole Rice, 17–45. Turnhout: Brepols, 2013.

———. *Fruit of the Orchard: Reading Catherine of Siena in Late Medieval and Early Modern England.* Toronto: University of Toronto Press, 2019.

———. "Gender, Confession, and Authority: Oxford, Bodleian Library, MS Douce 114 in the Fifteenth Century." In *After Arundel: Religious Writing in Fifteenth-Century England*, edited by Vincent Gillespie and Kantik Ghosh, 415–28. Turnhout: Brepols, 2011.

———. "The Many Misattributions of Catherine of Siena: Beyond *The Orchard* in England." *Journal of Medieval Religious Cultures* 41, no. 1 (2015): 67–84.

———. *Three Women of Liege: A Critical Edition of and Commentary on the Middle English Lives of Elizabeth of Spalbeek, Christina Mirabilis, and Marie d'Oignies.* Turnhout: Brepols, 2008.

Brown, Peter. "The Saint as Exemplar in Late Antiquity." *Representations* 2 (1983): 1–25.

Brownlee, Kevin, Tony Hunt, Ian Johnson, Nigel F. Palmer, and James Simpson. "Vernacular Literary Consciousness *c.* 1100–*c.* 1500: French, German and English Evidence." In *The Cambridge History of Literary Criticism*, vol. 2, *The Middle Ages*, edited by Alastair Minnis and Ian Johnson, 422–71. Cambridge: Cambridge University Press, 2009.

Bryan, Jennifer. *Looking Inward: Devotional Reading and the Private Self in Late Medieval England.* Philadelphia: University of Pennsylvania Press, 2008.

Büchner, Christine. *Die Transformation des Einheitsdenkens Meister Eckharts bei Heinrich Seuse und Johannes Tauler.* Stuttgart: W. Kohlhammer Verlag, 2007.

Bugbee, John. "Sight and Sound in *St Erkenwald*: On Theodicy and the Senses." *Medium Ævum* 77, no. 2 (2008): 202–21.

Bugyis, Katie. "Through the Looking Glass: Reflections of Christ's 'Trewe Louers' in Nicholas Love's *Mirror of the Blessed Life of Jesus Christ*." In *Devotional Culture in Late Medieval England and Europe*, edited by Stephen Kelly and Ryan Perry, 461–85. Turnhout: Brepols, 2014.

Bühler, Curt. "At Thy Golg First eut of the hous vlysse the saynge thus." *Studies in the Renaissance* 6 (1959): 223–35.

Bychowski, Gabrielle. "Trans Literature: Transgender Histories and Genres of Embodiment, Medieval and Post-Medieval." PhD diss., George Washington University, 2017.

Bynum, Caroline Walker. *Christian Materiality: An Essay on Religion in Late Medieval Europe*. Cambridge, MA: Zone Press, 2011.

———. *Docere verbo et exemplo: An Aspect of Twelfth-Century Spirituality*. Missoula, MT: Scholars Press, 1979.

———. *Holy Feast and Holy Fast: The Religious Significance of Food to Medieval Women*. Berkeley: University of California Press, 1987.

———. *Wonderful Blood: Theology and Practice in Late Medieval Northern Germany and Beyond*. Philadelphia: University of Pennsylvania Press, 2006.

Caferro, William. *John Hawkwood: An English Mercenary in Fourteenth-Century Italy*. Baltimore: Johns Hopkins University Press, 2006.

Cannon, Christopher. "Proverbs and the Wisdom of Literature: *The Proverbs of Alfred* and Chaucer's *Tale of Melibee*." *Textual Practice* 24, no. 3 (2010): 407–34.

Caravale, Giorgio. *Beyond the Inquisition: Ambrogio Catarino Politi and the Origins of the Counter-Reformation*. Notre Dame, IN: University of Notre Dame Press, 2017.

Carley, James P., and Ann M. Hutchison. "William Peto, O.F.M.Obs., and the 1556 Edition of *The folowinge of Chryste*: Background and Context." *Journal of the Early Book Society* 17 (2014): 94–118.

Caron, Anne Marie, R.S.M. "Mechthild of Hackeborn, Prophet of Divine Praise: To Sing God's Praise, to Live God's Song." *Cistercian Studies Quarterly* 36 (2001): 145–61.

Catto, Jeremy. "Written English: The Making of the Language, 1370–1400." *Past & Present* 179 (2003): 24–59.

Cavanaugh, Susan H. "A Study of Books Privately Owned in England, 1300–1450." PhD diss., University of Pennsylvania, 1980.

Cefalu, Paul. *The Johannine Renaissance in Early Modern English Literature and Theology*. Oxford: Oxford University Press, 2017.

Certeau, Michel de. *The Mystic Fable*. Vol. 1, *The Sixteenth and Seventeenth Centuries*. Translated by Michael B. Smith. Chicago: University of Chicago Press, 1992.

Champollion, Claire. "Zum intellektuellen Wortschatz Heinrich Seuses OP." In *Heinrich Seuse: Studien zum 600. Todestag, 1366–1966*, edited by Ephrem Filthaut, O.P., 77–89. Köln: Albertus Magnus Verlag, 1966.

Chance, Jane. "Gender Subversion and Linguistic Castration in Fifteenth-Century English Translations of Christine de Pizan." In *Violence against Women in Medieval Texts*, edited by Anna Roberts, 161–94. Gainesville: University Press of Florida, 1998.

———. "St. Catherine of Siena in Late Medieval Britain: Feminizing Literary Reception through Gender and Class." *Annali d'Italianistica* 13 (1995): 163–203.

Chenu, Marie-Dominique. "Auctor, Actor, Autor." *Bulletin du Cange* 3 (1927): 81–86.

Ciabattoni, Francesco. *Dante's Journey to Polyphony*. Toronto: University of Toronto Press, 2010.

Clancy, Thomas, S.J. "Spiritual Publications of English Jesuits, 1615–1640." *Recusant History* 19 (1989): 426–46.

Clark, Elizabeth A. "The Celibate Bridegroom and His Virginal Brides: Metaphor and the Marriage of Jesus in Early Christian Ascetic Exegesis." *Church History* 77, no. 1 (2008): 1–25.

Clark, John, ed. *Augustine Baker, O.S.B.: Collections I–III and "The Twelve Mortifications of Harphius."* Analecta Cartusiana 119, no. 21. Salzburg: Institut für Anglistik und Amerikanistik, 2004.

Clarke, Elizabeth. *Politics, Religion, and the Song of Songs in Seventeenth-Century England*. New York: Palgrave Macmillan, 2011.

Coakley, John W. *Women, Men, and Spiritual Power: Female Saints and Their Male Collaborators*. New York: Columbia University Press, 2006.

Cook, Megan. *The Poet and the Antiquaries: Chaucerian Scholarship and the Rise of Literary History, 1532–1635*. Philadelphia: University of Pennsylvania Press, 2019.

Cooper, Helen. "Translation and Adaptation." In *A Concise Companion to Middle English Literature*, edited by Marilyn Corrie, 166–87. Chichester: Wiley-Blackwell, 2009.

Corens, Liesbeth. "Catholic Nuns and English Identities: English Protestant Travellers on the English Convents in the Low Countries, 1660–1730." *Recusant History* 30, no. 3 (2011): 441–59.

Cousins, Ewert. "The Humanity and the Passion of Christ." In *Christian Spirituality: High Middle Ages and Reformation*, edited by Jill Raitt, 375–91. New York: Crossroad, 1987.

Craig, Leigh Ann. *Wandering Women and Holy Matrons: Women as Pilgrims in the Later Middle Ages*. Leiden: Brill, 2009.

Crane, David. "English Translations of the *Imitatio Christi* in the Sixteenth and Seventeenth Centuries." *Recusant History* 13 (1975): 79–100.

Cré, Marleen. "Further Thoughts on M. N.'s Middle English Translation of Marguerite's *Mirouer des simples âmes anienties*." In *A Companion to Marguerite Porete and The Mirror of Simple Souls*, edited by Wendy Terry and Robert Stauffer, 240–63. Leiden: Brill, 2017.

———. *Vernacular Mysticism in the Charterhouse: A Study of London, British Library, MS Additional 37790*. Turnhout: Brepols, 2006.

Cruz, Anne J. "Transgendering the Mystical Voice: Angela de Foligno, San Juan, Santa Teresa, Luisa de Carvajal." In *Echoes and Inscriptions: Comparative Approaches to Early Modern Spanish Literatures*, edited by Barbara Simerka and Christopher Weimer, 127–41. Lewisburg, PA: Bucknell University Press, 2000.

Curtius, Ernst Robert. *European Literature and the Latin Middle Ages*. Translated by Willard R. Trask. Princeton, NJ: Princeton University Press, 1990.

Da Costa, Alexandra. *Reforming Printing: Syon Abbey's Defence of Orthodoxy, 1525–1534*. Oxford: Oxford University Press, 2012.

Dailey, Alice. *The English Martyr from Reformation to Revolution*. Notre Dame, IN: University of Notre Dame Press, 2012.

Davidson, Clifford. "The Bodley *Christ's Burial* and *Christ's Resurrection*: Vernacular Dramas for Good Friday and Easter." *European Medieval Drama* 7 (2004): 51–67.

Davis, Carmel. *Mysticism and Space: Space and Spatiality in the Works of Richard Rolle, the "Cloud of Unknowing" Author, and Julian of Norwich*. Washington, DC: Catholic University of America Press, 2008.

Dean, Ruth. "Manuscripts of St Elizabeth of Schönau in England." *Modern Language Review* 32, no. 1 (1937): 62–71.

Dear, Natalie. "Representations of Continental Mysticism in British Library MS. Additional 37790: Mystical Union's Relationship with Courtly Love." PhD diss., University of Calgary, 2005.

Dearnley, Elizabeth. *Translators and Their Prologues in Medieval England*. Cambridge: D. S. Brewer, 2016.

Debongnie, Pierre. "Henri Suso et l'Imitation de Jesus-Christ." *Revue d'ascétique et de mystique* 21 (1940): 242–68.

Delaissé, L. M. J. *Le manuscrit autographe de Thomas à Kempis et "L'imitation de Jésus Christ": Examen archéologique et édition diplomatique du Bruxellensis 5855–61*. Paris: Éditions Érasme, 1956.

Delaveau, Martine, and Yann Sordet. *Un succès de librairie européen: l'Imitatio Christi, 1470–1850*. Paris: Éditions des Cendres, 2012.

Della Croce, Giovanna. *Enrico Suso: La sua vita, la sua fortuna in Italia*. Milan: Editrice Àncora, 1971.

De Looze, Laurence. *Pseudo-autobiography in the Middle Ages: Juan Ruiz, Guillaume de Machaut, Jean Froissart, and Geoffrey Chaucer*. Gainesville: University Press of Florida, 1997.

Demers, Patricia. "'God may open more than man maye vnderstande': Lady Margaret Beaufort's Translation of the *De Imitatione Christi*." *Renaissance and Reformation/Renaissance et Réforme* 35, no. 4 (2012): 45–61.

Denery, Dallas G. "From Sacred Mystery to Divine Deception: Robert Holkot, John Wyclif and the Transformation of Fourteenth-Century Eucharistic Discourse." *Journal of Religious History* 29, no. 2 (2005): 129–44.

Denise, Sister Mary. "'The Orchard of Syon': An Introduction." *Traditio* 14 (1958): 269–93.

Deschamps, J. "De Middelnederlandse vertalingen en bewerkingen van de *Hundert Betrachtungen und Begehrungen* van Henricus Suso." *Ons geestelijk erf* 63 (1989): 309–69.

DeVun, Leah. "The Jesus Hermaphrodite: Science and Sex Difference in Premodern Europe." *Journal of the History of Ideas* 69, no. 2 (2008): 193–218.

Dolan, Frances. *Whores of Babylon: Catholicism, Gender, and Seventeenth-Century Print Culture.* Notre Dame, IN: University of Notre Dame Press, 1999.

Dombrowski, Daniel A. *Contemporary Athletics and Ancient Greek Ideals.* Chicago: University of Chicago Press, 2009.

Doolan, Gregory. *Aquinas on the Divine Ideas as Exemplar Causes.* Washington, DC: Catholic University of America Press, 2008.

Doyle, A. I. "Carthusian Participation in the Movement of Works of Richard Rolle between England and Other Parts of Europe in the 14th and 15th Centuries." In *Kartäusermystik und -mystiker*, edited by James Hogg, 2:109–20. Salzburg: Institut für Anglistik und Amerikanistik, 1981.

———. "A Survey of the Origins and Circulation of Theological Writings in English in the 14th, 15th, and Early 16th Centuries with Special Consideration of the Role of the Clergy Therein." D Phil diss., University of Cambridge, 1953.

Doyno, Mary. *The Lay Saint: Charity and Charismatic Authority in Medieval Italy, 1150–1350.* Ithaca, NY: Cornell University Press, 2019.

Duffy, Eamon. *Marking the Hours: English People & Their Prayers, 1240–1570.* New Haven, CT: Yale University Press, 2006.

Dutton, Elisabeth. *Julian of Norwich: The Influence of Late-Medieval Devotional Compilations.* Woodbridge: D. S. Brewer, 2008.

Edwards, A. S. G. "Continental Influences on London Printing and Reading in the Fifteenth and Early Sixteenth Centuries." In *London and Europe in the Later Middle Ages*, edited by Julia Boffey and Pamela King, 229–56. London: Queen Mary and Westfield College, University of London, 1995.

Eire, Carlos. "Early Modern Catholic Piety in Translation." In *Cultural Translation in Early Modern Europe*, edited by Peter Burke and R. Po-chia Hsia, 83–100. Cambridge: Cambridge University Press, 2007.

Ellis, Roger. "The Juvenile Translations of Elizabeth Tudor." *Translation and Literature* 18, no. 2 (2009): 157–80.

———. "Translation and Frontiers in Late Medieval England: Caxton, Kempe, and Mandeville." In *Frontiers in the Middle Ages: Proceedings of the Third European Congress of Medieval Studies*, edited by O. Merisalo, 559–583. Louvain-le-Neuve: Fédération internationale des instituts d'études médiévales, 2006.

Engh, Line. *Gendered Identities in Bernard of Clairvaux's Sermons on the Song of Songs: Performing the Bride.* Turnhout: Brepols, 2014.

Erler, Mary. *Reading and Writing during the Dissolution: Monks, Friars, and Nuns, 1530–1558*. Cambridge: Cambridge University Press, 2013.

Falls, David. *Nicholas Love's "Mirror" and Late Medieval Devotio-Literary Culture*. London: Routledge, 2016.

Fawtier, R. "Catheriniana." *Mélanges d'archéologie et d'histoire* 34 (1914): 3–96.

Feiss, Hugh, O.S.B, ed. *On Love: A Selection of Works of Hugh, Adam, Achard, Richard, and Godfrey of St. Victor*. Turnhout: Brepols, 2011.

Fitzgibbons, Moira. "Critical Pleasure, Visceral Literacy, and *The Prik of Conscience*." *Pedagogy* 13, no. 2 (2013): 245–66.

Flasch, Kurt. *Meister Eckhart: Philosopher of Christianity*. New Haven, CT: Yale University Press, 2015.

Flasdieck, H. M. "Mittelenglische Verse vom deutschen Niederrhein." In *Studies for William A. Read: A Miscellany Presented by Some of His Colleagues and Friends*, edited by Nathaniel M. Caffee and Thomas A. Kirby, 35–66. Baton Rouge: Louisiana State University Press, 1940.

Fleck, Andrew. "'Ick verstaw you niet': Performing Foreign Tongues on the Early Modern English Stage." *Medieval & Renaissance Drama in England* 20 (2007): 204–21.

Fleming, John V. "Medieval European Autobiography." In *The Cambridge Companion to Autobiography*, edited by Maria DiBattista and Emily O. Wittman, 35–48. Cambridge: Cambridge University Press, 2014.

Foster, Allyson. "*A Shorte Treatyse of Contemplacyon*: The Book of Margery Kempe in Its Early Print Contexts." In *A Companion to the Book of Margery Kempe*, edited by John Arnold and Katherine Lewis, 95–112. Cambridge: D. S. Brewer, 2004.

Fuhrmann, Wolfgang. *Herz und Stimme: Innerlichkeit, Affect und Gesang im Mittelalter*. Kassel: Bärenreiter, 2004.

Fuller, Ross. *The Brotherhood of the Common Life and Its Influence*. Albany: State University of New York Press, 1995.

Gaffney, James. *Augustine Baker's Inner Light: A Study in Recusant Spirituality*. Scranton, PA: University of Scranton Press, 1989.

Garrett, Greg. *Holy Superheroes! Exploring the Sacred in Comics, Graphic Novels, and Film*. 2nd ed. Louisville, KY: Westminster John Knox Press, 2008.

Gatch, Milton. "Mysticism and Satire in the Morality of *Wisdom*." *Philological Quarterly* 53, no. 3 (1974): 342–62.

Gayk, Shannon. *Image, Text, and Religious Reform in Fifteenth-Century England*. Cambridge: Cambridge University Press, 2010.

Ghosh, Kantik. *The Wycliffite Heresy: Authority and the Interpretation of Texts*. Cambridge: Cambridge University Press, 2002.

Gillespie, Vincent. "Anonymous Devotional Writings." In *A Companion to Middle English Prose*, edited by A. S. G. Edwards, 127–51. Cambridge: D. S. Brewer, 2004.

———. "Chichele's Church: Vernacular Theology in England after Thomas Arundel." In *After Arundel: Religious Writing in Fifteenth-Century England*, edited by Vincent Gillespie and Kantik Ghosh, 3–42. Turnhout: Brepols, 2011.

———. "Dial M for Mystic: Mystical Texts in the Library of Syon Abbey and the Spirituality of the Syon Brethren." In *The Medieval Mystical Tradition in England: Exeter Symposium VI*, edited by Marion Glasscoe, 241–68. Cambridge: D. S. Brewer, 1999.

———. "The Haunted Text: Reflections in the Mirour to Deuote Peple." In *Medieval Texts and Contexts*, edited by Denis Renevey and Graham Caie, 136–66. New York: Routledge, 2008.

———. "Mystic's Foot: Rolle and Affectivity." In *The Medieval Mystical Tradition in England: Papers Read at Dartington Hall, July 1982*, edited by Marion Glasscoe, 199–230. Exeter: University of Exeter Press, 1982.

———. "Postcards from the Edge: Interpreting the Ineffable in the Middle English Mystics." In *Interpretation, Medieval and Modern*, edited by Piero Boitani and Anna Torti, 137–65. Cambridge: D. S. Brewer, 1993.

———. "Syon and the New Learning." In *The Religious Orders in Pre-Reformation England*, edited by James G. Clark, 75–95. Woodbridge: Boydell & Brewer, 2002.

Gillespie, Vincent, and A. I. Doyle. *Syon Abbey, with the Libraries of the Carthusians*. London: British Library, 2001.

Gillespie, Vincent, and Samuel Fanous, eds. *The Cambridge Companion to Medieval English Mysticism*. Cambridge: University of Cambridge Press, 2011.

Goodrich, Jaime. *Faithful Translators: Authorship, Gender, and Religion in Early Modern England*. Evanston, IL: Northwestern University Press, 2014.

Green, Jonathan, and Frank McIntyre. "Lost Incunable Editions: Closing in on an Estimate." In *Lost Books: Reconstructing the Print World of Pre-Industrial Europe*, edited by Flavia Bruni and Andrew Pettegree, 33–72. Leiden: Brill, 2016.

Green, Jonathan, F. McIntyre, and P. Needham. "The Shape of Incunable Survival and Statistical Estimation of Lost Editions." *Papers of the Bibliographical Society of America* 105, no. 2 (2011): 141–75.

Green, Richard. *Works of John and Charles Wesley—A bibliography: containing an exact account of all the publications issued by the brothers Wesley, arranged in chronological order, with a list of the early editions*. London: C. H. Kelly, 1896.

Greenblatt, Stephen, with Ines Županov, Reinhard Meyer-Kalkus, Heike Paul, Pál Nyíri, and Friederike Pannewick. *Cultural Mobility: A Manifesto*. Cambridge: Cambridge University Press, 2010.

Gregory, Brad. "The 'True and Zealouse Seruice of God': Robert Parsons, Edmund Bunny, and *The First Booke of the Christian Exercise*." *Journal of Ecclesiastical History* 45, no. 2 (1994): 238–68.

Gregory, Rabia. *Marrying Jesus in Medieval and Early Modern Northern Europe: Popular Culture and Religious Reform*. London: Routledge, 2016.

————. "Marrying Jesus: Brides and the Bridegroom in Medieval Women's Religious Literature." PhD diss., University of North Carolina, Chapel Hill, 2007.

Grisé, Catherine. "Holy Women in Print: Continental Female Mystics and the English Mystical Tradition." In *The Medieval Mystical Tradition in England: Symposium VII—Papers Read at Charney Manor, July 2004*, edited by E. A. Jones, 83–95. Cambridge: D. S. Brewer, 2004.

————. "'In the Blessid Vyneȝerd of oure Holy Saueour': Female Religious Readers and Textual Reception in the *Myroure of Oure Ladye* and the *Orcherd of Syon*." In *The Medieval Mystical Tradition in England, Ireland, and Wales. Papers Read at Charney Manor, July 1999*, edited by Marion Glasscoe, 193–211. Cambridge: D. S. Brewer, 1999.

————. "Proliferation and Purification: The Use of Books for Nuns." In *After Arundel: Religious Writing in Fifteenth-Century England*, edited by Vincent Gillespie and Kantik Ghosh, 503–19. Turnhout: Brepols, 2011.

————. "Translating Tears in *The Orcherd of Syon*." In *Booldly bot meekly: Essays on the Theory and Practice of Translation in the Middle Ages in Honour of Roger Ellis*, edited by Catherine Batt and René Tixier, 265–78. Turnhout: Brepols, 2018.

Grundmann, Herbert. *Religiöse Bewegungen im Mittelalter: Untersuchungen über die geschichtlichen Zusammenhänge zwischen der Ketzerei, den Bettelorden und der religiösen Frauenbewegung im 12. und 13. Jahrhundert und über die geschichtlichen Grundlagen der deutschen Mystik*. Darmstadt: Wissenschaftliche Buchgesellschaft, 1977; orig. published Berlin, 1935.

Guggisberg, Hans R. *Sebastian Castellio, 1515–1563: Humanist and Defender of Religious Toleration in a Confessional Age*. Translated by Bruce Gordon. Aldershot: Ashgate: 2003.

Gunn, Steven, and Antheun Janse, eds. *The Court as a Stage: England and the Low Countries in the Later Middle Ages*. Woodbridge: Boydell Press, 2006.

Haas, Alois. *Geistliches Mittelalter*. Freiburg, Switzerland: Universitätsverlag Freiburg Schweiz, 1984.

————. *Kunst rechter Gelassenheit: Themen und Schwerpunkte von Heinrich Seuses Mystik*. Bern: Peter Lang, 1995.

————. *Nim din selbes war: Studien zur Lehre von der Selbsterkenntnis bei Meister Eckhart, Johannes Tauler, und Heinrich Seuse*. Freiburg, Switzerland: Universitätsverlag Freiburg Schweiz, 1971.

Habsburg, Maximilian von. *Catholic and Protestant Translations of the "Imitatio Christi," 1425–1650: From Late Medieval Classic to Early Modern Bestseller*. Aldershot: Ashgate, 2011.

Hackett, Benedict. *William Flete, O.S.A., and Catherine of Siena: Masters of Fourteenth Century Spirituality*. Villanova, PA: Augustinian Press, 1992.

Haigh, Christopher. *English Reformations: Religion, Politics, and Society under the Tudors*. Oxford: Oxford University Press, 1993.

Hamburger, Jeffrey. "Heinrich Seuse, *'Das Exemplar.'*" In *Katalog der deutschsprachigen illustrierten Handschriften des Mittelalters*, edited by Norbert Ott, 156–92. Munich: Bayerische Akademie der Wissenschaften, 2008.

———. "The Iconicity of Script." *Word & Image* 27, no. 3 (2011): 249–61.

———. *Script as Image.* Leuven: Peeters, 2014.

———. *The Visual and the Visionary: Art and Spirituality in Late Medieval Germany.* New York: Zone Books, 1998.

Hamm, Berndt. "*Normative Zentrierung*—eine gemeinsame Vision von Malern und Literaten in Zeitalter der Renaissance." In *Künstler und Literat: Schrift- und Buchkultur in der europäischen Renaissance*, edited by Bodo Guthmüller, Berndt Hamm, and Andreas Tönnesmann, 46–74. Wiesbaden: Harrassowitz, 2006.

———. *The Reformation of Faith in the Context of Late-Medieval Theology and Piety.* Leiden: Brill, 2004.

———. "Was ist Frömmigkeitstheologie? Überlegungen zum 14. bis 16. Jahrhundert." In *Praxis Pietatis: Beiträge zu Theologie und Frömmigkeit in der frühen Neuzeit*, edited by Hans-Jörg Nieden and Marcel Nieden, 9–45. Stuttgart: W. Kohlhammer Verlag, 1999.

Hanna, Ralph. "English Biblical Texts before Lollardy and Their Fate." In *Lollards and Their Influence in Late Medieval England*, edited by Fiona Somerset, Jill Havens, and Derrick Pitard, 141–54. Woodbridge: Boydell Press, 2003.

———. *The English Manuscripts of Richard Rolle: A Descriptive Catalogue.* Exeter: University of Exeter Press, 2010.

———. "Producing Magdalene College MS lat. 93." *Yearbook of English Studies* 33 (2003): 142–55.

———. "The Transmission of Richard Rolle's Latin Works." *The Library* 14 (2013): 313–33.

Harrap, David Alexander. "The Phenomena of Prayer: The Reception of the *Imitatio Christi* in England (1438–c.1600)." PhD diss., Queen Mary University of London, 2016.

Hartke, Austen. *Transforming: The Bible & the Lives of Transgender Christians.* Louisville, KY: Westminster John Knox Press, 2018.

Hascher-Burger, Ulrike. "Religious Song and Devotional Culture in Northern Germany." In *A Companion to Mysticism and Devotion in Northern Germany in the Late Middle Ages*, edited by Elizabeth Andersen, Henrike Lähnemann, and Anne Simon, 261–83. Leiden: Brill, 2014.

———. *Singen für die Seligkeit: Studien zu einer Liedersammlung der Devotio moderna: Zwolle, Historisch Centrum Overijssel, coll. Emmanuelshuizen, cat. VI. Mit Edition und Faksimile.* Leiden: Brill, 2007.

Havens, Jill C. "A Narrative of Faith: Middle English Devotional Anthologies and Religious Practice." *Journal of the Early Book Society* 7 (2004): 67–84.

Hayes, T. Wilson. "John Everard and Nicholas of Cusa's *Idiota*." *Notes & Queries* 28, no. 1 (1981): 47–49.

———. "Nicholas of Cusa and Popular Literacy in Seventeenth-Century England." *Studies in Philology* 84, no. 1 (1987): 80–94.

Heffernan, Carol F. "The Middle English *Orcherd of Syon* in Late Medieval England: A Reconsideration." *Magistra* 22, no. 1 (2016): 3–24.

Heijting, Willem. "The Media in Reformation Historiography." In *Between Lay Piety and Academic Theology: Studies Presented to Christoph Burger on the Occasion of His 65th Birthday*, edited by Ulrike Hascher-Burger, August den Hollander, and Wim Janse, 415–32. Leiden: Brill, 2010.

Hellinga, Lotte. "Importation of Books Printed on the Continent into England and Scotland before c. 1520." In *Printing the Written Word: The Social History of Books, circa 1450–1520*, edited by Sandra Hindman, 205–24. Ithaca, NY: Cornell University Press, 1991.

Hellinga, Wytze, and Lotte Hellinga. "Between Two Languages: Caxton's Translation of Reynaert de Vos." In *Studies in Seventeenth-Century English Literature, History and Bibliography*, edited by G. A. M. Janssens and F. G. A. M. Aarts, 119–32. Amsterdam: Rodopi, 1984.

Highly, Christopher. *Catholics Writing the Nation in Early Modern Britain and Ireland*. Oxford: Oxford University Press, 2008.

Hill, Alexandra. *Lost Books and Printing in London, 1557–1640: An Analysis of the Stationers' Company Register*. Leiden: Brill, 2018.

Hill, Geoffrey. *The Orchards of Syon*. Washington, DC: Counterpoint, 2002.

Hiscock, Andrew. "'A supernal liuely fayth': Katherine Parr and the Authoring of Devotion." *Women's Writing* 9, no. 2 (2002): 177–98.

Hodgson, Phyllis. "*The Orcherd of Syon* and the English Mystical Tradition." *Proceedings of the British Academy* 50 (1964): 229–49.

Hoffman, C. Fenno. "Catherine Parr as a Woman of Letters." *Huntington Library Quarterly* 23, no. 4 (1960): 349–67.

Hofmann, Georg. "Seuses Werke in deutschsprachigen Handschriften des späten Mittelalters." *Fuldaer Geschichtsblätter: Zeitschrift des Fuldaer Geschichtsvereins* 45, nos. 4–6 (1969): 113–206.

Hollywood, Amy. *Acute Melancholia and Other Essays*. New York: Columbia University Press, 2016.

Holsinger, Bruce. *Music, Body, and Desire in Medieval Culture: Hildegard of Bingen to Chaucer*. Stanford, CA: Stanford University Press, 2001.

Hosington, Brenda. "Lady Margaret Beaufort's Translations as Mirrors of Practical Piety." In *English Women, Religion, and Textual Production, 1500–1625*, edited by Micheline White, 185–204. Burlington, VT: Ashgate, 2011.

———. "The Young Princess Elizabeth, Neo-Latin, and the Power of the Written Word." In *Elizabeth I in Writing: Language, Power and Representation in Early*

Modern England, edited by Donatella Montini and Iolanda Plescia, 11–36. New York: Palgrave Macmillan, 2018.

Hoskins, Edgar. *Horæ Beatæ Mariæ Virginis, or, Sarum and York Primers: with kindred books and Primers of the reformed Roman use, together with an introduction.* London: Longmans, Green, and Co., 1901.

Houliston, Victor. *Catholic Resistance in Elizabethan England: Robert Persons's Jesuit Polemic, 1580–1610.* Aldershot: Ashgate, 2007.

———. "Why Robert Persons Would Not Be Pacified: Edmund Bunny's Theft of *The Book of Resolution.*" In *The Reckoned Expense: Edmund Campion and the Early English Jesuits,* edited by Thomas McCoog, S.J., 159–77. Woodbridge: Boydell Press, 1996.

Howes, H. "In Search of Clearer Water: An Exploration of Water Imagery in Late Medieval Devotional Prose Addressed to Women." PhD diss., Queen Mary University of London, 2016.

Hsy, Jonathan. *Trading Tongues: Merchants, Multilingualism, and Medieval Literature.* Columbus: Ohio State University Press, 2013.

Hudson, Elizabeth K. "English Protestants and the *imitatio Christi,* 1580–1620." *Sixteenth-Century Journal* 19, no. 4 (1988): 541–58.

Hunt, Paul Robert. "John Everard: A Study of His Life, Thought, and Preaching." PhD diss., University of California, Los Angeles, 1977.

Hvidt, Niels Christian. *Christian Prophecy: The Post-Biblical Tradition.* Oxford: Oxford University Press, 2007.

Iguchi, Atsushi. "A Study of Vernacular Devotional Translation in Late-Medieval England." PhD diss., University of Cambridge, 2008.

Jacobs, Andrew. *Christ Circumcised: A Study in Early Christian History and Difference.* Philadelphia: University of Pennsylvania Press, 2012.

James, Sarah. "A Previously Unnoticed Extract of Suso's *Horologium Sapientiae* in English." *Notes & Queries* 59, no. 1 (2012): 28–30.

———. "Rereading Henry Suso and Eucharistic Theology in Fifteenth-Century England." *Review of English Studies* 63, no. 262 (2012): 732–42.

Johnson, Eleanor. *Staging Contemplation: Participatory Theology in Middle English Prose, Verse, and Drama.* Chicago: University of Chicago Press, 2018.

Johnson, Ian. *The Middle English Life of Christ: Academic Discourse, Translation, and Vernacular Theology.* Turnhout: Brepols, 2013.

———. "Prologue and Practice: Middle English Lives of Christ." In *The Medieval Translator,* vol. 1, *The Theory and Practice of Translation in the Middle Ages,* edited by Roger Ellis, 69–85. Cambridge: D. S. Brewer, 1989.

———. "Translational Topographies of Language and Imagination in Nicholas Love's *Mirror* and *A Mirror to Devout People.*" In *The Medieval Translator,* vol. 15, *In Principio Fuit Interpres,* edited by Alessandra Petrina, 237–46. Turnhout: Brepols, 2013.

Jones, E. A. "A Chapter from Richard Rolle in Two Fifteenth-Century Compilations." *Leeds Studies in English* 27 (1997): 139–62.

———. *England's Last Medieval Monastery: Syon Abbey, 1415–2015.* Leominster: Gracewing, 2015.

Jones, E. A., and Alexandra Walsham, eds. *Syon Abbey and Its Books: Reading, Writing and Religion, c. 1400–1700.* Woodbridge: Boydell Press, 2010.

Jørgensen, Johannes. *Catherine of Siena.* Translated by Ingeborg Lund. Eugene, OR: Wipf & Stock, 2012.

Kamath, Stephanie A. V. G. *Authorship and First-Person Allegory in Late Medieval France and England.* Rochester: Boydell & Brewer, 2012.

Kapfhammer, Gerald, Wolf-Dietrich Löhr, and Barbara Nitsche, eds. *Autorbilder: Zur Medialität literarischer Kommunikation in Mittelalter und Früher Neuzeit.* Münster: Rhema-Verlag, 2007.

Karáth, Tamás. *"Altum sapere:* The Risks of Authority and the Responsibility of Knowledge in Late Medieval English Extramural Literary Texts." PhD diss., Eötvös Loránd University, 2008.

Karnes, Michelle. *Imagination, Meditation, and Cognition in the Middle Ages.* Chicago: University of Chicago Press, 2011.

Keiser, George. "The Mystics and the Early English Printers: The Economics of Devotionalism." In *The Medieval Mystical Tradition in England: Papers Read at Dartington Hall, July 1987,* edited by Marion Glasscoe, 9–26. Cambridge: D. S. Brewer, 1988.

———. "Patronage and Piety in Fifteenth Century England: Margaret, Duchess of Clarence, Simon Wynter and Beinecke MS 317." *Yale University Library Gazette* 60–61 (1985): 32–46.

Keller, Hildegard Elisabeth. *Die Stunde des Hundes: Auf dem mystischen Weg zu Gott.* Schlieren, Switzerland: NZZ Fretz, 2007.

———. "Kolophon im Herzen: Von beschrifteten Mönchen an den Rändern der Paläographie." *Das Mittelalter* 7 (2002): 157–82.

———. "Zorn—Prüfstein der Exemplarität? Eine Fallstudie zum *Exemplar* und seinen Paratexten." In *Anima und sêle: Darstellungen und Systematisierungen von Seele im Mittelalter,* edited by Katharina Philipowski and Anne Prior 221–48. Berlin: Erich Schmidt Verlag, 2006.

Kelly, Stephen, and Salvador Ryan, "Devotional Cosmopolitanism in Fifteenth-Century England." In *After Arundel: Religious Writing in Fifteenth-Century England,* edited by Vincent Gillespie and Kantik Ghosh, 363–80. Turnhout: Brepols, 2011.

Kennedy, Kathleen E. "Reintroducing the English Books of Hours, or 'English Primers.'" *Speculum* 89, no. 3 (2014): 693–723.

Kerby-Fulton, Kathryn. *Books under Suspicion: Censorship and Tolerance of Revelatory Writing in Late Medieval England.* Notre Dame, IN: University of Notre Dame Press, 2006.

————. "Langland and the Bibliographic Ego." In *Written Work: Langland, Labor, and Authorship*, edited by Stephen Justice and Kathryn Kerby-Fulton, 67–143. Philadelphia: University of Pennsylvania Press, 1997.

Kieckhefer, Richard. "Major Currents in Late Medieval Devotion." In *Christian Spirituality: High Middle Ages and Reformation*, edited by Jill Raitt, 75–108. New York: Crossroads, 1987.

————. *There Once Was a Serpent: A History of Theology in Limericks*. Winchester: O Books, 2010.

————. *Unquiet Souls: Fourteenth-Century Saints and Their Religious Milieu*. Chicago: University of Chicago Press, 1984.

Kimmelman, Burt. *The Poetics of Authorship in the Later Middle Ages: The Emergence of the Modern Literary Persona*. New York: Peter Lang, 1996.

Kinch, Ashby. *Imago Mortis: Mediating Images of Death in Late Medieval Culture*. Leiden: Brill, 2013.

King, John N. *Foxe's "Book of Martyrs" and Early Modern Print Culture*. Cambridge: Cambridge University Press, 2006.

Kirakosian, Racha. "Musical Heaven and Heavenly Music: At the Crossroads of Liturgical Music and Mystical Texts." *Viator* 48, no. 1 (2017): 121–44.

Kirk, Jordan. "The Hideous Noise of Prayer: *The Cloud of Unknowing* on the Syllable-Word." *Exemplaria* 28, no. 2 (2016): 97–117.

Klaniczay, Gábor. "Legends as Life Strategies of Aspirant Saints in the Later Middle Ages." *Journal of Folklore Research* 26, no. 2 (1989): 151–71.

Knapp, Ethan. *The Bureaucratic Muse: Thomas Hoccleve and the Literature of Late Medieval England*. University Park: Pennsylvania State University Press, 2001.

Knight, Stephen. "The Social Function of the Middle English Romances." In *Medieval Literature: Criticism, Ideology, and History*, edited by David Aers, 99–122. New York: St. Martin's Press, 1986.

Köbele, Susanne. *Bilder der unbegriffenen Wahrheit: Zur Struktur mystischer Rede im Spannungsfeld von Latein und Volkssprache*. Tübingen: A. Francke Verlag, 1993.

Kraebel, Andrew. *Biblical Translation and Commentary in Later Medieval England: Experiments in Interpretation*. Cambridge: Cambridge University Press, 2020.

Krug, Rebecca. "*The Fifteen Oes*." In *Cultures of Piety: Medieval English Devotional Literature in Translation*, edited by Anne Clark Bartlett and Thomas Bestul, 107–117. Ithaca, NY: Cornell University Press, 1999.

————. *Reading Families: Women's Literate Practice in Late Medieval England*. Ithaca, NY: Cornell University Press, 2002.

Kubsch, Florian. *Crossing Boundaries in Early Modern England: Translations of Thomas à Kempis's "De imitatione Christi" (1500–1700)*. Zürich: Lit Verlag, 2018.

Kujawa-Holbrook, Sheryl. "Katherine Parr and Reformed Religion." *Anglican and Episcopal History* 72, no. 1 (2003): 55–78.

Kurtz, B. P. "The Relation of Occleve's *Lerne to Dye* to Its Source." *PMLA* 40 (1925): 252–75.

Lampinen, Olli. "Just Friends? Richard Rolle and the Possibility of Christian Friendship between Men and Women." Master's thesis, University of Helsinki, 2014.

Lane, Jason D. *Luther's Epistle of Straw: The Voice of St. James in Reformation Preaching*. Berlin: De Gruyter, 2018.

Langdell, Sebastian. *Thomas Hoccleve: Religious Reform, Transnational Poetics, and the Invention of Chaucer*. Liverpool: Liverpool University Press, 2018.

Largier, Niklaus. "Der Körper der Schrift: Bild und Text am Beispiel einer Seuse-Handschrift des 15. Jahrhunderts." In *Mittelalter: Neue Wege durch einen alten Kontinent*, edited by Jan-Dirk Müller and Horst Wenzel, 241–72. Stuttgart: Hirzel, 1999.

Lawler, Thomas. "Fruitful Business: Medieval and Renaissance Elements in the Devotional Method of St. John Fisher." *Medievalia et humanistica* 4 (1973): 145–59.

Lay, Jenna. *Beyond the Cloister: Catholic Englishwomen and Early Modern Literary Culture*. Philadelphia: University of Pennsylvania Press, 2016.

Leach, Elizabeth Eva. *Sung Birds: Music, Nature, and Poetry in the Later Middle Ages*. Ithaca, NY: Cornell University Press, 2007.

Lee, Paul. *Nunneries, Learning and Spirituality in Late Medieval English Society: The Dominican Priory of Dartford*. Woodbridge: Boydell & Brewer, 2000.

Lehmijoki-Garner, Maiju, ed. and trans. *Dominican Penitent Women*. Mahwah, NJ: Paulist Press, 2005.

Lerer, Seth. *Error and the Academic Self: The Scholarly Imagination, Medieval to Modern*. New York: Columbia University Press, 2003.

Lerner, Robert. "New Light on the Mirror of Simple Souls." *Speculum* 85 (2010): 91–116.

Lewis, Gertrud Jaron. *By Women, for Women, about Women: The Sister-Books of Fourteenth-Century Germany*. Toronto: Pontifical Institute of Mediaeval Studies, 1995.

Lovatt, Roger. "Henry Suso and the Medieval Mystical Tradition in England." In *The Medieval Mystical Tradition in England: Papers Read at Dartington Hall, July 1982*, edited by Marion Glasscoe, 47–62. Exeter: University of Exeter Press, 1982.

———. "*The Imitation of Christ* in Late Medieval England." *Transactions of the Royal Historical Society* 18 (1968): 97–121.

———. "The Influence of the Religious Literature of Germany and the Low Countries on English Spirituality, c. 1350–1475." PhD diss., University of Oxford, 1965.

———. "The Library of John Blacman and Contemporary Carthusian Spirituality." *Journal of Ecclesiastical History* 43, no. 2 (1992): 195–230.

Luongo, F. Thomas. "Cloistering Catherine: Religious Identity in Raymond of Capua's *Legenda Maior* of Catherine of Siena." *Studies in Medieval and Renaissance History* 3 (2006): 25–69.

———. "The Historical Reception of Catherine of Siena." In *A Companion to Catherine of Siena*, edited by Carolyn Muessig, George Ferzoco, and Beverly Mayne Kienzle, 23–45. Leiden: Brill, 2012.

———. *The Saintly Politics of Catherine of Siena.* Ithaca, NY: Cornell University Press, 2006.

Lutton, Robert. *Lollardy and Orthodox Religion in Pre-Reformation England.* Woodbridge: Boydell Press, 2006.

———. "'Love this Name that is IHC': Vernacular Prayers, Hymns and Lyrics to the Holy Name of Jesus in Pre-Reformation England." In *Vernacularity in England and Wales, c. 1300–1550*, edited by Elizabeth Salter and Helen Wicker, 119–45. Turnhout: Brepols, 2011.

———. "The Name of Jesus, Nicholas Love's *Mirror*, and Christocentric Devotion in Late Medieval England." In *The Pseudo-Bonaventuran Lives of Christ: Exploring the Middle English Tradition*, edited by Ian Johnson and Allan F. Westphall, 19–53. Turnhout: Brepols, 2013.

Lux-Sterritt, Laurence. *English Benedictine Nuns in Exile in the Seventeenth Century: Living Spirituality.* Manchester: Manchester University Press, 2017.

Mack, Phyllis. *Visionary Women: Ecstatic Prophecy in Seventeenth-Century England.* Berkeley: University of California Press, 1992.

Macmillan, Sarah. "Asceticism in Late-Medieval Religious Writing: Oxford, Bodleian Library, MS Douce 114." PhD diss., University of Birmingham, 2010.

———. "Mortifying the Mind: Asceticism, Mysticism, and Oxford, Bodleian Library, MS Douce 114." In *The Medieval Mystical Tradition: Papers Read at Charney Manor, July 2011*, edited by E. A. Jones, 109–24. Rochester: Boydell & Brewer, 2013.

Manter, Lisa. "Rolle Playing: 'And the Word Became Flesh.'" In *The Vernacular Spirit: Essays on Medieval Religious Literature*, edited by Renate Blumenfeld-Kosinski, Duncan Robertson, and Nancy Bradley Warren, 15–37. New York: Palgrave, 2002.

Margry, Peter Jan, ed. *Shrines and Pilgrimage in the Modern World: New Itineraries into the Sacred.* Amsterdam: Amsterdam University Press, 2008.

Masten, Jeffrey. *Textual Intercourse: Collaboration, Authorship, and Sexualities in Renaissance Drama.* Cambridge: Cambridge University Press, 1999.

McDonald, Nicola, ed. *Pulp Fictions of Medieval England: Essays in Popular Romance.* Manchester: Manchester University Press, 2004.

McDonie, R. Jacob. "Performing Friendship in Richard Rolle's *Incendium Amoris*." *New Medieval Literatures* 17 (2017): 81–114.

McGinn, Bernard. *The Mystical Thought of Meister Eckhart: The Man from Whom God Hid Nothing.* New York: Herder & Herder, 2001.

———. *The Presence of God: A History of Western Christian Mysticism*. Vol. 4, *The Harvest of Mysticism in Medieval Germany*. New York: Crossroad, 2005.

———. *The Varieties of Vernacular Mysticism, 1350–1550*. Vol. 5 of *The Presence of God: A History of Western Christian Mysticism*. New York: Herder & Herder, 2014.

McHugh, Jess. *Americanon: An Unexpected U.S. History in Thirteen Bestselling Books*. New York: Dutton, 2021.

McIlroy, Claire. *The English Prose Treatises of Richard Rolle*. Rochester: D. S. Brewer, 2004.

McNamer, Sarah. *Affective Meditation and the Invention of Medieval Compassion*. Philadelphia: University of Pennsylvania Press, 2009.

———. *Meditations on the Life of Christ: The Short Italian Text*. Notre Dame, IN: University of Notre Dame Press, 2018.

———, ed. *The Two Middle English Translations of the Revelations of St. Elizabeth of Hungary*. Heidelberg: Universitätsverlag C. Winter, 1996.

McNulty, Robert. "The Protestant Version of Robert Parsons' 'The First Booke of the Christian Exercise.'" *Huntington Library Quarterly* 22 (1959): 271–300.

Meredith, Peter. "The Bodley *Burial* and *Resurrection*: Late English Liturgical Drama?" In *Between Folk and Liturgy*, edited by Alan Fletcher and Wim Hüsken, 133–56. Amsterdam: Rodopi, 1997.

Mertens, Thom. "Collatio und Codex im Bereich der Devotio Moderna." In *Der Codex in Gebrauch*, edited by Christel Meier, 163–82. Munich: Fink, 1996.

Metzler, Irina. *Disability in Medieval Europe: Thinking about Physical Impairment during the High Middle Ages, c. 1100–1400*. London: Routledge, 2006.

Milway, Michael. "Forgotten Best-Sellers from the Dawn of the Reformation." In *Continuity and Change: The Harvest of Late Medieval and Reformation History*, edited by Robert J. Bast and Andrew C. Gow, 113–42. Leiden: Brill, 2000.

Minnis, Alastair. *Medieval Theory of Authorship: Scholastic Literary Attitudes in the Later Middle Ages*. Aldershot: Wildwood House, 1988.

Mitchell, Jerome. *Thomas Hoccleve: A Study in Early Fifteenth-Century English Poetic*. Urbana: University of Illinois Press, 1986.

Monks, Peter Rolfe. *The Brussels Horloge de Sapience: Iconography and Text of Brussels, Bibliothèque Royale, MS. IV 111, With an Edition of the Déclaration des Hystoires and a Translation by K.V. Sinclair*. Leiden: E. J. Brill, 1990.

Monta, Susannah Brietz. *Martyrdom and Literature in Early Modern England*. Cambridge: Cambridge University Press, 2005.

Mooney, Catherine. "Wondrous Words: Catherine of Siena's Miraculous Reading and Writing According to the Early Sources." In *Catherine of Siena: Creation of a Cult*, edited by Jeffrey Hamburger and Gabriela Signori, 263–90. Turnhout: Brepols, 2013.

Morley, Stephanie. "Translating Lady Margaret Beaufort: A Case for Translation as Compensatory Power." *The Medieval Translator* 12 (2009): 251–61.

Mortimer, Ruth. "St. Catherine of Siena and the Printed Book." *Papers of the Bibliographic Society of America* 86 (1992): 11–22.

Moss, Candida R. *The Other Christs: Imitating Jesus in Ancient Christian Ideologies of Martyrdom*. Oxford: Oxford University Press, 2010.

Mossman, Stephen. *Marquard von Lindau and the Challenges of Religious Life in Late Medieval Germany: The Passion, the Eucharist, the Virgin Mary*. Oxford: Oxford University Press, 2010.

Mueller, Janel. "Complications of Intertextuality: John Fisher, Katherine Parr, and 'The Book of the Crucifix.'" In *Texts and Cultural Change in Early Modern England*, edited by Cedric Brown and Arthur Marotti, 15–36. New York: Palgrave Macmillan, 1997.

———. "Devotion as Difference: Intertextuality in Queen Katherine Parr's 'Prayers or Meditations' (1545)." *Huntington Library Quarterly* 53, no. 3 (1990): 171–97.

Muldoon, Andrew. "Recusants, Church-Papists, and 'Comfortable' Missionaries: Assessing the Post-Reformation English Catholic Community." *Catholic Historical Review* 86, no. 2 (2000): 242–57.

Murdoch, John. *Classified Catalogue of Tamil Printed Books*. Madras: Christian Vernacular Education Society, 1865.

Murray, Alexander. "Should the Middle Ages Be Abolished?" *Essays in Medieval Studies* 21 (2004): 1–22.

Narveson, Kate. "Authority, Scripture, and Typography in Lady Grace Mildmay's Manuscript Meditations." In *English Women, Religion, and Textual Production, 1500–1625*, edited by Micheline White, 167–84. London: Taylor & Francis, 2011.

Neddermeyer, Uwe. "*Radix Studii et Speculum Vitae*: Verbreitung und Rezeption der 'Imitatio Christi' in Handschriften und Drucken bis zur Reformation." In *Studien zum 15. Jahrhundert: Festschrift für Erich Meuthen*, edited by Johannes Helmrath and Heribert Müller, 1:457–81. Munich: R. Oldenbourg Verlag, 1994.

Nelstrop, Louise. *On Deification and Sacred Eloquence: Richard Rolle and Julian of Norwich*. Abingdon: Routledge, 2020.

Newman, Barbara. "Exchanging Hearts: A Medievalist Looks at Transplant Surgery." In *Rethinking the Medieval Legacy for Contemporary Theology*, edited by Anselm Min, 17–42. Notre Dame, IN: University of Notre Dame Press, 2014.

———. *God and the Goddesses: Vision, Poetry, and Belief in the Middle Ages*. Philadelphia: University of Pennsylvania Press, 2003.

———. "On the Ethics of Feminist Historiography." *Exemplaria* 2, no. 2 (1990): 702–6.

Nicholas, David. *The Northern Lands: Germanic Europe, c. 1270–c. 1500*. Chichester: Wiley-Blackwell, 2009.

Noffke, Suzanne, O.P. "The Physical in the Mystical Writings of Catherine of Siena." *Annali d'italianistica* 13 (1995): 109–29.

Norman, Marion. "Dame Gertrude More and the English Mystical Tradition." *Recusant History* 13 (1976): 196–211.

Nugent, Elizabeth, ed. *The Thought and Culture of the English Renaissance: An Anthology of Tudor Prose, 1481–1555*. Cambridge: Cambridge University Press, 1956.

Outler, Albert C. *John Wesley*. Oxford: Oxford University Press, 1980.

Ouy, Gilbert. *La Librairie des frères captifs: Les manuscrits de Charles d'Orléans et Jean d'Angoulême*. Turnhout: Brepols, 2007.

Palmer, Nigel. "'Antiseusiana: *Vita Christi* and Passion Meditation before the *Devotio Moderna*." In *Inwardness, Individualization, and Religious Agency in the Late Medieval Low Countries: Studies in the* Devotio Moderna *and Its Contexts*, edited by Rijcklof Hofman, Charles Caspers, Peter Nissen, Mathilde van Dijk, and Johan Oosterman, 87–120. Turnhout: Brepols, 2020.

Panzig, Erik. "Lateinische und deutsche Terminologie in der Theologie Meister Eckharts." *Meister-Eckhart-Jahrbuch* 1 (2007): 157–66.

Papka, Claudia Rattazzi. "The Written Woman Writes: Caterina da Siena between History and Hagiography, Body and Text." *Annali d'italianistica* 13 (1995): 131–49.

Parsons, Gerald. *The Cult of Saint Catherine of Siena: A Study in Civil Religion*. Aldershot: Ashgate, 2008.

Patterson, Lee. "'What Is Me?': Self and Society in the Poetry of Thomas Hoccleve." *Studies in the Age of Chaucer* 23 (2001): 437–70.

Patterson, Paul. "Preaching with the Hands: Carthusian Book Production and the *Speculum devotorum*." In *Medieval Latin and Middle English Literature: Essays in Honor of Jill Mann*, edited by Christopher Cannon and Maura Nolan, 134–51. Rochester, NY: Boydell & Brewer, 2011.

Pederson, Randall. *Unity in Diversity: English Puritans and the Puritan Reformation, 1603–1689*. Leiden: Brill, 2014.

Perkins, Nicholas. *Hoccleve's Regiment of Princes: Counsel and Constraint*. Cambridge: D. S. Brewer, 2001.

Perry, Nandra. *Imitatio Christi: The Poetics of Piety in Early Modern England*. Notre Dame, IN: University of Notre Dame Press, 2014.

Peters, Ursula. *Das Ich im Bild: Die Figur des Autors in volkssprachigen Bilderhandschriften des 13. bis 16. Jahrhunderts*. Köln: Böhlau, 2008.

Pettegree, Andrew. "French Books at the Frankfurt Fair." In *The French Book and the European Book World*, edited by Andrew Pettegree, 129–76. Leiden: Brill, 2007.

Pfaff, R. W. *New Liturgical Feasts in Later Medieval England*. Oxford: Clarendon, 1970.

Philipps, Susan. *Transforming Talk: The Problem with Gossip in Late Medieval England*. University Park: Pennsylvania State University Press, 2007.

Pietschmann, Klaus. "Religion and the Senses in Fifteenth-Century Europe" (translated by James Steichen). In *The Cambridge History of Fifteenth-Century Music*, edited by Anna Maria Busse Burger and Jesse Rodin, 40–52. Cambridge: Cambridge University Press, 2015.

Pietschmann, Klaus, and Steven Rozenski. "Singing the Self: The Autobiography of the Fifteenth-Century German Singer and Composer Johannes von Soest." *Early Music History* 29 (2010): 119–58.

Pollard, William. "Richard Rolle and the 'Eye of the Heart.'" In *Mysticism and Spirituality in Medieval England*, edited by William Pollard and Robert Boenig, 85–105. Cambridge: D. S. Brewer, 1997.

Polo de Beaulieu, Marie-Anne. *Education, prédication, et cultures au Moyen Âge: Essais sur Jean Gobi le Jeune (†1350)*. Lyon: Presses Universitaires de Lyon, 1999.

Poor, Sara. *Mechthild of Magdeburg and Her Book: Gender and the Making of Textual Authority*. Philadelphia: University of Pennsylvania Press, 2004.

Powell, Susan. *The Birgittines of Syon Abbey: Preaching and Print*. Turnhout: Brepols, 2017.

Prendergast, Thomas. "Revenant Chaucer: Early Modern Celebrity." In *Chaucer and Fame: Reputation and Reception*, edited by Isabel Davis and Catherine Nall, 185–201. Rochester, NY: Boydell & Brewer, 2015.

Ragazzi, Grazia Mangano. *Obeying the Truth: Discretion in the Spiritual Writings of Saint Catherine of Siena*. Oxford: Oxford University Press, 2014.

Rambuss, Richard. "Pleasure and Devotion: The Body of Jesus and Seventeenth-Century Religious Lyric." In *Queering the Renaissance*, edited by Jonathan Goldberg, 253–79. Durham, NC: Duke University Press, 1994.

Renevey, Denis. "Anglo-Norman and Middle English Translations and Adaptations of the Hymn *Dulcis Iesu Memoria*." In *The Medieval Translator*, edited by Roger Ellis and René Tixier, 5:264–83. Turnhout: Brepols, 1996.

———. *Language, Self and Love: Hermeneutics in the Writings of Richard Rolle and the Commentaries on the Song of Songs*. Cardiff: University of Wales Press, 2001.

———. "Name above Names: The Devotion to the Name of Jesus from Richard Rolle to Walter Hilton's *Scale of Perfection I*." In *The Medieval Mystical Tradition: England, Ireland and Wales*, edited by Marion Glasscoe, 103–21. Cambridge: D. S. Brewer, 1999.

———. "The Name Poured Out: Margins, Illuminations and Miniatures as Evidence for the Practice of Devotions to the Name of Jesus in Late Medieval England." In *The Mystical Tradition and the Carthusians*, edited by James Hogg, 9:127–47. Salzburg: Institut für Anglistik und Amerikanistik, 1996.

———. "Richard Rolle." In *Approaching Medieval English Anchoritic and Mystical Texts*, edited by Dee Dyas, Valerie Edden, and Roger Ellis, 63–74. Cambridge: D. S. Brewer, 2005.

Rex, Richard. *The Theology of John Fisher*. Cambridge: Cambridge University Press, 1991.

Rhodes, J. T. "The Body of Christ in English Eucharistic Devotion, c. 1500–c. 1620." In *New Science out of Old Books: Studies in Manuscripts and Early Printed Books in Honour of I. A. Doyle*, edited by Richard Beadle and A. J. Piper, 388–419. Aldershot: Ashgate, 1995.

———. "Prayers of the Passion: From Jordanus of Quedlinburg to John Fewterer of Syon." *Durham University Journal* 85 (1993): 27–38.

———. "Syon Abbey and Its Religious Publications in the Sixteenth Century." *Journal of Ecclesiastical History* 44, no. 1 (1993): 11–25.

Riddy, Felicity. "'Women Talking of the Things of God': A Late Medieval Subculture." In *Women & Literature in Britain, 1150–1500*, edited by Carol M. Meale, 104–27. Cambridge: Cambridge University Press, 1993.

Riehle, Wolfgang. *The Middle English Mystics*. Translated by Bernard Standring. London: Routledge and Kegan Paul, 1981.

———. *The Secret Within: Hermits, Recluses, and Spiritual Outsiders in Medieval England*. Translated by Charity Scott-Stokes. Ithaca, NY: Cornell University Press, 2014.

Ritchey, Sara. *Holy Matter: Changing Perceptions of the Material World in Late Medieval Christianity*. Ithaca, NY: Cornell University Press, 2014.

———. "Wessel Gansfort, John Mombaer, and Medieval Technologies of the Self: Affective Meditation in a Fifteenth-Century Emotional Community." *Fifteenth-Century Studies* 38 (2013): 153–74.

Rivers, Isabel. *Vanity Fair and the Celestial City: Dissenting, Methodist, and Evangelical Literary Culture in England, 1720–1800*. Oxford: Oxford University Press, 2018.

Robson, Michael. *The Franciscans in the Middle Ages*. Woodbridge: Boydell, 2006.

Roman, Christopher. "*The Dialogue* of Catherine of Siena: A Charity Born of Solitude." *Magistra* 21, no. 1 (2015): 110–31.

———. "Opening the Inner Doors: Richard Rolle and the Space of the Soul." *Mystics Quarterly* 32, no. 3–4 (2006): 19–45.

———. *Queering Richard Rolle*. New York: Palgrave, 2018.

Rose-Lefmann, Deborah. "Lady Love, King, Minstrel: Courtly Depictions of Jesus or God in Late-Medieval Vernacular Mystical Literature." In *Arthurian Literature and Christianity: Notes from the Twentieth Century*, edited by Peter Meister, 138–58. New York: Garland, 1999.

Rothenberg, David. *The Flower of Paradise: Marian Devotion and Secular Song in Medieval and Renaissance Music*. Oxford: Oxford University Press, 2011.

Rowntree, C. B. *A Carthusian World View: Bodleian MS e Museo 160*. Salzburg: Institut für Anglistik und Amerikanistik, 1990.

Rozenski, Steven. "Authority and Exemplarity in Henry Suso and Richard Rolle." In *The Medieval Mystical Tradition: Papers Read at Charney Manor, July 2011*, edited by E. A. Jones, 93–108. Rochester: Boydell & Brewer, 2013.

————. "Ave Ave Ave [Ave]: Bruder Hans and the Multilingual Poetics of Exuberance." *New Medieval Literatures* 20 (2020): 107–42.

————. *"The Chastising of God's Children* from Manuscript to Print." *Études Anglaises* 66, no. 2 (2013): 369–78.

————. "Henry Suso and Richard Rolle: Devotional Mobility and Translation in Late-Medieval England and Germany." PhD diss., Harvard University, 2012.

————. "Henry Suso's *Horologium Sapientiae* in Fifteenth-Century France: Images of Reading and Writing in Brussels Royal Library MS IV 111." *Word & Image* 26, no. 4 (2010): 364–80.

————. "Music, Mysticism, and the Task of Popularization: The Case of Meister Eckhart and Henry Suso." In *Musik der mittelalterlichen Metropole: Räume, Identitäten und Kontexte der Musik in Köln und Mainz, ca. 900–1400*, edited by Fabian Kolb, 477–90. Kassel: Merseberg Verlag, 2016.

————. "The Visual, the Textual, and the Auditory in Henry Suso's *Vita* or *Life of the Servant.*" *Mystics Quarterly* 34, no. 1–2 (2008): 35–72.

————. "'Your Ensaumple and Your Mirour': Hoccleve's Amplification of the Imagery and Intimacy of Henry Suso's *Ars Moriendi.*" *Parergon* 25, no. 2 (2008): 1–16.

Sabia-Tanis, Justin. *Trans-Gender: Theology, Ministry, and Communities of Faith.* 2nd ed. Eugene, OR: Wipf & Stock, 2018.

Saenger, Paul. "Books of Hours and the Reading Habits of the Later Middle Ages." In *The Culture of Print: Power and the Uses of Print in Early Modern Europe*, edited by Roger Chartier, 141–73. New York: Polity Press, 1989.

Sanok, Catherine. "Saints' Lives and the Literary after Arundel." In *After Arundel: Religious Writing in Fifteenth-Century England*, edited by Vincent Gillespie and Kantik Ghosh, 469–86. Turnhout: Brepols, 2011.

Sargent, Michael. "The Anxiety of Authority, the Fear of Translation: The Prologues to *The Myroure of Oure Ladye.*" In *Booldly bot meekly: Essays on the Theory and Practice of Translation in the Middle Ages in Honour of Roger Ellis*, edited by Catherine Batt and René Tixier, 231–44. Turnhout: Brepols, 2018.

————. "Mystical Writings and Dramatic Texts in Late Medieval England." *Religion & Literature* 37, no. 2 (2005): 77–98.

————. "Ruusbroec in England: *The Chastising of God's Children* and Related Works." In *Historia et spiritualitas cartusiensis: Colloquiii Quarti Internationalis acta, Gandavi, Antverpiae, Brugis, 16–19 Sept. 1982*, 303–12. Destelbergen: De Grauwe, 1982.

————. "Versions of the Life of Christ: Nicholas Love's *Mirror* and Related Works." *Poetica* 42 (1995): 39–70.

————. "What Do the Numbers Mean? Observations on Some Patterns of Middle English Manuscript Transmission." In *Design and Distribution of Late Medieval Manuscripts in England*, edited by Margaret Connolly and Linne Mooney, 205–44. York: York Medieval Press, 2008.

Sauer, Michelle. "Cross-Dressing Souls: Same-Sex Desire and the Mystic Tradition in *A Talkyng of the Loue of God.*" In *Intersections of Sexuality and the Divine in Medieval Culture: The Word Made Flesh*, edited by Susannah Chewning, 157–82. Aldershot: Ashgate, 2005.

Scheepsma, Wybren. *The Limburg Sermons: Preaching in the Medieval Low Countries at the Turn of the Fourteenth Century*, edited by David F. Johnson. Leiden: Brill, 2008.

Schepers, Kees. "Ruusbroec in Latin: Impulses and Impediments." In *A Companion to John of Ruusbroec*, edited by John Arblaster and Rob Faesen, 237–85. Leiden: Brill, 2014.

Schleich, G. "Auf den Spuren Susos in England." *Archiv für das Studium der neueren Sprachen und Literaturen*, n.s., 156 (1929): 184–94.

———. "Über die Enstehungszeit und den Verfasser der mittelenglischen Bearbeitung von Susos *Horologium.*" *Archiv für das Studium der neueren Sprachen und Literaturen*, n.s., 157 (1930): 26–34.

Schmoldt, Benno. *Die deutsche Begriffssprache Meister Eckharts: Studien zur philosophischen terminologie des Mittelhochdeutschen.* Heidelberg: Quelle & Meyer, 1954.

Schultze, Dirk. "Henry Suso's *Treatise on the Sacrament* in Cambridge, St. John's College G.25: An Edition." *Anglia* 132, no. 3 (2014): 439–72.

———. "Spiritual Teaching by Catherine of Siena in BL Harley 2409: An Edition." *Anglia* 136, no. 2 (2018): 296–325.

———. "Wisdom in the Margins: Text and Paratext in *The Seven Points of True Love and Everlasting Wisdom.*" *Études anglaises* 66, no. 3 (2013): 341–56.

Schwanda, Tom. *Soul Recreation: The Contemplative-Mystical Piety of Puritanism.* Eugene, OR: Pickwick Publications, 2012.

Schwartz, Regina. *Loving Justice, Living Shakespeare.* Oxford: Oxford University Press, 2016.

———. *Sacramental Poetics at the Dawn of Secularism: When God Left the World.* Palo Alto, CA: Stanford University Press, 2008.

Scott, Karen. "'*Io Caterina*': Ecclesiastical Politics and Oral Culture in the Letters of Catherine of Siena." In *Dear Sister: Medieval Women and the Epistolary Genre*, edited by Karen Cherewatuk and Ulrike Wiethaus, 87–121. Philadelphia: University of Pennsylvania Press, 1993.

———. "Mystical Death, Bodily Death: Catherine of Siena and Raymond of Capua on the Mystic's Encounter with God." In *Gendered Voices: Medieval Saints and Their Interpreters*, edited by Catherine Mooney, 136–67. Philadelphia: University of Pennsylvania Press, 1999.

———. "Not Only with Words, but with Deeds: The Role of Speech in Catherine of Siena's Understanding of Her Mission." PhD diss., University of California, Berkeley, 1989.

———. "St. Catherine of Siena, 'Apostola.'" *Church History* 61, no. 1 (1992): 34–46.

Sears, Elizabeth. "The Iconography of Auditory Perception in the Early Middle Ages: On Psalm Illustration and Psalm Exegesis." In *The Second Sense: Studies in Hearing and Musical Judgment from Antiquity to the Seventeenth Century*, edited by Charles Burnett, Michael Fend, and Penelope Gouk, 19–42. London: Warburg Institute, 1991.

Seelhorst, Jörg. *Autoreferentialität und Transformation: Zur Funktion mystischen Sprechens bei Mechthild von Magdeburg, Meister Eckhart, und Heinrich Seuse.* Tübingen: A. Francke Verlag, 2003.

Selman, Rebecca. "Hearing Voices? Reading *Horologium Sapientiae* and *The Seven Poyntes of Trewe Wisdom.*" In *The Medieval Translator/Traduire au Moyen Age*, edited by Roger Ellis, René Tixier, and Bernd Weitemeier, 6:254–69. Turnhout: Brepols, 1998.

———. "Spirituality and Sex Change: *Horologium Sapientiae* and *Speculum Devotorum.*" In *Writing Religious Women: Female Spiritual and Textual Practices in Late Medieval England*, edited by Denis Renevey and Christiania Whitehead, 63–79. Cardiff: University of Wales Press, 2000.

———. "Voices and Wisdom: A Study of Henry Suso's *Horologium Sapientiae* in Some Late Medieval English Religious Texts." PhD diss., University of Exeter, 1998.

Sexon, Sophie. "Gender-Querying Christ's Wounds: A Non-Binary Interpretation of Christ's Body in Late Medieval Imagery." In *Trans and Genderqueer Subjects in Medieval Hagiography*, edited by Alicia Spencer-Hall and Blake Gutt, 133–53. Amsterdam: Amsterdam University Press, 2021.

Shackle, Emma. "The Effect of Twinship on the Mysticism of Catherine of Siena (1347–1380): A Vergotean Analysis." *Archiv für Religionspsychologie/Archive for the Psychology of Religion* 25 (2003): 129–41.

Shuger, Debora. "Literature and the Church." In *The Cambridge History of Early Modern English Literature*, edited by David Loewenstein and Janel Mueller, 512–43. Cambridge: Cambridge University Press, 2002.

Simpson, James. *Burning to Read: English Fundamentalism and its Reformation Opponents.* Cambridge, MA: Harvard University Press, 2007.

———. "Diachronic History and the Shortcomings of Medieval Studies." In *Reading the Medieval in Early Modern England*, edited by Gordon McMullan and David Matthews, 1–30. Cambridge: Cambridge University Press, 2007.

———. "Madness and Texts: Hoccleve's 'Series.'" In *Chaucer and Fifteenth Century Poetry*, edited by Julia Boffey and Janet Cowen, 15–29. London: King's College London Centre for Late Antique and Medieval Studies, 1991.

———. *The Oxford English Literary History.* Vol. 2, *(1350–1547): Reform and Cultural Revolution.* Oxford: Oxford University Press, 2002.

Skouen, Tina. *The Value of Time in Early Modern English Literature.* New York: Routledge, 2018.

Smart, Walter Kay. "Some English and Latin Sources and Parallels for the Morality of Wisdom." PhD diss., University of Chicago, 1912.

Smith, Rachel J. D. *Excessive Saints: Gender, Narrative, and Theological Invention in Thomas of Cantimpré's Mystical Hagiographies*. New York: Columbia University Press, 2018.

Smoller, Laura Ackerman. *The Saint and the Chopped-Up Baby: The Cult of Saint Vincent Ferrer in Medieval and Early Modern Europe*. Ithaca, NY: Cornell University Press, 2014.

Smyth, Karen. *Imaginings of Time in Lydgate and Hoccleve's Verse*. Aldershot: Ashgate, 2011.

———. "Reading Misreadings in Thomas Hoccleve's Series." *English Studies* 87, no. 1 (2006): 3–22.

Soer, G. B. de. "The Relationship of the Latin Versions of Ruysbroek's 'Die Geestelike Brulocht' to 'The Chastising of God's Children.'" *Mediaeval Studies* 21 (1959): 129–46.

Spearing, A. C. *Medieval Autographies: The "I" of the Text*. Notre Dame, IN: University of Notre Dame Press, 2012.

———. "Language and Its Limits: *The Cloud of Unknowing* and *Pearl*." In *Approaching Medieval English Anchoritic and Mystical Texts*, edited by Dee Dyas, Valerie Edden, and Roger Ellis, 75–86. Woodbridge: D. S. Brewer, 2005.

Staubach, Nikolaus. "*Diversa raptim undique collecta*: Das Rapiarium im geistlichen Reformprogramm der Devotio moderna." In *Literarische Formen des Mittelalters: Florilegien, Kompilationen, Kollektionen*, edited by Kaspar Elm, 115–47. Wiesbaden: Harrassowitz, 2000.

———. "Eine unendliche Geschichte? Der Streit um die Autorschaft der 'Imitatio Christi.'" In *Aus dem Winkel in die Welt: Die Bücher des Thomas von Kempen und ihre Schicksale*, edited by Ulrike Bodemann and Nikolaus Staubach, 9–35. Frankfurt a.M.: Peter Lang, 2006.

Steer, Georg. "Bernhard von Clairvaux als theologische Autorität für Meister Eckhart, Johannes Tauler, und Heinrich Seuse." In *Bernhard von Clairvaux: Rezeption und Wirkung im Mittelalter und in der Neuzeit*, edited by Kaspar Elm, 235–59. Wiesbaden: Harrassowitz, 1994.

Stevens, John. *Words and Music in the Middle Ages*. Cambridge: Cambridge University Press, 1986.

Straubhaar-Jones, J. Christian. "The Rivalry of the Secular and the Spiritual in the Masculine Personae of Henry Suso's *The Life of the Servant*." In *Rivalrous Masculinities: New Directions in Medieval Gender Studies*, edited by Ann Marie Rasmussen, 42–56. Notre Dame, IN: University of Notre Dame Press, 2019.

———. "Understanding the Visuality of a Medieval Visionary: Fourteenth-Century Dominican Henry Suso's Interwoven Concepts of Divine Image, Gendered Identity, and Epistemology." PhD diss., University of North Carolina, Chapel Hill, and Duke University, 2015.

Summit, Jennifer. *Lost Property: The Woman Writer and English Literary History, 1380–1589*. Chicago: University of Chicago Press, 2000.

Sutherland, Annie. "Biblical Text and Spiritual Experience in the English Epistles of Richard Rolle." *Review of English Studies* 56 (2005): 695–711.

———. "The Chastising of God's Children: A Neglected Text." In *Text and Controversy from Wyclif to Bale: Essays in Honour of Anne Hudson*, edited by Helen Barr and Ann M. Hutchison, 353–73. Turnhout: Brepols, 2005.

———. "'Comfortable Wordis': The Role of the Bible in *The Doctrine of the Hert*." In *A Companion to the "Doctrine of the Hert,"* edited by Denis Renevey and Christiania Whitehead, 109–30. Liverpool: Liverpool University Press, 2010.

Swanson, R. N. "Passion and Practice: The Social and Ecclesiastical Implications of Passion Devotion in the Late Middle Ages." In *The Broken Body: Passion Devotion in Late-Medieval Culture*, edited by A. A. Macdonald, H. N. B. Ridderbos, and R. M. Schlusemann, 1–30. Groningen: Egbert Forsten, 1998.

Tagliaferri, Lisa. "Lyrical Mysticism: The Writing and Reception of Catherine of Siena." PhD diss., City University of New York, 2017.

Tarvers, Josephine Koster. "'Thys ys my mystrys boke': English Women as Readers and Writers in Late Medieval England." *Studies in Medieval Culture* 31 (1992): 305–27.

Tavárez, David. "Nahua Intellectuals, Franciscan Scholars, and the *Devotio Moderna* in Colonial Mexico." *The Americas* 70, no. 2 (2013): 203–35.

Temple, Liam P. "The Mysticism of Augustine Baker, OSB: A Reconsideration." *Reformation & Renaissance Review* 19, no. 3 (2017): 213–30.

Thorp, Nigel. *The Glory of the Page: Medieval and Renaissance Illuminated Manuscripts from Glasgow University Library*. Oxford: Oxford University Press, 1987.

Tinsley, David. *The Scourge and the Cross: Ascetic Mentalities of the Later Middle Ages*. Leuven: Peeters, 2010.

Tobin, Frank. "Henry Suso and Elsbeth Stagel: Was the *Vita* a Cooperative Effort?" In *Gendered Voices: Medieval Saints and Their Interpreters*, edited by Catherine Mooney, 118–35. Philadelphia: University of Pennsylvania Press, 1999.

———. *Meister Eckhart: Thought and Language*. Philadelphia: University of Pennsylvania Press, 1986.

Trusen, Winfried. *Der Prozeß gegen Meister Eckhart: Vorgeschichte, Verlauf und Folgen*. Paderborn: Ferdinand Schöningh, 1988.

Turner, Denys. *The Darkness of God: Negativity in Christian Mysticism*. Cambridge: Cambridge University Press, 1995.

Twycross, Meg. "'Transvestism' in the Mystery Plays." *Medieval English Theatre* 5 (1983): 123–80.

Tylus, Jane. *Reclaiming Catherine of Siena: Literacy, Literature, and the Signs of Others*. Chicago: University of Chicago Press, 2009.

————. "Writing versus Voice: Tommaso Caffarini and the Production of a Literate Catherine." In *Catherine of Siena: Creation of a Cult*, edited by Jeffrey Hamburger and Gabriela Signori, 291–312. Turnhout: Brepols, 2013.

Ulrich, Peter. *Imitatio et configuratio: Die philosophia spiritualis Heinrich Seuses als Theologie der Nachfolge des Christus passus.* Regensburg: Verlag Friedrich Pustet, 1995.

Underwood, Malcolm, and Michael K. Jones. *The King's Mother: Lady Margaret Beaufort, Countess of Richmond and Derby*. Cambridge: Cambridge University Press, 1992.

Undset, Sigrid. *Catherine of Siena*. Translated by Kate Austin-Lund. New York: Sheed and Ward, 1954.

Vander Veen, Brian. "The *Vitae* of Bodleian Library MS Douce 114." PhD diss., University of Nottingham, 2007.

Van Deusen, Natalie. " 'Doubleday affaren': The Story of Sigrid Undset's *Catarina av Siena*." *Scandinavian Studies* 87, no. 3 (2015): 383–400.

Van Dussen, Michael. *From England to Bohemia: Heresy and Communication in the Later Middle Ages*. Cambridge: Cambridge University Press, 2012.

————. "Richard Rolle's Latin Psalter in Central European Manuscripts." *Medium Ævum* 87, no. 1 (2018): 41–71.

Van Engen, John. "Multiple Options: The World of the Fifteenth-Century Church." *Church History* 77, no. 2 (2008): 257–84.

————. "New Devotion in the Low Countries." *Ons geestelijk erf* 77 (2005): 235–63.

————. *Sisters and Brothers of the Common Life: The Devotio Moderna and the World of the Later Middle Ages*. Philadelphia: University of Philadelphia Press, 2008.

Vauchez, André. *Catherine of Siena: A Life of Passion and Purpose*. Translated by Michael F. Cusato. Mahwah, NJ: Paulist Press, 2018.

————. *Sainthood in the Later Middle Ages*. Translated by Jean Birrell. Cambridge: Cambridge University Press, 1989.

Voaden, Rosalynn, ed. *Prophets Abroad: The Reception of Continental Holy Women in Late-Medieval England*. Cambridge: D. S. Brewer, 1996.

Vuille, Juliette. " 'Towche me not': Uneasiness in the Translation of the *noli me tangere* Episode in the Late Medieval English Period." In *The Medieval Translator*, vol. 15, *In Principio Fuit Interpres*, edited by Alessandra Petrina, 213–23. Turnhout: Brepols, 2013.

Vulić, Kathryn. "*Þe Pater Noster of Richard Ermyte* and the *Topos* of the Female Audience." *Mystics Quarterly* 34, no. 3–4 (2008): 1–43.

Wadley, T. P. *Notes or Abstracts of the Wills contained in the Volume entitled the Great Orphan Book and Book of Wills, in the Council House at Bristol*. Bristol: Bristol and Gloucestershire Society, 1886.

Walker, Claire. "The Experience of Exile in Early Modern English Convents." *Parergon* 34, no. 2 (2017): 159–77.

Wallace, David, ed. *Europe: A Literary History, 1348–1418.* Oxford: Oxford University Press, 2016.

———. "In Flaundres." *Studies in the Age of Chaucer* 19 (1997): 63–91.

———. "Mystics and Followers in Siena and East Anglia: A Study in Taxonomy, Class and Cultural Mediation." In *The Medieval Mystical Tradition in England: Papers Read at Dartington Hall, July 1984*, edited by Marion Glasscoe, 169–91. Cambridge: D. S. Brewer, 1984.

Wallace, Lewis. "Bearded Woman, Female Christ: Gendered Transformations in the Legends and Cult of Saint Wilgefortis." *Journal of Feminist Studies in Religion* 30, no. 1 (2014): 43–63.

Walsh, Laura. "Ecclesia Reconsidered: Two Premodern Encounters with the Feminine Church." *Journal of Feminist Studies in Religion* 33, no. 2 (2017): 73–91.

Walsham, Alexandra. *Church Papists: Catholicism, Conformity and Confessional Polemic in Early Modern England.* London: Royal Historical Society, 1993.

———. *The Reformation of the Landscape: Religion, Identity, and Memory in Early Modern Britain and Ireland.* Oxford: Oxford University Press, 2011.

Ward, Laviece Cox. "The *E Museo* 160 Manuscript: Writing and Reading as Remedy." In *The Mystical Tradition and the Carthusians*, edited by James Hogg, 4:68–87. Salzburg: Institut für Anglistik und Amerikanistik, 1995.

———. "Historiography in an Early Sixteenth-Century English Manuscript, *e Museo 160.*" *Medieval Perspectives* 3, no. 1 (1990): 281–91.

———. "Historiography on the Eve of the Reformation." In *The Work of Dissimilitude: Essays from the Sixth Citadel Conference on Medieval and Renaissance Literature*, edited by David G. Allen and Robert A. White, 81–90. Newark: University of Delaware Press, 1992.

———. "A Study of MS e Museo 160, a Middle English Devotional History." PhD diss., University of Colorado-Boulder, 1978.

Warnar, Geert. *Ruusbroec: Literature and Mysticism in the Fourteenth Century.* Edited by Diane Webb. Leiden: Brill, 2007.

Warnicke, Retha. "Lady Mildmay's Journal: A Study in Autobiography and Meditation in Reformation England." *Sixteenth Century Journal* 20, no. 1 (1989): 55–68.

Warning, Rainer. "Seeing and Hearing in Ancient and Medieval Epiphany." In *Rethinking the Medieval Senses: Heritage, Fascinations, Frames*, edited by Stephen G. Nichols, Andreas Kablitz, and Alison Calhoun, 102–16. Baltimore: Johns Hopkins University Press, 2008.

Warren, Michael J. *Birds in Medieval English Poetry: Metaphors, Realities, Transformations.* Rochester: Boydell & Brewer, 2018.

Warren, Nancy Bradley. *Chaucer and Religious Controversies in the Medieval and Early Modern Eras.* Notre Dame, IN: University of Notre Dame Press, 2019.

———. *The Embodied Word: Female Spiritualities, Contested Orthodoxies, and Religious Cultures, 1350–1700*. Notre Dame, IN: University of Notre Dame Press, 2010.

———. "Owning the Middle Ages: History, Trauma, and English Identity." In *Renaissance Retrospections: Tudor Views of the Middle Ages*, edited by Sarah A. Kelen, 174–97. Kalamazoo, MI: Medieval Institute Publications, 2013.

———. "Tudor Religious Cultures in Practice: The Piety and Politics of Grace Mildmay and Her Circle." *Literature Compass* 3, no. 5 (2006): 1011–43.

Watkins, Reneé Neu. "Two Women Visionaries and Death: Catherine of Siena and Julian of Norwich." *Numen* 30, no. 2 (1983): 174–98.

Watson, Nicholas. "Censorship and Cultural Change in Late-Medieval England: Vernacular Theology, the Oxford Translation Debate, and Arundel's Constitutions of 1409." *Speculum* 70, no. 4 (1995): 822–64.

———. "Melting into God the English Way: Deification in the Middle English Version of Marguerite Porete's *Mirouer des simples âmes anienties*." In *Prophets Abroad: The Reception of Continental Holy Women in Late-Medieval England*, edited by Rosalynn Voaden, 19–50. Cambridge: D. S. Brewer, 1996.

———. *Richard Rolle and the Invention of Authority*. Cambridge: Cambridge University Press, 1991.

———. "Theories of Translation." In *The Oxford History of Literary Translation in English*, vol. 1, *To 1550*, edited by Roger Ellis, 71–92. Oxford: Oxford University Press, 2008.

Watson, Nicholas, Jocelyn Wogan-Browne, Andrew Taylor, and Ruth Evans, eds. *The Idea of the Vernacular: An Anthology of Middle English Literary Theory, 1280–1520*. University Park: Pennsylvania State University Press, 1999.

Watt, David. *The Making of Thomas Hoccleve's "Series."* Liverpool: University of Liverpool Press, 2013.

Watt, Diane. *Secretaries of God: Women Prophets in Late Medieval and Early Modern England*. Cambridge: D. S. Brewer, 1997.

Webb, Heather. "Catherine of Siena's Heart." *Speculum* 80, no. 3 (2005): 802–17.

Westlake, Elizabeth. "Learn to Live and Learn to Die: Heinrich Suso's *Scire Mori* in Fifteenth Century England." PhD diss., University of Birmingham, 1993.

Wheatley, Edward. "The Developing Corpus of Literary Translation." In *The Oxford History of Literary Translation in English*, vol. 1, *To 1550*, edited by Roger Ellis, 174–89. Oxford: Oxford University Press, 2008.

White, James. "Hungering for Maleness: Catherine of Siena and the Medieval Public Sphere." *Religious Studies and Theology* 33, no. 2 (2014): 157–71.

White, Micheline. "The Psalms, War, and Royal Iconography: Katherine Parr's *Psalms or Prayers* (1544) and Henry VIII as David." *Renaissance Studies* 29, no. 4 (2015): 554–75.

Whittington, Karl. "Medieval Intersex in Theory, Practice, and Representation." *postmedieval* 9 (2018): 231–47.

Wichgraf, Wiltrud. "Susos *Horologium Sapientiae* in England nach Handschriften des 15. Jahrhunderts." *Anglia: Zeitschrift für Englische Philologie* 53, no. 1–2 (1929): 123–33; 53, no. 3 (1929): 345–73.

Wild, Cornelia. *Göttliche Stimme, irdische Schrift: Dante, Petrarca und Caterina da Siena*. Berlin: Walter de Gruyter, 2017.

Williams, Franklin B., Jr. "Lost Books of Tudor England." *The Library* 33, no. 1 (1978): 1–14.

Williams, Ulla, ed. *Die Alemannischen Vitaspatrum*. Tübingen: Max Niemeyer Verlag, 1996.

Williams-Krapp, Werner. "Henry Suso's *Vita* between Mystagogy and Hagiography." In *Seeing and Knowing: Women and Learning in Medieval Europe 1200–1500*, edited by Anneke B. Mulder-Bakker, 35–47. Turnhout: Brepols, 2004.

Willing, Antje. *Heinrich Seuses "Büchlein der ewigen Weisheit": Vorstudien zu einer kritischen Neuausgabe*. Berlin: Erich Schmidt Verlag, 2019.

Winstead, Karen. *Virgin Martyrs: Legends of Sainthood in Late Medieval England*. Ithaca, NY: Cornell University Press, 1997.

Wolf, Kenneth Baxter. *The Poverty of Riches: Saint Francis of Assisi Reconsidered*. Oxford: Oxford University Press, 2003.

Wolfe, Heather. "Reading Bells and Loose Papers: Reading and Writing Practices of the English Benedictine Nuns of Cambrai and Paris." In *Early Modern Women's Manuscript Writing: Selected Papers from the Trinity/Trent Colloquium*, edited by Victoria Burke and Jonathan Gibson, 135–56. Aldershot: Ashgate, 2004.

Woodward, Walter. *Prospero's America: John Winthrop, Jr., Alchemy, and the Creation of New England Culture, 1606–1676*. Chapel Hill: University of North Carolina Press, 2011.

Yarrow, Simon. *Saints: A Very Short Introduction*. Oxford: Oxford University Press, 2018.

Yeoh, Paul. "*Saint's Everlasting Rest:* The Martyrdom of Maggie Tulliver." *Studies in the Novel* 41, no. 1 (2009): 1–21.

Zeeman (Salter), Elizabeth. "Two Middle English Versions of a Prayer to the Sacrament." *Archiv für das Studium der neueren Sprachen und Literaturen* 194 (1957): 113–21.

Ziegeler, Hans-Joachim, and Stephanie Altrock. "Vom *diener der ewigen wisheit* zum Autor Heinrich Seuse: Autorschaft und Medienwandel in den illustrierten Handschriften und Drucken von Heinrich Seuses 'Exemplar.'" In *Text und Kultur: Mittelalterliche Literatur 1150–1450*, edited by Ursula Peters, 150–81. Stuttgart: Verlag J. B. Metzler, 2001.

Zieman, Katherine. "The Perils of *Canor*: Mystical Authority, Alliteration, and Extragrammatical Meaning in Rolle, the *Cloud*-Author, and Hilton." *Yearbook of Langland Studies* 22 (2008): 131–63.

Zweig, Stefan. *The Right to Heresy: Castellio against Calvin*. Translated by Eden Paul and Cedar Paul. New York: Viking Press, 1936.

INDEX

Steven Rozenski is an assistant professor of English at the University of Rochester. He is co-editor of *Devotional Interaction in Medieval England and Its Afterlives*.